PERFORMING IRAN

PERFORMING IRAN

Culture, Performance, Theatre

Edited by
Babak Rahimi

I.B.TAURIS
LONDON • NEW YORK • OXFORD • NEW DELHI • SYDNEY

I.B. TAURIS
Bloomsbury Publishing Plc
50 Bedford Square, London, WC1B 3DP, UK
1385 Broadway, New York, NY 10018, USA
29 Earlsfort Terrace, Dublin 2, Ireland

BLOOMSBURY, I.B. TAURIS and the I.B. Tauris logo are trademarks of
Bloomsbury Publishing Plc

First published in Great Britain 2022
This paperback edition published 2023

Copyright © Babak Rahimi, 2022

Babak Rahimi and contributors have asserted their right under the Copyright, Designs and Patents Act, 1988, to be identified as Author of this work.

Copyright Individual Chapters © 2021 Babak Rahimi, Soodabeh Malekzadeh Erdaji, Shahrokh Yadegari, Joshua Charney, Mahmood Karimi Hakak, Roxanne Varzi, Staci Gem Sheiwiller, Amy Motlagh, Siavash Rokni, Torange Yeghiazarian, Rana Salimi, Heather Rastovac-Akbarzadeh

For legal purposes the Acknowledgements on p. xvi constitute
an extension of this copyright page.

Cover image courtesy of Sanya Ghaderi.

All rights reserved. No part of this publication may be reproduced or transmitted in any form or by any means, electronic or mechanical, including photocopying, recording, or any information storage or retrieval system, without prior permission in writing from the publishers.

Bloomsbury Publishing Plc does not have any control over, or responsibility for, any third-party websites referred to or in this book. All internet addresses given in this book were correct at the time of going to press. The author and publisher regret any inconvenience caused if addresses have changed or sites have ceased to exist, but can accept no responsibility for any such changes.

A catalogue record for this book is available from the British Library.

A catalog record for this book is available from the Library of Congress.

ISBN:	HB:	978-1-7845-3561-2
	PB:	978-0-7556-3514-6
	ePDF:	978-0-7556-3511-5
	eBook:	978-0-7556-3512-2

Typeset by Integra Software Services Pvt., Ltd.

To find out more about our authors and books visit www.bloomsbury.com
and sign up for our newsletters.

*To Poneh Rahimi,
the kindest sister*

CONTENTS

List of Figures	ix
List of Contributors	x
Notes on Transliteration	xiv
Acknowledgements	xvi

INTRODUCTION   1

Part I
PERFORMING TRADITION: PAST TRACES IN THE PRESENT

Chapter 1
MINSTRELS: THE WISE TEACHERS OF ANCIENT IRAN
    Soodabeh Malekzadeh   39

Chapter 2
THE SCARLET STONE: AN INFATUATED WISDOM
    Shahrokh Yadegari   45

Chapter 3
THE QUESTION OF AUDIENCE IN ABBAS KIAROSTAMI'S *A LOOK TO TA'ZIEH*
    Babak Rahimi   57

Part II
PERFORMING (POST-REVOLUTIONARY) IRAN: SPACE, STAGE AND THEATRE

Chapter 4
THE SHIRAZ ARTS FESTIVAL AND THE SLIDE TOWARDS REVOLUTION
    Joshua Charney   77

Chapter 5
IRAN IS THE STAGE AND YOUTH ITS MAJOR PLAYERS: SEVEN-YEAR EDUCATIONAL EXCURSION INTO IRAN'S SOCIO-THEATRE
    Mahmood Karimi Hakak   87

Chapter 6
ACTING OUT: HAMED TAHERI AND THE TRANSFORMATIVE POWER OF IRANIAN UNDERGROUND THEATRE
    Roxanne Varzi   105

Chapter 7
DISRUPTING BODIES, NEGOTIATING SPACES: PERFORMANCE ART IN TEHRAN
    Staci Gem Scheiwiller   113

Chapter 8
'NOW IT'S YOUR TURN TO SEE': JAFAR PANAHI'S CINEMATIC INTERVENTION IN HUMAN RIGHTS DISCOURSE
    Amy Motlagh   129

Chapter 9
PERSISTENCE AS PERFORMATIVE: A BRIEF HISTORY OF THE EVOLUTION OF TWO ROCK MUSIC SCENES IN IRAN
    Siavash Rokni   139

Part III
RESTAGING IRAN IN DIASPORA SPACES

Chapter 10
PROBING THE WOUNDS OF HISTORY: *444 DAYS*, A WORLD PREMIERE IN SAN FRANCISCO
    Babak Rahimi and Torange Yeghiazarian   157

Chapter 11
PERFORMING GLIMPSES OF THE PAST: THE POLITICAL IMPLICATIONS OF DANCE IN NOWRUZ PARADES
    Rana Salimi   169

Chapter 12
NEW MEDIA PERFORMANCE AND (AR)TICULATIONS OF THE SELF: CONVERSATION WITH AMIR BARADARAN
    Heather Rastovac-Akbarzadeh   181

Notes   196
Bibliography   238
Index   240

FIGURES

0.1	Nasr Theatre, Lalehzar Street, Tehran, Courtesy of Babak Rahimi	2
0.2	*The Merchant of Venice*, directed by Majid Rezvani, performed in the Zoroastrian Club in Tehran 19 April 1928	14
0.3	*A Midsummer Night's Dream*, translated and directed by Mahmood Karimi Hakak, Tehran, 1999	25
0.4	The theatrical poster of David Mamet's *A Life in the Theatre* (1977), Tehran, 2015, Faranak Irani	30
2.1	Intensity graph of scenes in stage adaptation of *The Scarlet Stone*	52
2.2	The projections for the opening of the piece. Photo: Jim Carmody	53
2.3	Projections for 'Rostam's hunt'. Photo: Jim Carmody	53
2.4	Real-time animated graphics rise in the backdrop when Sohrab confronts Tahmineh about his father and decides to attack Iran. Photo, Jim Carmody	54
3.1	*Look at Me*, Tehran, Iran. Photo: Babak Rahimi	65
7.1	Neda Razavipour. *Dream Set*, 2004. Performance, Tehran. Photograph taken by Abbas Kowsari. Courtesy of the artist	114
7.2	Bavand Behpoor. Dada Student Performance, 2012. Tehran. Courtesy of the artist	119
7.3	Bavand Behpoor. Dada Student Performance, 2012. Tehran. Courtesy of the artist	120
7.4	Poster of Nooshin Naficy's *The Remaining Scent: Spices*, 2014. Khaneh-ye Honarmandān, Tehran. Photograph taken by the author	123
7.5	Neda Razavipour. *Self-Service*, 2009. Performance, Azad Gallery, Tehran. Courtesy of the artist	124
7.6	Sohrab Kashani. *The Adventures of Super Sohrab*, 2014. Performance, Geneva. Courtesy of the artist	125
7.7	Sohrab Kashani. *The Adventures of Super Sohrab*, 2011. Performance, Istanbul. Courtesy of the artist	126
7.8	Barbad Golshiri. *Cura: The Rise and Fall of Aplasticism*, 2011. Performance, Solyanka State Gallery, *Fourth Moscow Biennial*. Courtesy of the artist and Aaran Gallery	127

CONTRIBUTORS

Joshua Charney is a performer, composer and musicologist based in California. He received his PhD in music from UC San Diego, where he completed his dissertation entitled *The Shiraz Arts Festival: Cultural Democracy, National Identity, and Revolution in Iranian Performance, 1967–1977*. He is an active researcher who has lectured and presented papers on contemporary jazz in Iran, musical improvisation in post-war America and the corporate soundscapes of Southern California. Charney also composes and plays piano in the Sibarg Ensemble, a group that creates a unique hybrid of traditional Iranian music, chamber music and jazz.

Mahmood Karimi Hakak, MFA, SED, is a poet, author, translator and professor of theatre whose scholarly and artistic works are centred on intercultural dialogue and peacebuilding. He has produced, directed and designed over seventy stage and screen productions, a number of which have received international acclaim at such festivals as Tehran, Edinburgh, the Netherlands, Delhi, Montreal, New York and Los Angeles. He is the recipient of eight artistic and scholarly awards including The Critic's Award (1999), Raymond Kennedy Award (2005) and Fulbright (2009–10). His 2010 translation of Hafez, *51 Ghazals by Hafez* (with Bill Wolak), was nominated for ALTA's best translation of poetry. Karimi Hakak's literary credits include seven plays, two books of poetry, five translations and numerous articles and essays. His most recent play, *Is the One I Love Everywhere?* (2020), is a dialogue between Jalal-al Din Rumi, Forough Farrokhzad and six American youths. Mahmood is the artistic director of Mahak International Artists Inc, CEO of Café Dialogue LLC, and the founder and president of Free Culture Invisible www.freecultureinvisible.com. Professor Karimi Hakak has taught at Rutgers, Towson and Southern Methodist universities in the United States, as well as Azad, Soore, Tehran and Teachers Training universities in Iran. He presently serves as Professor of Creative Arts at Siena College in New York. www.mahmoodkarimihakak.org

Soodabeh Malekzadeh is Development Analyst for the University of California, Irvine. She also owns and operates a private copyediting firm in Costa Mesa, California. Malekzadeh holds a PhD and an MA in history from the University of California Irvine. She earned her MA in Ancient Languages and Cultures from Shiraz University, where she also received her BA in English Literature.

Amy Motlagh is Associate Professor of Comparative Literature and Middle East/South Asia Studies, and the inaugural Bita Daryabari Presidential Chair in Persian Language and Literature at UC Davis. Motlagh's first book was *Burying*

the Beloved: Gender, Fiction and Reform in Modern Iran (Stanford University Press, 2012), and her other publications focus on topics including Iranian cinema, genre and narrative, ideologies of gender and race and life-writing in the Iranian diaspora. She is currently at work on two projects dealing, respectively, with Iranian cinema and human rights discourse and with the influence of American ideologies of race on modern Persian literature.

Babak Rahimi is the director of the Program for the Study of Religion at the University of California, San Diego. His monograph, *Theater-State and Formation of the Early Modern Public Sphere in Iran: Studies on Safavid Muharram Rituals, 1590–1641 C.E.* (Brill, 2011), traces the origins of the Iranian public sphere in the early-seventeenth-century Safavid Empire with a focus on the relationship between state-building, urban space and ritual culture. Rahimi is also the co-editor (David Faris) of *Social Media in Iran* (SUNY Press, 2015) and co-editor (Armando Salvatore and Roberto Tottoli) of *The Wiley Blackwell History of Islam* (Wiley Blackwell, 2018), *Muslim Pilgrimage in the Modern World* (Peyman Eshaghi, co-editor, University of North Carolina Press, 2019). Rahimi's research interests concern the relationship between culture, religion and technology. The historical and social contexts that inspire his research range from early modern Islamicate societies to the Global South.

Heather Rastovac-Akbarzadeh is a scholar, artist, and educator with two decades of experience as a researcher, dancer-choreographer, artistic director, curator, and dramaturg among diasporic MENA/SWANA communities. Heather earned her Ph.D. in Performance Studies from UC Berkeley with a Designated Emphasis in Women, Gender and Sexuality, where she completed a dissertation on diasporic Iranian dancers and performance artists. Following her doctoral studies, she was the Mellon Postdoctoral Fellow in Dance Studies in the Department of Theater and Performance Studies at Stanford University (2016–2018) and the University of California Chancellor's Postdoctoral Fellow in the Department of Asian American Studies at UC Davis (2018–2020). She is currently working on her first book manuscript, *Choreographing the Iranian Diaspora: Dance, Spectatorship, and the War on Terror*, which has been selected for the Dance Studies Association's 'Series in Dance History' 2019 First-time Author Mentorship Program. www.heatherrastovac.com

Siavash Rokni is a teacher, researcher, translator, editor, musician and doctoral candidate at the University of Québec in Montreal in Communication (UQÀM). He is the winner of an FRQSC doctoral bursary and FARE scholarship. His master's thesis focused on Networked Protesting Crowds during the 2009 green movement in Iran, and his PhD research focuses on the rise of the Talfiqi music genre in the post Iranian revolution music scene. Siavash has published articles on various subjects, including social movement theory, academic creativity and music in both English and French. He has been the guest editor for *Commposite* journal and *Stream* journal as English and French editor, and he has translated multiple academic articles from French to English. Siavash is a classical flutist, jazz saxophonist and composer of ensemble music. He is a member of *Le grand ensemble de Flûte de Montréal* and the founder and head chef of *Ma table persane/ My Persian Table*, an initiative that showcases Iranian regional cuisine through pop-up events and cooking classes.

Rana Salimi received her PhD from UC, San Diego. Her specialty is in theatre and performance in the Middle East with a focus on performativity of violence, the role of media and the intersection of culture and politics through the lens of performance studies. She is the recipient of Melon Dissertation Award for her thesis on 'Political Performance of Violence: Palestinian Female Bombers and the Politics of Visual Representation' at UC San Diego. Dr Salimi has published 'Harem entertainers: Female performers in Qajar courts' in *Performing Iran; Cultural Identity and Theatrical Performance* and 'The female bomber's body in performance' in *New Theatre Quarterly*. Her articles have also appeared in *Theatre Forum* and Cornell University Press. Currently, she is a lecturer in University of San Diego, Department of Theatre.

Staci Gem Scheiwiller is Associate Professor of Modern Art History in the Art Department at California State University, Stanislaus. She received her PhD in the History of Art from the University of California, Santa Barbara, in 2009. Her field is Modern and Contemporary Art with an emphasis in Iranian art and photography and a minor field in Islamic Art. She is currently writing her second monograph, in which she continues her research on gender and sexuality in nineteenth-century Iranian photography, hopefully composing the most feminist manifesto on this topic. Her most recent publications include *Liminalities of Gender and Sexuality in Nineteenth-Century Iranian Photography: Desirous Bodies* (Routledge, 2017); an edited volume with Markus Ritter, titled *The Indigenous Lens? Early Photography in the near and Middle East* (De Gruyter, 2017); and another edited volume, *Performing the Iranian State: Visual Culture and Representations of Iranian Identity* (Anthem Press, 2013).

Roxanne Varzi is a writer, artist, filmmaker, playwright and Full professor of anthropology at the University of California Irvine. She held the first Fulbright to Iran since the Revolution and was the youngest distinguished senior Iranian visiting fellow at St. Antony's College, Oxford University. Her writing has been published in *The London Review of Books*, *Le Monde Diplomatique*, *The Annals of Political and Social Science*, *Feminist Review*, *Public Culture* and *American Anthropologist*. She is the author of *Warring Souls: Media, Martyrdom and Youth in post-Revolution Iran*, Duke University Press, 2006 and 2016 Independent Publishers Gold Medal Award-winning Novel *Last Scene Underground: An Ethnographic Novel of Iran*, Stanford University Press.

Shahrokh Yadegari, composer and sound designer, has collaborated with such artists as Peter Sellars, Robert Woodruff, Ann Hamilton, Christine Brewer, Gabor

Tompa, Maya Beiser, Steven Schick, Lucie Tiberghien, Shahrokh Moshkin Ghalam, Keyavash Nourai and Siamak Shajarian. He has performed, and his productions, compositions and designs have been presented internationally in such venues as the Carnegie Hall, Royce Hall, Festival of Arts and Ideas, OFF-D'Avignon Festival, International Theatre Festival in Cluj Romania, Ravinia Festival, Ruhr-Triennale, Vienna Festival, Holland Festival, Tirgan Festival, Forum Barcelona, Japan America Theatre, The Pulitzer Foundation for the Arts and the Institut für Neue Musik und Musikerziehung (Darmstadt). He is one of the founders and the artistic director of Kereshmeh Records and Persian Arts Society, organizations dedicated to the preservation and dissemination of Persian traditional and new music. Yadegari is currently on the faculty of the department of Music at UC San Diego and the director of the Sonic Arts Research and Development group and the Initiative for Digital Exploration of Arts and Sciences (IDEAS) at the Qualcomm Institute (UCSD's branch of the California Institute for Telecommunication and Information Technology).

Torange Yeghiazarian is the founding artistic director of Golden Thread Productions, the first American theatre company focused on the Middle East, where she launched such visionary programmes as ReOrient Festival and Forum, New Threads, Fairytale Players and What Do the Women Say?, and timely initiatives such as Islam 101 and Project Alo? In her capacity as an artistic director, Torange helped build the careers of numerous artists and helped launch the Middle East North African Theater Makers Alliance (MENATMA), the first national organization advocating for the MENA theater community. A playwright, director and translator, Torange contributed a case study chapter to 'Casting a Movement', forthcoming from Routledge, 2019. She translated a number of contemporary plays from Iran, including *A Moment of Silence* by Mohammad Yaghoubi (winner of Best Play at Toronto Fringe) and *The Language of Wild Berries* by Naghmeh Samini. Her translation and stage adaptation of Nizami's 'Leyla & Majnun' is published on Gleeditions.com. She has published in *The Drama Review, American Theatre Magazine, AmerAsia Journal*, and has contributed to *Encyclopedia of Women and Islamic Cultures and Cambridge World Encyclopedia of Stage Actors*. Born in Iran and of Armenian heritage, Torange holds a master's degree in theatre arts from San Francisco State University.

Notes on Transliteration

Transcription

Persian and Arabic

ء	ʾ
ب	b
پ	p / -
ت	t
ث	th
ج	j
چ	ch / -
ح	ḥ
خ	kh
د	d
ذ	ẕ
ر	r
ز	z
ژ	zh
س	s
ش	sh
ص	ṣ
ض	ż
ط	ṭ
ظ	ẓ
ع	ʿ
غ	gh
ف	f
ق	q
ک	k
گ	g / -

Notes on Transliteration

ل	l
م	m
ن	n
و	v / w
ه	h
ى	y
ة	-at
ال	al-, 'l-
ّ	Double consonant

Vowels and Diphthongs

Long ا	ā
Long و	ū
Long ي	ī
Short ا	a
Short ʾ	o
Short ٜ	e
Short ى	i
ىَ	ai
وَ	au
ى	ei
و	eu
يه / ية	-ieh

ACKNOWLEDGEMENTS

This collection of studies arises out of a conference held at the University of California, San Diego, on 21 February 2014. I am deeply grateful to Shahrokh Yadegari, also a contributor to this volume, who provided the logistical support in organizing the conference on the subject of 'Performing Iran'. My thanks also go to my colleague and friend, Amelia Glaser, who kindly helped with the conference. I owe special thanks to Fatemeh Shams, who helped with the translation of Abbas Kiarostami's poem, which appears in Chapter 3. Many thanks are also due to Mahmood Karimi Hakak and Torange Yeghiazarian, also contributors to this volume, who, in a variety of ways, were abundantly helpful and supportive. I am also deeply grateful to Nasser Rahmaninejad, whose immense knowledge helped me better understand Iranian theatre. I particularly want to thank Behnam Aboutorabia, Reza Kouchek Zadeh, Ida Meftahi and Marjan Moosavi for their help with the introduction. Special thanks to Soodabeh Malekzadeh for her diligent work in copyediting the volume. Thanks are also due to Maryam Mianji for introducing me to Sayna Ghaderi, whose photo appears on the book cover. Ghaderi's photography is reflective of the innovative form of performance culture that this volume seeks to identify. Ali Gheissari, mentor and a true scholar, like always, was helpful in many ways. I owe special thanks to Shahla Talebi and her profound insights for a section in the introduction. I am deeply grateful to my wife, Mehrnaz Eizadyrad, and my son, Ardeshir Rahimi, for always being there to support me. Finally, I would like to thank the contributors, who have generously provided their expertise on the subject of theatre and the broader question of performance in Iran. I am deeply grateful to each of these remarkable scholars for the unique ways they have enriched this book by sharing their experience and knowledge. Our collective hope is to (re)present Iran from the prism of expressive action, marked by a pulsating sense of the new that is not the continuum of past and present but the yet to come.

With the aim of scholarly thoroughness, the present volume adopts a system of transliteration of Persian inspired by the model used by the *International Journal of Middle East Studies* (*IJMES*), with modifications and elimination of most diacritical marks, except when translation passages from the original text are included. In addition, all years mentioned in the volume relate to the Common Era unless otherwise stated.

I may have said, or may still say, to the contrary or otherwise, on this subject. But I have always spoken, no doubt always shall, of things that never existed, or that existed if you insist, no doubt always will, but not with the existence I ascribe to them.

Samuel Beckett, *First Love*

INTRODUCTION

If you were to visit Lalehzar Street in Central Tehran, while strolling past the numerous electronic appliance shops, you may find yourself looking up at the deteriorating buildings, many of which date back to the late Qajar period when the urban elite and *flâneur* would frequent the fashionable street for an experience of 'modern life'.[1] As you walk this rather busy street, once lined with cafes, cinemas, hotels and restaurants, towards the southern end of the thoroughfare, you would find a relief sculpture of an unveiled female figure, with breasts upward, holding a harp and facing the snow-capped mountains of Northern Tehran.[2] Here the paling Art Deco facade of the grey building, decorated on top with a damaged neon sign that reads 'Tehran Theatre', is a fading reminder of one of the oldest theatres in Iran.[3] The Nasr Theatre, named after Seyyed Ali Nasr (1894–1962), a celebrated director and playwright, and the person responsible for the establishment of the first permanent troupe and the institution for actor training, was among the most popular theatres located on this historic boulevard.[4] Abandoned since 2002, the Nasr Theatre is a reminder of a once-bustling theatre life, symbolic of a culture informed by a sense of modernness in its urban form (Figure 0.1).[5]

Known as the 'graveyard' of cinema and theatre, Lalehzar evokes a sense of dreary decay, not a mere trace of a bygone era but a decomposing space in public display. The street, which famously promoted a revolution in leisure in the Iranian society and drew a heterogeneous mix of denizens and visitors to the city, now serves as a site of historical ruins, despite its vibrancy in commerce and heavy traffic. Some of the distinctive modern features of Lalehzar were the outcome of deep-seated social transformations that spanned across the globe in a fast-changing era of wars and technologies of mass destruction in what Eric Hobsbawm famously described as 'the short twentieth century' (1914–91).[6] Speed in historical time in a globalizing world of consumption matched the fluctuating metropolitan styles of life, wherein spaces of conspicuous consumption emerged in connection with multiple forms of communication and information flow. New technologies, such as cinema, phonograph, photography and therewith the transformation of subjective and social experiences, created new audio and visual publics registered in the theatrics of commodity culture, such as shop window displays, as key signified markers of Lalehzar sociability.

Figure 0.1 Nasr Theatre, Lalehzar Street, Tehran, Courtesy of Babak Rahimi.

Lalehzar is also a haunted site of forgotten beginnings. It was at Tehran's Grand Hotel, where, in 1921, Iran's first female actor and theatre director, Varto Terian (1896–1974), staged and popularized the satirical play *Jaʿfar Khan az farang amadeh* (*Jafar Khan Has Returned from the West*).[7] In 1939, Lalehzar saw the establishment of the first training institution for actors, Honarestan-e

Honarpishegi-e Tehran (The Tehran Acting School), where Seyed Ali Nasr invited leading actors, artists, dramatists, musicians and psychologists to train actors.[8] Between 1947 and 1949, when Iranians were experiencing relative freedom of expression following the Anglo-Soviet occupation, the Ferdowsi Theatre, under the directorship of Abdolhossein Nooshin (1906–71), saw, for the first time, the staging of technically cutting-edge performances of European plays, revolutionizing the theatrical culture of modernist form for a wide range of audiences and performers in Iran.[9] In February 1980, the Nasr Theatre saw the first staging of Dario Fo's 1974 subversive play, *Can't Pay? Won't Pay!*, produced and performed by the Iran Theatre Association and directed by Nasser Rahmaninejad, on the occasion of the anniversary of the revolution.[10]

Ephemeral in nature, new beginnings can equally shape future histories to come. To understand such futurity, one must look beyond Lalehzar's abandoned playhouses. In historical terms, the modernist shift in the Ferdowsi Theatre had a significant impact on experimental theatre as anti-colonial and socialist currents emerged in the 1950s and 1960s in Iran and around the globe. After the 1979 Revolution, cities such as Tabriz and Rasht, where theatre performances were first staged in the late Qajar period because of their geographical proximity to the Caucasus and Russia, saw the growth of new post-revolutionary theatrical genres with a focus on connected themes such as revolution, war and youth. Promoted by private and state sectors, provincial performance troupes operated in tandem with local festivals, publication venues, online ticketing services and theatre halls in the production of diverse dramatic and literary genres, including new translations and staging of European and Latin American theatres.[11]

Especially since the end of the Iran-Iraq War (1980–8), marked by the election of the reformist president, Mohammad Khatami (1943–), in 1997, a post-revolutionary performance culture has emerged in Tehran and other cities of Iran. With theatre as a salient cultural art form, the growing array of cultural spaces have included vibrant performing spaces where various staging practices attract a new generation of audiences with a diverse range of social backgrounds. Despite censorship, and a regime of regulation of artistic production that dates back to the Qajar period, which is certainly not unique to Iran, together with US-led sanctions with its economic impact on cultural industries, post-revolutionary Iran boasts one of the most innovative performance and theatre cultures in West Asia. The creative performance of translated and indigenous works, by established or emerging writers, performed by theatre groups match a range of shows from creative remakes of Iranian traditional rituals to the restaging of Shakespearian dramas. Likewise, the Iranian diaspora theatre mirrors the diversity of Iran-based theatres in its attempts to address questions of alienation, identity and migration in shifting transnational contexts.

Such cultural shift owed much to a new generation of Iranian directors, dramatists and performers who do theatre and performance, at large, as a critical reflection upon questions of quotidian and mythical concerns, addressing the broader condition of modernity drawn from lived realities of post-revolutionary contexts. Described by Alain Badiou as 'the most complete of the arts', theatre, closely imbricated in architectural performances, has historically served as a social force marked in embodied and symbolic practices for change.[12] In its multimedia form in relation to creative collaboration, theatre as a distinct 'medium' has fostered the perception of autonomy based on enactments and translatability of dialogue and speculation, predicated on conceptions of self-cultivation and progress.[13] Theatre during the revolutionary periods has served in the production of alternative modes of expression and radical staging, neither of which are sanctioned or promoted by the state, as evident in the burst of theatre culture during the Constitutional Revolution (1905–11) and street theatre in 1979 Revolution.

In the modernist imaginary, theatre signifies the material or spectral enactment of live drama between actors and audiences, (re)presentational in performing narrative and transformational as a set of cultural practices.[14] The notion of the theatrical as a means of subjective change is not unique to 'modernity', as a multidimensional concept based on historical and institutional processes.[15] However, the modernity of theatre, either in its proscenium stage or experimental empty stage, lies in the production of distinct knowledge, paradoxically, anchored in the staging possibility of going beyond the determinacy of history through the awareness of historicity of a relivable past. And such awareness is inherently political for its vision of what is possible. Theatre is politics by other means, and this is because, in the words of Augusto Boal following the famed Aristotelian axiom, 'all activities of man are political and theater is one of them.'[16]

In reference to theatre as politics, a crucial strand in the distinct conception of theatre in Iran resembles the Enlightenment notions of theatre, famously described by Denis Diderot as an emotive means to mould the morality of citizens in the body politics in progressive time.[17] Particularly evident during the Constitutional Revolution, the emerging playwrights and theatre troupes had taken on the task of staging performances as educational projects for the moral progress and sovereignty of Iran undergoing change. The pedagogical understanding of theatre, partly in an important sense, reflected a new conception of nationhood as an endangered 'motherland' and in need of protection by familial solidarity.[18] If public theatres as spaces of conviviality had not yet disappeared in urban Iran, the question of theatre as a new performance genre had opened up a cultural field for political action.

In 1908, Mirza Reza Khan Nai'ni (1873–1932), a constitutionalist author, would identify theatre in *Ruznameh-ye Te'atre* (Theatre Newspaper), along with schools and newspapers, as one of the three key principles of 'modernity and civilisation'.[19] The civilizational value of theatre, he argued, is the projection of 'good and the evil attitudes and activities on stage in order to raise awareness among the audience'.[20] For constitutionalists, in particular, theatre would serve as a site of moral refinement, and ultimately enhancing the rational consciousness in being (or becoming) modern. Equally important would be the educational force of theatre that identifies a cultural struggle of indigenous configuration against foreign ailment and internal infections that have wreaked havoc on Iranian body politics since antiquity.

The discourse on the efficacy of theatre as an educational experience would reappear in the Pahlavi era (1925–79). A 1939 advertisement on the establishment of Honarestan-e Honarpishegi-e Tehran (The Tehran Acting School) in the Etela'at newspaper would echo Mirza Reza Khan Nai'ni's 1908 statement. 'The collective desire of modernists from earlier years', the anonymous author would argue, 'has been for play and theatre houses to serve in the promotion of training and refinement of people's morality and through theatre acquaint people's consciousness with life's truths and spirituality, so plays and theatre houses can become large educational places for the training of people's thought and soul'.[21] Necessary in the realization of theatre's potential for educational self-growth is the enhancement of educational training sites for dramatic arts, which the Tehran Acting School purported to offer. To actualize theatre, performance needs to be professionalized.

Aside from the impact of the professionalization of theatre that saw its advancement in the Pahlavi period, the intellectual discourse on theatre must be viewed in connection with major socio-economic and political changes in the interwar period. To modernists of varied political leanings who fought against monarchical authoritarianism in the post-Constitutional period, theatre's significance was pronounced in the moral shaping of conscious citizens who became participants in a modernizing Iran. In its post-revolutionary variant, by extension, the field of theatre culture, and broadly speaking performance cultures, has inherited varied modernist imaginaries that primarily point towards a commitment to self-knowledge through staged performance. In a significant sense, the moral project that continues to inform theatrical practices in Iran, as the basis of conventions and experimentations, goes beyond the nation-state paradigm and, moreover, invites us to understand performance not as mere self-expression but the repertoire of performing the nation as a living, acting construct, hence the notion: 'performing Iran'.[22]

This book concerns itself with the question of performance, in particular theatre, as embodied practices, but does not limit its scope of analysis to conventional notions of theatre as a collaborative form of dramatic performances. It also attempts to go beyond the theoretical frameworks of the congruence of national culture as a stable entity, found in some approaches in regional studies. The main aim is to decentre the practice of theatre and by and large performance in line with the embodied knowledge that generates agency through dramatic enactments. While the study of theatre in Iran is a major theme, this book is ultimately concerned in how artistic and aesthetic performances produce meaningful sites of self-reflexivity.

Performing Iran: Culture, Performance, Theatre is a collection of chapters that, in their permutation, advance a study of performances that highlight the reflexivity of performance in changing practices. Such reflexivity is transferred and produced in local and global conditions, national and diaspora settings, yet tied to trans-local processes, from which theatrical traditions have invariably emerged to be reinvented in response to shifting contexts. In scholarly terms, the question of performance and, in particular, theatre in Iran is one that has received less attention than cinema. The tremendous interest in the Iranian cinema, by and large, has to do with the politics of cinematic production in post-revolutionary Iran, which has seen a proliferation of internationally acclaimed works, especially since the end of Iran-Iraq War (1980–8). There is also the aspect of commodification of cultural production in their packaged multiform technologies, which cinema has served as a privileged manufactured product for wider viewership and easier access.[23] Cultural production has enabled the entertainment repertoire of cinema, with its easy access to global audiences, to overshadow theatre's aesthetics of live immediacy and cultural transference in local settings.

Also advanced here is a conception of 'culture' that defies assumptions of ideology or resistance.[24] Culture is also less about the mere ensemble of expressive schemes in artistic, musical, ceremonial or theatrical productions and more about affective processes that shape distinct embodied publics.[25] As wide-ranging processes in what Raymond Williams famously called 'a whole way of life,' the emphasis on performance sustains a paradigmatic notion of action embedded in historical and social settings.[26] It is therefore no surprise that history is a major theme in this book (especially in the first part of the volume).

Moreover, performance variances, as expressed in theatre, are rejected as locked-up practices of cultural totalities, while overlooking the lived practices of class, gender, sexuality, status and state power. Equally important are the ephemeral spaces, ranging from shifting art galleries to traveling theatre troupes, and from commemorative rites to street performances, that configure embodied knowledge. Such practices, however, are always contingent to social realities through which performance is documented, recorded, reported and reinvented in the circulation of representations and reenactments.

What are the social realities of culture that are represented and reenacted in theatre and performance at large? And what sites of political and social agency do such cultural processes entail in the course of shifting historical contexts?

It is with the question of 'modern' that we begin, and with this beginning we trace the genesis of Iranian theatre in the nineteenth century.[27] This is the historical period during which Iran's encounters with colonial modernity (as a feature of modernity as a socio-historical global process at large) and technologies of standardization set the stage for deep tensions between Qajar modernization and revolutionary politics in the early twentieth century. Theatre in Iran, specifically, was informed by the shifting boundaries of political legitimacy guided by a moral paradigm of progress that became increasingly articulated by a network of artists, intellectuals, journalists and political figures in the late nineteenth century. Yet the extent to which such moral paradigms were reinterpreted in the course of history is primarily tied to contested institutional frameworks through which social change emerged in culturally specific forms of imaginaries – ways of conceiving conflict, order and change in temporal horizons. More importantly, the moral paradigm can be associated with the reinvention of traditions and the formation of new practices that shaped Iran into a revolutionary society in the beginning of the twentieth century.

Rest assured, what follows is not a comprehensive attempt at mapping out a historical account of Iranian theatre, needless to say, performance culture at large as a way to provide a context for the chapters in this volume. The account may seem grand in scale, but the proposed conceptual history is limited to cultural features in Iran since the nineteenth century that overlaps with global processes in the emergence of global theatre. Much will be left out, but in the hope that the rhizomatic discussion of ceaseless interaction of performance practices across time and space will open new lines of thinking in how performance can be conceptualized in transnational Iranian history.

From (invented) traditions to (post-)revolutionary theatre

Known for his detailed and lucid description of travels to Europe and Asia, the Qajar mystic and traveller Hajji Mohammad Ali Pirzadeh Na'ini (1835–1904) would write the following observation of the Parisian theatres in his *Safarnameh* or travelogue (1886–9): 'in all neighbourhoods in the city of Paris a number of highly reputable theatres can be found where people frequent every night and spend fortunes.' In an account detailed on the crowded life inside the Parisian theatres, he would add, "Even some go as far as paying a lump sum of money in the beginning of the year so they can have assigned seating for every night when attending theatre, as many are excited and eager to go to the theatre."[28] In Hajji Pirzadeh's account, Parisian theatres, in particular the opera house Palais Garnier, exemplify the most popular sites for entertainment-seeking Parisians, who show sheer exuberance in their collective interest in theatre as a popular activity.[29] However, the cultural life of Parisian theatres, Hajji Pirzadeh notes, is not just about the performers and their audiences but about the organization of the entertainment spaces, in particular the seating arrangements that are as intricate as the decor and lightening used to enhance the experience of visiting the *tamasha-khaneh* (house of spectacles). Theatre, for Hajji Pirzadeh, is as fascinating an architectural spectacle as the social life revolving around it.[30]

At the time of Hajji Pirzadeh's visit to Paris, the theatre culture of the Third Republic (1870–1940) marked the rise of new leisure space in the aftermath of Haussmann's reconstruction of the capital between 1853 and 1870. In light of radical urban changes, Parisians participated in an incipient mass culture of arts, architecture and fashion tied to new modes of cultural representation. The new spaces of urban networks reflected changing patterns of consumption coloured by new aesthetic sensibilities. Along with the construction of shopping arcades and department stores, new avenues such as the Avenue de l'Opéra, which led to Charles Garnier's Opera House, offered Parisians and visitors a visual feast of monumental spaces.[31]

By the late nineteenth century, theatre as an architectural space also had become monumental.[32] New spatial structures achieved the optical performance of new staging practices, an inheritance of late eighteenth-century Enlightenment with roots in the Italian Renaissance indoor theatres such as the Teatro Olympico in Vicenza (1585).[33] Such ocular theatrical spaces combined architectural, internal decor and prop techniques, and also an economy of entertainment consumption, in the form of purchasing tickets, that were, by and large, unfamiliar to a visiting Iranian traveller such as Hajji Pirzadeh. Here the intricate connection between theatre and city space is significant. With roots in Baroque and classical courtly theatre, late nineteenth-century French theatre represented the most consolidated form of architectural theatrical space based on the proscenium stage, Renaissance horseshow auditorium and organized seating arrangements, reflective of what Richard Preiss has called 'leisure industries' that through monetary transactions provide services for 'future experience', a product not yet produced but promised in a near future.[34] To meet the demand of its growing popularity, Parisian theatres owed much to the engineering and technological advancements of energy industrializations such as the 1881 installation of electricity, which allowed optical spectacles in the auditorium of Palais Garnier.[35]

The ability to control light, along with the lavish scene spectacles for realist effects and revolving stage-settings, accommodated the growing cultural appetites of a range of audiences such as working-class and middle-class members of French society.[36] In a significant sense, the Parisian theatre life, in words of Henry James in 1876, was not merely about entertainment but an essential feature of French identity: 'an institution, connected through a dozen open doors with literature, art, and society'.[37] While mass production of newspapers helped with the promotion of theatre shows, ranging from ballet to opera, the French railways provided transportation to theatre troupes to stage shows beyond Paris for diverse audiences. Moreover, new design patterns in architecture, industrial technology and urbanization defined a new era of bourgeois spaces of cultural consumption, which theatres, along with stylish café and elegant restaurants, best exemplified.[38]

In contrast to the described urban spatialization was Qajar Iran, where indoor auditoriums and proscenium stage theatres were yet to emerge as symptomatic of changes in patterns of consumption. In historical terms, Iranian cities would experience the de-territorialized cultures of consumerism in connection with new patterns of labour and markets caused by tepid modernization schemes, initiated by the Qajars, only in the late nineteenth century. It was in consumptive spaces, though limited in major urban centres, in particular Tehran, that spatial distinctions between work and leisure would eventually emerge to play an integral role in a new metropolitan order of modern living. Such distinction signalled new practices of urban sociability that spanned across the globe, in which the emerging middle class of Iran also sought to participate.[39]

Theatres as popular spaces of conviviality and experimentation, specifically architectural structures in which different dramatic performances were viewed, would locate common expressions to values of an emerging urban (petit) bourgeoisie population, which also coincided with the increasing presence of the working class as new audiences who flooded the cities from the rural areas in the late nineteenth century.[40] However, emerging theatrical spaces significantly owed to new engineering and technological advancements in staging practices. Gas or electric lightening of indoor playhouses created a self-enclosed theatrical ambience with naturalistic features, in what Raymond Williams described as 'theatrical environments', for the changing leisurely taste of urban spectators.[41] And, more importantly, public theatres were yet to become endowed with revolutionary fervour through drama as social critique, evident in the flourishing of theatre in the constitutional revolutionary period.

Under the Qajars, urban houses comprised of *arg* (inner fortress) and living spaces were divided into districts populated by networks of families based in neighbourhoods, and connected with narrow, winding streets, public baths, squares and local mosques.[42] More advanced in literary and cultural production, especially in the early Qajar period, Shiraz and Tabriz, especially Tabriz, due to its proximity to Ottoman and Russian-controlled Caucasus regions, sustained commercial and communication networks. Public spectacles (*namayesh*) in the form of gaming and comical entertainment during annual festivals or everyday spectacles such as *kheimeh-shab-bazi* (puppet shows) and *ma'rekeh-giri* (displays of strength) took place in alleys, on streets or at bazaars: daily/nightly public sites interwoven to residential districts.[43] Other performances such as slapstick comedies, *kachalak-bazi* (bald rogues), *pahlavan kachal* (the bald and generous champion/hero) or *baqqal-bazi* (grocer play) were staged at private homes or teahouses, with the latter serving primarily as a homosocial gathering space dating back to the Safavid period.[44] Likewise, lesser-known traditions such as *bazi-ha-ye namayeshi* identify comic performances that are primarily created and performed by women.[45]

The fluidity of the city necessitates fluid performances. Comic performances in humorous dance and narratives based on folk traditions were practised among traveling entertainers who saw an apogee in popularity in the Qajar period.[46] Ephemeral in practice, *ruhowzi* (on the pool) represented a type of satirical and musical show that was performed on wooden boards over small pools in the yards of private homes and inns. As a distinct comical genre with racial denotations, the blackface comical performance, *siah-bazi*, which staged the subversive relation of a domestic servant with his master, created a carnivalesque space where the life of hierarchy would briefly escape its official furrows and would enact festive possibilities.[47]

Under Qajar rule, the most important performances were staged at the city squares (*meidan*), where collective mourning or state rituals, such as military parades or executions, would take place. Of equal importance to popular performances were *pardeh-khwani*, or off-a-curtain storytelling sessions, and *naqqali*, or dramatic storytelling in verse or prose, performed at coffeehouses, private domains or caravansaries, where the audiences would also include foreign travellers. Among Kurdish populations, oral performances, along with a variety of ritual ceremonies, signified diverse traditions across the Iranian landmass.[48] In cities such as Isfahan, Kermanshah and Tehran, coffeehouses served as homosocial spaces, congregated by male customers who gave audience to *naqqali* and stories about Shi'i Imams, in particular Ali, the cousin and son-in-law of the Prophet, and Hossein, his son.[49] Similar to coffeehouses as homosocial spaces of conviviality, *zur-khaneh* (house of strength) identified as a repository site of *javanmardi* (young-manliness) ethics, as elaborated by Philippe Rochard and Denis Jallat, performed through 'codified fight games and traditional calisthenics' and characterized by spiritual overtones.⁵⁰

As a Shi'i Twelver (Imami) state, the Qajar's most popular form of performance was *ta'zieh*, the ritual dramas that in elegies recount the martyrdom of Hossein ibn Ali (626–680), the grandson of Prophet Mohammad, at the battle of Karbala in 680. Performed across cities and villages, the popularity of *ta'zieh* grew immensely during the reign of Naser al-Din Shah (1848–96) when permanent sites called *takkiyeh*, which were used for staging *ta'zieh*, spread throughout the country. The construction of Takkiyeh Dowlat (1868–9) introduced a major transformation in Iran's foremost traditional ritual performance, *ta'zieh*, as the new *takkiyeh* attained a royal status and a fixed spatial setting.⁵¹ The royal *ta'zieh* presented new entertainment features into the rituals and also embodied an innovative architectural building that most likely was modelled after the Parisian Opera House, a place where Nasir al-Din Shah had visited during his European travels.⁵²

As a result of economic reforms that included the introduction of new communication technologies, in particular the telegraph system in 1861, Tehran underwent two major urban plans. As Vahid Vahdat has shown, the 1855 plan entailed moderate changes to the city structure with 'eclectic expression' that revealed a new urban life.⁵³ Based on Renaissance urban structures, the new design involved the expansion of a distinct urban theatricality with the construction of European neoclassic architecture. Along with the construction of state buildings such as telegraph houses, hospitals, the city hall, the post office and especially streets as new commercial hubs, the second plan occurred under the supervision of Dar al-Fonun, the technical school founded in 1851, and was the most unique urban product of the Naseri-era urbanization.⁵⁴ The significance of the change was not just because Dar al-Fonun represented Iran's first institution of higher learning, modelled after European technical schools, but also for the theatre space inside the school, where dramatic performances of Hans Christian Anderson and Molière were translated and staged for ambassadors, ministers and other state officials.⁵⁵ The incorporation of gas lanterns in the Dar al-Fonun theatre would indicate an early example of in-door staging for selective visibility and mood setting for realist effects in Iran.⁵⁶ Other official spaces of performance included the royal court, where the translation of Molière's five-act comedy *L'Avare (The Miser)* was also staged for state audiences.⁵⁷

Although most early performances were organized at private homes or the royal court, by 1878, the theatrical performance was staged by a group of Armenians who had studied in Europe. The 1880 establishment of the Association of Theatre Lovers (Anjoman-e dustdaran-e te'atr) in the Armenian quarter of Tehran presented the first civic ensemble of troupe, director and enthusiasts.⁵⁸ In fact, Armenian theatre practitioners from Azerbaijan, Gilan and Tehran led the way in the performance of European plays in translation in Tabriz, Rasht, Isfahan and Armenian villages such as Haftvan, where several plays were performed between 1894 and 1900.⁵⁹ By the turn of the century, theatre shows in cities such as Tabriz and Tehran were partly organized by diasporic networks that traversed across Armenia, Azerbaijan, Britain, France, Georgia and Russia. Similar to cinematic production in urban Iran, the transnational operatives behind theatre production marked the emergence of what Golbarg Rekabtalaei has called 'Iranian cosmopolitanism', a process led by diaspora networks who participated in reimagining Iran according to modernist conceptions of moral progress and technological futurity.[60]

It was, however, with the satirical plays of modernist Mirza Fath-Ali Akhondzadeh (1812–78), written in Azari and translated into Persian by Mirza Jafar Qarachehdaghi (1834–93) that European-inspired drama was born as a performing art of modernist persuasion in Iran. The comic collections known as *Tamthilat* (*The Comedies*) are Akhondzadeh's ground-breaking contribution to Iranian theatre. First performed in Tbilisi and Moscow, the plays are emblematic of Enlightenment ideals, offering satirical critique of sociocultural norms and governmental ineptitude of the Qajars as a way to attain a rational order based on secular education, gender equality and rule of law.[61] Based in the Russian Caucasus, Akhondzadeh is exemplary of a diaspora activist/playwright/reformer whose secularist approach appropriated theatre as a didactic medium for social change.[62] Moreover, the translation of his works into Russian speaks of a literary modernity of transnational importance with neoclassical comical and Russian realism playing an integral role in early Iranian theatre.[63]

Mirza Aqa Tabrizi (1825?–1900?), a civil servant and an admirer of Akhondzadeh, authored the first plays in Persian. With his first plays published in Tabriz in 1908 and two other plays mistakenly published under the name of Mirza Malkam Khan in Berlin in 1922, Mirza Aqa Tabrizi wrote his works in descriptive narrative as a way to depict the social reality of his era, and hence not presentable for the stage.[64] Despite technical problems, which came under criticism by Akhondzadeh, Tabrizi's plays were noteworthy for their blunt criticism of the Qajar government and society, which also prevented them from being performed in Iran.[65] In a radical way, Tabrizi's writings anticipated Iranian drama literature in the twentieth century. Plays such as *Ashraf Khan* and *The Method of Government of Zaman Khan of Borujerd in 1820–1* explore themes such as moral corruption, bribery and the financial exploitation of people by corrupt politicians, written in comical boldness with a disregard for conventions, comparable to the works of Nikolai Gogol (1809–52).[66]

Equally important was the rise of theatrical criticism. For instance, the May 5, 1908 publication of Ruzname-ye Teʻatre (*Theatre Newspaper*) marked the publication of reviews and commentaries solely on theatre, covering various topics such as the religious lawfulness of theatre as a moral art form.[67] Similar articles and reviews on drama sought to legitimate theatre and at times echoed the critical discourses on moral and political corruption in Iranian society.

The late nineteenth and early twentieth centuries were also decades of significant political crisis for Iran. As the Qajar monarchy sought to maintain power amid British and Russian imperial rivalry in the region, a political force encompassed of a broad coalition of groups, such as the new intelligentsia, reformist clerics, merchants and guilds, who demanded new political opening for a constitutional order. In what led to the Constitutional Revolution of 1905–11, the new political environment gave way to a flourishing of theatrical spaces throughout Iran. In the wake of the Constitutional Revolution, the publication and staging of numerous plays by theatrical troupes saw the growing popularity of performances in places such as The Hall of Zahir al-Dowleh in Tehran.[68]

Theatre's popularity was also evident among the Sufi order, *Anjoman-e Okhovvat*, led by Zahir al-Dowleh, the son-in-law of Nasir al-Din Shah. In 1907 the reformist-leaning mystical brotherhood staged a pantomime performance within Zahir al-Dowleh's private domain near Lalehzar Street. The pantomime depicted the Shah on the throne with a body laying at his feet and clothed in richly embellished garments. The clothes and jewellery were then one by one stolen by foreigners such as English and Russian ambassadors, until a group of people made the king aware of the collective plunder and, in response, the Shah and his followers made the thieves go away.[69] Though with roots in *lal-bazi* (play of the mute), the 1907 pantomime was performed in the period's broad interest in theatre as a form of political expression.[70]

In what Kamran Sepehran has described as the 'theatricality of revolution', the Constitutional-era theatre combined a critical spirit for change and a didactic sensibility for public education, where the growing print culture played an integral role in its promotion.[71] Especially in the later stages of the revolution, theatre groups and constitutionalist playwrights staged plays in closed yet especially open spaces such as Amin al-Dowleh Park, where they advanced revolutionary conceptions of patriotism in addition to minority and women's rights.[72] In the immediate years after the revolution, theatre flourished in Tehran, as the capital underwent further expansion with the formation of new public spaces, such as administrative, educational and commercial centres, a process that slowly began in the late nineteenth century. Even smaller cities such as Rasht saw popular performances organized by rising theatre groups, such as the National Performance and Conference Company (Sherkat-e Namayesh va Konferans, Teʿatr-e Melli).[73] Independent from state support, the popularity of theatre performances was so great that they somewhat resembled the crowded theatres of Paris, though highly politicized and also minus the seating and organized schedules, which Hajji Pirzadeh so admired about the Parisian theatres.[74] Ironically, in 1924 when the British Orientalist Edward G. Browne (1862–1926) declared that the tradition of drama has 'not succeeded in establishing itself in Persia even to the extent which it has done in Turkey', Iranian theatre had become one of the most popular forms of performance.[75]

The 1921 coup d'etat of Reza Khan, who in 1925 established the Pahlavi monarchy, inaugurated an era of centralized modernization. Cultural engineering played a key role in the Pahlavi modernization programme, which included the expansion of the urban middle class with claims to national prosperity and capitalistic modernity. Tied to economic and industrial growth, the Pahlavi urbanization plan played an integral role in the creation of new city spaces of leisure, where not only the middle class but also urban workers can participate as consumer audiences. The early Pahlavi theatre combined the performance of translated European works, musical comedies and Iranian historical plays.[76]

Themes of foreign conquest, moral disease and a call for national rejuvenation are common among a number of plays during this period. Sadeq Hedayat's *Parvin Dokhtar-e Sasan* (1928) and *Maziar* (1933) exemplify historical dramas with nationalistic overtones in their focus on the seventh-century Arab invasion of Iran. Operettas by Reza Kamal (1898–1937) (best known by the pseudonym Shahrzad) and Mirzadah Eshqi (1831–1924) staged romantic narratives about the nation, which derived its popular legitimacy as a living, organic entity, emanating from a monarchical sovereignty. With appeal among the urban elite, European influences were ostensible in the popularity of ballet schools and public performances, which mostly originated in the migration of several dance artists to Iran after the October Revolution of 1917.[77] Meanwhile, the range of performing arts shared a common feature with post-Enlightenment cultural imaginary present in many nation-building experiences across the globe.[78] Musical performances such as *Madar-e Vatan* (*Mother Homeland* 1923) staged an alternative nationalistic imaginary based on what Mohammad Tavakoli-Targhi has called 'the matriotic counter-state discourse' in its depiction of nation as a disease-infected mother, juxtaposed to the official conception of a male monarch as the healthy embodiment of the nation.[79]

With roots in educational reforms that included *Nehzat-e Tarjomeh* (Translation Movement), launched by Amir Kabir (1807–52) with the establishment of Dar al-Fonun, post-Constitutional Iran saw the staging of numerous (re)translations of European dramatic works.[80] The performance of neoclassical works of Molière and realist plays of Alexander Ostrovsky benefited less from literal translation than moral substance, one that, in their adaptation to Iranian sensibilities, would evoke an ethical sense of self-criticism with strong educational objectives. In the specific case of Molière, as Edward G. Browne notes, plays such as *Le Misanthrope* (*Gozaresh-e Mardomgoriz*) would undergo changes in name and plot, including characters, even insertion of Persian proverbs in the dialogues.[81] While translated works of Molière appealed to the Iranian intellectuals for their critical commentary on religion and politics, the translations were also creatively rewritten and performed so as to avoid censorship by the monarchy.[82]

By the Constitutional period translation became less restricted to the whims of monarchy and more oriented towards opening new spaces of political expression. As part of an 'independent print culture', to use the words of Farzin Vejdani, the staging of foreign works allowed a distinct way of performing modernity through the very act of translation.[83] The formation of what can be identified as new translational publics, shaped by a growing number of theatre troupes, bespoke of being (or becoming) modern on theatrical platforms where European fashionable styles of hair and dress corresponded to experiences of feeling modern. As depicted in the 1928 photo of *The Merchant of Venice*, performed in the Zoroastrian Club in Tehran (Figure 0.2), theatre in translation served as a way of fashioning modern Iranianness, a significant departure from merely adapting received European performances to preconceived notions of Iranian taste.[84]

The spatial life of theatrical locality underwent change as well. Here again the transforming metropolis played a major role. In the early Pahlavi period, Lalehzar would become the most iconic place for performing arts, as cafes, cabarets and

Figure 0.2 *The Merchant of Venice*, directed by Majid Rezvani, performed in the Zoroastrian Club in Tehran 19 April 1928.⁸⁵

commercial cinemas represented the most fashionable places for Iranians of different social backgrounds to frequent. With twenty theatrical troupes in Tehran alone, Lalehzar boasted a number of venues, of which the Grand Hotel and Namayeshgah-e Markazi-ye Lalehzar (The Central Theatre of Lalehzar) represented two of its most popular sites. Between 1930 and the early 1940s, city spaces underwent change as new urban regulations and architectural projects marked a significant political means for reconstructing the cultural heritage by fusing pre-Islamic past with modernism, alongside major social reforms.⁸⁶ The 1936 unveiling decree enabled new spaces of conviviality for women and led to a social trajectory which Ida Meftahi describes as the 'intrusion of female sexuality into public space and onto the theatre stage'.⁸⁷ Such 'intrusion' would initially emerge in 1924 when Qamar al-Moluk Vaziri (1905–59), one of the first unveiled female singers, performed a poetic song in front of a mostly male audience at the Grand Hotel on Lalehzar Street.⁸⁸

The 1920s and 1930s marked two important developments in Iranian theatre and performance culture at large. In 1925 Seyyed Ali Nasr established the Sheraket-eh Komedi-yeh Irani (The Iranian Comedy Company), a theatre troupe comprised of experienced actors who would gain national fame for performing plays such as *Arusi-ye Hossein Aqa* (*The Wedding of Mr. Hossein*) in 1939. Inspired by the Comédie-Française, the Iranian Comedy Company focused on didactic performances with modernist stances on social change, in particular gender reform. The company would also represent the first professional theatre group with monthly shows at the Grand Hotel Theatre and the first troupe to permit women to perform on stage.[89]

By the 1930s musical performances would increasingly include female dancers and singers, creating eroticized spaces of conviviality primarily for male audiences.[90] The 'intrusion' would also initiate what G. J. Breyley and Sasan Fatemi call the spread of *motrebi*, or musical cultural milieu of lowbrow entertainers in Lalehzar.[91] The popular *motrebi* (minstrel) performances and operettas in Persian with historical and romantic themes would become a common scene in Lalehzar throughout the Pahlavi period, when an increased number of working-class audiences would frequent the nightly cafe-restaurant and cabaret scenes.[92]

In the later Pahlavi period (1941–79), the eruption of theatrical productions by Iranian dramatists signified a growing theatrical culture that reflected the changing times. Four significant transformations took place in the post-occupation Iran. The first development was the Sovietization of the Iranian political culture that saw its apogee with the establishment of Tudeh Party in 1941.[93] As a member of Tudeh Party, Abdolhossein Nooshin developed a stellar reputation as a leading theatre practitioner in the production and staging of a range of European plays, such as Marcel Pagnol's *Topaze* (1928), which offered a moral critique of capitalistic systems in response to the Great Crash of 1929.[94]

Nooshin's attempt to shape stage production into an educational space also entailed the professionalization of Iranian theatre, in particular, the development of mise-en-scène, which highlights the enhanced performance of stage visualization in relation with the audience.[95] His influence also included the adaptability of Persian into stage performance and providing monthly financial support to his actors, which included talented female performers such as Turan Mehrzad (1930–) and Mahin Deihim (1925–2001).[96] Under Nooshin's mentorship at the Farhang Theatre in the 1940s and later at the Russian state Institute of Performing Arts, Mostafa Oskooi (1924–2005) and Mahin Oskooi (1930–2006) continued the professionalization of Iranian theatre with the introduction of Stanislavsky's method acting through their pedagogical and performance activities at the Anahita Art Training College especially from 1959 to 1964.[97]

The second development was the state sponsorship of 'high culture' performances. In the aftermath of the 1953 coup, which saw the overthrow of the democratically elected prime minister, Mohammad Mosaddegh (1882–1967), the Pahlavi repressive regime of censorship operated in tandem with the urban construction of monumental spaces, similar to what was earlier discussed in reference to nineteenth-century Paris. The building of the performing arts complex, Roodaki Hall, in 1967, where musical, operatic and ballet performances were staged as national events, defined a new spatial production in the hierarchy of the arts in nation-building.[98] As an extension of Mohammad Reza Shah's White Revolution, as a series of reforms launched in 1963, the construction of the City Theatre of Tehran in 1972 and the Tehran Museum of Contemporary Art in 1977 identified the expansive re-ordering of the hierarchy in the production of culture that directly impacted ways in which the new middle class could have access to 'arts' as a state commodity in urban display.

Monumentalization erases the past-ness of the past in the crystallization of new cultural spaces of national distinction. Major state processions, such as the 2500th Anniversary Celebrations of the founding of the Persian Empire in 1971, served as important performative spectacles to monumentalize a new national history based on a dramatized pre-Islamic past.[99] Meanwhile, the institutionalization of the Shiraz Arts Festival (1967–77) launched a period of stage production in national culture. The state-sponsored festivals involved various venues and a range of performances: avant-garde or jazz music from the United States to the performance of a number of Iranian avant-garde plays directed by Arby Ovanessian (1942–). Yet given its high visibility as a cultural event, the most salient development was marked by the staging of arts and performances deemed as 'traditional' into reified cultural commodities in display for both Iranian and international audiences. The performance of *musiqi-ye asil* (authentic music), *naqqali*, provincial music and especially *taʿzieh* played an integral role in the festival for staging a repertoire of cultural practices perceived indigenous and distinct to an imagined authentic Iran.

Transmitting a constructed memory of indigenous performance involves the mediated processes to envisage culture as an expression of an imagined nation. In the later Pahlavi period, this transmitting process was informed by the televised broadcasting of the Shiraz Festival, which signalled a third development, that is, the mass mediatization of performance culture.[100] The diffusion of radio in the 1930s and introduction of television in 1958 unleashed a nationwide process of imparting mass media to a large population through new technologies in Iran. Despite cinema's growing popularity, music and theatre, in particular, benefited from radio in the 1940s and, later, television in the 1960s, when Iranian society underwent significant change through consumerism and the mediatization of culture, which generated a new primacy of industrial metropolis.[101] During this period, the growth of popularity of radio theatre shows can be described as the radiozation of theatre, a performance tradition that is still practised in contemporary Iran.[102] The 1968 televised staging of the allegorical play, *Shahr-e Qesseh* (*The City of Tales*), written and directed by Bijan Mofid (1935–84), and performed at the Shiraz Festival, for example, provided a critical social and political commentary of Pahlavi modernization, through musical performances and a parable of animal characters.[103] Recorded and distributed on cassette tape and VHS throughout the 1970s and 1980s, the play became most popular among revolutionaries and also post-revolutionary dissidents who saw the satirical depiction of the clerics in the story as an apt critique of the newly established Islamic Republic.

Shahr-e Qesseh is also exemplary of a form of theatre that appeared from the 1950s to the 1960s and saw the reappropriation of 'traditional' performances into new theatrical expressions. First, *Shahr-e Qesseh* creatively adapted folk stories and the *ruhowzi* genre into a subversive avant-garde performance that also represented a national epic of critical substance. Likewise, playwrights such as Abbas Javanmard (1929–2020), the founder of the Goruh-e Honar-e Melli (The National Art Group) in 1955, which included major playwrights active in the production of numerous plays, advocated for indigenous Iranian theatre by incorporating traditional performances such as *ta'zieh* through the National Arts Group (1956–73).[104] The 1957 staging of *Af'i-ye talayi* (*The Golden Serpent*) by Ali Nasirian (1935–) best exemplified a post-1953 play that incorporated coffee performances of *hoqqeh-bazi* (conjuror) and traditional public spectacles of masculine strength, such as *ma'rekeh-giri* and *mar-giri* (snake charming).[105] Tradition, in this context, was not just (re)invented but made into a new national cultural consciousness.

Yet perhaps the most important development was the proliferation of independent theatre groups, identified by networks of artists, actors, intelligentsia, translators and producers who staged innovative performance of plays that addressed key social and philosophical problems amid Pahlavi modernization. In contrast to how the Tudeh Party ascribed post-1953 Iranian theatre as 'degeneration', the staging of plays by writers such as Gholam-Hossein Sa'edi (1936–85), who published under the penname Gowhar Morad, Hamid Samandarian (1931–2012), and Akbar Radi (1939–2007) represented an ongoing Iran-based production of performances that also coincided with the production of translation and staging of non-Iranian, in particular European works by various established theatre groups, such as the Armenian Theatre troupe led by Shahin Sarkissian (1910–66).[106] The realist plays of Radi such as *Marg dar payiz* (*Death in the Autumn*) (1966) and *Az posht-e shisheha* (*From behind the Windows*) (1966) reflect a palpable influence by Anton Chekhov and Henrik Ibsen, two of the most popular European playwrights in Iran.[107] For most realist plays, venues such as Talar Sangelaj (established in 1965) saw the performance of rising actors/playwrights such as Ali Nasirian (1935–) and Ezzatollah Entezami (1924–2018). Meanwhile, the avant-garde theatre of Bahram Beyzaie (1938–) and his appropriation of indigenous performances concurred with a new wave of global experimental theatrical production that appealed to new artistic circles and broader public, marked by a generational shift in line with an expanding educational sector in urban Iran.[108]

The 1960s rise in theatre production reflected a fundamental shift in rural-urban relations and the growth of an urban middle-class population that experienced new tastes, desires and patterns in leisure consumption and intellectual vitality. In various instances, and in appeal to the new middle class with a taste for alternatives, theatre emerged as a critical, subversive space associated with oppositional activities. Plays by Sa'edi such as *Shahadat* (*Witness*) (1962), *Entezar* (*Waiting*) (1964) and *Choob-beh-dastha-ye Varazil* (*The Club-wielders of Varazil*) (1965) displayed a mix of realist and surrealist genres with a critical exploration in the psychological dimensions of everyday Iran, with implicit critique of Pahlavi modernization.[109] Informed by contemporary revolutionary social movements in other parts of the world, dissident theatre was an embrace of an aesthetic-expressive universality that perceived performance as a means of creating self-consciousness and a space to educate and bring about change for alternative politics.

In a similar vein, the emergence of experimental performances paved the path towards a new kind of theatre. Established in 1969, Kargah-e Namayesh (The Theatre Workshop) embodied the first experimental theatre, in what has been called 'the new wave of theatre', where plays by Iranian experimental playwrights such as Ismael Khalaj (1945–) and European playwrights such as Eugène Ionesco and Samuel Beckett would be performed with the sponsorship of NITV.[110] The major directors of the workshop were Iraj Anvar (1939–) and Arby Ovanessian, who remained in contact with European directors such as Tadeusz Kantor (1915–90), Jerzy Grotowski and Peter Brook through the Shiraz Arts Festival.[111] Absurdist plays such as *Pajuheshi zharf va setorg dar sangvareha-ye gharn-e bistom o panjom-e zamin-shenasi ya chardahom, bistom farghi nemikonad* (*A Deep, Big, and New Research on the Fossils of the 25th Genealogy Period, or the 14th, 20th, There Is No Difference*) (1966) by Abbas Nalbandian (1947–89) articulated the budding anti-realist genres that also signalled an aesthetic revolutionary shift evident in the 'new wave' of Iranian cinema in the 1960s.[112] Theatre professionals in the absurdist genre were particularly influenced by intellectual currents, including existential themes embodied in the artwork of emerging artists such as Parviz Tanavoli (1937–), who viewed modernization as increasingly empty and devoid of value.[113] Beyond Kargah-e Namayesh, Bahman Forsi (1934–), with his groundbreaking absurdist play, *Goldan* (*The Vase*), 1960, showed a striving to cast off accepted notions of reality in favour of an existential quest for self-knowledge amid an inescapable era of technological determinism.[114]

During expansive urbanization and demographic change, emerging female playwrights and translators would push beyond the actor performance role. As directors and playwrights, Khojasteh Kiya (1933–) and Farideh Farjam (1935–) represented a new generation of dramatists who addressed historical and social themes, especially the status of women in relation to social class.[115] In the 1970s Manijeh Mohamedi (1944–), a noted director, would stage street performances in Tehran and also translate the works of Iranian playwrights such as Sa'edi into English.[116] Across a range of venues, women playwrights and directors had become active participants in the production of culture.[117]

The Pahlavi-era theatre also provided a crucial conceptual model for post-revolutionary theatre practitioners. The ideal was a modernist imaginary that saw theatre as a collaborative expressive medium for emergent meanings and self-perceptions while reinterpreting indigenous traditions in response to changing socio-political circumstances. Such a modernist response would involve a range of critiques on the direction being taken by rapid industrialization and regimes of censorship under Pahlavi modernization; they also included a blunt assessment of transforming social relations based on new patterns of work and class.

This critical feature is mostly evident in Sa'edi's plays. In *Karbafakha dar Sangar* (*Workaholics in the Trenches*) (1960), he depicts the impact of a mining company on the everyday life of rural Iran. Sa'edi's play is a forthright critique of the ideology of technological progress with implications on psychological and social relations in Iranian life.[118] Likewise, the 1974 staging of Maksim Gorky's *The Petty Bourgeois* (1902) in Rasht by the Iranian Theatre Group embodied a critical enactment of class relations and state power from the pre-revolutionary to the early revolutionary periods.[119]

A sadly understudied form of performance in the context of Iranian history is prison theatre. Especially in the pre-revolutionary period, theatre in prison spaces identified invisible sites of incarceration. It also constituted specific forms of repressed sociability where informal performance would serve an emotive process under confinement. In Nasser Rahmaninejad's pre-revolutionary prison account, we read about the adaptation of Chekhov's 1884 short story, *The Chameleon*, performed at Qasr Prison.[120] In Shahla Talebi's haunting prison memoir, we learn about makeshift stage decorations made by female prisoners for nightly performances at Qasr Prison.[121] Written by one of the prisoners, the (unnamed) play depicted a middle-class family life and their superficial aspirations, a performance rich in detail and rife with depth and subtlety. Talebi describes, 'For me more than the play itself, the attempt to create the stage, the curtain, the setting of the apartment, the details, the way they were made in a collective work, and the reaction of the prison head and the guards who could not believe their eyes have stayed as vivid memories.'[122] The spontaneous and improvised in prison theatre informs the staging of hidden revolts that herald the coming of open rebellions on city streets, and the two mentioned examples certainly presaged the coming of the most mass-based revolt in world history: the revolution of 1979.

If theatre is the transfiguration of the empty space into a stage of performance, revolution is then the dramatization of excess change, real and imaginary, into the public domains of the living and the dead, that is, squares, streets, parks and cemeteries.[123] The myriad street demonstrations that served as iconic images of the 1979 Revolution provoke an examination of mass protest as an urban theatrical performance of historic significance.[124] Through technologies of visualization that reveal a 'people' in rebellion, revolutionary action signals an ocular performance that hinges on the relationship between the visible protestors and the delocalized audiences, who give witness to the performative force of mass revolt. In so far as performance and visibility open up the dialectics between movement and memory, posters of martyrs, clerics, intellectuals carried by demonstrators or stencils on the walls of city streets constitute the absorptive power of multiple imageries, partially phantasmatic and always mediated through experiences that the political can be reimagined.[125]

We may reflect on street protests as the first instances of open street theatre in the early revolutionary period, roughly speaking 1979 to 1980. Streets as transient spaces designed for traffic and pedestrian mobility are transformed into a spectacle of revolt, affective sites of outrage in defiance of the status quo. It is no surprise that some of the most intriguing street performances were staged during the revolutionary period. Rahmaninejad recalls student-led performances at parks and streets, although of 'shallow content and abysmal theatrical skills', which limited their appeal to public audiences.[126] Rahmaninejad also directed several street performances, including plays by Bertolt Brecht.[127] Leftist playwright Saeed Soltanpour staged his *Abbas Agha Karegar-e Iran Nasional* (Abbas Aqa, the Worker of Iran National Company), a play about a worker at the Iran National automobile plant, in 1980.[128]

As the revolution faded in light of the consolidation of the Islamic Republic between 1980 and 1983, limited number of theatres served as venues to stage limited performances. Lalehzar performance culture, in particular, underwent dramatic change with the state takeover of all theatre venues.[129] Home to commercial life of cabaret and dance entertainment in the late Pahlavi period, Lalehzar saw a major transformation with the purging of 'Western influences' under the state policy of 'cultural revolution' (*enqelab-e farhangi*), as art and theatre began to serve revolutionary ends.[130] In 1980, Komiteh Emdad Imam Khomeini (The Imam Khomeini Relief Foundation), a state-supported charitable organization, took over the Nasr theatre, and in 1987 a number of theatre performances were staged by playwright and director Hasan Azimi (1947–). In terms of theatrical genres, Nasr theatre saw the combined performances of comical shows such as *siah-bazi* and translated works of Molière. Yet the range of performances was limited to the new state's cultural policies that saw theatre, in particular, as means for 'awakening the impoverished nations of the world'.[131]

With the opening of universities in 1983, some of the first theatrical shows were performed at the Theatre Department of the University of Tehran. The performance of *Yerma* by Federico García Lorca, a subversive play known for its criticism of the gender repression and sexual morality of Catholic Spain, is indicative of the ineffective censorship regime during this period.[132] In the early revolutionary period, a more important development was the introduction of *defa'-e Moqaddas*, or Sacred Defence theatre, a new genre that revolved around themes of memory, martyrdom and revolutionary ethics in response to the Iran-Iraq War (1980–8). As Iranians faced a major military conflict with the traumatization of shared consciousness, the Sacred Defence, as part of a broader military-revolutionary genre of *te'atr-e arzeshi* ('value-laden theatre'), became the best-funded production in the Iranian theatrical landscape.[133] Plays such as *Marg-e digari* (*The Death of Another*) (1981) and *Tir-e gheib* (*Invisible Arrow*) (1982) by the famed movie-director Mohsen Makhmalbaf (1957–) explored themes of death, war and mystical experience. *Taʿzieh* also saw a dramatized politicization, as its narrative and staging practices were reconfigured to match themes pertinent to the ongoing war, memorializing the 'living martyrs' of the frontlines where the Karbala story could be reenacted on stage.[134] However, as Liliane Anjo has observed, since their inception in 1980s a range of *defa'-e Moqaddas* performances have been 'ambivalent' in themes since some have also included critical depictions of the war considered by the state as 'sacred'.[135]

But it was with the institutionalization of revolutionary ideology when theatre reemerged as a popular art form in urban Iran. In the aftermath of the revolution, two major developments took place in the field of theatrical production. First, by 1982, post-revolutionary theatre became increasingly tied to state-sponsored events, known as the Fadjr International Theatre Festival (FITF), where local and international theatrical works were featured on stage.[136]

The significance of the festival is three-fold. First, it identifies a form of state ceremonial performance that annually commemorates the 1979 Revolution on the 22nd of *Bahman* (February).[137] Second, as noted by Marjan Moosavi, FITF should be viewed as part of the revolutionary project to 'solidify Iran's in Islamic ideology', and especially since its second phase, which began in 1997, reached out to the international theatre as a way to 'cultivate global relationships'.[138] Third, under the supervision of the Ministry of Culture and Islamic Guidance (MCIG), the festival gradually became a political battlefield between vying political factions, a central feature of the newly established Islamic Republic.[139] Factional politics became most evident during the early Reformist Period (1997–2002), when the more open cultural policies of President Mohammad Khatami led to an increase in theatre performances and, accordingly, audiences during the festivals. The festivals became a contentious site to combat conservative repression in other institutions, in particular print media and the legislative branch. Although less restricted than cinema, based on the perception that only a 'cultured' minority give audience to the distinct art form, the festival also serves as a medium of censorship, as the ministry continues to determine changing policies of permitted staged performance.[140]

Second, in their reinvented form, traditions of performance saw a new trajectory in post-war Iran. In 1989, the MCIG organized the first Traditional Theatre Festival, followed by other cultural festivals, such as the First national Painting Biennial in 1991.[141] The 1989 festival included familiar performances in *ruhowzi* genre, ranging from *siah-bazi* to *baqqal-bazi*, which appealed to a relatively large audience. The 1993 First Congress on *taʿzieh* shows the expansion of the Pahlavi-era interest in the rituals as cultural heritage to be studied and performed as theatre.[142] Space is limited to unpack the politics in the cultural production of reinvented traditions. But just to scratch the surface of this development, recalling the Pahlavi era, we can argue that the post-revolutionary attempt to perform tradition entailed an ideological desire to sustain the dynamism of an imagined past preserved in the performances. With the 1985 album *Bidad* (a word ambivalent in meaning: *without-voice, injustice or sensational havoc*) by Mohammad-Reza Shajarian (1940–2020), classical Persian music based on the repertoire of melodies, *radif*, however, presented a distinct example of a 'traditional' performance perceived by many as a subtle expression of dissent.[143] Traditions in performance were registered through not merely state cultural institutions but the opening of spaces of protest by various networks of artists, filmmakers, musicians and theatre practitioners.

By the 1990s, as Iran experienced an era of economic reconstruction under the presidency of Akbar Hashemi Rafsanjani (1934–2017), theatre's slow growth became tied to deep-seated societal transformation. The 1980s population boom, together with the advent of a younger population bulge, was coloured by an underlying educational transformation, initiated by Rafsanjani's pragmatist administration with investments in universities and promotion of scientific-industrial institutions.[144] The most significant development in the field of cultural production was the relative loosening of state control over public discourse in media and intellectual life, helping key figures such as Abdol Karim Soroush (1945–) to offer a systematic critique of Islamist ideology. The privatization initiatives, especially in the mobilization of private capital in urbanization, entailed changes in public spaces. Iranian cities experienced change similar to the Pahlavi period, albeit less global connections as a result of the broadening of sanctions put in place by the United States in 1995.

However, unlike the Pahlavi period, Tehran and other major cities did not undergo a major construction of new monumental spaces of cultural significance. For the most part, the Pahlavi-era theatres such as Mehrab, Sangelaj Vahdat (formerly known as Roodaki) and the City Theatre (Teʿatr-e Shahr) continued to stage performances. Theatrical productions certainly increased during the 1990s, but faced major obstacles because of censorship, at times imposed as a production was about to be staged, and also shortage of venues, which served as a form of control.[145] As a result of infighting between pragmatist and hardliner factions, *Pech-pechha-ye posht-eh nabard* (*The Whispers behind the Frontline*), a play by Alireza Naderi (1961–) about soldiers who experience doubt and angst amid the war with Iraq, was halted by the Basiji paramilitary forces at the Mowlavi Hall.[146] The factional politics over censorship though did not overshadow the growth of the middle class and its flourishing political prominence during the post-war period. Such growth also entailed cultural transformations, at times supported by the state. The development included an emergent musical culture, in what singer-songwriter-intellectual Mohsen Namjoo has ironically observed as 'independent music': a cultural field that originally received state support but later broke away into a distinct expressive movement.[147]

By the late 1990s the confluence of growth in urban life and increases in literacy across class, gender and ethnicity had pushed for greater openness in politics and, by extension, culture. Political change tied to the class dynamics of post-revolutionary society became most patently visible in 1997, when Khatami won a landslide presidential election. The rise of reformists (*eslah-talaban*), armed with the discourse of 'civil society' and 'dialogue between civilisations', boosted state investments in cultural infrastructures that, in turn, enhanced middle-class participation.[148] Khatami, who led the MCIG under Rafsanjani's administration, expanded a more open cultural policy based on *osul-e siasat-e farhangi* (principles of cultural policy) that included limitations on state promotion of Islam through culture and easing on restriction over print media, films and theatre.[149] The introduction of internet to the educational and later commercial sectors in the late 1990s also contributed to alternative social spaces. Such spaces set the stage in the introduction of new cultural products with increased expressions in digital performance, ranging from blogs to online publication of dramatic and literary works.[150]

The 'theatre boom' during the Reform period was a watershed moment in the history of Iranian theatre. First, state subsidies for cultural productions and theatre were marked by a sharp increase of 1000 per cent between 1997 and 2001.[151] Khatami's new cultural policy included the establishment of Khaneh Teʿatr (Theatre Forum), which brought together actors, critics, directors, playwrights and other theatrical practitioners into a professional organization in 1999.[152] The cultural policy also gave rise to new theatre groups such as the Mehr Theatre Group, founded by the internationally award-winning playwright/director Amir Reza Koohestani (1979–), heralded the birth of innovative plays such as *Dancing on Glasses* (2001) and *The Latest Experiences* (2003). In 2000 playwrights/directors such as Mohammad Charmshir (1960–) and actor Atila Pesyani (1957–) staged an adaptation of three Shakespearean plays in the *Three Rewritings of Shakespeare* that articulated a critical view of contemporary Iranian society.[153] As noted earlier, the FITF also saw a considerable increase in audiences, especially since the 1999 inclusion of international theatre groups in the festivals, a development that coincided with an upsurge in plays and innovative new performances beyond the festivals. During her 2003 visit to the 21st FITF, Moosavi describes the FITF audiences as the following:

> The news had spread far and wide: a Canadian group of artists had come to perform *Macbeth*. As a student of English in Iran, I believed it was a once-in-a-lifetime chance to watch Shakespeare performed by native English speakers. Arriving at the venue, I never imagined there would be 200 enthusiastic spectators squished into such a small space, which ushers struggled to keep clear for the performance.[154]

Here the relationship between the Iranian audience and the Canadian performers in the unfolding of a Shakespearean play should not be reduced to one of consumption of a theatrical production, but viewed in itself an intercultural performance in a theatrical event, an attempt to overcome the isolationism of the early revolutionary period.

The staging of translated works has and continues to be a critical feature of Iranian theatrical traditions since the late Qajar period. In an analytical conception, translation is based on two interconnected processes: first, the act of translation as a semantic function to interpret a play written in a foreign language; and second, the reproduction of the translated play into a performance of self-interpretation. The 'self' here is ambiguous as vernacular languages are hardly self-enclosed of linguist purities but multiple and intersectional, as every language, Jacques Derrida famously claimed, is 'a language of the other'.[155] In this view, translation can be understood as the interplay between the self and the other, and textual ways translated works spark off into new oral and literary expressions across and beyond languages, especially within the national construct. In the case of Shakespearian plays, for example, as evident in the early twentieth century, the 1900 translation of *The Taming of the Shrew* was rendered from a French translation of English to Persian, three languages with complex interlinguistic cross-fertilizations across Afro-Eurasia.[156]

But translation is also tempered by what can be officially sanctioned to be said in performative ways. Censorship, in many ways, has played a key role in translational practices. Especially since the early Pahlavi period, censorship of theatre would be officially supervised through a complex bureaucratic process, as aptly described by Christoph Werner in the case of the Red Lion and Sun Theatre in Tabriz.[157] Stage performances had to adapt to the official language, which critically excluded Azeri-Turkish. Likewise in the post-revolutionary period, the staging of *Richard III*, performed by Davood Rashidi (1933–2016) in 1999, and *Hamlet*, directed by Mikail Shahrestani (1963–) in 2000 and *Macbeth* bt Hamid Reza Naeemi (1974–) in 2005, are exemplary of cultural adaptations of the Shakespearean plays into Persian, while aligning with the vicissitudes of censorship regulations. Yet a key feature in translation production that spanned beyond the Reformist period was the subtle and, at times, explicit critique that the performances brought forth on the political and social issues related to the post-revolutionary condition.[158] Translation, paradoxically, involves subversion in the process of censorship. Translation as a way to circumvent state regulation over cultural production became evident in numerous plays such as Mostafa Rahimi's 1993 *Hamlet*. Rahimi's *Hamlet* not only evaded censorship rules through a careful translation of the English text but also innovatively mythologized the Danish prince similar to Iranian heroic figures. Despite constant inspector supervisions, Mahmood Karimi Hakak's *A Midsummer Night's Dream* at the 1999 Fadjr Theatre Festival (figure 0.3) included various staging tactics, described in the following account by the director:

> Here is an example: An 'inspector', bragging that he held an MA in theater, suggested that in order to avoid un-Islamic relationship between man and woman, I should have Lysander and Hermia marry each other before they escape into the woods! Imagine! The entire play happens because these two young lovers are not allowed to marry each other. That is why they run into the woods to escape to where 'the sharp Athenian law/Cannot pursue' them. Another censor objected to the proximity of a male and female characters on stage. 'From where I am sitting' he said, 'they seemed to touch each other!' I pointed out to him that, 'You can actually see that there's a distance of over three feet between these two actors, and that they did not touch.' He responded, 'Yes, "I" know they did not touch. But some people in the audience may think they touched.' There was no use explaining to this gentleman that theater is the art of make-believe, so I moved the two actors farther apart from one another.[159]

Karimi Hakak's repositioning of Lysander and Hermia's proximity, as a way to sidestep the inspector's request based on his perception of Islamic morals, accentuates the negotiated ways directorial authority retranslates scenes from a play (Figure 0.3). Nonetheless, translation depends on the creative adaption to regulations and, as in this case, subversive reframing of censorship regulations.

Working at the intersection of multiple practices, translation involves the constant realignment of writing and repertoire through which performance can be restaged in shifting contexts and for multiple audiences. As shown by Ali-Reza Mirsajadi, in response to Iran's volatile political life, the socio-political appeal of *Hamlet* has introduced a number of creative retranslation and restaging of the Shakespearean tragedy. The 2012 *Hamlet*, directed by Reza Gooran (1979–), exemplifies a retranslation performance in shifting frame perspectives. The play, written by Mohammad Charmshir (1960–), cross-fertilizes the Shakespearian play with Iranian design in an avant-garde reframing of the story through the perspective of Ophelia, the young noblewoman and the potential wife of Hamlet.[160] Equally innovative is *The Seven Trials of Hamlet* (2016) for its use of blackface minstrel motifs to underscore the comedic aspects of the late Elizabethan play

Figure 0.3 *A Midsummer Night's Dream*, translated and directed by Mahmood Karimi Hakak, Tehran, 1999.

for a post-2009 Iranian audience.[161] Here one can also mention *Unpermitted Whispers* by Azadeh Ganjeh (1983–), whose innovative adaptations of three female characters in Shakespeare's plays, Katherina, Ophelia and Desdemona, highlight a form of 'mobile theatre' with shifts in perspectives through multiple taxi rides in Tehran while addressing socio-political concerns of contemporary Iranian society.[162]

With the rise of what Anoushiravan Ehteshmi and Mahjoob Zweiri call the 'neoconservative' administration of Mahmood Ahmadinejad (1956–) and the expansion of censorship, theatre in translation became most apparent in the staging of experimental works.[163] The focus on experimentation included two features: the staging of a genre in literary drama with underlying symbolic or implicit meanings that could be interpreted in politically dissident or philosophically existential ways, and organizationally, the proliferation of smaller theatre troupes that employed minimalistic theatre productions in various venues.[164] Absurdist plays of Albert Camus, and, especially, Samuel Beckett, were forged largely in suppression of cultural practices amid hardliner takeover, especially after the 2009 contested elections, which saw the reelection of Ahmadinejad.

In one of the most intriguing translated plays in the post-Reformist period, mostly performed by a new generation of dramatists, *Waiting for Godot*, a tragicomedy parable of the human condition, enjoyed an astonishing popularity. Performed between a capricious tone and a minimalism of symbolical staging practices, the Iranian version of the *Waiting for Godot* served as a performative commentary on the absurdity of life in post-revolutionary times. By stressing the essential futility of human endeavour, endless wait draws upon an unrealized future under farcical circumstances.

In the 2013 version of Goruh-e Teʿatr-e Lahzeh, the staged performance of the *Waiting for Godot* is rethought through an Iranian perspective with the merging of Persian classical music and *siah-bazi*.¹⁶⁵ In a tale of infinite hope and non-redemptive suffering in response to the perpetual postponement of the future, the two characters, Vladimir (Didi) and Estragon (Gogo), are retranslated to perform two masculine characters, *siah* (blackface) and *pahlavan* (champion), interchangeable in disoriented identities, who await the hopeful arrival of *ostad/osta* (master).¹⁶⁶ The *pahlavan* character is thin, tall, a pretender to a self-assured championship. He amuses himself and his companion, *siah*, who is actually not a blackface (deliberatively done so as to undermine the blackness signifier of the character) with whimsical songs and word plays in a basically hopeless situation while he waits for *osta*. The absurdist play in *siah-bazi* is both to 'maintain' traditional performances and also to update it into a (post)modern theatrical expression.¹⁶⁷ Although performed based on a more direct translation of the play, similar themes of stagnant change with no end in sight also resonate with the January 2014 version of the play, directed by Homayoon Ghanizadeh (1980–) at the City Theatre, reflecting, in what Rana Salimi describes, the 'static situation of the country and the incompetence of the government'.¹⁶⁸

For all the genre variations in the post-Reform theatre, restaging the past as a critique of the present saw its greatest manifestation on the streets and the squares of Iranian cities during the contested presidential elections in 2009. At various junctures in post-election uprisings, the contentious streets protests that rocked Iranian cities mimicked the 1979 Revolution, not as mere reenactments in imitation but in citational performances of the past revolution as a relived event. From daily street demonstrations at major symbolic urban sites to nightly rooftop protests, from renditions of songs dating back to the 1979 Revolution to posters of martyrs, the new generation, though not entirely tied to a social class, defined the Green Movement by staging the largest theatre of dissent.¹⁶⁹ Here one could equally argue that the brutal repression of the demonstrations staged a performance in a regime of terror that defines a state of exception manifested to which the sovereign can operate outside of the law.

Yet dissent, essentially transgressive, spans across borders. Since the 1979 Revolution, Iranian theatre practitioners in diaspora have staged performances in a variety of genres. The modes of critique that early post-revolutionary diaspora theatre employed relied on styles of performance that were primarily self-critical, perhaps as a way to understand the revolutionary event that had radically changed Iranian lives.¹⁷⁰ The theatre activities took place very soon after the revolution. Early 1980s saw the regrouping of the Iranian Theatre Society in Paris, led by exiled Rahmaninejad and Sa'edi.¹⁷¹ Plays such as *The Ass* (1984), written, directed and performed by the famed Los Angeles-based actor-director-screenwriter Parviz Sayyad (1939–), exemplify early critical theatre in exile.¹⁷² Dissident theatre was echoed in the diaspora staging of Bezyaie's *Chahar Sandoq* (1979) (*Four Boxes*), directed by Rahmaninejad in the Unites States.¹⁷³

Performed at Siena College, New York, in 2011, playwright and director Mahmood Karimi Hakak's remake of *Hamlet* is tribute to the 2009 Green Movement. Set against post-revolutionary Iran, in this diaspora version of the Shakespearian play, retitled *HamletIRAN*, Hamlet appears as a young woman within the Iranian Green Movement, daughter of the late prime minister, Mohammad Mossadegh, who is murdered by his brother, the former president, Ahmadinejad.[174] On her dying breath, she begs her school friend, Horatio, to 'tell [her] story':

O, I die, Horatio;
The potent poison quite o'er-crows my spirit:
I cannot live to hear the word of the people;
But I do prophesy that election shall be theirs.
So speak this, to those who need to see what comes:
Each vote, each citizen, has my dying voice.

While Ophelia is modelled after Neda Aghasoltan, Polonius and Laertes represent the forces of tyranny. From this unequivocally critical perspective, *HamletIRAN* exemplifies a politically charged repertoire of performances in remaking a Shakespearian play in exile.

As demonstrated in Part III of this volume, diasporic theatre also transcends politics and addresses the precarious condition of identity in reference to class, migration, sexuality and transnationality. Themes of gender and migration, for instance, are depicted in the works of Sweden-based Farnaz Arbabi (1977–), whose 2006 rewriting of Vilhelm Moberg's 1949 *The Emigrants*, into a stage performance, explores the perilous challenges of migration from Bosnia in Sweden.[175] The staging of diaspora theatre need to be understood as discourses that sustain complex impulses within them, some reflective and others, in organizational terms, transnationally collaborative.[176] The staging of the Persian translation of Yasmina Evelyne Agnes Reza's (1959–) *Le Dieu du Carnage* (*The God of Carnage*), by the German-based director and playwright Alireza Koushk Jalali (1958–), in the City Theatre in 2008 shows the artistic collaborative networks across borders.

In the immediate aftermath of the post-election protests, key government institutions, under the control of the neoconservative factions, oversaw censorship and regulation of culture and media.[177] However, with the election of the pragmatic administration of Hasan Rouhani (1948–), a wider opening resulted from the state's loosening of its grip on certain cultural practices. The relaxing of state control operated in accretion of privatization in the field of culture. However, the impact of privatization, which began during the Rafsanjani's period, was not merely the lessening of state control over the economy but a push in state incentives for growth of the private sector. The boost in privatization witnessed the enlargement of domestic markets based on a neoliberal model of economy that views culture as a consumer commodity. As the service sector benefited from privatization, culture, as commodity, saw the advance of commercialism across arts, cinema, music and theatre.

But 'privatization', a term later elaborated, was not at first tied to commercial venture. The genesis of privatized theatre can be traced back to the second Ahmadinejad administration (2009–13), when theatre practitioners, upon graduation from university, would form unofficial performance venues, also known as 'pelatoo', where they would rehearse and informally stage plays outside of university spaces.[178] Without official license, required by formal theatre productions, these small venues would gradually form into workshops with permits for drama education. Theatre Mon, an old bathhouse turned into a performance stage in Tehran, served as the first venue for the incipient workshops. Many of the performances were experimental, although later (between 2012 and 2014), with the growth of new venues, different forms of theatre were also staged. Yet the workshop-theatres were not underground performances since they were officially sanctioned with state permits to train in limited, smaller performances for educational purposes.[179] Early pelatoos were inherently ephemeral, situated or perhaps anti-monumental as an alternative to established theatre sanctioned by the state.

By 2014, however, the workshop venues, mostly concentrated in Tehran, were transformed into more stable, recognizable spaces for ticket-purchase audiences. On 22 February 2014 Tamashakhaneh Ostad Mashayekhi in central Tehran staged the first public performance of private theatre. In what became known as, aptly put by Mostafa Koushki (1984–), *te'atr-e gheyre dolati* ('non-government theatre'), the newly formed theatre venue, with a large seating capacity, opened up a new chapter in post-revolutionary theatre.[180] Since 2014, a number of larger venues were set up – such as Te'atr-e Mostaghel-e Tehran, established in 2015 – and these venues showcased plays in diverse genres for primarily a younger audience.[181] By 2018–19 the venues sprang up throughout the country, including smaller cities, such as Bushehr and Ilam.[182]

The genesis of the privatization of some theatre venues can be traced to 2010 when experimental plays such as *Investigating a Silent Party*, directed by Reza Hadad (1969–), were staged at the Iranshahr Theatre Hall. The new model of theatre production was modelled independent from state-sponsorship and revolved around contracts between the private and public venues with the production team, most of the times led by the theatre director. While theatre concurrently grew in diverse genres in (sub)cultural spheres across urban Iran, the privatization trend in theatre expanded along with conspicuous consumption among certain segments of the urban population.[183] With increasing costs of tickets, performances such as the musical adaptation of Charles Dickens' *Oliver Twist*, staged at the Vahdat Hall in 2018, have become emblematic of the changing patterns of theatre consumption.[184] The irony of such Broadway-like spectacles is that some of the producers are the former state officials who once limited theatre but now profit from it as a large-budget shows.[185] In complex network ways, the lines that separate *te'atr-e gheyre dolati* from the state are hardly distinguishable.

Commercial theatres underpin a transition to what Harvey has called 'extroverted form of urbanism', as theatre becomes increasingly politically passive in the face of commodification of urban life forms.[186] Concurrently, the growth of e-commerce, in particular the popularity of the Tiwall app, has provided an online venue for interactive commentary, review posts and ticket sales, easing access to a range of theatre performances.[187] The virtualization of theatre has, in many ways, less to do with the possibility of 'digital performance' and more to do with the cultural production of theatre organization, in which a new cultural reality becomes constructed through 'cyberspace', and without physical constraints.

It is also worth pointing out that the privatization of theatre is a complex process since it involves multilayer practices that cannot be reduced to economic capital. In fact, the term 'privatization of theatre' requires reconceptualization since it assumes a liberalization paradigm of a transition from 'public' to 'private' ownership, based on a contract model of social order in which labour, cultural or otherwise, is reduced to exchange commodity. Here, however, by 'privatization' I mean the opening of the field of practice with network ties with state and capital in its various shapes, especially the cultural ones. The field of practice, in this sense, encompasses networks of theatre practitioners who operate at mostly smaller theatre venues with quasi-official status. The reference to theatre spaces is important since it relates to the growth of a distinct production culture of theatre, which, following John. T. Caldwell, underscores the reflexive and negotiated cultural practices that shape theatre into the mediated sphere of audiences as consumers.[188] Production culture involves network of economies, commercial representations, technologies and stage productions, along with material products that make theatre possible as a field of cultural practice.

By way of an example, the material and design production of theatrical posters for advertisement has represented one of the most notable aspects of production culture of theatre. With roots in early Iranian theatre, theatrical posters convey complex aesthetic and philosophical themes, while participating in the broader consumer culture of advertisements. The ornamental, figurative, at times abstract design styles, spawned by diverse graphic traditions across the globe, combine the pictorial conventions of graphic design with the dramatic flow of diverse theatrical plays.[189] With key figures such as Morteza Momayez (1936–2005), known as the father of Iranian graphic design and influenced by Swiss and Polish poster movement, the design cultures of theatrical posters have combined centuries-old visual traditions with new typographic and imagery approaches. The incorporation of various aesthetic techniques involves complex poetic, narrative and philosophical themes that, by and large, define post-revolutionary theatre.

Designed by Faranak Irani (1988–) for the 2015 production of David Mamet's *A Life in the Theatre* (1977) in Tehran, the theatrical poster in Figure 0.4 is an outstanding exemplary of a manufactured product that, in its digital and print material form, showcases a reflexive imagery of a dramatic play in a novel graphic design. The figurative abstract design of the poster concerns the philosophical theme of *A Life in the Theatre*, a play about the relationship of two stage actors, one older and fading with fame, and another younger actor, rising to his success. Mamet's self-reflexive play addresses the essence of life in ceaseless cycles, which theatre equally embodies as a perpetual drama of birth and decay. Irani elaborates on her design in the following: 'A Life in the Theatre is about the life of an actor behind stage and also on stage, as the play ultimately wants to show that there is no difference between the two.' Referencing the myth of Sisyphus and the absurd condition of life, she explains, 'I placed a mask behind the actor's face, which in reality is his/her own face. The two figures, pushing and letting down the rocks

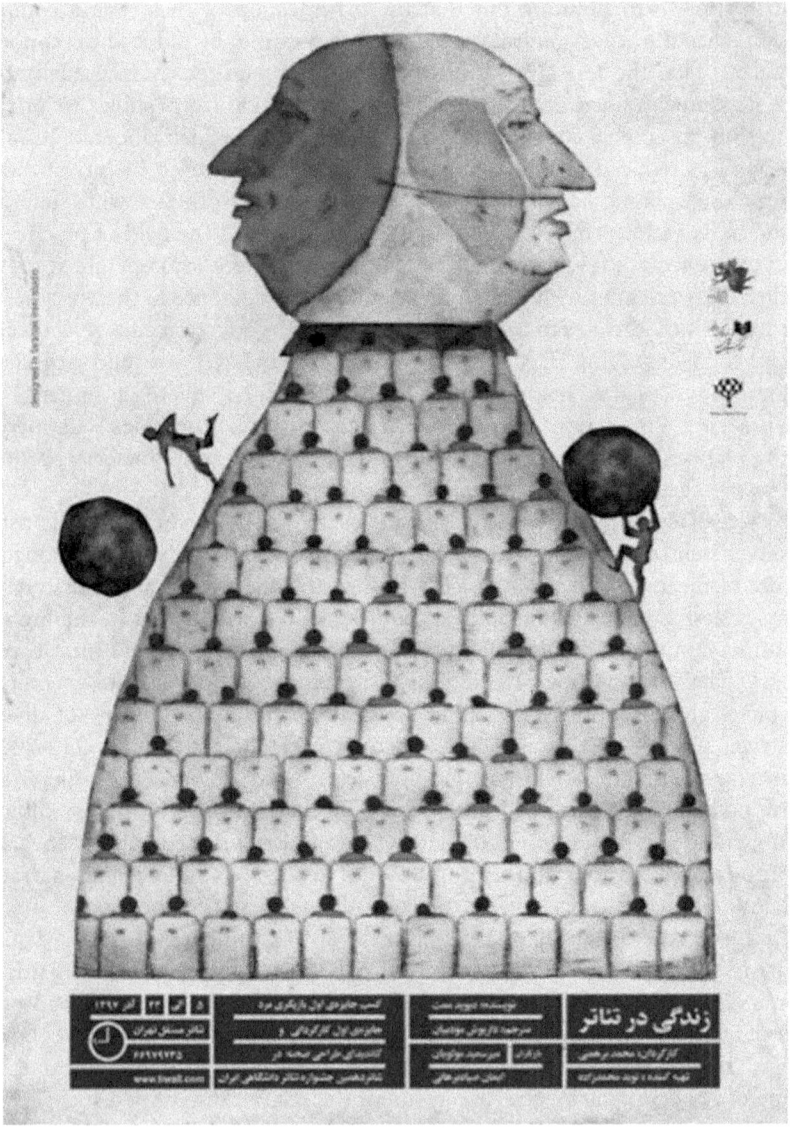

Figure 0.4 The theatrical poster of David Mamet's *A Life in the Theatre* (1977), Tehran, 2015, Faranak Irani.

[on the theatre space] represent the cycle of life, which is also present in theatre.'[190] Theatre here is not just a representation of life but also the enactment of life, and nothing more. It is as though Irani wants to remind us that the only reality is the life of theatre, which the poster and its design not only depict but also perform it as life.

The post-revolutionary poster production represents an aspect of the material culture that was spurred by the growth of the print industry in the twentieth century. Although the convergence of print media and theatre production is not new, the proliferation of publications on theatre, either as journal or book publications, can be viewed as an extension of the production culture of theatre. Despite financial and production challenges caused by economic problems, the Iranian publishing industry, indirectly tied to state apparatus through regulative measures, has taken notice of the market in theatre knowledge. The continued publication of key journals such as *Namayesh* (founded 1958) and newer book publications such as *Theatre and Society* (2019), by playwright and director Reza Kouchek Zadeh (1976–), attest to a vibrant and wide readership public that increasingly participates in digital publications.[191] In what John B. Thompson has called the 'hidden revolution', the digitization of theatre publications in the form of e-books and PDFs has entailed disruptive transformations in formats across different personalized computers and reading experiences in unprecedented ways.[192] The measure of such disruptive patterns in production cultures is yet to be studied in the emergence of digital theatre in years to come.

All in all, the proliferation of independent theatres involves the accommodation of diverse segments of Iranian population, including subcultural theatre audiences and fans with a keen interest in a range of theatres, alternative and commercial. By 2016, theatre performances increased to 842 shows.[193] As of 2017, there were more venues for stage performances than cinema, which is indicative of a major growth in theatre culture, although still with limited audiences.[194] Yet privatization also entails the absence of state support, which can be devastating to smaller, less funded theatre organization at times of economic crisis or pandemics, which led to the 2020 countrywide lockdown. The future of Iranian theatre remains as uncertain as it first emerged in the late nineteenth century. And yet, as this volume aims to show, there is promise for new experiences and interpretations in (re)making Iranian theatre in national and diaspora contexts.

Structure of the book

The contour of the contemporary life of Iranian performance is vast. For the most part, a thorough study would not just include a historical narrative, as generically provided in the previous section, but provide a critical understanding of the complexities of everyday and (in)visible institutional forms of performances, which can include state power. The present volume therefore primarily looks at Iranian artistic and theatre performances, with a keen eye on the production of culture. The importance of the relationship between culture and performance lies in how theatrical action becomes mediated by material conditions and interpretative paradigms that, in turn, are shaped by intersections of age, class, ethnicity, gender, family, migration, nationality, sexuality and status. This is mostly evident in the examples from the previous section in the rise of various theatre groups in post-Constitutional period. Aside from contested definitions and functions of performance, contemporary Iranian theatre in its historical formation can be described as a set of practices that intersects between various fields of performances, and in doing so, illuminates modes of being and becoming modern that redefine Iranianness in embodied, diaporic, multiple and translatable ways.[195]

Divided into three parts, the following chapters examine the past and contemporary reconstructions of performing traditions, with theatre as a dramatic art form. The first part, 'Performing tradition: The past in the present', aims at understanding how Iranian literary and performance traditions are reconfigured to shape cultural memory. In this transformational sense, memory transmits across historical time through storytellers, eulogists or mourners. Yet transmission is hardly about a linear continuity, but disruptions, reiterations and re-inventions that make performance possible. Transmitted knowledge through performance traditions also allow for new interpretative paradigms in shifting historical contexts.

In Chapter 1, Soodabeh Malekzadeh examines the social history of the Iranian storytelling tradition and *naqqali*, tracing the origins of such 'performances' in Iran to the pre-Islamic period. Malekzadeh argues that, even within its pre-modern context, such performances were utilized as didactic tools for social instruction and at times 'royal intervention' and argues that the roots of *naqqali* have extended in Iranian history as archival practices in the transmission of cultural memory and the continuity of Iranian 'ideals and traditions'. In Chapter 2, Shahrokh Yadegari continues Malekzadeh's discussion on storytelling traditions such as *naqqali*, *Shahnameh-khwani* (Reading of verses of the *Shahnameh*) and *Pardeh-dari/Pardeh-khwani* (screen-keeping/screen-reading). Yadegari's chapter is a study of his own restaging of Siavash Kasrai's *Mohre-ye Sorkh* (*The Scarlet Stone*), which he did in collaboration with dancer-choreographer Shahrokh Moshkin-Ghalam. *Mohre-ye Sorkh* brings to light the theatrical intricacies of Shahnameh's battle between Rostam and Sohrab, where Kasrai addresses the question of the reproduction of epic texts through performance in renarrative of the 1979 revolution. In Kasrai's poetic rendition, Sohrab confronts Ferdowsi for his tragic death and asks about the futility of his quest for justice. *Mohre-ye Sorkh* is a critical rendition of the revolutionary current that had begun to devour its own children, an apt metaphor for the tragedy of Rostam and Sohrab.

Yadegari portrays this heroic future in his restaging of the two stories, classical and modern, in the poetic body language of dance-theatre and a narrator's voice. Through interactive and theatrical audio-visual technologies, which are technically designed not to overtake the traditional narrative, we relook at Ferdowsi's mythological tale in an innovative presentation of an ancient story performed for a contemporary audience. Chapter 3, which is a study of Kiarostami's *A Look to ta'zieh* by Babak Rahimi, expands on the role of multimedia technologies in ways as *ta'zieh* can be reframed for a modern understanding that can appeal to multiple audiences. In fact, as Rahimi argues, Kiarostami's *ta'zieh* audiences are performers in a communal ritual that invites them to rethink their subjectivity in connected and multi-perspective ways. The mostly non-Iranian audiences of Kiarostami's *ta'zieh* are explained in terms of shaping a transcultural space of performance perspectives, which fuses oral traditions with digital modern platforms.

The second part, 'Performing (post-revolutionary) Iran: Space, stage and theatre', explores the negotiation of performance and place, where competing notions of identity are articulated in (in)visible ways in their post-revolutionary contexts. In contrast to the previous section, performance is less about the reinvention of older traditions and more about the production of new practices that express a modernity of performative kind.

In his study of the annual music (Chapter 4), theatre, art and film festival, known as the Shiraz Arts Festival (1967–77), and conceptualized by Farah Pahlavi, Charney describes a range of performances at the festivals that conjured varied response from Iranian and non-Iranian audiences. The festivals, Charney argues, 'uniquely offered a creative and experimental space within a dictatorship'. And this creativity revealed a cross-cultural space that connected the past with the present as a cultural symbol of Pahlavi modernity, viewed by Islamist and Marxist revolutionaries as decadent and corrupt. In terms of the creative potential of theatre, as a dramatist, director and a scholar, Mahmood Karimi Hakak (Chapter 5) provides a rare personal glimpse onto the early revolutionary Iranian theatre. With personal narrative as oral history, Karimi Hakak's study is also significant for his use of a personal narrative that serves both as oral history and also performance of identity in response to intractable political situation that renders artistic expression an act of defiance, in particular among the youth.

In Chapter 6, Roxanne Varzi takes up such concern for performance as political engagement in her study of post-war theatre that emerged with the youth culture of early Reformist period (1997–2001). Hamed Taheri and his theatre group exemplify a new trend for translation, in particular the works of Polish stage director and theorist Jerzy Grotowski. The study of Taheri's reinterpretation of Grotowski enunciates an intimate connection between physical site, body and performance, with theatre serving as a therapeutic space of cultural importance in contemporary Iranian Theatre. The merging with the here-and-now, the earthly existence wherein embodied sensations take control over experience as Taheri's plays invite a participatory response from the audience, is also evident in *ta'zieh* performances. Note that Joshua Charney also addresses the question of space and performance in the production of cultural identity, bringing together these chapters in terms of space as performance.

Staci Gem Scheiwiller's study of performance art in central and north regions of Tehran (Chapter 7), where the largest art scenes and markets are located, frames the question of Iranian performance in the interactive contexts around the relationship between the bodies of artists and their audiences. She locates the performative frameworks that shape the ways in which the artists' embodied practices are viewed in contested ways, redefining specific urban spaces, where they are viewed for responsive audiences. Unique to Scheiwiller's chapter is the study of Iran's performance art, which, as she argues, is closely tied to avant-garde anti-institutional Dadaist experiments of early twentieth century. Equally unique to the Iranian case is the strategic ways artistic production is negotiated through what Scheiwiller describes as public, private, gallery and translational spaces.

Chapters 8 and 9 by Amy Motlagh and Siavash Rokni look at how filmmakers and musicians intervene in making indigenous performances for multiple viewers while rejecting state ideologies. In Motlagh's study, cinema of contemporary Iran performs a dual function: first, it advocates for an alternative to global conception of human rights and, second, it offers a critical discourse on the Islamic Republic's critique on the discourse of human rights. This ambiguity reveals a push for autonomy, which the art of cinematic performance best articulates in Iran's growing film industry. This chapter provides important insight on how domestic production culture, as in the case of Jafar Pahani's cinema, is intricately tied to national and transnational legal performatives (or rather 'spectacles') on justice and rights but also how cinematic critique of a concept, such as 'human rights', can be understood as a distinct act of performance. Rokni's study of two generations of rock musicians in the Reformist period in Tehran and Mashhad also looks at the indigenization of rock music not as an act of resistance but 'persistence'. The process involves the attempt to carve out new spaces of performances for a new generation of Iranians who desire autonomy and yet connectivity with the broader world. For Rokni, the rise of rock music culture and its gradual acceptance in the Islamic Republic was a result of a tenacious presence that negotiated spaces of expression for the younger musicians. Presence is a form of performance, a framework of action to redefine the public in the context of a broader national project.

The final part of this book includes three chapters that discuss the rearticulation of Iranian diaspora through performance. In his interview with Torange Yeghiazarian, the founding artistic director of Golden Thread Productions in San Francisco, Rahimi probes the question of diaspora theatre in Chapter 10. As Yeghiazarian elaborates in her account of diaspora theatre in the Bay Area, *444 Days*, the third and final play in her trilogy on the 1979 Revolution and its impact on the Iranian-American community, she explores complex emotions in relation with political conflict on the individual level. Modelled after the Asian American and Latino-American theatres, the Golden Thread exemplifies a diaspora-run theatre company with the aim to build 'a Middle Eastern American theatre'. The biennial ReOrient Festivals showcase forums and plays that have become sites of community formation and also spaces for claiming my diaspora narrative by women who also express identity as Americans.

In 'Performing glimpses of the past: The political implications of dance in Nowruz Parades' (Chapter 11), Rana Salimi addresses the question of diaspora identity by shedding light on the politics of dance and music performances during the Nowruz dance parades of New York. What the process of reimagining identity through cultural events involves is the construction of exclusive cultural spaces wherein a secular Iranian identity is affirmed through performance. She concludes, 'by excluding more conservative or more stigmatised segments of the exilic community, the organisers draw an imaginary line between Oriental Iran as it is portrayed in the west (backward and fundamentalist) and an idealised Iran (Europeanised and modernised) as it was imagined by the Pahlavi kings of the twentieth century.' The reproduction of culture in terms of class and religious identity contrasts to the Golden Thread, where the question of performance becomes an opportunity for building inclusive communities, where Iranian Americans can participate as both performers and audiences.

The relationship between art performance and diaspora identity is pursued by Heather Rastovac-Akbarzadeh in '(AR)ticulations of the Self: A Conversation with Amir Baradaran' (Chapter 12), with a particular reference to Augmented Reality (AR) technology to cite 'a provocation and a proposition' of an artistic movement which conceptual artist Amir Baradaran calls 'FutARism'. As an interactive technology that expands the experience of physical reality through prism of digital information, the application of AR for performance enables Baradaran to produce 'a spectator-participants speculative' that critically reconfigures the relationship between the embodied, technological and creative production, and also gendered identities in racialized and (trans)national settings. Rastovac-Akbarzadeh's 2015 interview with Baradaran reveals how AR technology performance can make visible the queer body of Muslim Iranians whose presence is normatively marginalized in the hegemonic Iranian nationalist and Euro-American cultural imaginary.

Baradaran rendering of Rumi's stanza *man na manam na man manam* ('I am not I, neither am I, I') presents the shaping of a negative space for diaspora positionality. His *(AR)ticulations of the Self* stages the re-performance of identity through AR technologies in the construction of queer diasporic and new, enhanced modes of experiences. And it is in this enhanced experience that the present book seeks to provide, with its various studies of performances by diverse Iranians situated in different localities, historical contexts, projected towards future possibilities. Since all texts pose the limit of their own possibility, as Roland Barthes reminds us, diverse Iranian performances, diasporic or otherwise, constitute new experiences of identity in limits of imperceptible reality.

In broad terms, to understand performance is to recognize the practice of contested experiences and interpretations of individuals and communities that are made explicit or concealed through a repertoire of situated enactments in social life. From gestures, speech-acts and habits to art, fashion, film, music and theatre, performance both shapes and is reshaped by cultural practices that paradoxically reiterate norms and open up sites of critique in possibilities for contested identities. The notion of performance draws the intractable question of identity that is re-presented and re-materialized in mediations between discursive frames that interpret the world and experiences that perpetually re-delineate modes of social identity in terms of sex, class, gender, race, sexuality and national character.

The historical and social contours of performance in 'Iran' as a contentiously imagined nation are no exceptions to how intersectional identities, associated with changing notions of nationhood, have and continue to emerge in a variety of locations around the globe. Performances by Iranians traversing across localities share a range of themes and practices that include (re)translation of literary and dramatic texts, reinvention of traditional performances, restaging of art, music or plays in multiple sites of visibilities (street art) and invisibilities (underground theatre). Known for its rich dramatic traditions, the modernity of Iranian culture is tied to complex processes through which Iranians of diverse backgrounds have and continue to critically rethink self and reality. Such processes involve embodied practices in transhistorical structures that are linked to state and transnational models of identities and also contested (sub or counter) cultural fields. Theatrical cultures are as complex as the practices of identity that are interwoven into contested histories of (trans)national cultures.

Part I

PERFORMING TRADITION: PAST TRACES IN THE PRESENT

1

MINSTRELS: THE WISE TEACHERS OF ANCIENT IRAN

Soodabeh Malekzadeh

Stories live in your blood and bones, follow the seasons and light candles on the darkest night – every storyteller knows she or he is also a teacher.[1]

—Patti Davis

Iranian storytelling traditions are mirror images of the past, present and future of the Iranian people and their worldviews. They serve as a system that stores socio-cultural values and ensures their transmission through time and even geographical location. Whether in the form of prose or poetry, such traditions are ultimately performative literature. They are enacted with dramatic elements such as voice and tone manipulation, episodes of audience/performer interaction, and a reliance on the audience's power of visualization through the use of powerful literary devices. Performed songs and stories ranged from epic heroic deeds to tales of love and heartbreak and were either part of long traditions of myth and folklore or improvised to suit their time and social space. Iranian storytellers also possessed a profound understanding of the cultural needs of their community and time, strategically basing their performative content on a desired socio-cultural outcome.

In the context of ancient Iran, storytellers played two crucial roles that will be discussed in this chapter. First, they were responsible for the transmission of socio-cultural principles to younger generations and hence served as cultural teachers. Shahrzad – the protagonist of the overarching plot of *Hezar Afsan*, the central framework for *One Thousand and One Nights* – is one of the most famed storytellers in the world of global fiction.[2] Shahrzad is not merely a storyteller, though, but a skilled performer and instructor as well.[3]

> [She] had perused the books, annals and legends of preceding Kings and the stories, examples and instances of bygone men and things; indeed, it was said that she had collected a thousand books of histories relating to antique races and departed rulers. She had perused the works of the poets and knew them by heart; she had studied philosophy and the sciences, arts and accomplishments; and she was pleasant and polite, wise and witty, well read and well bred.[4]

The second function of storytellers, especially those employed by the royal court, was to serve as messengers. While entertaining courtiers was their primary function, they were also instrumental in conveying 'distressful' news to the sovereign and in turn maintaining peace and order at court – a role that has more or less been overlooked. The queen of *One Thousand and One Nights*, Shahrzad, tactfully and diplomatically uses her performative storytelling skills to soothe the pains of the mad king and stops him from shedding more blood.[5] It is precisely this role that sets Shahrzad apart from her global peers.

Moreover, Iranian storytelling, as a performative art, was most frequently accompanied by music. Hence the term 'minstrel' may be more suitable for this social role. Xenophon, the Greek historian and the a mercenary of Cyrus the Younger, writes that 'even to this day, the barbarians [Persians] tell in *story and in song* that Cyrus was most handsome in person, most generous of heart, most devoted to learning and most ambitious, so that he endured all sorts of labor and faced all sorts of danger [...]'.[6] The Parthian *gosān* and the Sasanian *khunyāgar* also held a similar position.[7]

The minstrels of ancient Iran operated in both public and royal spaces. Xenophon, who lived amongst the Persians, does not differentiate between royal and public spaces when speaking of Iranian minstrelsy, which allows us to assume that the heroic stories echoed through palaces and humble cottages alike.[8] While minstrels are commonly depicted at the royal court, we know from later sources that they also frequently performed at communal spaces known as *meydan*, or the town square. Later, specifically as the result of increasing urbanization during the Safavid period, we see the emergence of a more enclosed space known as the *Qahveh Khane* or the coffee house where events such as *Shahnameh-khwani* or *naqqali* would be performed.[9] While operating in two different spaces, both royal and public forms of minstrelsy complemented one another and touched on similar values, rendering the binary between the two types of literature as insignificant. The 'mirror for princes' genre, for example, may well have been an instructional tool for all Iranians and not just members of the royal family. What made such literature timeless was that it allowed each individual or social group to use it in their own distinct way as their imagined communal and individual identities were shaped and reshaped by stories handed down by one generation after another.

Cultural instruction through minstrelsy

Storytelling acts as a system that reinforces the transmission of cultural and ideological traditions, customs and beliefs.[10] It also serves as a prototype for social expression and communication, providing 'culturally acceptable models of behaviour'.[11] Strabo, the Greek philosopher and historian, alludes to the role of Iranian minstrels as teachers and touches upon the theme of 'didacticism' when dealing with the topic of tales and stories. Strabo writes, 'They [the Persians], use as teachers of science their wisest men, who also interweave their teachings with the mythical element, thus reducing that element to a *useful purpose* and rehearse both with song and without song the deeds both of the gods and of the noblest men.'[12] While the pleasure of listening to a well-told story of adventure and bravery is more than obvious, such stories were held valuable mainly because of what they taught the youth; lessons of valour, glory and how to be an honourable human.[13] Hannaway adds that 'in Persian romances, both popular and courtly, instruction is combined with entertainment. Listeners are instructed in the traditional social and moral values of the Iranian common people […] Popular romances thus complement courtly romances in preserving and transmitting traditional values'.[14] Storytelling then, in turn, reinforces those values and promotes their social implementation. In a cycle of invention and reinvention, traditional values become fundamental in keeping storytelling as a performative art alive and thriving. Could the survival and eternality of ancient stories and tales have been due to their core cultural messages or the thread of 'instruction and didacticism' which is woven into the plot of the story?[15] Gorgāni writes that *Vis o Rāmin* is not only beautiful and popular amongst all people but is also highly didactic, emphasizing the value of the lessons and teachings hidden beneath the surface of the story and concealed within its symbolism.[16]

Minstrels as tactful messengers

Delving deeper into the role of minstrels at court, one comes upon a unique and interesting function, where they used their literary, performative and cultural knowledge to gently prevent possible predicaments from causing disruptions.[17] First we learn of their high status at court, which meant they were privy to the most intimate affairs and rumours that took place in the dark corners of the palace.[18] Also, aside from knowing 'many stories capable of charming mortals […] [and] spreading the deeds of men and gods', Iranian minstrels were tactful messengers and bearers of emotionally disruptive news to the king.[19] It is through the interaction, sometimes invisible, between the performer and the audience that the minstrel achieves such control over his audiences' emotions.[20]

Athenaeus, the Greek author, writes that the minstrels of the Median court were not only aware of the valour and might of Cyrus himself but also had inside information about the looming war that was about to change the history of the Iranian mainland. Athenaeus sheds lights on the high courtly status of such men, and their role as tactical messengers. He writes,

> Astyages was having a feast at that point with his friends, and a man named Angares – he was the most distinguished bard – who had been invited in, sang the other, conventional songs, and at the end said that a great beast, even bolder than a wild boar, had been allowed to escape into the swamps; if it got control of the territory around there, it would soon have no difficulty fighting large numbers of men. When Astyages asked, 'what kind of beast are you referring to?' The bard said that he meant Cyrus the Persian.[21]

Who else is more in tune with the power of words, heroic tales, legends and music than the minstrel? Who else can take the most tragic, disturbing or distressful accounts and convey them in the most delicate, heartfelt and appropriate manner?

Vis o Rāmin provides us with another example of such responsibility. During a night of feasting and entertainment, the royal *gosān* must inform the king of a disturbing news. The *gosān* begins with merry songs and beautiful melodies and slowly begins improvising a tale of infidelity. He uses literary devices, such as metaphors and symbolism, to gently let the king know of his wife Vis's infidelity.[22]

Bārbad, the minstrel of the Sasanian king Khosro II, uses a similar strategy to let the king of kings know that his favourite horse, Shabdiz, has passed away. Bārbad 'improvised a song about Shabdiz, filled with symbolic insinuations and indirect references that he was no longer amongst them. He sang of how Shabdiz would never again run the fields, or graze the meadows, nor will he ever have another taste the sweetness of a serene slumber'.[23] The soothing sound of Barbad's harp, his gentle voice and his knowledge of Khosro's temperament allowed him to deliver the news in the least shocking and disruptive manner. Khosro listened calmly and, finally, turned to his beloved minstrel and said: 'so he [Shabdiz] has passed'.[24] The last time we hear of Sasanian minstrels is when the House of Sāsān is fleeing Ctesiphon, taking with them their trusted messengers, performers and teachers, the *Khunyāgars*.

Minstrelsy in the post-Sasanian period

The high status of Iranian minstrels underwent much adjustment in the post-Sasanian centuries as Iran gradually left behind the world of Late Antiquity and stepped into a new era of change and appropriation.[25] However, as Anthony Shay states, the move from Sasanian Persia, in a very cultural term, to Islamic Near East was not 'as if someone turned off the lights after the battle of Nahavand in 642 CE and [...] the next day dawned Islamic: everyone wore Islamic clothing [...] and lived an Islamic lifestyle'.[26] Storytellers, as traditional preservers and transmitters of cultural values, stayed active and central, despite going through a wave of religious and literary hostility that interestingly had already existed in the region before the Arab conquest of Iran, if not amongst Iranians.[27] Minstrelsy, while evolving and/or covering new subjects, continued to be an essential part of the Iranian society and culture. Even in the post-Sasanian era, we can say that the role of minstrels very much resembled that of Sasanian times. We hear of the famed *khunyāgars* in the service of the Umayyads, Abbasids and later Turkic rulers. For example, Ebrahim Moseli and his son Eshaq were not only elite courtiers but also highly respected minstrels.[28]

The Iranian minstrels' exquisite art and skills brought them fame, wealth and influence. However, history still owes these individuals a much greater applause for their role as the protectors, transmitters and instructors of Iranian traditional and cultural values. Especially in post-Sasanian times, their skills allowed them to sing of the values of a nation conquered and subjugated, whose culture was vulnerable to erosion and erasure. Ultimately, Iranian minstrels were the soothsayers who gradually breathe life into a 'socio-cultural' entity that is in transition and ultimately have a fundamental role in the creation of a hybrid culture that guarantees the survival of a 'past' that could have easily been subjected to oblivion.

2

THE SCARLET STONE: AN INFATUATED WISDOM

Shahrokh Yadegari

This chapter discusses the stage production of *The Scarlet Stone*, which is based on Abolqasem Ferdowsi's *Shahnameh* and *Mohreye Sorkh*, the last work of the contemporary Iranian poet, Siavash Kasrai.[1] Both stories are engaged with the political history of Iran: one recounts a very ancient history in the form of mythology, and the other grapples with certain key events since the 1979 Iranian Revolution in modern poetic form. *The Scarlet Stone* is a multidisciplinary dance-theatre performance which presents the ancient Persian performative storytelling tradition of *naqqali* using modern theatrical settings with technologically advanced designs. In this chapter, we focus on the relationship between the old and the new regarding the issues of political identity, performative traditions and artistic expressions in the production of *The Scarlet Stone*.

Ferdowsi wrote the *Shahnameh* in Persian about a thousand years ago when the Persian language was almost extinct due to the Arab invasion of Iran and the subsequent banning of the use of the language in the region. Containing around 60,000 lines of poetry, the *Shahnameh* is a collection of some of the most famous and influential mythological stories of the Persian-speaking region. Mixing mythology with some accounts of historical facts, it begins with the creation of the world and ends with the conquest of Persia by the Arabs in the seventh century CE, which resulted in establishment of Islam theocratically as the religion of the region years later. The name used for the region in the *Shahnameh* is Iran, which has been the endonym for the country known as Persia to the world, prior to 1935. The epic of the *Shahnameh* (The Book of Kings) recounts the story of Iranian kings and heroes in the context of their relation with neighbouring regions. One of the most famous stories of the *Shahnameh* is the story of 'Rostam and Sohrab'. Rostam is the strongest and the ultimate hero of Iran – similar to Hercules, but as a full human being overseen by Simorgh, the mythological fantastic bird that symbolises knowledge and wisdom. Sohrab is Rostam's love child, whom Rostam kills in the battlefield in ignorance. Many of the stories of the *Shahnameh* are found in other older documents; however, *Rostam and Sohrab* is one of the few stories which cannot be found in any other older document. While the synopsis of this story is extremely well-known in Iran, its details are less known among the masses.

Poetry is arguably one of the most developed and cherished art forms in Iran. For about 900 years, the poetic tradition of Iran following the *Shahnameh* continued to be politically and socially aware, however, not directly and with few specifically identified signifiers. In this period, often signifiers such as wine, pleasure, the beloved and beauty were used to discuss contemporary social and political problems. A fundamental literary movement, largely attributed to Nima Yushij (1895–1959, aka Nima), began in the 1920s among young Iranian poets. This apparent revolution in the poetic form, similar to the movement of modernity in the West, questioned the strict rules in formal structures of poetry and found a relatively quick acceptance in the literary circles of the 1940s. In the preface to Ahmad Karimi Hakkak's *An Anthology of Modern Persian Poetry*, Ehsan Yarshater writes:

> His [Nima's] poetry became known only when a group of gifted younger poets proclaimed him the leader of their movement and set out to exemplify his principles in their own work [...] In their poetry not only were the traditional meters and rhyme patterns were thrown overboard, but more important, the whole world of medieval imagery.[2]

Karimi Hakkak has also noted that this literary movement not only broke the rules of formal meter structures in poetry but also brought about a fundamental change in the model of employment of symbols and significations in direct engagement of poetry with social, economic and political standings of the society.[3] Similar to the modern movement of the West, the traditional constraints, such as meter and rhyme, as well as medieval imagery no longer played a dominant role in the construction of poetry. Unlike classical Persian poetry, the 'new' poetry directly engaged with contemporary social, economic and political issues, and most modern Iranian poets reflected their political views directly in their work. Among them, Siavash Kasrai, one of Nima's disciples, stands out for his political life, especially with his active involvement with the Tudeh Communist Party.

The 1979 Iranian Revolution is considered one of the most popular revolutions in history in terms of the portion of the population who had an active participation role in the process of the revolution. In *The Unthinkable Revolution in Iran*, Charles Kurzman writes 'indeed, the Iranian Revolution was one of the most popular upheavals in world history: 10 percent or more of the Iranian population participated in the demonstrations and general strikes that toppled Shah Mohammad Reza Pahlavi.'[4] Many groups from different political inclinations came together with the common goal of ousting the current monarchy regime at the time, and by December 1978, individual protests on the streets of Iran drew several million anti-Shah demonstrators. After the consolidation of power by the fundamentalists shortly after the revolution, many groups who fought for the revolution, among them also the leftists who supported the theocratic regime, found themselves in a precarious position. During February 1983, the leaders of the Tudeh Party were arrested, and the Party was disbanded, effectively turning the country to a single-party state. The arrests were followed by the appearance of the Tudeh Party leaders on television confessing to 'treason' against the country.[5] With the fear of being persecuted by the Islamic Republic of Iran, Siavash Kasrai fled Iran in 1983 and lived in Kabul until 1987, when he moved to Moscow. Arguably discussing his own life and denouncing the activities of the Tudeh Party, Kasrai wrote *Mohreye Sorkh* in Moscow in 1992. He then moved to Vienna in 1995 and published the work in the same year. In *Mohreye Sorkh*, Kasrai problematizes his political struggles, the movement of the left and what he believed to be any heroic act based on infatuation and righteousness, in the context of the story of *Rostam and Sohrab*.

The story

The stage production of *The Scarlet Stone* begins with what is recounted in the *Shahnameh* and ends with Siavash Kasrai's depiction of Sohrab's hallucinations after being stabbed by his father Rostam, in the battlefield. The story in the *Shahnameh* begins with Rostam, the strongest warrior alive, becoming introspective and going hunting. He finds himself close to the border of Turan, the historically adversarial neighbouring land. After hunting and having a feast, he falls asleep. Upon waking up, Rostam then finds his horse missing. He follows the footsteps of his horse and arrives at Samangan, a city in Turan. Fearing Rostam's revenge, the king of Samangan invites Rostam to be his guest of honour for the night and assures that he will find Rostam's horse by the next morning. In the middle of the night, Tahmineh, the king's daughter, who had heard of Rostam's heroism, comes to Rostam's bedchamber, declaring her love for him and her wishes to bear his child. They spend the night together in secret, and upon leaving in the morning, as a gift and a sign for identity, Rostam gives Tahmineh a famous gem from his arm-ring, to be wrapped around their child's arm if the child is a boy or to be braided in her hair if the child is a girl. Tahmineh gives birth to a son and names him Sohrab.

Sohrab grows quickly to be one of the dominating officers of Turan in his youth. Realizing his unique strength, Sohrab confronts Tahmineh to learn about his father's identity. When Sohrab finds out that he is the son of Rostam, he decides to attack and conquer Iran, and hand kingship to his father Rostam. He also plans to return and attack Turan and put himself on its throne as he declares, 'If Rostam is my father and I am his son, then no one else in all the world should wear the crown.'[6] The king of Turan learns of Sohrab's plan; hoping Sohrab would kill Rostam, he surrounds Sohrab with officers to make sure that Sohrab and Rostam do not recognize each other in the battlefield. The king also plans on killing Sohrab afterwards.

Sohrab heads towards Iran with a large army. At the border, he fights Godafarid, a brave Iranian warrior who has disguised herself as a man. Upon the revelation during the fight that Gordafarid is a woman, Sohrab falls in love with her, but cannot attain her. Gordafarid runs away from Sohrab and warns him that his life will be in great danger once Rostam arrives at the border. Days later, Sohrab fights his father Rostam, without either of them knowing the identity of the other. In the battleground, Sohrab and Rostam sense their relationship; however, whenever Sohrab inquires about Rostam's identity, to protect the national security of Iran and fearing defeat, Rostam denies his own identity. Rostam manages to stab Sohrab with trickery, and it is at this time that Sohrab reveals his identity and shows Rostam the gem on his arm-ring. Realizing he has stabbed his own son, Rostam returns to the palace and requests a healing potion from the king. The king, fearing dethronement by the strong father and son, denies Rostam the potion and Sohrab thus dies.

The Mohreye Sorkh poem

Mohreye Sorkh is an epic long-poem[7] which restages the mythological story of *Rostam and Sohrab* and begins with Sohrab's hallucinations while he is on the ground, drowned in blood, and Rostam is away looking for the healing potion. The most important characters of Sohrab's life appear to him one by one. First, Tahmineh, his mother, arrives mourning the quick death of the child whom she had wished would bring peace and unification to the region. Sohrab consoles his mother and asks her to care for Rostam as he thinks 'Rostam is now a desperate and lonely man'. After Tahmineh leaves, Rostam appears. He pleads ignorance and argues that the burden of the protection of the national security of Iran closed his eyes to all the signs. Rostam wanders off and Sohrab asks for Gordafarid, the wise woman, who, even though felt for Sohrab, did not become entangled with his infatuation and impulsive tendencies. Kasrai's treatment of Gordafarid's character speaks of the respect he had for passion and love, even when he was questioning his own infatuations and impulsive beliefs. In Sohrab's hallucinations, Gordafarid declares her love for him, but also notes that this love was unnecessary and futile. However, Sohrab believes that his death is more meaningful when he has 'tasted love'.[8]

In the climax of Kasrai's poem, Ferdowsi also appears to Sohrab. Sohrab confronts Ferdowsi for his hasty, premature and tragic death, and ponders the meaning (or meaninglessness) of his futile quest for peace and justice, a question, which resonates with the sentiments of many who fought for the 1979 revolution and saw its usurpation by the fundamentalist Islamist factions.

In the production of *The Scarlet Stone*, segments of the text of the *Mohreye Sorkh* poem which supported the narrative and referenced the political struggles of the 1979 revolution were used. The text depicting the confrontation between Sohrab and Ferdowsi, of which we used the most portion, portrays Kasrai's most philosophically and politically tangible introspection in the text. Possibly most directly related to the social and political climate during the crackdown on Tudeh Party, and the confessions of the Party leaders, Sohrab asks Ferdowsi:

> Father and son
> Swords raised against one another
> Yet no staying hand
> No warning sign
> No thread of kinship

No trace of affection
…
Those who are silent
With their lips sealed
Obedient they are
But to which master
Who crafted them
Did not their silence
Add fuel to the fire.⁹

Ferdowsi's response is one of responsibility and commitment to one's belief through wisdom and searching for enlightenment in one's roots. He replies:

> Be calm
Once as a hero
You set out on a dangerous path
No longer should you complain
No longer should you lament
Be now a hero
And like a hero – End this story'¹⁰
…
'Sohrab – That stone which adorns your arm
That talisman
Yes – It is the mark of a world hero
He who wears this mighty sign
Unwittingly affects the world¹¹
…
Listen to me, Sohrab
Enlightenment is your remedy
The rocky spring of knowledge
Is your place¹²
…
Whether good or whether bad
Whether joyous or whether sad
It is your cradle
It is your Shahnameh
The story of your roots.¹³

The reference to the *Shahnameh*, with its political and historical stance against the theocratic rule of Islam and the Arabs in Iran, as a venue for solution, sheds more light on Kasrai's sentiments about what happened after the 1979 revolution. The preface to the *Mohreye Sorkh* contains a considerable amount of context in regard to Kasrai's intentions for writing this poem. While one may look at *Mohreye Sorkh as* a strong critique of the activities of the Tudeh Party and those of its leaders during the 1979 revolution and years afterwards, ultimately Kasrai sees the need for future as a heroic acceptance of responsibility. In the stage production of *The Scarlet Stone*, we end the story with the line below in the preface of *Mohreye Sorkh*:

> Why lament and wail. We reap the fruits of what we sow. Whoever had stars in his eyes and hope in his heart, has faded into the tormenting shadow of loneliness and despair. Where is the missing key to this dungeon?[14]

The production style of storytelling

The production of *The Scarlet Stone* is the fruit of years of collaboration of the author with dancer-choreographer Shahrokh Moshkin-Ghalam. We both were interested in finding a piece which could engage with social and political issues of Iran without ourselves taking a specific political position. We both felt that *Mohreye Sorkh* could provide us the context we needed for our artistic exploration. The connection between the modern poetry of Kasrai and the ancient poetry of *Shahnameh* also resonated with our artistic aesthetics.

Some of the oldest Iranian performance traditions are *naqqali* (storytelling), *Shahnameh-khwani* (reading of verses of the *Shahnameh*) and *Pardeh-dari/Pardeh-khwani* (screen-keeping/screen-reading). The *Shahnameh* has historically been the source for such performances, although during post-Arab-conquest years different forms of religious drama have also taken similar forms.[15] These performances have traditionally been held in coffeehouses, on streets and, in some cases, in royal courts and private gatherings of the affluent. The *naqqal* (storyteller) usually performs alone in front of a painting or a large screen (*pardeh*) which depicts one or more stories of the *Shahnameh*. In *Shahnameh-khwani* the verses of the *Shahnameh* are recited verbatim in contrast to *naqqali*, where the delivery can take many different forms from literary to colloquial and improvisational, drawing from multiple sources of past collections and performances. One of the popular forms used in *naqqali* is the *Bahr-e Tavil* (which is a text constructed freely based on rhythms of the classical poetry known as *Ozan-e 'aruzi*) or *Nasr-e Mosajja'* (freely rhymed prose). All these performances include dramatic gestures and sometimes live instrumental and vocal music. Theatrical design elements, such as set, costume, lighting and sound, are often very minimal, and the main force of the performance is found in the *naqqāl*'s depth of knowledge and performative mastery.

Using advanced interactive and theatrical audio-visual technologies and juxtaposing the classical and 'new' Persian poetry, *The Scarlet Stone* has been conceived to be a contemporary presentation of an ancient art form with modern aesthetics. Great care has been taken to stay committed to important principles of *naqqali* and not allow technological design elements to usurp the traditional forms, while at the same time not allowing traditional values to impose a nostalgic quality over the modern and technological elements of the piece.

The production is in the language of dance-theatre with a narrator. In the first two-thirds, the only speaking character is the storyteller, while towards the end other characters speak as well. Telling the story in a strictly chronological manner based on the two texts presented two major problems. The first problem was a formal performative and dramatic one, which resulted from the difference between the moods of the two texts. The second problem was the stark manifestation of the contrast in the poetic forms between these two texts. The text from the *Shahnameh* includes two extensive and energetic fight scenes – Sohrab and Gordafarid, and Rostam and Sohrab. Dramatically speaking, had all the events been presented chronologically in this production, the two most intense sections of the performance would follow one another back to back. *Mohreye Sorkh* has a very introspective and sombre mood. While it is full of poetic imagery, it lacks dramatic and intense physical context for the stage, especially for a performance told in the language of dance-theatre. Thus, the switch from the text of *Shahnameh* to the *Mohreye Sorkh* sections would be an abrupt change from the classical text with intense and epic energy to modern poetry as a long, heavy and sombre ending. In other words, the two climactic parts would be presented before halfway into the performance, leaving the last half of the piece as a very long cadence. The form as such would be untenable for a live performance. To solve this problem, we adapted the story to be told from the point of view and in the mind of the injured Sohrab vividly remembering the events of his life.

All of the *Shahnameh* is written in twenty-two syllable verses. This form is often used in long Persian poems, but the presentation of such form for an extended period on stage could negatively affect the attention span of the audience. Sections of *Mohreye Sorkh and* ancient prose (such as sections of *Bahr-e Tavil and Nasr-e Mosajja'*), which have more varied rhythmical constructions, are juxtaposed in multiple sections before the stabbing of Sohrab, specifically to create variations in vocal forms of the storyteller. To address the formal matter of the timings of climaxes, the fight with Rostam is presented twice, first in an abstract form depicting Sohrab's inner turmoil and entanglements with the event and second as a real physical battle, in which the full weight of the stabbing of Sohrab by Rostam is presented to the audience. Figure 2.1 presents the intensity graph of the scenes in the performance. While the introduction of Rostam, and his dance with Tahmineh, is a strong, joyous and sensual opening, the capturing of Gordafarid by Sohrab is a highly emotional moment, which is followed by the abstract fight of Rostam and Sohrab. The final energetic climax comes after we have experienced the mournful and tragic sections of the fallen Sohrab with Tahmineh and Rostam. In his dialogue with Rostam, Sohrab remembers the fight once more vividly, and the scene ends with Sohrab being stabbed and slowly carried away by Rostam. Before Ferdowsi arrives on stage, Sohrab asks for Gordafarid. The scene with the ghost of Gordafarid, suggesting a mixture of grief and passion, is quiet and soft and is underscored by highly emotional electronic sounds.

The role of storyteller (*naqqal*) had traditionally and strictly been played by men in Iran. In the past years a number of female actors and scholars have been able to break this barrier. In this production, Fatemeh Habibizad, who uses the stage name of Gordafarid, was cast to play the role of the storyteller, and Ferdowsi is a representation of the role of women in the various social resistance movements

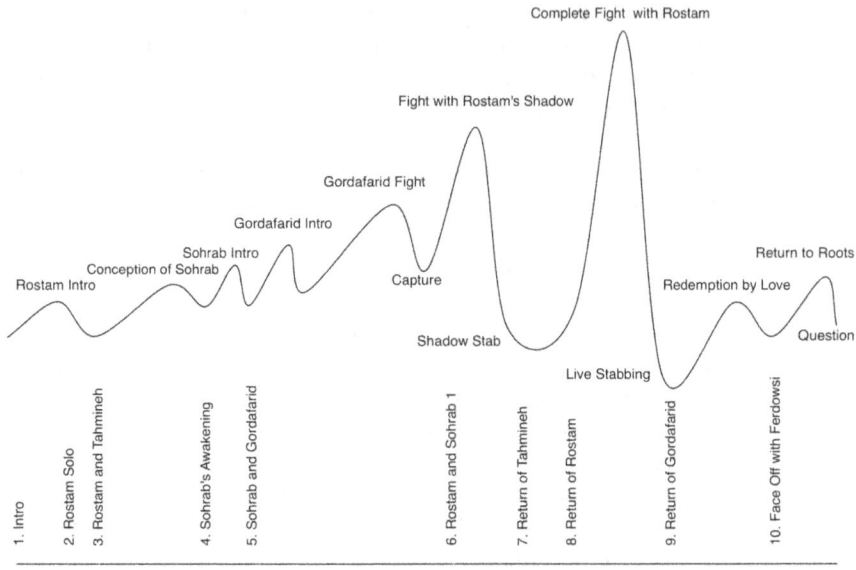

Figure 2.1 Intensity graph of scenes in stage adaptation of *The Scarlet Stone*.

in Iran. The adaptation introductions of the Shahnameh in the piece were done in collaboration with Gordafarid.

The Persian calligraphy and drawings and their animatic evolution through interactive video (using Isadora software) replace the traditional backdrop for the storyteller.[16] While the concept is old, the rendition of the animations and moving projections are very advanced in their expression and in terms of their technological construction. The set designed by Ian Wallace is composed of multi-layered scrims upon which calligraphy of the poetry fills the background as three-dimensional moving paintings. Figure 2.2 is a photograph of the stage which depicts the projections for the opening of the piece, and Figure 2.3 shows the first change in the background for 'Rostam's hunt' scene.

Various visual symbols were used in the production of the projections to relate abstractly to each character, such as 'water' for Sohrab, 'fire' for Rostam, 'wind' for Tahmineh and 'hair' for Gordafarid. The evolution of these graphics and the animatic movement of the background at times were controlled by parameters obtained through real-time analysis of the music or vocal signal of the storyteller. Thus, the projection backdrops mirror the intensity of the scene and behave like a movie, but one that follows and accommodates for variations (or even improvisations) in performances on stage. In some sections of the performance, the storyteller is present on stage and recounts the story as the dancers act or portray the dramatic elements. Figure 2.4 is a photograph of the scene where Sohrab confronts his mother about his father and, upon learning that he is the son of Rostam, decides to attack Iran. In this scene the storyteller stands centre-

Figure 2.2 The projections for the opening of the piece. Photo: Jim Carmody.

Figure 2.3 Projections for 'Rostam's hunt'. Photo: Jim Carmody.

upstage and speaks on behalf of both Sohrab and Tahmineh. The blue graphics, representing the 'water' sign for Sohrab, rise based on a running intensity average value extracted from the vocal signal of the storyteller.

Figure 2.4 Real-time animated graphics rise in the backdrop when Sohrab confronts Tahmineh about his father and decides to attack Iran. Photo, Jim Carmody.

The music

Similar to many of the other elements of the production, the music for *The Scarlet Stone* is a fusion of old traditional elements with modern forms and renditions. The aesthetics and principles of Persian traditional music and regional music of Iran are mixed with electronics and modern approaches without compromising the identity of either form. Traditional instruments of Iran such as the *balaban*, *tanbur*, *sorna*, *daf* and *tonbak*, as well as the violin, cello and electronics, are used to produce a new sound and musical form without losing the Persian/Iranian character of the music. The product is a music that is at times seductive and introspective and at times climactic and energetic. Most of the music used in the show are original and have been composed and produced specifically for this piece. Much of the piece is underscored, and the music is used as a formal tool for storytelling and dance. Each character is associated with the sound of at least one instrument. Rostam is associated with the tanbur and the cello. Among the tanbur players of Kurdistan, it is believed that Rostam played the tanbur in his fourth hurdle (*khan-e chaharom*). The cello is used to represent the power of Rostam. Sohrab is associated with three timbres: the *tabla*, as a foreign sound; the tanbur, as the sound related to Rostam; and the voice, as a sign of his love for Gordafarid. Tahmineh is associated with the *balaban*. The sound for Gordafarid is the voice of Azam Ali, which portrays power, grace and, at the same time, great wisdom. Percussion instruments have generally been used for the battle sections or during the early upbeat dance of Tahmineh and Rostam.

Critical and political implications

Ferdowsi tells the story of Rostam and Sohrab with great detail without declaring either of them clearly as the victim or the aggressor. What drives the story is a strong context around the life of these two characters. The collusion of the leftist movements with the Islamic fundamentalists during the 1979 revolution played an important role in the success of the revolution and handing the power to the clergies. Having been a vocal part of that relationship, Kasrai lived a controversial life. In this production we neither judge nor defend him, but we portray his words and the hope he envisions. While the stage production of *The Scarlet Stone* deals with a political, historical, social and mythological subject, it does not have a specific stance by which right and wrong are clearly delineated. This matter is not only an approach in the building of the storyline of the piece but also a structural one in building the space of collaboration among all the artists involved and the space of interpretation for audiences who may have specific beliefs or inclinations. The gem that Rostam gives Tahmineh after their night together has no colour in the *Shahnameh*. The colour red given to this stone by Kasrai may be interpreted as Leftist ideals or it could be the colour of blood, representing nationalistic or heroic passion.

What is clear is that in this work, Kasrai is confronting some of his own Leftist ideals and actions he took based on those ideals. He also does not clearly depict a line by which right and wrong could be separated. Even more vague is the position and meaning of the colour red. In the last pages of *Mohreye Sorkh*, Ferdowsi reveals to Sohrab why he had to endure such difficulties. The phrase of this revelation, which was the centre of many conversations among the collaborators on this piece, could be read in three different ways, by just changing the emphasis on various words. The first form would be that Sohrab went through all the trouble so that the impassioned would no longer approach the red shining light, implying a negative tendency towards the Left. The second form would be that Sohrab went through all the trouble, so that the impassioned would be guided by the red shining light, implying a positive tendency towards Leftist ideals, and finally, the third form, which we used and found to be what Kasrai had meant, is that Sohrab had to go through all the difficulties so that the impassioned would be able to see the effects of the red shining light in their path, implying a neutral approach to Leftist ideals.[17]

In the production process and the performances of *The Scarlet Stone*,[18] we paid great attention to developing a collaborative environment among all the artists without a need for a specific political declaration for the piece as a whole or for the symbols found in the piece. The focus has been the integral artistic expression of the piece to allow the audience to draw their own conclusions. It has been our hope that this piece would be a catalyst for communication among Iranians and those interested in the socio-political life of Iran.

3

THE QUESTION OF AUDIENCE IN ABBAS KIAROSTAMI'S *A LOOK TO TA'ZIEH*

Babak Rahimi

We grew weary of reality
Truth, far from sight.

—Kiarostami[1]

Ta'zieh has often been described as the only 'indigenous theatre' in Islamicate societies.[2] However, as a commemorative ritual of social significance, *ta'zieh* considerably differs from theatre. Introduced from Europe to North Africa and West Asia in the nineteenth century, theatre is the collaborative form of performing art based on the culture industry that produces performances at specific sites to be viewed on a range of stages by a target audience. Although contingent to context and operational function, theatre is performed, to recall a key term used by Richard Schenchner, for 'entertainment', a choreographed event to amuse audiences as consumer participants in an industry of cultural production.[3] Theatre is the stage of spectacle.

Somewhat similar to older forms of public ritual such as puppet theatre, storytelling events such as *naqqali* (in Iran), *al-halaqa* (in Morocco), parades and urban games, *ta'zieh* is a ritual of communal character that has integrally involved audience-actor participation in a range of everyday spatial sites, such as household domains, village squares and urban neighbourhoods.[4] Shape-shifting, spontaneous and at times improvised, with aspects of entertainment, *ta'zieh* reflects the porous, lived experiences of non-professional performers who participate as actors-spectators-organizers-producers of the drama of sacred life ingrained in uncertainty and demise of temporal reality. The distinct dramatic expressions of *ta'zieh* involve the fusion of affective experiences to create a shared space of alternative reality, however ephemeral, beyond the limits of the theatrical frame – spaces that range from proscenium stages to open-air auditoriums.

This chapter engages with the dramatic aspects of *ta'zieh* through Abbas Kiarostami's video installation, *A Look to ta'zieh*, so as to frame the encounter between performance and performer in a reinterpretation of the audience. Here the term 'ritual' underlines the multi-dimensional set of practices that combine emotive and reflective performances in the construction of reality.[5] The drama of *ta'zieh*, reframed through Kiarostami's video installation, is the performance of everyday presences as practices of collective orientation that bring about a new awareness in emotive ways. The *ta'zieh* audiences, I argue, are the performing actors who reinterpret reality through an affective distance in the expression of community as an ongoing performance.[6] Meanwhile, the cinematization of *ta'zieh* in the form of Kiarostami's video depictions of the audiences signifies an alternate audience-actor relationship, as the viewer of the *ta'zieh*, audiences enact the rituals in interpreting the emotions through distance. Such self-reflexivity is the recognition of radical contingencies that undo individuated perception and, therefore, defamiliarize reality for something different, a feature also found in Kiarostami's cinematic works.

'The Living Ritual:' A re-look at Ta'zieh

Performed during the month of Moharram in the Islamic lunar calendar, *ta'zieh* (also *shabih-khwani*) is a repertoire of commemorative rituals that reenacts the martyrdom of Prophet Mohammad's grandson, Hossein ibn Ali (626–680), in the battle of Karbala in 680 CE.[7] Though the popular practices vary from South Asia to the Caribbean, in its specific Shi'i Twelver Iranian form, *ta'zieh* as mourning drama has developed into intricate narrative oratory, poetic retellings and representational arts of an imagined battlefield at Karbala, where Hossein and his followers' martyrdom, by Caliph Yazid (647–683) and his army, attain a mythical status of cosmic significance.[8] Though mostly minimalist in form, the representational tropes of the rituals are indicative of a complex set of symbolic practices that embody messianic and redemptive ideals in reenactments of the Battle of Karbala. Yet the representational aspects are secondary to rituals as communal events with historical roots in Safavid urbanization.

In a historical sense, *ta'zieh* is best described as a post-Safavid urban construct.[9] The Safavid project that reshaped the Iranian landmass into a Perso-Shi'i *Imami* socio-political order also institutionalized several public rituals, the most important of which was Moharram, commemorative rites of Hossein's martyrdom at Karbala.[10] Especially during the Isfahani phase of Safavid rule (1589–1642), the urban features of Moharram included performance display of primarily male bodily acts of mourning tied to the spatial visibility of the new city as a Safavid imperium. The late Safavid period, under Sultan Hossein (1694–1722), saw the transformation of Moharram into a more dramatic staging of the ceremonies with the display of pageantries with participants as actors performing the story of Karbala on shifting and stationary podiums. The development of public dramatic narrations of Karbala characters from Kamal al-din Hossein Va'ez Kashefi's *Rowzat al-Shohada* (*Meadow of the Martyrs*), known as *rowzeh-khani* (recitation), is indicative of ritual stationary performances that paved the way for the development of *ta'zieh*.[11] However, as Peter J. Chelkowski has argued, the late Safavid Moharram dramas were not *ta'zieh* since they excluded poetical eulogies and textual lyrical performances so commonly associated to their current form.[12]

It is highly likely that the Moharram ambulatory processions merged with the stationary practices sometime during the eighteenth century, especially after the disintegration of the centralized state of Nader Shah (r. 1736–47), which gave way for the rituals to develop into distinct civic events of musical semblances and poetic oratory.[13] With the first documented depiction in the travel report of the English traveller William Francklin, who visited Shiraz in October 1787, *ta'zieh* emerged into an elaborate oral drama of stationary ritual.[14] What the later Zand and early Qajar variations of *ta'zieh* reveal is the intersection of public-street and square forums as central staging spaces of the rituals for villages or urban publics.[15] Such sites emphasized the convivial and interactive social basis of *ta'zieh*, by which the boundaries that separate the audience and the actors were constantly disrupted by the street-carnivalesque tendencies of the dramatic ceremonies, observed and performed by people of all walks of life. In the words of Matthew Arnold, spaces of *ta'zieh* are where 'the public meets the actor halfway'.[16]

With the construction of Takkiyeh Dowlat (1868–9) during the reign of Naser al-Din Shah (1848–96), *ta'zieh* underwent a dramatic transformation, as the new *takkiyeh* or the building site for the performances attained a royal status and a fixed spatial setting.[17] The royal *ta'zieh* introduced new entertainment features into the rituals, such as the *goriz* (digression) device that integrated non-Moharram narratives and *taqlid* (imitation) comical acts into the performances.[18] As a religious cultural artefact of the Qajars, *ta'zieh* was banned under Reza Shah, only to reappear as a national-cultural relic during the reign of Mohammad Reza Shah (r. 1941–79) when scholarly, pedagogical and theatrical interests in the performances grew among theatre practitioners and Iranian studies specialists.[19] The most important development appeared in the 1950s when *ta'zieh* served as a model for Iranian indigenous theatre as its perceived avant-garde features were incorporated into the theatrical works of leading dramatists such as Bahram Beyzaie (1938–) and Abbas Javanmard (1929–).[20] With the Shiraz Arts Festival (from 1967 to 1978) the popularity of *ta'zieh*, which was first featured with *ta'zieh Horr, Nemayesh-e Kohan-e Irani* in 1967, grew among non-Iranian playwrights such as Jerzy Grotowski (1933–99) and Peter Brook (1925–), who saw the technical and experimental features of the rituals as a means to rethink American and European theatres.[21]

Since the post-revolutionary period, *ta'zieh* has been staged and aspects of it have been incorporated into the growing theatrical culture of Iran or utilized for political or ideological purposes.[22] As noted earlier, the theatricalization of *ta'zieh* originates with the Takkiyeh Dowlat, designed from the advice of Jules Richard and most likely modelled after the Parisian Opera House under the reign of Naser al-din Shah Qajar (r. 1848–96).[23] However, the theatricality of *ta'zieh* since the Pahlavi period has considerably accentuated the representational-symbolic features of the ritual over its socially lived constitution where the audiences play an active role in the rituals. The perceived symbolic depths are, in fact, theatrical projections into the *ta'zieh* by (Iranian and non-Iranian) dramatists as a way to shape an innovative cultural art in response to modernity's cultural limitations.

While the overemphasis on acting and staging *ta'zieh* practices has seen the production of innovative studies on literary and theatricality of the performances, the field has yet failed to see a study of the dramaturgical performances of the audiences.[24] This is because the interest in the theatrics of *ta'zieh* comes from the outside, the non-ritual scholarly observer, who brackets off the rituals from the social practices that define them. Here, by 'social practices' I refer to performances and events that permeate the everyday/nightly life, similar to sporting games, marriage ceremonies, social meetings at cafes or at restaurants or pedestrian gatherings for social event on sidewalks. As ritual events, the blurring of sociability and performed emotions that both actors and audiences experience in *ta'zieh* overlap with the performative ways of being social actors in flexible and yet strategic ways. Here the notion 'performative' underscores the effective transformation that takes place in actor-audience participants, a change similar to a rite of passage such as a marriage ceremony that identifies, in words of John Langshaw Austin, 'the performance of an action'.[25] The 'action' here refers to what Schechner describes as the merging of 'symbolic and actual events' in which distinct forms of transformation (i.e. status, prestige, adulthood) takes place within the participants.[26] This is the main reason why Kiarostami correctly understood *ta'zieh* not as 'theatre' but as 'ritual', and sought to highlight the role of the spectators as performers in an attempt to demystify the rituals and emphasize its transformable features in the course of performances.[27]

Before we move to the question of audience, I would like to briefly underline two themes that highlight the social life of *ta'zieh* as ritual. Diana Taylor's notion of 'repertoire of performances' as gestures, dance, song, political processions or funerals in transferring knowledge, memory and subjective experiences through repetition serves as a guiding concept to understand *ta'zieh*'s framework of everyday performances in constituting the rituals.[28] The primacy of dramatic performance beyond text and situated in the everyday experience necessitates repeatable acts that range in cyclical, routine and reenactments of rhythmic orientation. Social encounter in the 'repertoire of performances' is the life of ritual.

First is the element of informality. Conveyed in gestures, humours, chats, improvised facial expressions and what Erving Goffman called routine 'face-work' as a display of verbal and non-verbal acts of interaction, *ta'zieh* maintains minute bodily practices that characterize the non-professional expression of performers, always symbolically divided between antagonists (Yazid's forces) and protagonists (Hossein's forces), as they verbally narrate dialogues and the story amid a crowd of mournful listeners who individually and collectively respond, interact and react to the physical movements of the performers.[29] This key feature of informality has been observed by many and identified as the disruptive feature of *ta'zieh*, and, in fact, a source of inspiration for theatrical innovation. Yet considering participation in the performances, we must understand, in an important sense, that *ta'zieh* performers do not perform as 'actors' but rather as ritual participants embedded in a community, though with an enhanced role as key players in the enactment of the narrative. In relation to the element of informality, likewise *ta'zieh* audiences also act as co-organizers and co-creators in the ritual process. The audience both organizes and views as ritual participants in the larger communal complex.

In a 2002 study I conducted in a village near the port of Bushehr, I noticed how *ta'zieh* actors who depicted characters in the Moharram story repetitively stepped outside of their roles and casually conversed with the watching crowd, who happened to be their neighbours or friends. The performers themselves were members of the village: backers, workers or high-school students performing in the battling armies of Hossein or Yazid. In this village context, the *ta'zieh* stage was a non-stage, personal and informal as in an open space in a neighbourhood where interaction is as immediate and spontaneous as any form of face-to-face encounter.[30] The symbolism in the drama is overshadowed by the frequent twinges of ordinary interactions that at times enter the 'stage' in unpredictable ways, marking it into a scene-shifting 'bare stage', in the words of Peter Brook, in a village square, which is not a square but a vacant site opened up for the rituals to become publicly visible.[31]

Informal performance also makes the formal notion of director and actor irrelevant. This is because the performing authors of the story are several; no single person leads the performances, while everyone, including the audiences, gives witness to the martyrdom story as performed in a collective consort, and because everyone who performs there has a clear understanding that no one is the person who he pretends to be. The distance is a performing awareness of what is real and what might be possible in the act of ritual performance. Hamid Dabashi has an intriguing depiction of *ta'zieh*, which is worth quoting:

> The director of Ta'ziyeh is always present (and often deliberately visible) on the stage, not because the actors would not know what to do without him, but because the audience needs assurance that this is just acting. The stage is not really a stage, not because the villagers and townspeople who stage the Ta'ziyeh are poor and cannot afford a proper amphitheatre, but because the stage must be an extension of the rest of the physical habitat of the actors and the audience – their ordinary realities fused into their acting. The actors often come on stage directly from their homes, alleys, streets, and markets. The stage never loses sight of its not-being-the-stage, of being a natural extension of reality. Non-actors can frequent the stage easily, while the actors fall in and out of character without any prior notice.[32]

In other words, the social lines that separate ritual space and everyday sites of interaction are very thin. The ritual dissonance in *ta'zieh* encompasses the staging of a non-stage that is permeable of ordinary people making the performances possible in the first place. This is partly why Kiarostami describes *ta'zieh* as a 'living ritual', with constant transgressions in recreating self and community in the dialectic of situated ordinariness and dramatic extraordinariness.[33]

Connected with informality is the element of interruption. In *ta'zieh*, not only actors step out of character but they do so not because of a theatrical strategy but a complete awareness of the performance's artificial process for an authentic experience. Interruption takes place as actors read out their lines off a paper held in hands or when they ask for a handkerchief to wipe their tears as they recite the eulogy to the fallen Imam and his companions.[34] The actor does not identify with the characters and he (and it is always a 'he') makes sure his audience knows this as well by undermining the role he performs in various breaks from character. Likewise, the literary story deviates in *goriz* dramatic device that is meant to expand the narrative horizon of *taʿzieh*, adding an unpredictable element to the storyline.[35] Even the ostensible literary performances in the form of oral eulogies are of non-literary characteristic, as the symbolic meaning of the poem defies immediate decipher by the listening audiences.[36] In its traditional performance, the props, costumes and decor (if any) are minimalist, often secondary to the bodily performances that reenact the story.[37] At times the play is paused so the actor can fix a prop amid the performance, as other performers continue with their oral narration or chat with a person in the crowd. Interruptions delineate *taʿzieh*. To perform *taʿzieh*, one needs to step out of the story to retell it, and in the process discover a new reality.

A Look to Taʿzieh: Audience as performer

The practice of stepping out of the story and breaking the fourth wall is a defining feature in Kiarostami's filmmaking practice. The transgressive shift from camera to the spectator, who becomes the subject of the cinematic experience, elucidates the agency of a heightened awareness that reality is contingent on fluid perspectives. And such fluidity breeds ambiguity in meaning, which depends on the audiences' view as they participate in the cinematic practice and, accordingly, trouble the ordinary senses of reality. Through indirection, Hamid Naficy argues that Kiarostami's spectators 'are always kept in an ambiguous position, having to constantly parse the truth of fiction from the fiction of realism'.[38] Kiarostami's films are endless vistas of interpretations based on the Socratic ethos of life examinations that embraces other lives, such that, in a dialogical process, would lead to further questionings without an end.

Consider the ending of *Taste of Cherry* (1997), where the image of nightly darkness, depicting the death of middle-aged man, Mr. Badii, changes to daylight, camcorder footage of soldiers' march and the film crew in the countryside field, where the movie was earlier recorded. At the end of the film, Mr. Badii, as an actor, transfigures into a displaced actor, perhaps an audience of his own film, a self-portrait of the director, Kiarostami. We, as the audience, are also reminded that this is just a construct, a mere film, which is actually not a film, perhaps an anti-film, devoid of allegories or symbols, undermining all claims to filmic authority. There is also the much-analysed film: *Close-Up* (1990). A surrealist cinematic-documentary achievement, *Close-Up* is a true story of Hossein Sabzian, an unemployed man who impersonates the famed director, Mohsen Makhmalbaf, in deceiving the Ahankhah family to believe they would star in his new film. In a collage of real and reenactment scenes of events that lead to Sabzian's arrest, the performers are the very characters in the real story. What, of course, becomes problematic in the story is the reality of 'real'. *Close-Up* fuses the boundaries of reality and fiction in ways that denaturalizes perceived self-knowledge and forces the audience to question the stability of reality. The complexity of being and seeing, or being viewed, is a central feature of Kiarostamian cinema.

Key to such complexity of being and seeing is reflexivity as an attempt to create distance with reality. In his *Under the Olive Tree* (1994), as Talajooy explains, Kiarostami 'creates powerful moments by displaying the distance between the actors and their roles, the process through which we create narratives to give meaning to our lives and the collapse of these narratives under the actualities of life'.[39] Together with *Original Copy* (2010) and other films such as *ABC Africa* (2001), Kiarostami constantly interrupts the relationship between audience, actor, director and the unfolding story through the way cinematic participants step out of character or story and create new relationships with the film and, more importantly, with themselves as participants. Self-reflexivity, as the unending process of self-shaping between co-actors, is an interpretative practice. Interpretation, in a sense, involves the breakdown of stable perceptions as meaning is perpetually projected into the perceived world, where knowledge becomes possible only through the other in the process of dialogical interaction. In doing so, interpretation allows autonomy in the possibility to re-arrange circumstances according to constant self-interpretation in varied ways of seeing.

The audience is at the axis in the space between cinematic experience and meaning. As an experimental case of cinematic reflexivity, or perhaps a theatrical form of filmmaking, Kiarostami's *Shirin* (2008) turns the camera away from the screen (as stage) to a close-up on the audiences (as actors), mostly notable female actors who play a pivotal role in this hyper-reflexive film. The ninety-two-minute film is a visual collage of changing frames of spectators who are shown one after another as *performing* audiences in varied emotional expressions that ultimately defamiliarize cinematic conventions, or in what Kiarostami calls the 'disappearance of direction' in the rejection of orthodox filmmaking.[40] Seated in an apparent dark movie theatre – actually recorded in the basement of Kiarostami's house in Tehran – the women appear to be watching the romance of *Khosrow and Shirin* by Nezami Ganjavi (1141–1209), while their faces are lit by an apparent screen, unseen to the viewer. Each performer-audience reacts to hand-made drawings installed above the camera, as if she is watching a film on screen. The illusion of film is achieved through a reflector so as 'to create lighting effects on their faces as if cast from the flicker of light on a screen'.[41] The story as we, the alter audience, hear was later composed and added to the film, while the audiences appear to react to moving images, giving the illusion of direct viewership. *Shirin* is a feast of editorial innovation and a theatricality of illusions.

The reflective distance between audio and visual perception in the illusion of a coherent narrative is co-created by Kiarostami, his crew, the cinematic editor and the actors as audiences and, of course, us, the viewers of *Shirin*, who watch a film that is hardly a film.[42] Both the depicted audience (actors) and the watching audience (us) participate in a cinematic imaginary that defies film in its conventional sense. As for the performing audience, he explains, 'I asked every actress to recall a personal episode – an intimate memory or emotion – and imagine a film in her mind based on that experience.'⁴³ Kiarostami would describe the film's objective to one of the audience-performers as the following: 'We have portraits of 80 to 90 women, while they are being themselves. No one's around them. No one's Looking at them; they are watching the screen. In fact, you are looking at yourself. Now, as spectators you are looking at yourselves as actors.'⁴⁴ The self as watcher becomes the mirror upon which the self becomes possible.

This hermeneutical inversion of audience as a self-seeing performer enables us to think of performance not as a practice of self-expression, in response to a symbolic narrative, but an interpretative act of subjunctive orientation. Narrative in the form of exchanged symbols and signs only becomes relevant as a discursive measure to remind (articulate) the limits of self-perception, but not to define it. The emotive enactments are revealed without articulation, concealing motivations behind the face as a mask. Meanwhile, through facial expression, the female audiences project their singular stories into the film in a dark theatre not as a form of 'acting' but as the experience of 'being', like perhaps the way we stroll through a park or read a book. This ordinary sense of affective enactment is less about expression and more about the experience of presence that opens up the possibility of remaking reality along new lines in mundane ways.⁴⁵ Watching *Shirin*, the seen audience as actor becomes a felt encounter rather than an 'immediate sight', to use an expression by John Berger.⁴⁶ In other words, the viewer equally becomes the interpreter of the audience who strategically expresses her emotions on the camera.⁴⁷

The audiences enact their role as they would in everyday circumstances, requiring them to perform across gender and status in shifting contexts. How such performances are displayed depends on the creative potential of the audiences and the extent to which they can effectively make (in)visible their desires, wishes, anxieties and sorrows in a public setting. Kiarostami explains this element of subjectivity with limitations of lived circumstances as the following:

> When you watch *Shirin* you are free to imagine whatever you want, but at the same time – because you are listening to *Khosrow and Shirin* or reading the subtitles, and watching the faces of these women – it could be that you are feeling precisely what I want you at any moment. Audiences have their freedom, but at the same time are confined within precise boundaries.⁴⁸

Authentic film is the mirror that shows liberty and discipline in the shaping of performance. And yet in every restricted situation, humans can self-present in complex ways. He explains, 'In the darkened theatre, we give everyone the chance to dream and to express his [sic] dream freely. If art succeeds in changing things and proposing new ideas, it can only do so via the free creativity of the people we are addressing, each individual member of the audience.'⁴⁹

While performing within the confines of institutions, either a movie theatre or a bureaucratic order (recall *The Report* 1977), we can embrace the affective potential to interpret beyond ourselves, perceptions-within-perceptions that push beyond the perceived ordinary, what appears self-evident but ultimately unstable as we frame our fluid, lived reality. In the photo gallery *Look at Me*, displayed in Tehran as part of the Louvre exhibit opening in the National Museum of Iran in 2018, Kiarostami deconstructs perception in a range of photographs he had taken during his visits to the Louvre Museum from 1996 to 2012.[50] Viewing photos of museum visitors taking photos of paintings open up new a perspective for the viewer. There is a kind of hall of mirrors at work here. The photographic images make perception external to a vanishing point of origin (recall *Certified Copy* 2010). Perception is subverted by stepping out of a fixed view and participating in a play of framed perspectives. Self-reflexivity is key here. The collapse in the boundaries between looking and what is looked at fuses the spectators into the frame, making the viewers view themselves as implicated in the aesthetic process.

Perception mirrors perception (see Figure 3.1). What follows then is an awareness that is shaped into multiple ways of looking that overlap, mingle, though, at times potentially collide, yet ultimately go beyond gazing. The revealed reality is self-referential through altering and shifting ways of seeing through and among multiple perceptions: in this case from one photographic image to another, producing the sensation of plasticity that defines a new reality, a process of its making through the practice of perception.

The connection between *ta'zieh* and *Shirin* is ostensible in the audience-performance nexus. As performers, audiences shape the narrative reenacted in the process of looking. Similar to *Shirin*, *A Look to ta'zieh* is a multi-layered

Figure 3.1 *Look at Me*, Tehran, Iran. Photo: Babak Rahimi.

perspective performance. The video installation, *A Look to taʿzieh*, originally staged in Rome in July 2003, includes six large screens around a stage in a former soap factory, where each screen shows close-up facial expressions of *taʿzieh* audiences in rural Iran.⁵¹ A smaller screen depicts *taʿzieh*, as Nacim Pak-Shiraz notes, visually underscoring the importance of the audience over the actors.⁵² The depicted spectators on the screen are edited to react to the performances, as they shed tears, at times cry and beat themselves in perceived response to the reenacted story of the martyrdom of Imam Hossein. The 2005 version, which I watched at the Victoria and Albert Museum in London, was a cinematic recording of the video installation performance, first shown in Brussels in 2004.⁵³ At the museum, the audiences were a mix of European and Iranian diaspora audiences, such as myself.

It is important to note that the recorded scenes are from a range of different *taʿzieh* enactments, including a village in the south of Tehran. The scenes from the female audiences, who were difficult to record at a 'live' *taʿzieh*, were based on footages of women from rural Tehran whom Kiarostami hired as they watched a VHS tape of the performances at his backyard garden.⁵⁴ The incorporation of backyard recordings into the video installation did not undermine the performances since so much of *taʿzieh* is based on disjoint interactions though still connected to the immersive emotions that define the ritual process. In a panel conversation with Ahmad Karimi Hakak and Geoff Andrew, following the 2005 Victoria and Albert Museum exhibition, Kiarostami explains the disjoint feature as the following:

> the fact that they were watching it on TV and not 'live' did not take away anything from the reality of the meaning of the process itself. In fact, one could see it as an extension of the distancing that occurs in *taʿzieh*. It [the mediated form] was no longer important to them. In fact, at some points the sun was so bright that you could barely see anything, but they still continued to cry by just hearing the words.⁵⁵

The 'distancing' that Kiarostami describes here is the creative awareness for the *taʿzieh* audiences to distinguish between real and fiction while at the same time performing spectatorship whenever expected in a given performance situation.

Social differences such as age, class and gender condition variation of audience performances loom large among the audiences. When in need of more footage, Kiarostami hires again several women for more recordings in his backyard. The story following the new hires is intriguing. Kiarostami describes:

> This time the organiser brought 30 women with her, 15 of whom were the old faces. I told her that I had already shot their faces, to which she responded, 'Well, they've come along anyway!' So we sat the old crowd on the side and the new ones in front of the camera. We served them tea and sweets and then got started. After a while I noticed the old ones who didn't have the camera on them were

much more emotional and weeping far more than the new batch! [Audience is laughing heartily by now] Whatever I'm saying is the truth! Once they were finished, their organiser came to me and charged even for the old group saying that they had done their share of crying anyway! Despite all of this, it is very difficult and complex to find out what is happening in their heads […] I didn't say all of this just to make you laugh! I wanted to demonstrate how people are far more complex than it appears.[56]

Since the Safavid era, it has been common to employ Moharram participants to mourn on behalf of a penitent benefactor. What is unique in this story, though, is not the economic transaction but the distinction in the display of mourning between the young and the older group of female mourners. Here the camera, as Kiarostami notes, is not the defining element as to why the younger participants do not emotionally respond to the performance on TV.[57] In fact, individuated and collective motivations and how they are performed through gender identity in relation to the act of mourning are hardly accessible to the observer. Why?

In critical conceptual terms, an explanation in terms of a single clear answer to the question of motive lends itself to an assumption of linearity of psychological trajectory in the ritual process. The reasons why a person participates and how she expresses a range of motivations in the act of ritual performance can be multiple, at times even unconscious to the participants in temporal and spatial contexts. More important to note is the creative element of mimicry that pervades all levels of ritual communication. The complexity lies in the creative ways in which a performing person, say an audience, mimics images, texts or narratives in shades of social interactions amid the ritual enactments with implicit and explicit effects. In an important sense, *distance* lies between what is mimicked and the motivation behind the act of mimicry. The strategic use of bodily and in particular masking practices, especially the act of lamenting, may not mirror the felt emotions; rather, they can represent masquerade performances, as displays of subversion in the context of a set of shifting power relations, in which gender plays a critical role.[58] The *ta'zieh* distanciation, therefore, is an interruption in emotional presences that splits what is real and how that reality can be performed through bodily expressions.

Audiences enact through various bodily performances and, in doing so, maintain varied motivations behind enact expressions that at times strategically hide motivations. Symbols fail to reveal meanings that become multifaceted through ritual interaction. In the 2002 field research in Bushehr, for example, I learned that men who participated in the Moharram rituals did so for their devotion to the martyred Imam but also for marriage blessings, employment prospects or personal health.[59] It goes without saying that other factors such as peer-pressure, status and gender identity played a central role as to why these men participated in Moharram. The facial projection in consort with the ritual enactment can mask multiple desires, hopes or anxieties on complex personal and social levels. In a dramaturgical sense, the face becomes a strategy in staging oneself, as ritual participants create distance between emotion and expression in ritually situated ways. Goffman famously described this strategy as 'impression management', the expressive communications one conveys to others, in particular to a group one belongs to, as an interplay between a 'front-stage' (where the self is made visible) and 'back-stage' (where the self remains hidden from view).[60] The management of facial expression is a social practice that lies between these two stages and, therefore, makes it possible for a person to convey accepted social norms, or at times break character to transgress them.

Kiarostami's *Shirin* is a reconstruction of *taʻzieh*'s performativity. In both cases, what the female participants reveal as an 'internal' feature of themselves becomes contingent to how they anticipate what we, the viewing audience, expect from them in the form of certain gendered bodily acts (e.g. crying). While the role of male-director as in the figure of Kiarostami cannot be ignored, there is agency in how gender performativity is strategically displayed for a specific narrative performance. The identity of the performing audience is, accordingly, sustained through a set of self-staged acts, in which the gendered stylization of the body becomes strategically visible. Yet the depicted women who manage self-expression based on personal experiences direct such strategic visibility.[61] Also linked to gender, the expectation of playing a specific role also appears in the beginning of the installation when the gender-segregated spectators casually chat among themselves, drink tea and laugh. As the story unfolds, the same spectators cry and beat their chests. The mourning stops with the story, as though it was all a show but the sort that the spectators also play an instantaneous role. The display of shifting emotions is testimony to the immediacy of the audiences' experience of rituals as living participants.

As his only theatrical staging, Kiarostami deliberately highlights key features of *taʻzieh*, most conspicuously the absence of a clear-cut boundary of a fixed and singular stage, which are actually the multiple screens that show involved audiences that ceaselessly interact with the play. He describes the boundary-less performance as 'an empty stage show', whereby the spectators lose themselves in a narrative that they act as mourners.[62] Here the video installation plays a spatial strategic role in the narrative arrangement that defies linearity of cinematic discourse by creating an immersive and yet fragmented ambience for the audiences. Equally important is the way perspective becomes grounded in the materiality of the screen. The audience, as performer, plays an active role as he or she frames the narrative through expressive emotions that alter on the screen. In many ways, the video installation signifies a performance that is inherently interactive since it displays the way the viewer becomes an extension of the plot. Yet the viewer performs not just because of giving witness to the narrative but also for partaking in a social event based on the construction of reciprocal relations, and shared within the quotidian spaces: markets, neighbourhood festivals, school celebrations or civic gatherings.

However, we must also acknowledge another audience. In its video installation form, which signifies a cinematic reinterpretation of *taʻzieh*, the viewers who watch the audiences also become, unconsciously though perhaps even consciously, the ritual participants. In watching the *taʻzieh* audiences, the viewers of the video installation become aware of the participatory nature of being an audience in the course of viewing, which I would argue lends to the possibility of empathy.[63] 'Why are they crying?' a man next to me asks his companion at the museum exhibit, a question that instantly opens up the possibility of projecting an emotion into the embodied person viewed on the screen.[64] The deconstructive turn comes as the cinema audiences of diverse background realize distance between themselves and the *ta'zieh* audiences, whose expressed emotions are maintained through distance from the screen, creating an ambiguous experience as to who is the performer and who is the audience in the video installation. The ambiguity also extends to how a viewer of a viewer is to be seen.[65] Distance in observation becomes an event of performance. In this inter-visual citationality, there is no single perspective, but a manifold of sights that make reality both visible and invisible to the viewer, a way of seeing beyond the gaze. The connection between narrativity and performances also becomes tenuous as self-reflexivity provokes interruption in the minds of cinematic viewers who leave the experience with more questions than answers. The element of interruption operates as a distancing device, detached from the perceived reality that in the course of ritual perception the audience would allow the ecstasy of being beside itself, and in the end, remain unknown to itself.

Here the factor of distance should not be confused with the Brechtian concept of distanciation.[66] For Brecht, the distancing effect, also known as alienation or estrangement effect, is a theatrical technique to defamiliarize the naturalized reality and reveal its historical contingencies for a new consciousness, ideally a revolutionary one that could potentially change the status quo. In Brechtian terms, by breaking the fourth wall, the manipulative strategies of fictive practices are unmasked, as audiences are discouraged from simply identifying with the characters and opening up a space for critical consciousness. The audience steps out of the perception of being a passive, unseen spectator, and transgresses the consumerist identity from which modern theatre has emerged, exposing the fact that acting is not neutral but an ideological practice.

In *ta'zieh* and its various performances, the spectators, however, are already aware of the manipulative strategies of the performance. There is also the awareness from the beginning that they actively participate in a communal event, not as passive spectators but multiple authors with the ability to contribute to the traditions as co-performers in a lived ritual. Moreover, as Majid Fallah-Zadeh has argued, the *ta'zieh* distance is one of emotional spontaneity that already exists in living experience, whereas distanciation is an intellectual attempt to interrupt the cultural hegemony of modern theatre, in the words of Brecht, to move 'above the level of the everyday' towards political emancipation.[67] Unlike audience-theatrical performances, such as Vyacheslav Ivanov's 'theatre of the future', in which the spectators are envisaged to mingle in the theatrical repertoire in a merging of stage and auditorium, or Augusto Boal's Forum Theatre and the notion of 'spect-actor', which incorporates the audience as both viewer and creator of dramatic meaning, *ta'zieh*'s performances do not break the fourth wall to reach out to the audiences, but from the outset are the stage upon which the performances become realized.[68]

For Kiarostami, distanciation in *ta'zieh* is the inventive stuff of reality that is already present to the audiences and can be discovered through self-reflexive practices such as cinema; for Bretch, reality is the manipulated arrangements that cause alienation and can be overcome through distanciation technique. Kiarostami explains,

> I found distanciation in *Tazieh* [...] although the audience is deeply close to the subject matter and believes in it, when they sit to watch the show, they forget about everything they knew before and accept an actor's claim that without changing decor, just by doing two laps around a circuit (usually in the desert or some dusty village), he has now come from Mecca to Medina.[69]

In other words, the suspension of belief is paradoxically an awareness of the unreality of the real, an anti-realist worldview that prevents the audience to become too committed to perceived reality with the potential of reconstruction for a new beginning.

The audiences reconstruct reality and in doing so refashion themselves. This is because the spectators, in Jacque Rancière references to *ta'zieh*, know the performance as much as do actors, directors and organizers, and such knowledge permits them to 'see, feel and understand something in as much as they compose their own poem'.[70] The prime technique of *ta'zieh* audience is the total presence of all participants, redistributing meaning across emotive expressions that are embedded in the flow of the performances as lived rituals. The refusal to postulate a stable reality is a central theme of *ta'zieh*, marked by the audience awareness that reality is inherently disjoint and a reconstruction of an endless vista of reinterpretations that defines life, and no more.

Conclusion

This chapter offered a theoretical response to the question of audience in Kiarostami's *A Look to ta'zieh*. It argued that *ta'zieh* audiences are more than passive spectators but active performers in a 'living ritual' that encompasses a community that mourns the loss of a revered Imam. In doing, the ritual process injects ambiguity into perceived reality as a reconstruction of human experience based on interpretation. In an open-ended formation of meaning, Kiarostami's *ta'zieh*, perhaps similar to anti-theatre of Brecht, offers a self-reflexive understanding of the spectator-performance relations. Through the distancing effect, the range of performances also invites into the rituals the absent audiences: those who may not be involved in the immediacy of spectatorship but nevertheless participate in an intimate experience of empathy and hence the self-transforming process of viewership as participation.

Kiarostami *reperforms* the *ta'zieh* as a ritual that binds the actors and audiences in an unrehearsed and spontaneous hold, in which they become connected in the reenactment of a shared story. Yet it is not the story that is integral to the ritual process but the embodied practices, that is, the presence of active practices, living and yet-to-be deceased bodies. The affective is the link between the self and the other, and the possibility of looking beyond mere sight limited to individuated perspective.

At the core of the performances, a trustful link is forged between the actors and spectators who come together based on not merely the narratives but the emotive linkages that push for an alternative subjectivity, enacted in the ritual space, beyond the individuated self and into an assemblage of dissonant emotions. What emerges, in turn, is a community of sorrow and joy that playfully depicts the loss of the Imam and his followers with an alternative look at themselves in a lived context. The agency of the audience lies in the ability to rebuild the world through self-reflexive interpretation, while the narrative drama of symbolic expression, as myth, a key expressive mode of the symbolic, attains a secondary importance in a ritual that takes place in a lived environment where audiences intimately partake as living performers with mixed emotions.

Zsolt Gyenge describes this radical self-reflexive feature in Kiarostami's cinematic works as the 'embodied gaze', the affective experience that opens up the spectator's awareness in the very act of looking.[71] Such perception is not an 'averted' but a counter-gaze to which looking transgresses its own very ocular projection.[72] 'Embodied gaze' is not a gaze at all but a way of seeing that undermines what Martin Jay calls the 'scopic regime of modernity' that is integral to the perspectivist paradigm.[73] Here the practice of looking becomes the very object of perception that shifts epistemic frame beyond the binary perception that divides internal and external realities.

In what can also be described as affective perception, the act of looking therefore can be described as relational, a form of presence possible only in relation with others. The affective implies the trans-individuated process that breaks down received binaries between self and other, and reality and fiction into a dream world of wonder: winding alleys, open roads and wide valleys in pursuit of the yet to be seen, though perpetually elusive.

Here the final scene of *Through the Olive Trees*, a film about the troubled courtship of an illiterate young man, Hossein, pursuing a student, Tahereh, both victims of an earthquake that has changed their lives, exemplifies a form of looking that troubles sight as a practice of perception. As Hossein runs after Tahereh down the hill, first, through a zig-zag pathway, then, the olive grove and later a grassy field, at the distant we see the girl appear to offer a reply to his marriage proposal. We do not know the response she gives. We then see the couple separate off into different directions and gradually disappear from the green field. In this final scene, narrative closure dissolves into the distance that defies visibility. Perhaps similar to a Chinese landscape painting, we look but only to find our viewing expand into a faraway distance, where seeing is no longer about what is visible but of being lost in a boundless world. Looking becomes an open field of interconnected, intermingled objects, trees, grass, colours and two small moving human figures that seem like a floating dream, visually sumptuous but visibly imperceptible, opaque, inaccessible. The more our sight searches into the distance, the farther the object of perception gets away from us. Vision blurs into the colours, and the music over an unresolvable frame that both moves and remains still.

While the gaze is undermined through embodiment, the spectator is equally dislodged as the author of sight, becoming a transient agent shaped by an experience, a shared pathos. In *A Look to ta'zieh*, Kiarostami also invites us to 'see' ritual performance not from our perspective but from the felt experience of the mourners – not to cognize the expressed poetry or even the story behind the rituals but to immerse in the expression of pain that can be felt, mostly heard from others in an encounter. The auditory aspect brings *ta'zieh* closer to its ritual form that revolves around the repertoire of rhetorical and stylistic elements of vocal performance. In an important way, the audio emphasizes the original performance of being an 'audience', those assembled at a public to listen and hear.

The invisible is audible. By transgressing our gaze onto the felt experience of the mourners as audience-listeners, we step out of the immediacy of our own senses into a shared and deafening void: the presence of an absence revealed in the pain of mourners we feel, we hear. Yet, looking still matters. Central to reflexive looking, as Gyenge's describes, is 'the unseen, hidden, traumatic Real that defines everything despite its apparent absence'.[74] The inherent artifice of Kiarostami's cinema, as Kenta McGrath reminds us, is the practice of what is not shown, images that hide and at times vanish into shifting frames of perception.[75] Similar to Ernest Hemingway's theory of omission, the unseen, omitted from the narrative, is meant to make the audience feel beyond what is perceived.[76] The inescapability of absence is what defines reality as a construct, which can only be recognized in reflexive perception.[77] The audience is the imperceptible truth.

To immerse in the pain of others offers the radical ethics of being-with-others-as-oneself, a dependency of emotions that makes life, in its multi-layeredness and fluidity, expressive, embodied but mostly interconnected. An audience to mourning is the claim to a shared or communicable experience that takes the form of ritual performance based on not a presumed collective unconscious or a national cultural character but an open-ended experience of togetherness. Note that the claim here does not read into *ta'zieh* a cosmopolitan ethos. One should recognize the intricate relations of class, gender, race or, broadly speaking, social practices embedded in power relations that shape uneven frameworks for understanding self and other. Yet, as an affective community, *ta'zieh*'s audience also bears implication of an ethics based on an alternate, imaginary, perception is disoriented from institutional identities and the givens of the socio-political reality towards relational interdependence.

Beyond the rituals, how does such ethics function in everyday context? The answer is the experience of defamiliarization. *A Look to ta'zieh* is an example of a reflexive performance of *open play* through which reality becomes other than the received ordinary, a fable of good and evil that sustains many lives – anticipatory of a potentiality that is open, indeterminate, always renewable, regenerative and ultimately reflexive. It is an open play because of the possibility of reiteration, through which human imagination responsively engages with the made-belief world, where the self becomes part of an ongoing game, renewed once the ritual game is over. Kiarostami's *ta'zieh* defamiliarizes reality to recast life into an irreversible form of ambiguity. Yet what emerges from this ambiguity is a created distance from the instituted fictional boundaries that tend to separate the audience from the performance. *Ta'zieh* is the in-between space where the audience is reperformed in an open future.

Part II

PERFORMING (POST-REVOLUTIONARY) IRAN: SPACE, STAGE AND THEATRE

4

THE SHIRAZ ARTS FESTIVAL AND THE SLIDE TOWARDS REVOLUTION

Joshua Charney

On 26 October 1967, the Shah Mohammad Reza Pahlavi and his wife, Queen Farah, left their home, the Kakh-e Marmar, and travelled by horse-drawn coach through the streets of Tehran to the Golestan Palace. On that Friday in October, the Shah of Iran was celebrating not only his forty-eighth birthday but also his coronation. While news cameras rolled, he sat on his throne wearing a gold crown in the style of Sassanian kings and carried a heavily jewelled sceptre in his right hand. The Empress sat beside him in a long white robe and a crown specially designed for the occasion by the French jeweller Van Cleef & Arpels.[1] Though the Shah had assumed the throne well over two decades previous, he thought it improper to crown himself until he felt Iran was on the path to progress. By 1967, the Shah's 'White Revolution', devised in 1963, began to yield discernible results. The literacy rate had increased, women were granted more rights, and the economy was steadily improving. The government, and the Queen, in particular, also took it upon themselves to establish new cultural programmes and improve existing ones. March of 1967 saw the launching of National Iranian Television (NITV) and the creation of the NITV Chamber Orchestra, while September saw the grand opening of the Shiraz-Persepolis Festival of Arts.[2] A brainchild of the Queen, The Shiraz Arts Festival, as it was also known, was an annual music, theatre, art and film festival that ran from 1967 to 1977 in and around the southwestern city of Shiraz. Highlights of the festival included performances by pianist Arthur Rubinstein, violinist Yehudi Menuhin, the Juilliard Quartet, Western experimentalist composers such as Karlheinz Stockhausen and John Cage, traditional music and dance from Indonesia, India, Vietnam and Senegal, as well as cutting-edge theatre presented by known directors such as Peter Brook and Robert Wilson. Conjointly, there was a focus on the Iranian arts, including modern, folk and classical Persian music.

When Queen Farah gave the inaugural address at the Shiraz Festival in 1967, she explained why an arts festival of this sort was important. Her goal was to create a platform that would expose Iranians to gifted artists from other countries, as well as allow Iranian artists to gain recognition both at home and abroad.[3] The Shah wished for Iran to be seen as a 'great' civilization, and the Shiraz Festival would prove Iran was achieving a 'high' cultural standard.[4] Furthermore, the objective was to generate intercultural development between the Occident and the Orient. Through the arts, the festival would forge 'a bridge connecting not only Iran's past and future, but also the East and the West'.[5] It was to be a 'cultural synthesis' of Iran's history and contemporary artistic expression with that of the Western world.[6]

Plans for the first festival began in 1966, when the Queen and her cousin, the soon-to-be-director of NITV, Reza Ghotbi, formed a board of directors that included, among others, the director of the Ministry of Culture and Arts – Zaven Hakopian – new wave Iranian film director Farrokh Ghaffari and Ghotbi himself.[7] Queen Farah's initial concept was to model the Shiraz Festival after the International Festival of Contemporary Arts in Royan, France.[8] The Queen had spent time in Paris in the late 1950s while attending the Ecole Speciale d'Architecture and, like many young Iranians at the time, believed France to be a hub for art and culture. Moreover, board members like Farrokh Ghaffari researched other festivals throughout Europe and Asia and travelled to remote regions of Iran to find significant artists that may have been lesser known to the Iranian public.[9]

Over the course of its ten years, the festival was both criticized and acclaimed by Westerners and Iranians. For some, it represented Iran's dedication to the arts and creativity, showcasing innovative composers, performers, directors and artists from around the world, while for others, it was a symbol of the leadership's embrace of a decadent modernism and advocacy of *gharbzadegi* or 'Westoxication' – Iran's loss of identity through imitation of Western culture. In retrospect, the festival may be seen as a motivator in the slide towards the Islamic Revolution of 1979.[10] This subversive motivation functioned in a multi-faceted capacity, as the festival opened itself up to criticism for government expenditure and programmed challenging and presumptively distasteful avant-garde works, while also presenting pieces that potentially aided in organizing the apparent public turbulence. Two notable performances, Iannis Xenakis's *Persepolis* and Mohammad Ghaffari's *ta'zieh*, proved provocative by retelling Iran's ancient historical narrative or connecting with Iran's Islamic history and empowering members of the Iranian public. Both consequently engaged with the growing revolutionary fabric of the 1970s.

In 1971, the festival commissioned Greek composer Iannis Xenakis (1922–2001) to compose and perform his multimedia spectacle, *Persepolis*. Many locals interpreted Xenakis's piece as both a celebration of the gluttonous and debauched regime and a skewed retelling of pre-Islamic Persian history. Five years later, in 1976, the festival presented the traditional Iranian Islamic drama known as *ta'zieh*, directed by Iranian actor and theatre director Mohammad Ghaffari. Placed in this historical and political context, *ta'zieh* became what Hamid Dabashi refers to as a 'theatre of protest' against an autocratic king.[11] Despite the surrounding controversies of the decade-long festival, these two productions referenced two separate perspectives and periods of Iranian history, and in doing so revealed specific underlying social and political issues that would eventually contribute to Iran's revolution. Through a visceral demonstration of sight and sound, both

Xenakis's *Persepolis* and Ghaffari's *ta'zieh* performances connected the historical and contemporary culture of Iran, as well as the East to the West, and in doing so became either representations of a problematic government and/or critiques of the regime itself. It was this kind of synthesis that rendered the Shiraz Festival a complex and controversial space.

The year 1971 marked Iannis Xenakis's third appearance at the festival. His previous works, such as *Nuits* for chorus (1968) and the percussion piece *Persephassa* (1969), were met with audience and critical acclaim. Xenakis, an accomplished architect, had even begun discussing with officials the possibility of designing a year-round 'scientific research centre' for the arts.[12] For the 1971 performance, Xenakis was commissioned to create a piece for the festival's inaugural event at the ancient ruins of Persepolis. On 26 August 1971, in the presence of the Queen, Xenakis premiered his highly anticipated *Persepolis*. *Kayhan International*, a widely circulated Iranian English language newspaper, published three articles on the work. The first was an interview with Xenakis and a description of the piece, the second was a review of the performance, and the third was a follow-up on the roundtable discussion that took place after the premiere. *Persepolis* was a fifty-minute eight-track tape, electroacoustic, sight-specific spectacle. Xenakis referred to these sorts of pieces as 'polytopes', because they explored multiple experiential dimensions. In the case of *Persepolis*, there was pre-recorded sound, spatialized throughout forty-eight speakers within six localized listening stations; there were also bonfires, projector lights and two red laser beams that traversed the broken palace. Xenakis controlled all sonic and visual parameters from a walkie-talkie.[13] During the performance, audience members were free to move around the historical site and experience the piece with their five senses. There were no live musicians involved, other than Persepolis herself. However, Xenakis did include 150 children with lit torches on a surrounding mountaintop, who spelled out the phrase, 'We bear the light of the earth'.[14] This phrase was coined by Xenakis in Persian, but was a reference, along with the torches, to the ancient Zoroastrian religion. For Xenakis, the light and the fire represented truth, as well as Ahura Mazda – the supreme Zoroastrian deity, while the children represented the people of Iran, their future and a hope for humanity, in general.[15]

In creating *Persepolis*, Xenakis was inspired by the history of Persia. In his programme notes, he referred to the piece as a '[s]ymbol of history's noise; unassailable rocks facing the assault of waves of civilisation'.[16] Xenakis incorporated the physical site into his piece to create a work that represented Iran's ability to maintain its civilization throughout a tumultuous history. A few months after the premiere, Xenakis would write that *Persepolis* was 'a tribute to Iran's past and her great Zoroastrian and Manichean revolutionaries'.[17] This added a political dimension to the work, something not uncommon for a composer that had been part of an armed resistance in Greece during the Second World War. *Persepolis* is recognized as an important work in Xenakis's catalogue and in the canon of site-specific works and sound installations. French music journalist and composer Maurice Fleuret, who was present at the premiere, called it 'a landmark in the evolution of one of the most speculative and general philosophies of our time', clearly observing a progressive significance to the work that would influence generations of composers and artists to come.[18]

Ultimately, however, *Persepolis* received a negative critical and audience response in Iran, not for its political ramifications or avant-garde nature but specifically for its telling of history. Articles published in *Kayhan* made the connection that a Greek was reenacting the burning and destruction of Persepolis, which was first accomplished by Alexander the Great over 2,000 years ago. The sounds ranged from 'thunder to the roar of a jet engine, from caravan bells to the faint echoes of cries of anguish buried under the debris of civilizations to highly abstract noises from the depths of space and time'.[19] These apocalyptic sounds emphasized the historical spectacle and the event was admittedly memorable and unique, but, according to one review, fundamentally oversimplified Iranian history through noise and a pseudo-narrative structure, even if it was trying to convey that Iran had stood strong through the centuries.[20]

The roundtable discussion following *Persepolis* revealed a similar, but harsher reaction from Iranians. People attacked Xenakis for insulting Iran by reenacting the destruction of Darius the Great's palace. Apparently, Iranian students, some of Xenakis's biggest supporters in previous years, were especially upset, drawing a parallel between the child torch bearers and Alexander's Macedonian troops.[21] During the roundtable, Xenakis's advocates resolved that the work was free of any narrative structure and restated that the fire was merely a symbol of the Zoroastrian deity, as well as knowledge and truth. The critics then questioned who brought in this fire, implying that it must have been the Macedonian invaders, a further insult. Other opponents pointed to the general artistic weakness of the electroacoustic music, stating that it 'does not yet provide any means of evaluation, its meaning is the one arbitrarily chosen by its maker'.[22] A 'visibly tired' Xenakis apparently did not clarify or elaborate on the piece, but rather repeated what had already been said in his program notes and in a preceding interview.[23]

The day after the premiere, the Queen was asked what *she* thought of Xenakis's *Persepolis*. Queen Farah responded,

> I liked Xenakis's work and I thought the idea was marvellous. All those lights on the hills. This was a unique event that could only happen at Persepolis. But as I said, I am not an authority on the subject. You can dislike it or like it.[24]

The Queen, speaking highly of the work, only articulated the artistic achievements and made no reference to the specific controversial historical allusions. She was also quick to distance herself from any definitive value judgement, allowing for audience members to interpret and evaluate the piece as they should see fit.

By Xenakis's admission, *Persepolis* links the past to the present. There is a curious encounter between cutting-edge technology and antiquity, in that the spectacle connects the modern and experimental soundtrack, with the ancient location.[25] In this way, it adheres to the festival's goal of linking Iran's past to its present, and even its future through the use of the child torch bearers. It also brings together East and West, in that Xenakis, a European composer – Greek by birth and also a resident of France, created a piece that focused thematically on Persian history. To add further complexity, the work, through these historical allusions, aligns with the Shah's political agenda by promoting autocracy and anti-Islamism. Not only did the Queen defend Xenakis's *Persepolis*, but in that same interview, she defended the Pahlavi dynasty by saying, 'monarchy has been a guarantee of national unity.'[26] She preceded this by diplomatically stating, 'I do not wish to say whether monarchy is good or bad', yet if her point was that monarchy keeps Iran united, then she must have believed it to be a beneficial political structure.[27] Furthermore, Queen Farah initially made this statement in order to defend an upcoming celebration.

One month after the premiere of Xenakis's spectacle, the Shah and his wife travelled to Persepolis to host the 2,500-year anniversary celebration of Iranian monarchy. The lavish festivity was a way to attach the Shah to the monarchy of Cyrus the Great, the founder of the Achaemenid Empire. The Shah wished to defend the monarchy's strength and persistence against constitutionalist and Marxist factions, as well as against a growing group of Iranians that believed Islam, not kingship, was at the centre of Iranian identity.[28] To counter constitutionalism, the anniversary would celebrate historical monarchy, internationally televising men dressed up as ancient Median soldiers. This was also an attempt to diminish the more radical Islamic groups by celebrating a pre-Islamic history – a Zoroastrian heritage – and ignoring the more recent Muslim past. This was not an isolated political manoeuvre by the Shah; in 1976, he changed the Iranian calendar from the Islamic Solar Hijri year 1355 to the Zoroastrian year 2535. It was a concern by some that the Shah might reveal himself to be, not a Muslim, but a Zoroastrian.[29] Ultimately, average Iranians viewed the 2,500-year anniversary as ostentatious at best and depraved at worst; either way, the event succeeded in further dividing the people from their king. Additionally, Persepolis, as a symbolic site, was and would be attacked by fundamental Islamic sects. After the revolution, the chief justice and cleric Sadegh Khalkhali sent men to destroy Persepolis because it had been a grandstand of the Shah and a symbol of infidelity.[30] Fortunately, locals fought off the militia with stones and the landmark remains to this day.[31]

With *Persepolis*, regardless of whether or not he was reenacting Alexander the Great's victory, Xenakis was admittedly celebrating Iran's pre-Islamic history and parading the ancient monarchy's strength to weather the storm. By doing this, he was also promoting the Shah and the lineage to which the Shah absorbed, and if the piece was celebrating the destruction of Persepolis by Alexander the Great, it was doing it with the Shah's endorsement, both financially and otherwise. The piece underlines the image that Khalkhali and other clerics resented.

Surprisingly, Xenakis's most public criticism came, not from Iran, but from Iranians living in Europe, and not on artistic grounds, but simply for participating in the government's Shiraz Festival. The playwright Serge Rezvani attacked Xenakis in the French daily newspaper *Le Monde* for participating in the festival 'happenings', while peasants had to sell their blankets in order for the festivities to take place. Xenakis responded in *Le Monde*, 24 November 1971, defending the festival, and noting that he, in fact, did not participate in the aforementioned 'festivities'. He went on to stress the hypocrisy of such a declaration, saying that '[d]emocracy is a fallacy, an artificially sweetened mythology in the mouths of all regimes, be they under the influence of overt dictators or camouflaged ones, throughout the world'.[32] After his 1971 appearance, Xenakis continued his plans to construct an arts centre in Iran, but because of further European criticism and increased reports of the Shah's human rights violations, he decided finally to end his relationship with the festival. In a 1976 letter to a member of the festival board of directors, Xenakis wrote:

> You know how attached I am to Iran, her history, her people. You know my joy when I realized projects in your festival, open to everyone. You also know of my friendship and loyalty to those who, like yourself, have made the Shiraz Persepolis Festival unique in the world. But, faced with inhuman and unnecessary police repression that the Shah and his government are inflicting on Iran's youth, I am incapable of lending any moral guarantee, regardless of how fragile that may be, since it is a matter of artist creation. Therefore, I refuse to participate in the festival.[33]

Persepolis marked Xenakis's last appearance at Shiraz, while the arts centre was never realized.

Persepolis was premiered in 1971. The year was an important marker in the 'slide' towards the Islamic revolution. In February of that year, thirteen armed guerrillas attacked a gendarmerie post in Siahkal along the Caspian Sea. In the raid, the guerrillas killed three policemen and freed two political prisoners. This kind of violent revolt influenced a forthcoming movement of aggressive upheaval against the regime. Over the course of the next eight years, hundreds of guerrillas and armed political dissidents were executed or killed in battle, an overwhelming majority of which were members of the young middle-class intelligentsia. Their discontentment sprung, not from the uneven socioeconomic development of the 1970s, but from a general aversion to the repressive regime.[34] By 1976, the country was only a few short years away from revolution. When the Shah had crowned himself in 1967, he was admittedly beginning to see the positive results of his 'White Revolution', named such because it was bloodless. It consisted of a six-point plan that included women's suffrage and land reformation that would give the peasants a larger share in the land. The Shah hoped to gain the support of the large peasant class population in order to empower the Pahlavi dynasty. In terms of the economy, Iranian oil was the largest source of the country's revenue. By the 1970s, the government was receiving around 80 per cent of its earnings from oil alone, though despite this, there remained other economic issues. By 1974, inflation exceeded 60 per cent and the population had almost quadrupled what it was in 1960. For this reason, rental costs had doubled in price by 1976 from what they were a few years earlier. Education improved, but universities didn't possess enough spots for prospective students.[35] Increasing disillusionment and resentment of the government naturally followed from the general population and certain artists began to speak out, even create political works, which were often banned.

By late 1975, twenty-two eminent Iranian artists were in jail for openly criticizing the government.[36] Reza Baraheni, a writer and member of the Writer's Association of Iran, spoke out against the Shah and spent 102 days in prison for it. In 1976, the *New York Times* published his description of what took place in captivity.

> I was given 75 blows from a wire whip on the bottom of my feet [...] People are hung upside down, their skulls are pressed, their spines are burned and their nails are plucked. Women are raped and children are slapped in front of their fathers.[37]

Because of this injustice, Baraheni and Eric Bentley, a British playwright, called for a boycott of the 1976 Shiraz Festival. Choreographer Merce Cunningham, who had performed at the festival in years previous, cancelled his 1976 appearance as did other artists and attendees. In a twist of irony, 1976 was the year the regime promised an 'open political space'. In the Shah's words, 'We shall have freedom of speech and freedom of press according to a new press law that may be adopted from any of the world's freest nations.'[38] Despite artists' cancellations and bad press, the festival went ahead as planned.

The focus of 1976 was the ritual drama *ta'zieh*. The word *ta'zieh* roughly translates to 'mourning', in that it is a passion play of sorts that mourns the death of the Muslim Imam Hossein at the Battle of Karbala in 680 CE.[39] This historical tale is what led to the split between Shi'i and Sunni, making *ta'zieh* a specifically Shi'i drama. Hossein's followers believed he was the rightful Caliph, as he was related to the prophet by blood. For the Shi'i, the standing Caliph, Yazid, the antagonist of most *ta'zieh*, wrongfully usurped power from Muhammad's bloodline. There are many *ta'zieh*, and although each one deals with the death of Hossein in some way, he is not necessarily the central character of the story. They are often performed during Moharram, the first month of the Islamic calendar. The Shiraz Festival of 1976 ran from mid to late August. It did not line up with Moharram, but nonetheless presented a cycle of seven *ta'zieh* productions, as well as an international symposium on the Persian drama, which included scholars from Iran, the United States, India, Turkey, Germany, Czechoslovakia, Lebanon, France and Tunisia.[40]

The history of *ta'zieh* in Iran has been complicated. It emerged in the middle of the eighteenth century as a fusion between Moharram processions and narrative recitations of Shi'i martyrs. It was performed at street intersections or in city squares and eventually moved into the *takkiyeh*, an open-air theatre built for *ta'zieh* performances.[41] In the first half of the twentieth century, the Shah's father, Reza Shah Pahlavi, sought to ban *ta'zieh* in an effort to neutralize Shi'ism and secularize the country.[42] Even though *ta'zieh* was still performed, though now relegated to the villages, it wouldn't get any significant attention until the Shiraz Festival. In fact, before 1967, it was an unofficial government protocol to abolish any public Shi'i ritual.[43] Because one of the goals of the festival was to examine Iran's past and further the traditional and folk forms, the programme could not ignore *ta'zieh*.

At the inaugural festival, Iranian film and theatre director Parviz Sayyad directed the first two public urban productions of *ta'zieh* since its prohibition in 1933.[44] When Sayyad returned to direct another *ta'zieh* in 1970, his production was harshly criticized by theatregoers and religious extremists. *Kayhan International* reported that 'the fanatics criticised him for what they called "his wanton playing with sacred drama"', while the theatre fans said he had 'insulted the sacred soul of drama'.[45] These attacks seemed to be on grounds of poor directing, more so than on *ta'zieh* itself.

For the 1976 *ta'zieh* cycle, the festival brought in the young actor and theatre director Mohammad Ghaffari. Ghaffari had actually participated in the festival in previous years, working with Peter Brook in 1971. Ghaffari even took Brook to see his first *ta'zieh*, to which Brook responded, 'This is what has been missing from the Western theatre for a long time.'[46] Ghaffari's approach to directing the *ta'zieh* cycle in 1976 was both traditional in its presentation and original in its process. Ghaffari had been interested in theatre since a very young age and had been researching and participating in *ta'zieh* since the age of eleven, when he was a child actor in Neishapur, Khorasan.[47] What was unique about Ghaffari's process in the 1976 production was that he wanted the best *ta'zieh* performers from around the country. Obvious as is it may seem, this was an uncommon practice; since *ta'zieh* had only been performed in small villages, productions of it featured local performers, almost like community theatre. According to Ghaffari, many people felt *ta'zieh* was archaic and unexciting, so he set out to prove otherwise. He spent a year travelling all over the country trying to find the best *ta'zieh* performers Iran had to offer. The protagonists in *ta'zieh* are required to be strong heroic singers whose voices can carry unaccompanied, while the villains who speak must speak loudly since they are without amplification. Furthermore, the music is not notated or written down, so compelling singers will have studied *ta'zieh* for several years, usually since childhood. The texts are documented but are often adapted to each performance. For this reason, Ghaffari was looking for people 'who retained the art of *ta'zieh*'.[48] Once he found his performers, he brought them to Shiraz and rehearsed eight to ten hours a day, six days a week, for three months. Since the performers were from different parts of Iran, they had learned different styles of singing, sword fighting and horseback riding. Ghaffari was faced with the task of blending these different styles while cutting and adapting the texts.[49]

In order for a *ta'zieh* to appeal to a wide Iranian audience, it needed to travel a line of ambiguity. In Islam, it is unacceptable to have actors play the part of an imam or the Prophet. *Ta'zieh* bypasses this by eliminating any impersonation of religious characters; the performers simply recite text. The production is self-consciously unreal. The actors have sides (excerpts of the text) in their hands, and even though they have their parts memorized, they do glance down and read the paper. They never fall in or out of character, because they always maintain their own identity; some of the performers might even be sipping tea on the side of the stage while waiting their turn to sing.[50] As for the music, Islam has had a complicated relationship with the art form. *Ta'zieh* singing is not unlike the *azan*, the Muslim call to prayer – unaccompanied, chant-like and with a spiritual dimension. It also reinforces the non-character by having the performers sing with a consistent powerful practice, regardless of whether the character is reflective, joyful or melancholy. The performer might be executing a loud trilling coloratura while his character is in the throes of death.[51] All this being said, the performance must remain emotional and entertaining. Ghaffari's *ta'ziehs* were large productions, using horses, swords and elaborate costumes. The final success of a *ta'zieh* is dependent upon its affect or emotional response from the audience. In Ghaffari's own words, 'if the audience is not openly weeping at strategic points, the rhetorical purpose of the drama will have failed'.[52] Ultimately, it is a mourning ritual, inclusive of its viewers.

Ghaffari's performances took place in Shiraz and in the small village of Kaftarak, about eight miles east of Shiraz. The productions were extremely popular, with about 70,000 people in attendance, including Westerners, dignitaries, the Iranian elite and local and remote villagers.[53] A review of the opening 1976 *ta'zieh* by an Iranian journalist read, 'The moving and excellently enacted *ta'zieh* left several members of the audience in tears and visibly enthralled almost all present.'[54] A performance of the *ta'zieh of the Martyrdom of Imam Hossein* was 'particularly noted by the festival guests for its success in electrifying the audience: many viewers wept aloud and beat their chests in the traditional mourning sign of Islam'.[55] *TDR* published a review of the *ta'zieh*, writing, 'Many Western observers were struck by the intense emotional reaction of the spectators – primarily wailing and breast-beating by the women. (The *ta'zieh* performances I attended were presented in an old stable in the hill village of Kaftarak; working people made up a large portion of the audience.)'[56] These sorts of comments measure the overwhelming success of Ghaffari's productions and remark on the appealingly unique aspect observed by the unfamiliar Western audience, who witnessed the affect this ritual drama had on its local spectators. Ghaffari believed the festival and its media exposure saved *ta'zieh* from extinction.[57]

The extremely popular and free-of-charge *ta'zieh* of 1976 also functioned as a 'theatre of protest', although unintentionally from its director. These stories, which focus on the Imam Hossein, regard him as a hero and martyr who gave his life in order to expose and protest government corruption and the dissemination of social immoralities. The characters Yazid, the evil Caliph who ordered Hossein's death in order to maintain power, and his general, Shemr, the one who carried out the murder, are *ta'zieh*'s villains. In a famous speech by the Ayatollah Khomeini in 1963, he went as far as to compare the Shah to Yazid. Khomeini accused the Shah of holding fraudulent elections, disregarding the Iranian constitution, denying freedom of speech, turning his back on the working-class merchants, thoughtlessly appeasing the United States known as 'The Great Satan' and, of course, crippling Iran's attachment to Islam.[58] After Khomeini's arrest and eventual exile, the comparisons continued and intensified, and not solely among religious extremists. Because of Hossein's struggle against corruption, Shi'ism was a perfectly accessible representation of the citizens' concurrent conflict. When the Islamic revolution materialized, groups of protesters identified Khomeini with Hossein and the Shah with Yazid – a corrupt demonic tyrant. *ta'zieh* contributed to the reinforcement of these identifications. According to Dabashi, 'As a *taʿzieh* was staged at the Shiraz Arts Festival, *taʿzieh* leitmotifs were fomenting revolutionary mobilizations in the streets and alleys, markets and squares of Iran.'⁵⁹ Even though the festival included *taʿzieh* to demonstrate its appreciation of the traditional Iranian arts and pay tribute to its Islamic history and partially placate the religious population, this inclusion likely had a negative effect on the regime, and, in turn, promoted a revolution. Despite a western boycott in 1976, tens of thousands of Iranians attended the Shiraz Arts Festival only to see a production of ritual theatre that incorporated pillars of Shi'i good and evil – symbols of a seemingly spiritual and heroic leader to come, the Ayatollah Khomeini, and an evil Shah who would soon be deposed.

The Shiraz Arts Festival would only see one more year of existence. The 1977 festival presented a controversial theatre piece by a Hungarian troupe that contained sexual content, which was blown out of proportion through media rumours. Khomeini himself even commented on it in exile, while denouncing the festival and the government. Because of the growing labour strikes and large public demonstrations, the twelfth festival, planned for September 1978, was cancelled. In January 1979, the Shah went into exile and by December of that same year, Ayatollah Khomeini was officially the Supreme Leader of the newly named Islamic Republic of Iran. Over the years, the Shiraz Festival received its share of criticism from the Iranian public at large. Muslim clerics were opposed to avant-garde or modern art, while leftists attacked the festival for being elitist and anti-populace.⁶⁰

Despite the criticism, the festival uniquely offered a creative and experimental space within a dictatorship. Its goal of bringing together East and West, connecting past to present, and establishing Iran as a bold agent in the world of arts was in many ways successful. Any style of art that was deemed culturally significant or that was on the cutting edge of the genre was, for the most part, included. It was the festival, as a symbol of modernism and decadence, that spurred dissent from members of the religious right and the intellectual left. Because, at the time, Iran had little exposure to Western contemporary music, Iranian composer Alireza Mashayekhi, for example, believed the festival took on 'the appearance of an invasion'.⁶¹ Yet, the role of performance at the Shiraz Festival served the government's cultural development program and aimed to unite the people by balancing different sides of Iranian identity. Xenakis's *Persepolis* revealed a dedication to modernization and the latest international artistic developments, as well as a thematic attachment to Iran's ancient history. Ghaffari's *taʿzieh* performances connected with the country's Shi'i identity, while reviving the traditional form through an innovative approach. Moreover, the relationships between these performances and their conflicting identities unavoidably contextualize the festival within the political backdrop of pre-revolutionary Iran. As products and practices of culture, the festival's contentious theatrics ultimately became representations of the decade's discord and resistance as Iran quickly slid further and further towards a revolution.

5

IRAN IS THE STAGE AND YOUTH ITS MAJOR PLAYERS: SEVEN-YEAR EDUCATIONAL EXCURSION INTO IRAN'S SOCIO-THEATRE

Mahmood Karimi Hakak

Since the devoted mystic never revealed the Divine secret.
I wonder where the wine-seller might have heard about it?

—Hafez

Since the Iranian uprising and Islamists' consolidation of power four decades ago, rarely a week has gone by without notable news emerging from Iran. Much has been written about the ideological backwardness of its leaders, the unpredictable nature of its government and the senseless brutality of its militia, as well as the progressive conviction of its artists and intellectuals, the rational behaviour of its political activists and protesters and the cultural and educational strength of its youth.

What follows is based not only on extensive research and tireless reading but also on personal observation and experience through repeated visits and a seven-year stay in Iran, as well as continuous communications with my friends, colleagues and students over the past thirty years. Although there is no shortage of negative remarks, I do not wish to mirror the numerous comments made on the absurdity of the Iranian regime. Instead, I would like to illustrate a young society's perception, tolerance, compassion, philanthropy and resilience.

There is little disagreement on the controversial and contradictory complexities ingrained within the Iranian society: a society that is spirited and forward-thinking, yet filled with superstitious beliefs and ideas and has repeatedly been subjugated by autocratic dictators and manipulated by oppressive religious despots.

The Iranian society is alive and breathing, regardless of how polluted the atmosphere is. It is a young society in both age and national consensus, with a home-grown, grassroots journey towards acceptance of differences and celebration of similarities. Contrary to patronizing views expressed by some neo-orientalists and warmongers who portray Iran incapable of evolution and see its prosperity in yet another outside interference, most Iranians are intelligent, educated and creative individuals who are well able to think for themselves and create their future with their own hands.

Like many other Iranians living abroad, I was glued to the TV during the months leading to the Shah's departure. Almost a decade earlier studying at Tehran University, I had witnessed and even participated in a number of anti-Shah rallies, but I never imagined such a landslide movement sweeping through the streets so swiftly. This juggernaut simply felt too fast and impulsive for my taste. Having lived among and around the mullahs as a young boy, I generally did not trust this group. Of course, there were exceptions, but from what I had heard about Khomeini, he was not one of them. So, I tried to learn more about him, a task that proved difficult with no internet or Google to help. Thus, I relied on the little he said and the lot that was said about him. His claim of not having any political ambition and his demeanour of never looking into the camera or at the interviewer made me feel uneasy. I was well familiar with the religious practice of *taqiya*, when a Shi'i Muslim may tell a lie as long as he believes that his dishonesty would result in a good deed. I knew from years of close acquaintance with this group that for Khomeini the Machiavellian theory of 'the end justifies the means' was a real tool to reach his goal of swaying the country towards a religious autocracy. And his promise of free gas, electricity and cash for every household made me even more suspicious.

However, seeing so many political and intellectual elites following his lead made me doubt my instincts. So, I attended as many political gatherings as I could regardless of their affiliation to 'the right, the left or the in-between', asked questions, raised concerns and searched for solutions. The more I observed, the less certain I was about the future direction of my country. Almost all opposition groups and activists supported Khomeini's call for the Shah to step down, but none offered a workable, planned and practical alternative. The notion that 'we must first get rid of the Shah and then decide the future' was too vague for me as a theatre practitioner who needs to know what the audience will see before they settle into their seats. Looking at the people running through streets of Tehran enthused by Khomeini's offer of political freedom and financial prosperity reminded me of a scene from one of Eisenstein's movies.

In this scene, a crowd of hungry people are gathered in a street corner. A cart guarded by a few soldiers carrying freshly chopped meat to the palace passes them by. The scent of fresh meat overwhelms this mass driving them to follow the meat cart frantically. The closer the crowd shadows, the more anxious the guards become. The chase continues to the palace gates. The cart enters, the gates close and the people swarm pressing against the palace fence. The fence gives in under pressure from the crowd. The hungry citizens rush in, destroying anything that stood in their way. The palace is conquered in just a few minutes. In Iran's case, however, it seemed to me that the people followed the 'promise' of the meat rather than its 'aroma'.

In a relatively short time, led by intellectuals and activists who each had their own agenda, masses of Iranians, mostly uneducated and unaware, poured into the streets of Tehran demanding the Shah's departure. Eventually, the Shah left and Khomeini returned. The words coming out of Iran for the first few months suggested an atmosphere of free expression where newsstands overflowed with all kinds of publications, people gathered freely to debate ideas and opinions, and every political view was openly expressed.

'It is democracy in action', a friend told me over the phone, 'you just have to come and see for yourself'. Ashamed of my hesitancy and feeling guilty about not having taken a more active role, I flew to Iran in August 1979 to support the rebuilding of the country. However, I encountered a very different scene. The newspaper stands existed and so did the gatherings, but there was an unexpected distraction on this stage. Gangs of bearded motorcyclists mysteriously appeared now and then, toppling stands, breaking up gatherings and beating people with chains, clubs and brass knuckles. Nonetheless, as soon as the thugs left, the stands were re-erected, groups re-assembled and youth re-joined the protective circle around women, shielding them from yet another attack.

I rarely slept during the next two months. Every day I walked the streets, read various publications, listened to theories and discussions about the future government and helped re-erect toppled newsstands, and at nights, I attended gatherings of artists, poets and intellectuals. I witnessed how the ideological gap between factions, both the educated and the ordinary citizens, not only widened but also gave way to bigotry, violence and backstabbing. In the meanwhile, the Islamists, largely unrestrained, took advantage of this in order to 'divide and conquer'.

I had three months left on my US student visa and needed to decide. Should I stay in Iran and join one of these groups (and there was none that I felt strongly about), or should I return to school in the United States? Confused, depressed and uncertain, I talked with my family, friends and mentors. With such a variety of opinions and advice, I kept shifting from one choice to the other. One night, I attended a meeting of the Association of Iranian Writers, where even an agreement on whether or not to move forward with a scheduled public poetry reading proved difficult to reach. After everyone left I shared my dilemma with the host, a prominent poet, whom I had come to know, respect and trust during his yearlong stay in the United States a few years earlier.

Listening attentively to the pros and cons, he said, 'Go while you can!' Then pointing out what I had just witnessed, he confirmed, 'we cannot even endure listening to one another', adding with a sigh, 'soon we will all be buried alive here'. Then, putting his hand on my shoulder, as if needing my support to rise from his chair, he repeated, 'Go! go and echo our cry to the world.'

Driving home that night as I passed wall paintings of Khomeini's image, I remembered a poem I had seen at the Holocaust Memorial Museum in Washington, DC:

First, they came for the Socialists, and I did not speak out
Because I was not a Socialist.
Then they came for the Trade Unionists, and I did not speak out
Because I was not a Trade Unionist.

Then they came for the Jews, and I did not speak out
Because I was not a Jew.
Then they came for me, and there was no one left to speak for me.

I left Iran on one of the last direct flights to New York a few days before the American Embassy in Tehran was taken hostage.

The Hostage Crisis, the Iran-Iraq War, the imprisonment and executions of political activists, including a few friends I had met in Iran, all made me feel depressed and useless. Ted Koppel's Nightline did not help, nor did the words of President Carter's mother who said, 'If I had a million dollars, I would look for someone to kill Ayatollah Khomeini.'[1] Even though I shared her annoyance, I, like many other Iranians, was the target of American slurs, abuse and even punches. However, politely confronting individuals, speaking at academic gatherings and travelling, I learned that given the opportunity to communicate face to face, the majority would understand that not every Iranian agrees with Khomeini and his followers in disrespecting international decrees and agreements.

Frustrated by images spread across American media and appreciating the feelings of helplessness expressed by my friends inside Iran, I pondered on how to honour the request of my mentor, the poet. So, I took it upon myself to travel across the country in the summer of 1980, telling everyone that 'I am Iranian', to see how they would react. The adventures of those ten weeks far exceed the scope of this short chapter. A few of those stories have already been turned into a play entitled, *Bombing the Cradle*, and the rest are still waiting to be told.[2] What is worth mentioning, however, is that this journey gave me a completely different perspective on my approach to developments in Iran and my life in the United States.

In 1984, while hitchhiking through Europe, I ended up in Turkey, where I suddenly felt the impulse to return to Iran. So, I took a bus from Istanbul to Tehran. After a six-day eventful ride, I arrived in Tehran on a Friday evening in late fall carrying only a slide portfolio of my theatre productions. At that time, my mother was visiting my brother in the United States. So, I called a relative who had keys to my mother's apartment and he requested that I take a taxi to his house. Later, he drove me around the city to see the long lines for gas, heating oil and bread. He also convinced me to stay with him during my time in Iran. In less than a week, my host's brother was executed by the government. Ironically, he had been a staunch anti-Shah activist, who had spent years in SAVAK prisons and had been released after the 1979 revolution. Less than a year later, he was captured again and sent back to prison, where under torture, he lost a lung and a kidney. According to his sister who had visited him a week earlier, his right foot was stripped to the bone as a result of excessive whipping. As it was typical in such cases, the authorities never released his body to the family. To add insult to injury, as was also the usual practice, the government charged the family for the bullet he had been executed with.[3] As if that was not enough, they were forbidden from any type of mourning nor were they to hold any memorial service for him. The relatives, however, did have a private ceremony, which also was disrupted by attacks and disturbance.

I stayed in Iran for four months travelling between Tehran and my hometown of Mashhad. During this time, I witnessed many atrocities by the agents of the regime, which by now had killed or imprisoned most of the opposition, forced many artists, intellectuals and activists to sign repentance letters and driven others behind walls of their houses depressed, drugged or intoxicated, thus consolidating absolute power. The bearded motorcyclists I encountered in my first visit had now organized into a brutal militia called the *Basij*, who monitored both the public and private lives of citizens. For example, I witnessed a male friend receive eighty lashes for having alcohol on his breath and saw a woman having her lips lacerated for wearing lipstick in public. Meanwhile, I repeatedly visited my mentor, the poet, who was now confined to the sanctuary of his home in the outskirt of Tehran. 'He keeps writing vehemently every day', his wife told me, 'with no hope of ever publishing another word'.

On the positive side, I could also see glimpses of hope. For example, I saw a theatre production of *One Flew over the Cuckoo's Nest*, which received extraordinary popularity attracting a packed audience of youth. The authorities closed down the production, but because of unprecedented public demand, it was allowed to continue, albeit in a much smaller venue, where it played to sold-out houses for months.

Although the war with Iraq and international sanctions had devastated the society, there still existed a sense of hope among many that once the war was over, people would confront the domestic totalitarian regime. The mullahs seemed to be nervous about this as well. Perhaps, as declared by many experts, including Banisadr, the Iranian president at the time, it was because of this fear that Khomeini extended the war as long as he could and hurriedly ordered the execution of over 3,500 opposition leaders one week before he figuratively 'drank poison' and signed the peace treaty.[4]

My 1984 visit to Iran had a very negative impact on me, both psychologically and emotionally. I could not stomach so much tyranny and pain, so like my host and many other friends, I found refuge in alcohol. The occasional drinking turned into a routine. What was worse is that I began blaming the people, including my own friends, for their fast and unstudied submission to Khomeini. I remember speaking to a leftist fellow graduate student who had accused me of being an agent of SAVAK back in the United States on the ground that I refused to support the mullahs. Now back in Iran, he lived in hiding and feared for his life. I said to him, 'You made your bed, so lay in it!' Although I immediately regretted what I had said and apologized for it, my friend responded with regret, 'you are absolutely right!' adding, 'and a whole nation is now paying for it!' I left Iran with a vow to never return.

The war ended in 1988, Khomeini died and the Constitution was amended to make the position of Supreme Leader permanent. As families buried their dead and cared for their wounded, fearful mullahs stiffened their grip on the society, greedy generals drained economic resources and corrupt politicians prolonged their misuse of power. Women were exploited and oppressed, youth were hungry and unemployed and the opposition was virtually silenced. The exiled activists, by and large, saw the remedy in another regime change, and since they could not agree on a single approach, each sought the help of a different foreign administration. These efforts, however, received very little support inside Iran, where people were tired of one revolution after another and would not trust any alternatives that included outside interference. The country was in ruins and there was very little hope for the future. However, as I learned a few years later, just like a phoenix that rises out of its own ashes, the Iranian society was reenergizing itself from within.

I, on the other hand, felt depressed, desperate and disheartened. To deal with my depression, I immersed myself in further investigation and research in a method of directing plays that I had started exploring as a graduate student in the late 1970s. Then I combined Sufi mystical practices with the Holy Actor, a technique developed by Polish director Jerzy Grotowski two decades earlier.[5] I had labelled this experiment *Ascetic Theatre*.

A year later, I landed my first full-time position as Assistant Professor of Theatre at Towson University. There I continued my research on the relationship between theatre and spirituality. In 1991, following two successful play productions in Baltimore, Maryland, I was commissioned to produce a new play for the Edinburgh Theater Festival, Fringe. I worked with seven American actors to create *Seven Stages: A Symphony in Seven Movements* based on the works by Jalaleddin Rumi and Forugh Farrokhzad. The production received outstanding reviews in Edinburgh, and I was invited to work with a Latvian theatre company using this newly developed technique the next summer. On my way to Latvia, I decided to stop in Tehran to see my ageing mother. I never made it to Latvia. The ten-day visit turned into a seven-year stay. This seven-year journey changed my perception of Iran forever and taught me much more about the resilience of my people than any history book I had ever read.

I landed in Tehran in June 1992. After the first day at my mother's, which included visits from all her neighbours in the other eleven apartments, I called my old friends, fellow students and professors. Many were no longer around: some were either in jail or out of the country and a few had been executed in the 1988 massacre. Some of my old professors asked if I would speak to their students. I welcomed the idea.

At one of these lectures, I was scolding the students for being lazy in comparison to those of my generation. A brave young woman stood up, and with a combination of pity, anger and envy, she rebuffed my reproach saying,

> you have come here bragging about what you knew and criticizing what we do not; how you worked hard on your studies and we do not; how you spent 24/7 in the theatre rehearsing and performing while we do not. What you fail to remember, 'sir', is that it was your generation that fashioned this revolution. We were just small kids at the time and had no part in your decision.

She continued, 'and as soon as your generation realized that this was not what they had expected, they left, leaving us to deal with the aftermath of what they had started'. Looking at the shocked faces around the room, she said, 'we did not ask for this, nor did we have the means to leave like you did'. She added with a sigh, 'all these years not many worthwhile books have been published. Our progressive artists and intellectuals, those who could not leave, ended up either dead or in jail or, as Forugh so eloquently observed, "swamps of alcohol and opium have dragged them down to their depths"'.[6] Pointing to her professor, she continued, 'with very few exceptions, we are being taught by those who are given the job not because of their knowledge but because of their loyalty to a certain ideology, or so they pretend'. Then, looking directly into my eyes, she protested, 'what many of us struggle with, "dear sir", is trying not to sell our bodies to pay for our tuition!' The class came to a standstill. 'I cannot believe that you have the audacity', she added, 'to come here and chastise us!' I was utterly dumbfounded and did not know what to do or say. After what seemed like hours of deafening silence, she lowered her head and, almost pleadingly, she said, 'and then of course you will leave too!'

Her words pierced my heart. I could not keep my balance. My feet gave in under the heavy weight of my wounded spirit. I dragged myself to the stage steps and, like a lantern folding onto itself, crumbled down. I could not control my tears. I felt my face become wet and burning while my entire body was soaked yet cold. It was as if I were immersed in a bathtub of freezing water up to my neck as a hot shower poured down my cheeks. I cried, loud and long. She cried too, and so did my former professor. Almost everyone in the class cried. It was an utterly depressing scene.

After a long time, I felt my professor's hand on my shoulder. I looked up. He looked old, much older than he was at the beginning of this session. His face was wrinkled like that of my eighty-year-old mother. He reached for my arm and helped me up. I stood up, wiped the tears off my face and looked in the girl's direction. She lifted her head and gazed into my eyes. In the shining mirror of her wet cheeks, I saw the images of my forefathers. I saw the courage and wisdom of Gordāfarid and the glowing face of Forugh Farrokhzad as she cried, 'and thus it is/ that one dies and another remains'.[7] I stood straight, took a deep breath and, with a shaking yet determined voice, promised her, myself and my former professor that I would not leave.

It was not long after that fateful lecture when I met a group of intelligent young women and men who took it upon themselves to educate me about my country and the people I had lost touch with. I soon learned that these Iranian youth are very different from my generation. These 'kids' knew how to live life, what to do when and who to approach in order to circumvent the limitations imposed by the regime. Although at the time their juggling seemed chaotic, I could see the potential of how they might achieve the art of forbearance, tolerance and coexistence through understanding and dialogue. I learned that unlike my generation, who knew what they did not want but for the most part did not know what they wanted, these young people know exactly what they did not want, but they also knew what they wanted. More importantly, they seemed to have a pretty good idea as to how to get there.

The limitations imposed by the Islamic government had, in my view, caused these people to return to their roots and reflect more upon their rich heritage. The shortage of translation of foreign books, the illegality of listening to and watching international media and the scarcity of well-educated teachers and mentors had a reverse effect on them. While, during my time, it was more popular to read theoretical influential publications such as the Marxist Manifesto, these young folks learned the notions of 'existence' and 'reality' from the symbolic metaphors of Rumi and Mollā-Sadrā.[8] Consequently, their approach to future prospects helped them cultivate a potential for a more holistic view of the country where various beliefs and ideologies could coexist: a worldview that many in my generation lacked.

For example, let's look at the difference between the 'revolutionary uprising' of 1979 and the 'evolutionary movement' that followed twenty years later. In the first occasion, individuals and groups struggled to replace one regime with another, insisting on their authoritarian doctrines as the only alternative. In the latter, people regardless of philosophy and belief gathered together to transform and amend the shortcomings of an administered ideology. The difference is also evident in the slogans used within the two struggles. In 1979 the slogans demanded explicit action, 'The Shah Must Leave'. Upon achieving this objective, the resolves were divided. Each group demanded their dogma, often subscribing to the notion of 'my way or the highway' as the next step. As a result, the one that was most structured and most brutal defeated others through various means, including the 'divide and conquer' strategy. The 2009 movement, brought about by the peoples' frustration with decades of dictatorship and over the rigged election of an undesirable president, started without a clear leader. People strolled quietly with covered faces as they carried signs that read 'Where Is My Vote?' The demonstrations were peaceful and the gestures metaphoric. No one sought a regime change and no group thought itself above the others. Then the crusade shifted. Self-appointed leaders emerged, hide-away opposition groups claimed ownership of the movement, each insisting on their particular dogma, and demanded another revolution. The regime responded with the only defence it knows: violence.

Iranian youth acknowledged that their legitimate call for freedom and justice had caused the loss of many innocent lives. Therefore, in order to avoid further misuse of power, they retreated to the drawing boards of communication and education, where people could recognize the value of negotiation, acceptance and coexistence. It was because of such wisdom that Iranians were able to prevent the trap that others in the region, perhaps blindly, fell into. While Iranians supported months of nonviolent marches and protests through which they insisted on their fundamental human rights, the images of the regime's brutality and murder spread throughout the world, giving birth to what we now call citizen journalism. The people, knowing that they do not want a repeat of the past bloodsheds, however, practised self-restraint, waiting for another opportunity for a peaceful transformation. Needless to say, the complexities of the rise and fall of the 2009 movement are not limited to the above observation; rather, it requires a much longer analysis that is beyond the endurance of this chapter.

To learn more about this generation of Iranians, I participated in all kinds of gatherings around Tehran: book discussions, yoga practices, political meetings, poetry readings, healing ceremonies, religious services and wild parties, as well as art exhibits, theatre productions and public and private film screenings. What I noticed taking part in these gatherings was that a vast majority of participants were much younger than me, and from diverse educational, social and economic backgrounds. Moreover, the social and political issues of the day, as well as plans and possibilities for the future, almost always dominated the conversations. I was surprised to see that while, during my time, every disagreement or argument ended in a fight, betrayal and animosity, they listened to each other patiently and acknowledged arguments. Even when harsh and impolite accusations occurred, they took the time to contemplate the opposing view and, if not convinced, agreed to disagree, promising to continue the dialogue in the future. Moreover, I realized that my young friends' information and knowledge were not limited to the political manifestos or social theories they studied. Rather, their opinions were often grounded in personal explorations and observations, and even experiences during circumstances where they had taken dangerous risks. They patiently welcomed almost everyone to their gatherings, and genuinely tried to learn about their social, religious, economic and political upbringing. They also respected, honoured and even participated in their rituals and ceremonies. They did this in order to identify what is needed to help them overcome boundaries that limited their ability to endure and appreciate those with whom they disagreed. The following is one example of such practices.

One July morning, after an all-night party where we drank and danced away from the watchful eyes of the *Basij*, my friends suggested that we drive to a *qameh-zani* ceremony where they knew the host.[9] I had taken part in ʿashura commemorations as a young boy and knew that the participants are highly religious.[10] As we drove to southern Tehran, where the more traditional and religious citizens live, I questioned the benefit of appearing in such ceremonies, especially considering that our appearances clearly showed our disbelief in the practice. 'None of us here believe in such backward practices', I said, 'then why even go?' One of my young friends responded, 'How else do you suppose we can understand and respect the mindsets and beliefs of those who do believe in it?' I asked, 'And why do we need to understand their mindset?' He responded patiently, 'Don't you think if we all want to live in the same society as one nation, we must at least respect one another?' I was speechless. Another added, 'Otherwise, we will continue facing what we have so far: one group rules forcing everyone else to abide by their laws.' The driver added, 'And there we go again, revolution after revolution!'

We arrived at the location at 5.30 a.m. I was surprised at how organized and orderly the ceremony was – even more surprised at how well and respectfully we were received, even though our mannerism and appearances were entirely different from those gathered there. Remembering an episode that had happened during my 1984 visit not too far from this place worried me. Back then I saw a young woman stopped by a *Basij* patrol car. Performing their religious duty of *amr-e beh ma'ruf*, they had objected to her wearing lipstick.[11] She apologized and attempted to wipe it off immediately. The female *Basiji*, however, insisted that she, herself, would wipe it off and she did. Suddenly a stream of blood gushed out of the poor girl's lips. The girl screamed with pain as the woman shouted, 'This is what you get for walking around with makeup, you whore!' They had hidden a razor blade inside the napkin. Now, looking at my female friends who did have makeup on and thinking of the smell of alcohol on our breath, I felt scared. Although we had chewed on dried tea and mint tablets and used all the usual remedies to hide the smell, I was sure speaking with us up close, people would realize that we had been drinking.

We followed the host and his family to other customary rituals of the day, which included a communal march through the streets. The marchers engaged in *sineh-zani* and *zanjir-zani* accompanied by the usual chants and hymns that recapitulated the events of 'ashura.[12] There was also *shabih-khwani*, during which one group of men dressed in red, who portrayed the assailant army, followed another group of men dressed in green and wearing *chador*, who represented the women in Hussein's camp.[13] Chanting along with the music, the first group attacked the second one violently. The violence seemed far from staged and reminded me of the brutality I had witnessed in 1979 when motorcycle gangs attacked women in streets. The assailants also shouted vicious and cruel words. Onlookers followed this chorus as they beat their chests, heads and cheeks vehemently. During every short break between the scenes, both the audience and the actors would begin crying and praying for forgiveness and mercy.

At lunch, our host invited us to eat with a family whose seven-year-old son participated in the flagellation rituals. We talked about Islam, the revolution and the government and, of course, my life in the America. I was visibly worried when a female companion's scarf slid off of her hair as she questioned the rationality of a small boy bleeding for someone who died 1,400 years ago. The host's young wife, however, delicately handled the situation by remarking how beautiful her hair was. Then when the argument was getting heated, the boy's father calmly resolved the quarrel by saying, '*isā be din-e khod, musā be din-e khod!*'[14] I was astonished. Listening to Moody Blues' *Night in White Satin* on the drive home, I thought people have come a long way since the early days of the revolution. It felt that something has changed in this society and the youth ought to be credited for this change. When I was dropped off at my mother's apartment, a friend noticed my bewilderment. She smiled and said, 'Didn't someone say "Revolution is not a dinner party." Well, change does not happen overnight. Does it?'[15] They drove away leaving me curious about the next lesson! The song echoed in my ear:

> Cold hearted orb that rules the night,
> Removes the colors from our sight,
> Red is grey and yellow white,
> But we decide which is right,
> And which is the illusion.

During fall 1994, I was invited to teach a course at Tehran University. Even though only a dozen students were registered, frequently many more were in the room.

I lectured on the contemporary theories and practices in the theatre and discussed innovative performances, some of which had originated at Shiraz Arts Festivals of the early 1970s, a globally respected event they knew very little about. Students showed interest and enthusiasm and often stayed later than the class time. A few even accompanied me to my mother's apartment, directly across the north gate of Tehran University, where we continued our conversations. Later in the semester, I was asked to apply for a full-time teaching position. I loved the idea, but reviewing the application, I noticed several personal questions that I did not feel I should answer. So, my teaching at Tehran University stopped.

Some of the students, however, did not give up and asked if we could have private lessons. So, I started my first workshop with nine young artists. We met twice a week at a painter's studio for about six months. The lessons began from where I always start, the self. In teaching theatre, I try to adopt the principles of Sufism to the relationship between the character and the actor. Believing that there exists a core of every character within the actor portraying it, I challenge him to recognize this essence and submit to it. Through meditation, improvisation and research, the actor will eventually identify the truth about the character, adjust it to the production's specific environment and hopefully conquer the multiplicity of its magnitudes. In this method, participants uncover their artistic potentials by exploring creative impulses and imaginative channelling. We also studied literature, arts and philosophies of our cultural past and their influence on contemporary thoughts and practices. In addition, we considered the role of the artist as change agent within a society infested with superstitions and contradictions by examining how theatre reveals the answer of the past to the questions of the present. These conversations often continued in the privacy of our homes and up onto the serene hilltops of Darakeh, where we strolled late at nights.[16] I must admit that our discoveries and discussions during this period were the basis for my interest and research on peacebuilding through the arts, a topic that has dominated my scholarship and academic work until the present time.

Joining these new friends, I found myself among some exceptionally talented young theatre artists whose creative investigations, though spontaneous and raw, reminded me of the New York theatre of the early 1960s. Some of these artists are now among leading filmmakers, actors, painters, authors and, of course, prisoners of conscience. The more I worked with them, the more I appreciated the young woman who had confronted me during my first lecture. Now I knew why I had stayed.

In a system where producing anything has more to do with your connections than your merits, passing through the labyrinth of the bureaucratic maze of presenting a play consumes more energy and time than the actual staging of it. Therefore, a great deal of determination and drive is needed to remain creatively productive. For a play to receive approval and funding and to perform in an official theatre, various permissions are needed. First, the script must be approved. Then the director, playwright, actors, designers, production staff and even the gofers must be approved. Even if all approvals are issued and play is rehearsed, still there is no guarantee that it will enjoy public performances, or complete its scheduled run. In the absence of any clear guidelines and criteria, the process of obtaining the necessary permits was not always the same for everyone. The less compliant and accommodating the artist, the more difficult it was to receive authorization. Therefore, while some productions were issued quick approval, reasonable budgets and major theatres to play in, others, often the works of young artists, were shoved into insect-infested damp basement corners with little or no support. In my experience, however, the latter proved to be more creative, inspirational and encouraging. Although it was more difficult for these young artists to obtain permits and stage plays, some of their semi-underground productions were daring, provocative and challenging. However, I did not limit myself to seeing only the works of the youth; rather, I tried to be open and attend as many productions as I could. Yet the more I saw, the more I was disappointed with the work and ethics of older theatre artists.

For example, at a production held at Vahdat Theatre and directed by a well-known director with over-the-top expensive scenery, about forty actors played to a house of less than 100.[17] At the talkback, in response to the audience's complaints, the director defended the production by stating that he did not care what they thought. When a young critic questioned his approach to the text, instead of addressing the issue, he burst out in anger, calling him uneducated, ignorant and disrespectful.

A few nights later, I went to see Jean Genet's *The Maids* performed to standing room only by three young women in a cramped, make-shift space underneath the steps of Teʿatr-e Shahr (City Theatre). At the talkback, the ensemble considered the audiences' scrutiny more eagerly than their praise. I joined the cast party where a couple of dozen actors, crew and friends gathered in a small apartment. Endorsing their creative approach, I suggested that they should learn to accept the audiences' approval just as they do their criticism. Thanking me, the director responded, 'With all due respect, don't you think if the play is to serve its audience, we need to pay more attention to what it is not communicating?' The ensemble agreed and continued debating the production's flaws and successes in an honest and non-judgemental manner.

I was disappointed once again when a famous poet took me to see a production that had received high reviews. We met four other reputable artists and intellectuals at the theatre and were ushered to our seats in the front row. It was a good production, but not one that I would give standing ovation. My companions, however, stood up and cheered loudly, especially when the director joined the cast on stage. Pulling me up by my shoulder, my poet friend said, 'Stand up, he is looking directly at you'. So, I stood up. Then we went backstage to meet with the director and the cast. My companions visibly tried to outdo each other in praising the play. The director asked what I thought and I said that there were many imaginative moments in the production. He smiled. We weren't more than a few hundred feet away from the theatre when someone in the group said, 'What a piece of shit that show was!' Another responded, 'What did you expect; the guy does not know his ass from his elbow!' My poet friend commented, 'I don't know how he gets these huge budgets for such lousy work.' A fourth person added, 'Well, he knows whose ass to kiss.' I was starting to feel sick to my stomach. Using a silly excuse, I split and took a cab home where a soothing bottle of homemade vodka was waiting for me.

Meanwhile, my friends and students, curious about how my approach to the training of actors would work in an actual theatre production, insisted that I should direct a play. I had previously approached the Center for Performing Arts with a proposal to stage a new adaptation of *The Epic of Gilgamesh*.[18] Although I was called into several meetings where I was received with respect and even fed good Kabab, no definite response was issued. I faced a wall of silence even in repeated follow-ups. I explained the situation to my young friends. They contacted people they knew but received the same treatment. Finally, one of them suggested, 'If Gilgamesh seems problematic, let us present them with another play.' We pitched three more projects during that year, yet, again received no official response. In addition to the above, we proposed over 100 plays during the next few years, all of which were treated in a similar fashion. It was only in 1998, once President Khatami took office, that I was given permission to direct a play: Shakespeare's *A Midsummer Night's Dream*.[19]

Unable to do theatre, I decided to produce a film in 1995. This film too was subject to multiple scrutiny and sabotage. The constant encouragement, persistent teamwork and selfless contribution of the young support staff were the only recollections worth remembering. Otherwise, the odyssey of *Common Plight*, incorporated deception, fraud, dishonesty, intimidation, obstruction and shenanigans, all designed to discourage and frustrate.

We all have our limits. I reached mine in the spring of 1996 following a personal and professional betrayal by someone I loved and trusted. So, I reserved a ticket to return to the United States and headed to the Ministry of Ershad to get an exit stamp on a few videos I had shot while in Iran.[20] Once again, something happened that made me postpone my departure. On the way to the ministry I shared a cab with a young woman who had seen my film during the only day it was permitted to screen. I told her about my frustrating experiences and how I felt that I was wasting my life in Iran. She talked about difficulties she faced in her research on the increasing number of street children and the helpless situation they were trapped in. When I asked if this research is related to her studies, she casually said, 'No, I studied lies.' Noticing my baffled look, she explained, 'I studied history, and history is nothing but lies.'

She knew the city well. So, we spent the next few months going to places I had only seen in pictures. We ate *Dizi* with menial workers at small rundown coffeehouses while listening to their stories about how they felt betrayed by the revolution.[21] I met people who lived in unbearable conditions: homeless veterans, jobless labourers, illiterate drug addicts, underage prostitutes and other disadvantaged people the society had shoved aside. My new friend also introduced me to other young people who were trying to help their fellow citizens. Again, a glimpse of hope shined into my otherwise empty life. Like others of her generation, her life story intrigued me. She was eight when the revolution had happened. Everything had transformed overnight. She could no longer play with the boys, show off her long curly hair or even wear the green sneakers she loved so much. Then, the Iraq-Iran war had started and she had turned to religion, seeking refuge in God as the only salvation from the repeated news of bombardments. As she grew older and experienced the treatment women received, she had realized the deceitfulness of religious leaders, the hypocrisy of school officials and the duplicity of the *Basiji* brothers. Therefore, although vigorously active in caring for the less fortunate, she was disheartened and depressed with a split identity between the two opposing worlds of her private life and public persona. Every night, as I climbed the Darakeh hilltops, I thought of her stories and similar ones I had heard over the years and delayed my departure another month. She and I got married in the fall 1996.

One summer afternoon, as I was working on a major article for Iran's leading film monthly, two young men knocked at my mother's door. 'We have come to study with you', said the one introducing himself as a son of a respected film director. I explained that I do not teach any longer, but the young men insisted. A few hours later, as I was getting ready to go for my nightly uphill stroll, I wished them good night and asked to be excused. The young men requested to come along and would not take no for an answer. We hiked up quietly for a couple of hours before we stopped at a little cabin where the attendant offered us tea and sweets. On the way down, they repeated their request and once again I refused, this time using the excuse that you can't have a theatre workshop with only two students. Months later I realized why they had insisted to stay with me that night. They had heard a rumour that the reason I was fired from teaching at the university and that my proposals were not accepted was because I am both an alcoholic and a drug addict. They also knew that I climbed up Darakeh almost every night. So, they were puzzled and wanted to find out the truth about me. Two weeks later, I was running a workshop with five men and five women in an old building we converted into a working studio. It was with these ten talented and energetic people that I found another opportunity to continue developing my experimentations with the *Ascetic Theatre*.

For the next ten months we met for five hours twice a week behind closed doors, where we explored the relationships between life and theatre. At times the synergy reached such heights of creativity that is the dream of every theatre artist. We worked in the evenings, climbed hilltops at nights and travelled to the fields where, in moments of ecstasy, we disappeared within the vastness of the universe. I often define the peak of ensemble exploration as reaching a state of an artistic orgy. We achieved that many times. Over two decades have passed since then and the participants in that workshop are now among international playwrights, directors, filmmakers and professors, as well as entrepreneurs and bureaucrats. While we all think of those days as inspiring and invigorating, no one has yet revealed the details of our experimentations, despite much curiosity.

My twin daughters were born in December 1997. Mohammad Khatami, a progressive clergy, was elected president and there were high hopes for the future. I was teaching full time at a newly established arts institute. In addition, I had joined two other friends to educate a group of liberal-minded high clergy, most of whom have since been disrobed and/or imprisoned, about the Western cinema.

Once again, believing that the time is right, my friends encouraged me to direct a play. This time, however, they secured all the preliminary permits. I translated Shakespeare's *A Midsummer Night's Dream* into Persian using four different styles of spoken Persian, each designated to a specific social class. Even though we had the stamp of approval from the minister of Ershad himself, we were given no advance on our budget, no place to rehearse and no assigned theatre to perform in. We contacted the theatre officials, and wrote letters, including one to the president himself, all to no avail. Some newly established progressive newspapers published articles and interviews questioning the lack of support for our team. I even appeared on a live TV programme criticizing the theatre authorities about lack of support for the creative works of the youth. It felt like a cultural battle ground, where a young theatre group is trying to maintain its dignity. Several times, I became discouraged and was ready to give up. Yet my young collaborators insisted in continuing to work in spite of all odds. So, putting egg boxes on the walls to limit the noise, we rehearsed in my mother's 300-square-feet living room. Ultimately, as evident in the documentary film *Dream Interrupted*, one of the most movement-oriented productions of Shakespeare's play was rehearsed sitting down.

The production was inspected a number of times during rehearsals; each time new limitations were imposed. Eventually, we received a permit for forty-five public performances. However, the play was raided and closed down during its fourth public performance on 23 February 1999. I was charged with the crime of 'Raping the Public Innocence' and summoned to the Court of Islamic Guidance. My three court appearances can simply be summarized as yet another frustrating tale of dishonesty, disorganization and intimidation. However, the experience made me further appreciate the wisdom of Iranian youth. As we entered the court on the first day, I saw a few dozen young people hanging around the building. I did not pay much attention to this until my third scheduled appearance a few months later, when I noticed that not only the crowd had multiplied but also many of the faces are the same I had seen on the other two occasions. In response to my curiosity, the young friend who accompanied me on every visit slickly brushed the question aside saying, 'Some cases do take a long time to resolve!'

My case, however, was never resolved and remained inconclusive. Nonetheless, my family and I received a number of death threats, the last of which was against our then eighteen-month-old twins. As we prepared to travel to Turkey to apply for my wife's visa, we were advised to take the ground route to avoid possible arrest at the airport away from public view. This time only a few young friends came to see us out at the bus terminal. As we said goodbye, I noticed that one of them was joining us on the bus. 'I am also going to Turkey', he said, making it sound like it had nothing to do with safeguarding us across the border. It was not until a year later that I learned that the people around the court building were, in fact, there to show their support and the young man escorting us to Turkey was the only one within our group who had completed the mandatory military service needed to possess a passport.

In visits after that, I was repeatedly reassured of the creatively consistent role Iranian youth, especially the women, played in the formation of lasting social change, one that rises through education, association and conversation. I saw how they strived towards the pragmatic notion of respect, tolerance and acceptance, which I never saw in my own generation. Even though, given the authority that rules Iran, it might be long before a total and comprehensive change takes place, Iran is steadfastly moving towards an unprecedented grassroots democracy that has been the dream of every activist, artist and educator for centuries.

The evidence for such progress was most visible in the aftermath of the rigged presidential election of 2009, when Iranians demanded change in an unprecedented peaceful uprising. The nonviolent march of millions all through Iran, dubbed as the Green Movement, was in complete contrast with the violent storms that paved the way for the formation of the Islamic Republic. The silent marchers carried placard slogans dissimilar to any other prior protests. The chants repeated in the *'ashura* ceremonies following the Green Movement were unlike any recited during the first twenty years of the Islamic regime. The ferocious reenactments of the events of *ashura*, as I had witnessed in the early 1990s, had given way to calls to 'Rise, for now is the time to come together'.[22] The beating of chests was replaced by clapping of hands – moreover, with such arrogant slogans as 'There is only one party and that is the party of Ali. There is only one leader and that is Khamenei'[23] was replaced with

> We are weary of your religion
> We loathe your manners
> We are offended by the callus on your foreheads
> And your ruthless hearts.[24]

As was illustrated in *No Land's Song*, a documentary film directed by Ayat Najafi, and presented at the 2015 Human Rights Watch Film Festival in New York City, the Iranian youth have learned the art of negotiation without submission.[25] At its screening, the film's director was asked to compare the experience of completing such provocative film, in spite of all impediments and pressures, to that of two decades earlier when *A Midsummer Night's Dream* was raided and closed down. He simply responded, 'Then they knew how to play us. Now we have learned how to play them.'

Let me conclude by reiterating my delight about the role that Iranian youth perform on the stage of Iran today, albeit some playing negative characters. The most important change, in my opinion, is that the old tradition of *Pedar-salari* (Patriarchy) has given way to a new practice of *Farzand-salari*.[26] The Western convention, at least in its theatrical illustration, springs from the myth of Oedipus, where the son replaces the father as a ruler. The Iranian tradition stems from the story of Rostam and Sohrab, where the father must overcome the son, even by deceit.[27] We have remained faithful to this convention throughout our history, revolution after revolution. It is this principle that made my generation follow the lies of an old con artist who claimed he had no political ambition of his own. And it is still this same outlook that makes some wish the present white-bearded despot realizes his errors and changes his ways. It is also because of this viewpoint that some, especially among the diaspora, believe political change is only possible if it descends from the top. Therefore, in their effort to bring about such a change, they often pursue self-appointed leaders who are supported by this or that foreign power. Through research, observation and personal contact, I have come to believe that the Iranian youth have no such illusion. Both in art and in life, they know they will not reach their deserved potential by following the ways of the past. They also know that they cannot inaugurate the prosperous future without understanding the foundation on which they are to build that. Thus, our young sisters and brothers study their cultural past much more rigorously than we did and follow the foreign manuals of a perfect society much less religiously than we did. I have nothing but admiration for this generation and nothing but high hope for the future of our beloved Iran.

6

ACTING OUT: HAMED TAHERI AND THE TRANSFORMATIVE POWER OF IRANIAN UNDERGROUND THEATRE

Roxanne Varzi

While the Iran-Iraq War ended by 1990, it wasn't until a decade later that evidence of an underground counterculture began to take shape in public spaces in Tehran.[1] In 2000 reform President Mohammad Khatami was beginning his second term in office, and despite struggles with a strengthening opposition in the government, he continued to create and foster an open public sphere that entailed reforms in the press, in education and gestures of friendship to the outside. However, his reforms were coupled by an ever-failing economy and disillusionment in the general public marked by a rise in drug use among wealthy teens, to the poor who gave their last pennies for the sludge at the bottom of a wealthy man's opium pipe. His presidency saw a rise in male and female prostitution, open discussions in the press occurred about HIV; while homosexuality and sex change operations were hot topics in the underground media. Twelve-step recovery programmes mushroomed and films from Iran acquired world acclaim. Philosophical and radical texts from abroad – Foucault, Derrida and Heidegger, to name just a few – were being translated into Persian and readily available on bookshelves to be sold to the masses. The New Age was on the rise with its Zsar Paulo Chuelo making an annual visit to Iran and yet a strong Islamic central government at odds with the president was (and still is) in place forcing many cultural producers to practise in the dark, literally underground.

The theatre in this atmosphere was beginning to come out of hiding and to be exported – a herculean task and much more difficult than sending a reel of 35mm film as the theatre consists of young military-aged bodies who need exit visas from Iran and entry visas into Europe. But that did not stop path-breaking directors like the young Hamed Taheri, who, in his barely illuminated square cinder-block dorm room at Tehran University, spent his nights reading and translating forbidden thoughts till dawn. His dorm was the same building that would soon become the scene of sit-ins and tear gas clouds hanging over bloodied students making their way towards waiting police vans or escape.[2]

By day Taheri studied twenty-year-old engineering texts: he learned his physics and pondered God's dice. He prowled the bookstores outside of Tehran University for musty second-hand French texts too complicated to be censored and too racy or subversive to be translated. He knew all the backroom book dealers who trusted him. He was twenty-one and had just missed the war, but not the scars – they marked his generation and continue to do so in constant public reminders of the boys his age who died, young martyrs, for their country, for him, so that he could become an engineer, but not so that he could follow his true vocation – the theatre.[3]

That year, on those particular evenings, Taheri spent hours alone with the text of Jean Genet's *The Blacks*, which he and Atefeh Talahi translated painstakingly from French to Persian.[4] He read the Frankfurt school, Benjamin, Adorno, he listened to Meredith Monk and soaked-up any semblance of counter-culture he could find. In 1999 the city was so thick with smog and rules so strict that breathing was barely possible let alone translating a gay European man's text with the hope of transforming it for Iranian public consumption – which he did do and to great acclaim.

Taheri's company first met as friends in an underground acting and movement class, which they took together for nearly nine years before embarking on an actual production for the stage, directed by Taheri and acted by his friends.[5] That first play was *Antigone* and it was produced after sixteen weeks of twelve-hour days of practice. At the time, the actors were between the ages of sixteen and twenty-one. The play ran thirty sold-out nightly performances. This was no ordinary *Antigone*, but one based on Mephisto and the Quran, Balinese movement and yoga. It was about a group of people on death row with black bags over their heads, forced to play Antigone before dying. The characters gathered in the waiting room of an execution chamber where one by one a shot was administered to their left arm, the bag was removed and they began to act – to come to life for a final performance.

What made Taheri's theatre so path-breaking and what he brought to post-Revolution Iranian theatre, in particular, was the incredibly taxing and physical bodywork of Jerzy Grotowski, a Polish stage director and theatrical theorist, who founded the Polish Laboratory Theatre in 1959. Taheri painstakingly translated Grotowski at twenty words a day with the help of an old dog-eared English dictionary. He not only imported Grotowski's acting exercises but also completely adhered to his ideas of a poor theatre. 'Poor' meant the stripping away of all that was unnecessary (costumes, sound effects, makeup, sets, lighting) and leaving a 'stripped' and vulnerable actor. Grotowski was also much attuned to physical space and worked with all black sets, devoid of any political messages – which worked very well for a group of Tehrani youth who were trying to turn inward and away from an abundance of murals and posters – in short, propaganda.[6]

A number of reasons made *The Blacks* an important event at this juncture in Iranian history not least of which was that the motivation behind theatre and performance was therapeutic. Earlier mysticism was used to justify dying in the war, but now in the theatre it's a rehabilitative force. Ironically, rehabilitation is still couched within the context of a very strong element of martyrdom as evidenced in the body work and choice of theatre Praxis, mainly Jerzy Grotowski's theatre of the poor.[7] In all, the final product was not so much a performance as a psychic transformation for both the players and the audience.

For Taheri's company, the first step towards a psychic transformation came with creating the physical space – which in their case was an old long-forgotten basement theatre that was built under the Tehran City Theatre. The theatre, which is still in use today, is a kidney bean-shaped, uterus-like, cylindrical structure that winds down into a labyrinth of catacomb-like rooms. Aside from low-hanging pipes that throw long shadows that blend with streaks of diesel across the dirty floors, everything, from the ceiling to the wall to the floor, is cement, including cement benches that are built right into the walls. Cleaning the space for use would be their first collaborative exercise. The actors had a very intense connection to the space. They called it 'Khāne-ye Khorshid', *House of the Sun*, alluding to a piece of poetry by Ahmad Shamlou called *Mother of the Sea*, which an actor from *The Blacks* quoted upon seeing the space: 'The heart is black from pain, so where is the Sun's house?' Fourteen months of practice, according to Taheri, gave every actor a sense of the place that became innate: the layout, the smell and the acoustics. By the time they were ready to perform in the small, unlit theatre, the actors could find each other in the dark due to familiarity with the acoustics. But the audience, on the other hand, was uncomfortable with the spooky space and the anonymous actors.

After the space was created, the next Grotowskian move Taheri made was to take the actors through rigorous exercises that would give them full control over their bodies. What was important to Grotowski was what the actor could do with his or her body and voice without aids and with only the visceral experience they had with the audience. According to Grotowski the actors should be illuminated through the use of shadows and candles – Taheri used both candles and flashlights. Grotowski thought make-up a trick, as the muscles of an actor's face are true movements from face to face. Of course, this notion is especially relevant in Iran, where half the population is only seen in the face and yet there is a strong religious unspoken edict not to look into the face of women – and where make-up is forbidden. The body is the most political entity in post-Revolution Iran. It is the bodies of the citizenry, how they move, dress, when and where they appear that can either threaten or uphold the state's definition of an Islamic subject. And the actor, depending only on the natural gifts of voice and body, can bring the sacred rituals of theatre and the themes of social transformation to this particular audience that is imprisoned in these same restrictions through body techniques that are both sparse and explosive.

The technique of the actor for both Grotowski and Taheri is not so much a collection of skills as an eradication of blocks. Taheri and others I interviewed in his company took very seriously the socio-psychic responsibility they assumed when they made the theatre more about the rehabilitation of the actor and audience, especially of the actor, than about entertainment. In Tehran, for Taheri's company, the primary motivation behind the theatre was therapeutic – for both the actors and the audience. According to Taheri, every one of his actors had some sort of complex that they needed to work through. For Grotowski, 'All these exercises are about breaking down resistance and blocks, everyone's is different so the training becomes personalized, you never know what to do, but what not to do. Living impulses must be liberated. Exercises keep us from falling into chaos.'[8] One actor said in an interview, 'Hamed is teaching us the idea that each muscle has its own pace, memory and brain.'⁹ Taheri used Grotowski's pearl diver analogy with his actors. He said, 'An actor is like a pearl diver. Each dive is meant to be a pearl search. Taheri's actor goes on to say, 'Even if there's a ten percent chance of finding an oyster, each time you find a pearl, it's like finding a childhood memory, that's when you understand your role.' His theatre was more than a performance. It was a form of therapy.

For Taheri, before there was ever any notion of performing, came the idea that the exercises and the rehearsals alone could rehabilitate the creative energy of those who participated and that this would be enough if they never found their way to an audience. Grotowski recalls:

> It was the Stalinist period, censorship was very heavy. Performances were censored, but not rehearsals and the rehearsals, were for me the most important thing. Something happened between a human being and another human being that is the actor and myself that touched this axis beyond any control from the outside. It means that the performance has always been less important that the work in the rehearsals.¹⁰

As I mentioned above, this therapeutic motivation was far from the then popular neorealist move that began to counter the war documentaries in Iranian cinema like Kiarostami and Panahi that took on the role of redefining and revitalizing the nation, especially for the outside post-war, but rather on a very individual level for both the actor and the audience.[11] Rather it was most evident in the intense physicality of the performance, which made Taheri's theatre an especially important event at this juncture in Iranian history when citizens were dealing with twenty years of an intense culture of martyrdom.[12]

Much like a physical martyrdom, this kind of theatre is very physical and demands a great deal from the body of the actor. There is an extreme physical aspect to the performance that is as much an act of masochism and martyrdom through a fragmentation and the destruction of the body. His work is not unlike the Vienna actionists, Grotowski, Butoh Theatre, and at times it becomes an act of masochism bordering on martyrdom. Pain comes to define everyday practice. The body is broken down at the same time that the soul is rejuvenated. It's uncannily close to the idea of martyrdom during the Iran-Iraq War where the body may die but the soul is only just beginning to live. But it functions for a very different purpose, which is to rehabilitate and to live more fully on earth. Ironically, rehabilitation is *still* couched within the context of a very strong element of martyrdom as evidenced in the bodywork and choice of Grotowski's theatre Praxis. Grotowski believed that theatre is a sacrificial act. An actor gives herself to the audience who, in turn, gives the actor their energy. The idea here is of the actor as a gift, as a sacrificial object that is offered to the audience. The audience, in turn, returns the energy, thus dismantling the wall between the actors and the players.

In order to encourage men to martyr themselves at the front, Iranian propaganda filmmakers at the war front showed the beauty of martyrdom. These filmmakers railed against neorealism because it showed the 'ugliness of human existence' and not the beautiful new Islamic reality.[13] Taheri, on the other hand, shows the ugly repercussions and the fragmented space post-war. He shows how the citizen becomes a refugee in his or her own mind. Whereas the war filmmakers attempted to create reality through montage, bringing together fragments of death to build a new (after) life, Taheri takes this apart and re-fragments it into strips of meaning that are relevant to living in the now.

Maybe it is because beauty has been defined in the visual media in Iran as martyrdom for so much of Taheri and his generation's life that he claims outright that he is not attracted to beauty. 'I don't trust beauty, it is an illusion.'[14] Taheri, who lived through the intense post-war years, says, 'Beautiful objects cannot take me beyond.' He cites Dante and being led into the Inferno. Grotowski's training regime was devised to avoid the beautiful if it does not foster truth – one must constantly attempt to reveal the darkness within. Theatre here is provocation.[15] When performance becomes a sacrificial act, the audience is even more tantamount to the experience – which is something we see in the war years in Iran: martyrdom is nothing without an audience as is the case with the cultural industry around martyrdom where every audience member is a potential martyr. For Taheri's actors the metaphoric death of self or the real death of an old psychic self, in a way, is its own kind of martyrdom and is what is gifted to the audience through the gruelling performance. It's a rejuvenating gift that opens up into a different and better life for the actors who have, alongside the audience, been reconstructed and re-enlivened.

Spirituality and mysticism remain at the centre of this kind of philosophic move. But it is a very different kind of mysticism than the one used in the war to kill the self. Here mysticism is meant to rehabilitate the self.[16] One of Taheri's actors described it as 'Reaching to shamanism where the audience was like a spirit that took over and possessed the actors and moved them to do certain things'. Grotowski never allowed films or photos of his theatre because it would destroy the spiritual experience. Taheri's theatre looked like a dervish lodge and sounded a bit like a mosque mixed with African drums and Hebrew spirituals. The element of dance gave it a 'whirling dervish' effect.

Making the theatre about rehabilitation of the actor and audience, especially of the actor rather than about entertainment, is a very serious socio-psychic responsibility to take on. Again, his direction comes from Grotowski:

> Order and harmony in the work of each actor are essential conditions without which a creative act cannot take place. Here we demand consistency. We demand it from the actors who come to the theatre consciously to try themselves out in something extreme, a challenge seeking a total response from every one of us. They come to test themselves in something very definite that reaches beyond the meaning of 'theatre' and is more like an act of living and way of existence.[17]

Theatre here is more than entertainment, but a pathway to understanding. Taheri called the performance a handshake with the audience; the actor was a doctor keeping the audience alive. According to Grotowski:

Theatre – through the actor's technique, his art in which the living organism strives for higher motives – provides an opportunity for what could be called integration, the discarding of masks, the revealing of the real substance: a totality of physical and mental reactions. This opportunity must be treated in a disciplined manner, with a full awareness of the responsibilities it involves. Here we can see the theatre's therapeutic function for people in our present day civilization… The actor's act – discarding half measures, revealing, and opening up, emerging from himself as opposed to closing up – is an invitation to the spectator. This act could be compared to an act of the most deeply rooted, genuine love between two human beings […] This act […] epitomizes the actor's deepest calling.[18]

Every show was different because of what the audience brought to it. According to Taheri, 'The things the audience sees is not necessarily in the actors.' The audience was given flashlights and that was the only light in the auditorium. The first three nights were based on a script, by the third night people were interacting and had found their way in. The audience was told in the programme notes to interact but the first three nights they needed reminding and direction. Eventually, the play elicited an amazing participatory response from the audience. Every night the performance changed depending on how the audience interacted with the actors. The actors enjoyed the fun unpredictable series of events from night to night. They looked forward to the show hours before it started. The audience was completely involved emotionally and intellectually and eventually became part of the action. They took the play, even during the humorous moments, extremely seriously. There was a lot at stake for them. It became a sort of group therapy. The actors were dealing with post-war emotions that were only just finding their first cathartic outlet.

In Tehran, people came back so often that they often memorized the dialogue, especially the Iranian elements added to Genet like a poem by Yadollah Royaee. According to the actors, February–March of 2000 was like entering heaven. The play departed from *The Blacks* and became a collective improv based on spirit of Genet. For example, one actor, Majid, played the accordion in a telephone booth-like structure. He had a rope attached to his neck and to another actor's neck so that when a coin started the accordion player's music, the musician lowered his head, causing the other actor to choke. From the booth Majid witnessed the audience's sympathy. First there were concerned looks, then tears, then letters, then people who began to tell him their problems, then came repeat audience members on other nights with gifts, letters and stares. He remembers a woman sobbing as she looked at him. Eventually one night, the mob broke down the booth and released the ropes.

Another actor, Navid's character, was stuck on the wall, buried in mud, only his eyes apparent. 'He freaked out the crowd the first few nights for it took them a good part of the performance to realise he was not a prop or sculpture', recalls Taheri. 'Eventually, one night the audience released him from his wall and washed his mud under the shower where another character was based […] getting wet night. He continues, 'A woman brought shampoo, a brush, and a towel and began to wash Majid. It was very sensually [...]' Taheri went up to her and said, 'Lady please be careful we don't want to get in trouble back off the touching', and she said, 'Shut-up you filthy spy, get the hell out of here. Anything goes here [...] everything is allowed'. One woman brought a book of poetry. Most nights there were seven actors and thirty-eight audience members. Towards the end the audience members became more and more famous as Iranian's artists found a cathartic and creative outlet. The play gradually turned into an improv collective performance piece, with now famous and controversial film actress Gholshifteh Farahani showing up to play the accordion and Hossein Panahi (actor and poet who died shortly after at the age of forty-five), drawing a heart on an actor. On the last night, 140 people crammed into the small subterranean theatre with musical instruments, poetry, cats and shampoo. Finally, the ultimate code was broken, and the women threw off their veils. They cried and hugged each other, in keeping with Grotowski's philosophy that demands that we 'violate accepted stereotypes – jarring as it is imaged in the human breath/body and inner impulses. The theatre creates shock in order that masks that we wear from day to day are lifted. Defiance of taboo, transgression rips off the mask, enabling us to give nakedly'.[19] Taheri's *The Blacks* was so popular that it continued to sell out for weeks before finally being shut down by the government.

Taheri's legacy was apparent some ten years later when I returned to Iran to look at the theatre scene where new avant-garde theatre produced not only in the Tehran City Theatre but at newer government-run venues, one of which is run by the city municipality called *The House of the Artists* and, like the City Theatre, is sold out in advance of almost every performance. What was fascinating is that the bodywork, the staging, the costumes and the exercises that Taheri translated from Grotowski have come to define the aesthetic of contemporary Iranian Theatre (and film, as actors who have done the exercises and worked in the Theatre are in high demand in the cinema). But what has been lost, especially because the government has so openly allowed the theatre to flourish in this manner, is the critique, the narrative meat that was equally important to works like *The Blacks*.

Since Taheri, the Grotowski method of acting, because of its sparsity and deep need for interpretation, has become a popular form of theatre. The government has allowed music and dance and a lot of razzmatazz that takes away from the fact that at the end of the night nothing important was said. The audience is dazzled and amazed at the mere fact that the performance was produced for the public, with no idea to what degree these surfaces have been eaten at from within. A legacy lost that was just barely in the making for a few short months in the work of Hamed Taheri.

7

DISRUPTING BODIES, NEGOTIATING SPACES:
PERFORMANCE ART IN TEHRAN

Staci Gem Scheiwiller

In 2004, artist Neda Razavipour sat on a curb side in Tehran, selling neatly packaged dolls in 'Dream Sets' to passers-by (Figure 7.1).[1] Displayed on a blanket as ready-to-buy black-market goods, potential consumers expressed confusion when inspecting the boxes: the baby doll's head was separated from its body and had detached arms. Beneath the body, the severed legs were that of a male action figure. Last but not least, the baby doll came with its very own grenade. Whether a feminist gesture, a reflection on personal experience or a critique of globalization and capitalist relations, Razavipour transformed into a peddler of mutilated plastic babies meant to be rebuilt for potential violence, thus mimicking the selling of street goods in order to reveal to her unsuspecting audience several underlying ideologies latent in contemporary Iranian society.[2]

Within the limited scope of this chapter, I will discuss real-time, phenomenological performance art, such as that of Razavipour, that occurs in post-revolutionary Iran between two or more ontological bodies (the artists and viewers) within the social, physical spaces of bodily interaction as opposed to digital performance art and video art, in which the human body is mediated through technology. I will also only cover performance art that happens in the central and north sections of the capital city of Tehran, which comprise the largest art scenes, art markets and commercial sectors in the country. I argue that performance art in Tehran is largely defined by two major general aspects that may function somewhat differently than performance art in other international forums. First, the historical bases of performance art in Iran are strongly rooted in Dada and Neo-Dada – not in the existential heroism of post–Second World War American Abstract Expressionism, the identity and body politics of the 1960s, the performing or dramatic arts (i.e. theatre) or indigenous traditions, such as *ta'zieh* (passion play); thus, the types of bodily confrontations are usually composed of the Dada-like absurd, the sarcastic, the iconoclastic, the repulsive, the defiant and the mundane as gestures of critique of various institutions and social practices. Second, there are typically four spaces available to Iranian performance art, including public spaces, private spaces (i.e. private residences and private

Figure 7.1 Neda Razavipour. *Dream Set*, 2004. Performance, Tehran. Photograph taken by Abbas Kowsari. Courtesy of the artist.

property), hybridized third spaces (e.g. commercial art galleries) and transnational spaces. All these spaces play dominant roles in determining *how* the artist's body is framed, disputed and disruptive in challenging social spheres and eliciting the viewer's responses – not simply as contrasting aspects of the local versus the global and perhaps more encompassing and broader than site-specificity.

Despite the nuances that differentiate performance art of one group or era from another, several characteristics are almost universal, as defined by RoseLee Goldberg:

> The work may be presented solo or with a group, with lighting, music or visuals made by the performance artist […] and performed in places ranging from an art gallery or museum to an 'alternative space', a theatre, café, bar, or street corner. Unlike theatre, the performer is the artist, seldom a character like an actor, and the content rarely follows a traditional plot or narrative. The performance might be a series of intimate gestures or large-scale visual theatre, lasting from a few minutes to many hours; it might be performed only once or repeated several times, with or without a prepared script, spontaneously improvised, or rehearsed over many months.[3]

As Goldberg points out, performance art does not lie within the realm of theatre for various reasons and cannot be conflated with the dramatic arts, such as performance artists not having to play a character or to follow a plot or narrative (they can – but these qualities do not define performance art); hence, this chapter is somewhat an anomaly in this volume's collection of chapters. As Goldberg notes, though, the two different art forms share similarities and can utilize performative gestures and physical spaces of the corporeal human body as ways to engage viewers and to press them to question particular socio-political ideologies that are typically 'invisible' and normalized. However, as mentioned later, performance art's origins only began in the twentieth century, developed by modern visual artists – and sometimes by poets, musicians and dancers – to critique society at large and the dominance of artistic institutions, capitalism and greed over what good art, artists and taste will be. Whereas theatre at times can be Kitsch, entertaining and for the masses, performance art *will always* operate subversively, critically and/or in a socially conscious manner.

There are several shared aspects of performance art in general but are distinguished in practice between various geopolitical entities and cultures and occur in their own ways. First, the ontological body is disruptive or called attention to. Second, the nature of performance art is generally a violent act as the body of the artist must become objectified as the medium of the artwork itself, an act that often differentiates performance art from happenings and relational-aesthetic works. The objectification of the body as a violent act assumes a radical transformation of a forceful or inordinate form; in an almost Cartesian manner, artists separate their consciousness from their bodies. And third, it requires an audience or viewer, whether willing or forced, to be located in some sort of temporal, socio-physical space. As discussed further, these qualities combined will make the situation of performance art in Tehran in contrast to performance art elsewhere and even to other smaller cities in Iran. Although all artwork is somehow reflective of ideological concerns of the societies that produce it, performance art is perhaps even more so as the body of the artist is the direct, immediate conduit through which the message of the artwork is conveyed.[4]

The literature on the history of performance art has often been framed in monolithic ways, as the diversity in the practices of performance art in international situations has not been fully explored, as noted by Thomas Berghuis and by Francesca Dal Lago's conversation with contemporary Chinese artists in regard to Chinese performance art and site-specificity.[5] One of the most notable examples of varied cultural receptions in performance art was Yoko Ono's *Cut-Piece* (1964), which received very different audience reactions in New York City, Kyoto and London despite Ono's attempts at uniformity – from potential life-threatening violence in Japan to striptease rowdiness in England. Another example includes when Gülsün Karamustafa (b.1946) in *Objects of Desire/A Suitcase Trade (100 Dollars Limit)* (1998) replicated a suitcase trade in Zurich, similar to those in Istanbul, and the informality of the street market became co-opted into a 'regulated organizational structure'.[6] Notwithstanding these useful observations on how *similar* performances were received in multiple spatial locations, thus showcasing the polysemic nature of performance art and the signage of the artist's body, most writers assume the integrity of the original performances, or that all performance seems to have a common modus operandi, and only the reception or framing of the environment will change (i.e. Ono's and Karamustafa's performances remained similar in each venue; the venues and audiences changed the receptions and adjusted the meanings of the works).[7]

Except for Berguis and Dal Lago, scholars have not really considered a whole set of cultural and political factors that would determine what the artist would perform, where and how, and in this way, performance art as part of a cultural production will change or be nuanced, not only according to the artist's locality, site-specificity and mobility but also on *how* that particular genre was constructed and generated in the first place. The transculturation of the genre worldwide, the negotiation between the artist's body and the viewer's body and the physical space itself will all invariably vary. The same performance artwork will not always operate in a similar manner when transferred elsewhere – not just because of an audience's physical composition at that moment and the spatial conditions that may differ but also due to a specific set of social and political 'force relations' that may or may not be present, which might even stop the performance from taking place.[8] The entire modus operandi of performance art will be determined by its socio-cultural location, including its aesthetics and how it will even become confrontational, not necessarily only changes in its intention, meaning and reception solely through dislocation.

There are also several origins of how performance art began, which have had an impact on how the genre has developed in various countries and cultures. Creation myths of performance art include early experiments in Italian Futurism, which praised war, modernity and the machine, and the tongue-in-cheek, anti-art, anti-institution, anti-war Dada performances, which were held at the Cabaret Voltaire in Zurich during the First World War (1914–17). Although Berghuis also mentions those early beginnings in relation to Chinese performance art, he discusses how performance art is bound up with the 1950s polemics of art critic Harold Rosenberg (1906–78), who posited the movement of American Abstract Expressionism as one that bridged 'art and life'.[9] This understanding of American modernism led to the artistic formations of Allan Kaprow's happenings, as well as the artist's body as the medium, paralleling the global social unrest of the 1960s that produced political mantras, such as 'the personal is political'.

Though not universal, it seems that performance art in Iran is more indebted to the anti-art, anti-institution Dadaist experiments than to the heroic American version, as noted by the Dadaist inspirations of Bavand Behpoor ('DADA' was written on a car in one performance),[10] the absurdity of Samuel Beckett (1906–89) for Barbad Golshiri (b.1982)[11] and the wisdom of Neo-Dadaist John Cage (1912–92) for Alireza Amirhajebi (b.1970), who has written extensively on him. Indeed, in a short history of performance art published in Iran proper, Mohammad Baqer Rezai locates the origins of the genre in early twentieth-century European movements, such as Futurism, Dadaism and Surrealism.[12] Despite the plethora of indigenous performing arts, performance art in Iran is more connected to outside movements than within. If performance artists, such as Amitis Motevalli (b.1969), who works in both Los Angeles and Tehran, incorporate more indigenous dramatic art forms into their work, it is by artistic choice and individual creative vision – not through the progression of the genre itself in Iran.¹³ In fact, the genre itself is literally called 'performance art' in Persian. While I have heard/read the direct translation of 'performance art' as *honar-e ejrā* used by some artists, such as by Bavand Behpoor (1980–), others consider this label to be incorrect, because it implies more academic, theatrical and dramatic arts – not the particular genre noted above, which is a part of new media and contemporary art in Iran.¹⁴

Public spaces in Tehran hold democratic potential for performance artistic expression, but these are not spaces that an artist can usurp willy-nilly, though Ali Madanipour argues that the public sphere in Tehran is generally weak due to the cosmopolitan anonymity of the city between strangers and the influx of many residents not originally from Tehran. In contrast to smaller cities, this condition of Tehran allows more freedom to utilize public spaces in individual ways – ideal for performance art and a critique of capitalist relations – but this set of circumstances also causes difficulties for the state in terms of regulation.¹⁵ Although the dataset is somewhat older now, Roxanne Varzi's observations are still relevant and resonate with my own research experiences, which have been mainly in Central Tehran: 'Iranians have […] cultivated a culture of sameness at the surface in order to appease the ruling clergy. Iranians have always been able to discern political sympathies, class […] and religious belief based on small indicators'.¹⁶ Hence, public spaces in Tehran, in general, have to be carefully negotiated by performance artists in ways that do not overstep the possibilities for expression. This means that the potential is there, but it is not always clear or easy to predict how the public will react to a performance – the subtle nuances of legality in a situation often depend on whom is in the public sphere on that particular day, watching the performance.

The 'first' known performance artist in Iran was Kamran Diba (1937–). He had orchestrated a recorded performance *Āb-bāz* at Seyhoun Gallery in 1966 with the help of Parviz Tanavoli (1937–) and an unnamed female participant (Roxana Saba?) – a work inspired by Dadaist precepts.¹⁷ In 1967, at the Zand (Ave) Gallery, he and photographer Ahmad Aali (1935–) photographed the shoes of all the attendees at the gallery. Diba had devised the idea based on the work of British artist Allen Jones (1937–) and on the childhood memory of Diba's mother, who designed her own shoes with much care and precision.¹⁸ Another artist during the Pahlavi era (r.1925–79) who experimented with performance art and site-specific art was Marco Grigorian (1925–2007). For example, in *A Place to Rest* and *Peace on Earth* (1977), Grigorian lies in a crater in the ground, which resembles a grave, giving the appearance that he is dead. Furthermore, the prominent Shiraz Arts Festival (1967–77) brought many artists together from various countries, making performance art a more visible possibility for Iranian artists despite the considerable overlap with theatre, dance and music performances. Artists who appeared at the festival and had made these performance cross-overs between several artistic genres included John Cage, Merce Cunningham (1919–2009) and Robert Wilson (b.1941). Though initially banned in the 1930s, *taʿzieh* also became a feature at the festival.¹⁹

For the arts in general, the Iranian Revolution (1978–9) and the following Iran-Iraq War (1980–8) stymied the private art scene although state-sponsored art, such as murals, films and *ta'zieh*, were encouraged. After the war, the 1990s became a flourishing decade in relation to the fine arts, particularly through the directorship of Alireza Sami Azar (1999–2005) of the Tehran Museum of Contemporary Art[20] and the political leadership of former president Khatami (elected 1997–2005). Artist Ali Ettehad noted that after 2000, interest in performance art increased but so did the exploration of all artistic media.[21] Art historians Helia Darabi and Elahe Helbig claim that, currently, new media art, such as performance art, is an accepted and appropriate means of artistic expression in Iran,[22] but a history of Iranian performance art is quite lacking as the histories on Contemporary Iranian Art as an Art History subfield tend to be more focused on objects (other than the artist's body). Generally, there is no market for performance art, and Ettehad cites the increased interest and viability of contemporary art on the art markets – both global and domestic – as a factor that has side-lined the production of performance art in Iran.[23] Indeed, as I had examined art auction catalogues of contemporary art from the Middle East, sold by Christie's, Bonham's and Sotheby's between the years 2006 and 2013, I did not see performance art 'relics' for sale. Since most of the contemporary art scene in Iran is privatized, producing performance art as 'non-commercial and non-sellable' is not encouraging,[24] thus further emphasizing the production of marketable objects to be sold worldwide as the dominant paradigm.

The four spaces of performance art in Iran: The Public

Performance art requires the body as the medium to be the canvas of expression and to be a visceral engagement at all times of the sensual, temporal and unedited. Because the physicality of the body is needed, whether it is the body of the artist and/or the viewer, actual time and space are needed to play out these disruptions of 'normal' ontological realities. However, most, if not all, spaces (public, private and otherwise) of a modern state are surveyed and monitored and hence regulate the bodies of citizens, especially while in public spaces, although private ones can be, and often are, just as panoptic, thus diluting any sense of rigid dichotomy between the two. With that said, performance art in public spaces in Iran can create legal upheavals even when the performance is not meant to provoke the authorities or to engage in politics in a confrontational manner. The reception of performance art can go awry especially when the masses, in general, do not always appreciate or understand avant-garde art – an issue that also deters the frequency of performance art, as confirmed by Ettehad.[25] According to Ettehad, he had proposed using a gallery space at the Bagh-e Muzeh-ye Qasr as one dedicated to performance art, but after only ten events, 'security forces came and put an end to our activities. They told us that the international media had begun covering our activities, whereas they preferred us to attract as little attention as possible and quickly end what we were doing'.[26]

In another example, Bavand Behpoor and his students were arrested while doing a street performance in Tehran, in this case, when they took their second performance to the carwash; the first performance had not been halted

(Figures 7.2 and 7.3).[27] Behpoor was offering a performance art workshop, and for the student project, they created and enacted a performance based on Dadaist principles. Behpoor was arrested along with his students, and when he explained the situation, he was told that his students were not performing art and that they were troublemakers.[28] Then, according to Behpoor, their court appearance coincided with the arraignments of prostitutes and murderers. The students ultimately paid large fines, but their case was not pursued further due to lack of evidence and conflicting reports. Moreover, during my conversations with several Tehran-based artists, they typically commented that there was not that much happening in terms of performance art, but Behpoor thinks the contrary and couches the lack of visibility in different terms:

> [T]here are many performances happening in Tehran [...] but also in provinces across the country. The problem is, performances worthy of the name, are very few and New Media Art [...] is becoming very kitsch and cliché at the moment [...] I would say all artists who do performances document them, but do not present them online (only on Facebook [...]) fearing the risk.[29]

The performance *Lady in Red* (2011)[30] that included many young women artists was, however, officially approved by the authorities to take place, and although there were moments when uniformed men asked them what they were doing, no woman was stopped from participating in the performance or taken in for

Figure 7.2 Bavand Behpoor. Dada Student Performance, 2012. Tehran. Courtesy of the artist.

Figure 7.3 Bavand Behpoor. Dada Student Performance, 2012. Tehran. Courtesy of the artist.

questioning.³¹ The event was organized by Mohammad Hosseini and took place every day during the summer and fall of 1390/2011, between 6 and 7 p.m. in Ferdowsi Square, Tehran.³² The artists were all dressed in red to commemorate Yaqut, the legendary 'lady in red' from the 1960s–1980s, who had supposedly waited for her long-lost lover on the sidewalks of the north side of Ferdowsi Square.³³ This public manifestation of women as potentially lovelorn and yearning was a bold performance and could be a symbol of love in Tehran – which is usually not the first association with the city – thus recontextualizing the city as one of romance and rendezvous or giving Tehran a sense of identity that makes it unique from other cities.³⁴ Yet Yaqut's tragic story also connotes unrequited love and unfulfilled promises by men,³⁵ which could be read as a subtle political or feminist critique – much more so than in the case of Behpoor whose students' misunderstood Dada performance was actually stopped.

The private

Because public spaces in Tehran must be negotiated carefully in performance art so as not to create suspicion or to make confused citizens overly upset, performances that directly and overtly push socio-political and cultural boundaries may be contained specifically within private spaces, such as personal residences and private property, and require an invitation to the event, which indicates a select audience who are sympathetic to the artist's intentions. In this way, the potential for the body to disrupt spaces open to the public and to challenge sociopolitical norms becomes more complicated as the artist is already dealing with a known set of friends, relatives and colleagues who may not be as shocked or baffled by the artist's actions. This set of circumstances also means that many directly provocative performances (as opposed to ones that are more elusive and metaphorical) go unseen and unrecorded. Likewise, because of the specific spatial and cultural contexts, the performance cannot simply be reproduced or restaged in transnational spaces, in which the audience members would not or could not relate to the spatial disruptions.

A case of a private performance took place in 2012 in a home in Central Tehran and was orchestrated by an up-and-coming artist.[36] The attendees were sitting and waiting for the performance to begin when a group of *Basiji*s entered the room. The audience was in panic and fear and women attempted to re-cover their heads, anxious that they would be arrested for being in that space although the performance had not taken place yet. Somehow, the event had been reported to the authorities – or so it was thought. It turned out that the men posed as *Basiji*s to intimidate and frighten the attendees were, in fact, part of the performance. The narrator of this incident, who had attended the performance, commented on the collective angst that the attendees had shared through past memories of being stopped or searched by members of the *Basij* or the *Komiteh* during the 1980s–1990s and thus instinctually went into an automatic mode of internalized panic.

In the case of this residential performance, the seeming infiltration of the state personified (or fetishized) in the bodies of the soldiers into a personal, private living space made the performance even more disturbing and volatile. The artist played on the notion, whether consciously or subconsciously, that the 'home' is usually the safer, less controlled space, while the public sphere is where one is under more scrutiny, when in actuality private space is just as readily co-opted and surveyed as the public one. Needless to say, the 'success' of this cutting-edge performance could have only happened within the intimate private spaces of Iran. Indeed, there are political implications of the performance, but it also calls attention to a specific set of life experiences that have defined three generations, which many of the *nasl-e chaharom* (the fourth generation) and generations afterward plus most foreigners cannot fully comprehend except vicariously through the stories of others.

The gallery

The commercial art gallery space occupies a third space, hybridized between the public and private in Tehran. The reason for this ambiguity is that almost all the galleries are privately owned and not regulated by the government although the state has jurisdiction to shut down any place of business at its discretion. What this means is that galleries are basically on their own and can show the artwork they please as long as it falls within the socio-political dictates of the state. In this way, private galleries are given quite a bit of freedom to choose their exhibitions and artists. Also, if they are not under suspicion or being investigated, they can succeed in showing controversial artwork or the work can be shown in a private room that has limited attendee access. Despite galleries not having to pay taxes on the artwork they sell,[37] the state still benefits from not closely monitoring galleries (but they can and do), and this is in part because a large number of galleries, some of which represent world-famous artists, bring quite a bit of cultural tourism and wealthy investors into Iran.[38]

The gallery system has been instrumental in supporting and promoting ontological body performance art as an artistic genre in Iran, and in recent years, performance art in the gallery scene in Tehran has gained momentum because it attracts more attendees to one gallery over another. In Tehran alone, there are around 150 art galleries, so the competition between them is stiff and intense.[39] If there are many openings in one night (usually on a Friday night), then one has to decide to see only a limited number, excluding the rest, especially since Tehran is a large, dispersed city with traffic. It would be difficult to impossible to see all the art openings around the city, especially on opposite ends since the operating hours of a show opening on Fridays are typically between 4 and 8 p.m. So, if an opening has an inaugurating performance, such as the show of Nooshin Naficy's *The Remaining Scent: Spices* (2014) at Khaneh-ye Honarmandān, which promoted a performance only at the opening, then that would be one of many incentives to choose this gallery over another (Figure 7.4).

Though not all performances are lavish or over the top in dress, dialogue or action, they can be thrilling or controversial, drawing in more attendees.[40] Since 2011, an exciting yearly festival entitled *30 Performances, 30 Artists, 30 days* has been promoted by curator Amir Rad at the East Art Gallery, which has been instrumental in creating a performance art scene in Tehran.[41] In one performance of the third festival that focused on the abject body, called *Euphoria* (2013), Alireza Amirhajebi licked clean the surface of the gallery floor and several attendees' shoes, intermittent with wiping them and smoking cigarettes.[42] The performance conveyed a facet of sensuality as the artist's tongue wiped the floor in strokes as if licking a human body, and then he dragged his own body all over the demarcated galley space. The mere act itself elicits visceral attraction and repulsion in any context but probably even more so in Iran, where the public space is seen as incredibly filthy that one would not even dare put one's face near the floor in a public gallery let alone use one's tongue to clean it in an almost lovemaking gesture. Moreover, pioneering performances, although still powerful and meaningful, can act as attractions in an otherwise-busy, compacted art scene as gallery goers want to see and to talk about the outrageous performances that they had witnessed the night before.

Returning to Razavipour, one of her most notable gallery performances was *Self-Service* (2009), actually a relational aesthetic piece,[43] in which visitors to the Azad Gallery were invited to cut off pieces of handmade Persian carpets at their discretion (Figure 7.5). Scissors and blades were placed beside the carpets, and after mutilating the rugs, the participants placed their remnants into

Figure 7.4 Poster of Nooshin Naficy's *The Remaining Scent: Spices*, 2014. Khaneh-ye Honarmandān, Tehran. Photograph taken by the author.

envelopes that had an excerpt from Plato's *Republic* (380 BCE) printed onto it.[44] Considering its first staging in Tehran in the fall of 2009, art historian Andrea Fitzpatrick has framed this work in light of the Green Movement (2009–10) as an allegorical work that speaks of violence as the slashing of Persian carpets is indeed a murderous and iconoclastic act. The shards of the carpet parallel the

Figure 7.5 Neda Razavipour. *Self-Service*, 2009. Performance, Azad Gallery, Tehran. Courtesy of the artist.

executed bodies in Plato's *Republic*, as well as the victims of political upheavals.[45] Indeed, the cutting of the carpets proved to be a difficult task,[46] much like severing flesh or body parts. However, themes of mutilation and fragmentation have appeared in Razavipour's work much earlier than 2009, such as in *Dream Set* (2004) noted above.

In understanding Razavipour's work, there seems to be a confluence of agents informing *Self-Service*, in addition to the traditional motif of the Iranian carpet, which has become quite iconic as of late in contemporary Iranian art, such as her training in theatre design and reliance on antiquity. In framing Iran as part of the global world, it seems that invoking themes of antiquity, even if minimally, can bridge Iran to the global community, reflecting Iran's heritage of the classical world. This response has been seen in theatre practices in Iran, including recent stagings of ancient plays, such as *Antigone* (441 BCE), as well as scholars in Iran referencing classicism as a meeting point between countries and cultures. In this regard, one could view *Self-Service* engaged in several dialogues, spanning all three venues of the global, local and transnational, despite the message and interpretation seeming to be specifically about Iran in allegorical fashion, which is probably why its repeated performance abroad has been so successful worldwide. In comparison, Fitzpatrick sees this work as inherently pointing to global dispersion, of 'dissemination without the promise of taking root or regrowth, exile without repatriation or return', as the irreparable shards of the carpets are taken away by visitors to destinations unknown.[47]

The transnational

Political repercussions and non-viability on the art markets are not the only obstacles when it comes to encouraging performance art in Iran. When I asked Motevalli why there was a lack of performance art on the art market, especially for 'Contemporary Iranian Art', she replied, 'Objects are easier to transport than bodies.'[48] Motevalli's response resonates with the difficulty for Iran-based artists who have sought visas, especially during harsh American and European sanctions. For instance, in October 2013, the Asia Society held a symposium entitled *Iran: Art and Discourse*, and both artist Sohrab Kashani (1989–) and art historian Hamid Keshmirshekan were scheduled to speak at the event, but because Kashani did not receive a visa to attend, and Keshmirshekan's visa came too late, both had to Skype into the symposium.[49] What this implies is that unless the relic of the performance can be sold on the market or exhibited in museums or galleries, performance art stays in Iran unless artists travel, such as Razavipour's *Self-Service*, which was reproduced globally, including Tehran, Roda Sten, Delhi and Paris, and Kashani's persona of *Super Sohrab* – the mundane hero who is a modern millennial on Facebook and Skype – which was performed in Geneva, Istanbul, Rustavi, Tehran and Yerevan (Figures 7.6 and 7.7).

In contrast, Barbad Golshiri's *Cura: The Rise and Fall of Aplasticism* (2011) was specifically performed in the Solyanka State Gallery as part of the *Fourth Moscow Biennial* and not meant to be repeated in Tehran despite Aaran Gallery's

Figure 7.6 Sohrab Kashani. *The Adventures of Super Sohrab*, 2014. Performance, Geneva. Courtesy of the artist.

Figure 7.7 Sohrab Kashani. *The Adventures of Super Sohrab*, 2011. Performance, Istanbul. Courtesy of the artist.

announcement of it (Figure 7.8).⁵⁰ The performance itself was very intense, both physically and philosophically, comprising several components. Golshiri was dressed in black head-to-toe and sat in a replica of Kazimir Malevich's showroom during the *Last Futurist Exhibition of Paintings 0.10* (1915), but only traces or shadows of the original artwork, as well as the nails, remained. Much like Malevich's black square that awaits liberation from the artist, Golshiri had a surgeon remove a small piece of skin from his torso, which was then cured (hence *cura*, as well as *kura* – a poetic address that indexes a blind person) and placed into another square that was white and framed in black – the black square's negative.⁵¹ As soon as gallery attendees felt the wound on Golshiri's body, which was coded in Braille, the lights turned off although the overall gallery lighting was dim. Art historian Abbas Daneshvari has described Golshiri's works as ones that deconstruct identity as Golshiri 'erases the presumed foundations of meaning and asserts the absence of essence'.⁵² In a performance that is quite poetic, the artist transforms by becoming one with the artwork, at once immersing and disappearing – indeed, Golshiri has remarked in an interview with Keshmirshekan, 'I replace this kind of "I" with a schizophrenic one lost in inter-textuality.'⁵³

Overall, through this chapter, I hope to have shed some light on performance art in Tehran, as well as nuance it further in relation to performance art produced in other contexts. The origins of performance art are diverse, and in Iran (Neo-)Dadaism has played a dominant role in shaping understandings of

Figure 7.8 Barbad Golshiri. *Cura: The Rise and Fall of Aplasticism*, 2011. Performance, Solyanka State Gallery, *Fourth Moscow Biennial*. Courtesy of the artist and Aaran Gallery.

performance art. Furthermore, performance art as an artistic genre was 'created' only in the twentieth century and is associated with the visual arts – not with theatre or other performing arts despite the similarities they may share. Particular to the Iranian case is that performance art is spatially negotiated somewhat differently than in other countries and cultures by manoeuvring strategically through four prominent spaces: the public, the private, the gallery and the transnational. These spaces require calculated manipulation as they relate to performing the body as an art object. The ways in which the artist disrupts social spaces and challenges viewers through phenomenological confrontations may be taken for granted in other contexts as similar employments of method cannot be applied so easily in Tehran.

As more specialized histories on performance art and site specificity continue to be written on within the discourses of Art History, the complexities of how the body is received and the ideological spaces, in which the body is formed, can be accounted for and incorporated into the narratives. For example, this chapter omitted discussions on gender, ethnicity, religion and class in relation to demarcating spatialized bodies of both the artist and the viewer in Iranian performance art, as these are subjects worthy of their own discussions. Likewise, how performance art operates and what sorts of performances are occurring in other Iranian cities leave much for future discussion and research. This chapter was only one step in the Anglophone world to delineate a few major precepts of performance art in contemporary Iranian art that invite more sophisticated readings of these performances.

8

'NOW IT'S YOUR TURN TO SEE': JAFAR PANAHI'S CINEMATIC INTERVENTION IN HUMAN RIGHTS DISCOURSE

Amy Motlagh

A political filmmaker [...] will always take a political stand. What I do is say to the viewer: 'Look, this is the society we live in. Now it's your turn to see – according to your own perception, your own point of view – where the roots of our shortcomings are; where the sources of our problems lie.' So, in short, through my films I do two things simultaneously: firstly, I nudge my society, so that it starts thinking about itself; and secondly, I provide history with a report.

—Jafar Panahi[1]

In some ways, Jafar Panahi's films appear to be perfect vehicles for the depiction and critique of human rights abuses. Realistic in style and focused steadily on the *mostazafan*, the wretched, of Iranian society, Panahi's films document the suffering of his characters. But the suffering these individuals experience is not the 'spectacular' violence of human rights violations and cannot be referred to any court of justice. Rather, Panahi's films compassionately present the everyday encounters with injustice of people in a society ostensibly committed to radical social justice, but for which there is no arena for redress.

In *Spectacular Rhetoric* (2011), human rights scholar Wendy Hesford proposes that 'the history of human rights can be told as a history of selective and differential visibility, which has positioned certain bodies, populations, and nations as objects of recognition and granted others the power and means to look and to confer recognition.'[2] For Hesford, it follows that the 'spectacle' of human rights representational activism is therefore aimed at making the 'invisible' 'visible' to recognizing nations, especially the United States. Such practices, in her view, may ultimately reproduce violations rather than prohibiting or foreclosing them because they enshrine practices such as witnessing and listening that ultimately validate and re-centre the personhood of the witness/listener rather than the 'victim's'.

Although Hesford primarily considers documentary films in her study, the Panahi feature films I examine here (produced during the Khatami era,

1997–2005) offer an interesting complication of her thesis in that, while they are obviously profoundly invested in 'visibility' and the question of human rights, they decline to offer representations of conventional human rights violation, by which I mean murder, rape and other forms of physical violence; they are also not made exclusively for US or international audiences' consumption. Instead, these films develop a different rhetoric, dramatizing quotidian violations of humanity without direct representation of violence, making an appeal for a view of human rights which transcends both internationalist discourse and the Iranian Republic of Iran's human rights counter-discourse.[3] In doing so, these films complicate our notion of the human rights 'victim', thus eluding one of the traps of representation and recognition that Hesford identifies.

Yet although these films dramatize and demand recognition of perceived injustices, they do not fit neatly into the victim/witness dyad that Hesford recapitulates. Rather, they refuse these easy categories, refusing to present the protagonists as abject victims or the violators as outright monsters; furthermore, they openly complicate the position of the viewer through their deployment of formal techniques, manipulation of genre and self-consciousness of multiple audiences. Subtly engaging the Islamic Republic of Iran's (IRI) human rights discourse of the *mostazafan*, or 'wretched', who are depicted by the IRI as the natural objects of an Islamic human rights discourse, these films do not utilize the 'spectacular rhetoric' of violence, but instead enact what I would call the logic of the quotidian. By following characters' daily, hourly, moment-to-moment encounters with injustice in a circumscribed time frame, these films offer an alternative theory of human rights violation and possible reparation.

Because the IRI has posited its own Islamic human rights discourse as a counter to internationalist human rights discourse, which the IRI paints as yet another form of Western imperialism that it must resist, one focus of these films' criticism is the hypocrisy of the IRI in purporting to develop an 'indigenous' human rights system with the objective to protect the *mostazafan*.[4] The rhetoric of resistance in the IRI regime's rejection of international human rights discourse may be appealing, particularly at this historical moment, when the echoes of Fanon in the notion of *mostazafan* feel reinvigorated by global debates about class, race and systemic violence. Yet, as the films discussed below demonstrate, the IRI regime's behaviour towards the ostensible object of its own human rights discourse is ambivalent and inconsistent. As these values were theoretically embedded in the institutions overseen by the IRI, and with which the characters in these films interact, these films both question the utility of the category of *mostazafan* and critique the way in which those identified by the regime as *mostazafan*, such as those in poverty and veterans of the Iran-Iraq War, are cut off from basic human rights by the material conditions created by the regime's policies and practices.

Selective visibility

In Iran, the restrictions and the expectations placed on film in the post-revolutionary period are enormous. The current censorship regime, embodied in the Ministry of Islamic Culture and Guidance (*Vezarat-e Farhang va Ershad-e Islami*; frequently referred to simply as 'Ershad'), and its sub-unit creative organ, the Farabi Cinema Foundation, as well as *Bonyad-e Mostazafan* (the Foundation for the Dispossessed), perhaps the most powerful non-governmental organization operating in Iran today, have sought to engender an Islamic cinema that embodies the principles of the revolution. This has taken both a prohibitive nature, in the form of censorship, and a creative nature, in the form of the Farabi Cinema Foundation, which historically has selected for training filmmakers in whom the values of the revolution could be instilled.[5] This strong ideological motivation and direction in the training process has had mixed results, producing films and filmmakers who have – overtly or inadvertently – challenged some of these values.[6] Films that have achieved international regard – such as *Where Is the Friend's House*, *The White Balloon*, *Children of Heaven* and *The Colour of Paradise*[7] – often feature children in principal roles and tend to emphasize the virtues of charity, faith, humility and mercy, all characterized as 'Islamic' values which the regime wishes to promote and extol.

However, as the diversity and transgressive nature of post-revolutionary Iranian cinema demonstrates, these values are difficult to legislate. The difficulty of translating and legally codifying in law the values of the revolution has also been demonstrated in the inconsistencies of Iran's legal system and its practices, which have, of necessity, reinstated laws struck down by the revolution in some areas while at the same time broadly interpreting new laws that give leeway to the state in prosecuting individuals or groups it perceives as threats to its authority.[8] Yet the possibility of mercy is codified in the IRI's criminal law and has been used not only to emphasize Islamic virtues domestically but also as a form of indigenous response to international human rights discourse.[9] Yet choices to withhold mercy can also be a form of the state exercising its sovereignty.[10]

One publicly, if awkwardly, staged invocation of this sovereignty has been the regime's treatment of Jafar Panahi, the celebrated director of films such as *Badkonak-e sefid* (*The White Balloon*), *Dayereh* (*The Circle*) and *Afsaid* (*Offside*).[11] In late 2010, Panahi was sentenced to six years of house arrest and a twenty-year ban from filmmaking as retribution for his very visible and international support for the 2009 election protests and his participation in the protests upon his return to Iran. Yet Panahi, under house arrest, has refused to take the sentence passively and indeed has mastered the full strength of international support to challenge the ruling. In 2012, he released the cheekily subversive *In Film Nist* (*This Is not a Film*), whose title is a playful reference to Magritte's *Ceci ne pas une pipe*.[12] The film takes as its subject Panahi's house arrest: it is set exclusively within the confines of Panahi's apartment building and Panahi elaborately performs his sentence, elaborately not 'filming': his son sets up the camera and a friend, the filmmaker Mojtaba Mirtahmasb, visits him to help with the more complicated scenes involving movement from room to room. Within these constraints, Panahi makes *This Is Not a Film* by *not* making a 'film' – Panahi himself uses only the digital camera on his iPhone to record footage; in other words, he does not formally violate the letter of the punishment accorded him, which he decries in a filmed telephone conversation with his lawyer.

However, Panahi has long been a critic of the regime, even though he was trained as a filmmaker in the post-revolutionary educational system and supported by work for the state-affiliated Iranian Broadcasting Channel 2. *This Is Not a Film* is in some ways the culmination of a critique that began years before. Panahi's films have been concerned from the beginning with justice, but also with the quotidian: his films are in the business of pointing out the contradictions not only in the IRI's revolutionary commitment to social justice but also in society's complicity with the regime, which includes not only outright affiliation or support but also simply declining to help, or to see.

While these films do exhibit what the audience is meant to understand as clear violations of these characters' humanity, part of what these films question is whether the violations rise to the category of human rights violations. Is attending a soccer match a human right? Is being able to board a bus without a chaperone or permission a human right? Is being treated kindly by others, allowed one's individual suffering, a human right? By refusing the overt categories of violence that Hesford suggests are dramatized in 'human rights documentaries', Panahi skilfully asks questions about humanity and the possibility of defending it in the face of everyday disregard.

But what if being seen is as problematic as not being seen? These three films demonstrate that visibility can be as, or more, dangerous than being unseen. *The Circle* is set in Tehran's cityscape, showing – as the title implies – journeys that ultimately lead futilely back to the same point at which they began. The film follows a group of women who are connected in ways that are at first obscure: they are dressed in what appears to be a uniform – a blue headscarf and garment, with a black chador that is taken on and off as needed whenever the women are trying to vanish into a crowd. Eventually, they become legible to the viewer as women who know each other from prison and are on their way to prison or have just gotten out. The constraints on them are as women *and* as future/former convicts, but the film suggests that the reasons they have been criminalized have to do with their gender status: in a society where most, if not all, freedoms are prohibited to 'unaccompanied' women, a woman wishing to have freedom of movement must, necessarily and ironically, break the law in order to be free. While this would seem to affirm the use of the 'veiled Muslim woman' as human rights victim critiqued by Hesford, Panahi offers a more complicated analysis of these women's situations and society's complicity with their persecution.

The film begins with the story of Solmaz Gholami, who has just given birth to a girl rather than to a boy. We never see Solmaz, but we watch her mother repeatedly ask the nurse whether the baby is really a girl. She then lies to Solmaz's in-laws, who have come with flowers, saying that she does not know if Solmaz has given birth yet, then privately telling her own family member that it is a girl and she should 'run and tell her uncle', as though to prepare for a crisis. The mother expects that the husband will, at best, divorce Solmaz; the worst is left to our imaginations. At the end of the film, our expectations are realized, though not substantiated, when we hear Solmaz's name being called in the prison cell where many of the film's protagonists end up. Has the time trajectory of the film been reversed to show us that Solmaz, too, is an ex-convict, or are we finding Solmaz now the victim or perpetrator of a crime that has landed her in prison?[13] The theme of birth continues, as we learn that Pari, another one of the women followed in the film, is pregnant and seeking an illegal abortion. She, in turn, watches another woman abandoning the daughter she loves, hoping that she will be taken in by a 'good family'. Instead, the two women watch from behind a car as the girl is taken into the custody of the state by the *Pasdaran*, the bearded militia who haunt the film in green fatigues and Toyota Safaris and whose presence the women dread and flee.

These women selectively become *chadoris*, cloaking themselves in its anonymity when they need to and making themselves indiscernible from the surrounding population. While the *chador* signifies in one way for Western audiences (oppression, etc.), its meaning in a domestic Iranian context is multivalent. For many, the *chador* is a useful tool, allowing them both to take up space and disappear. However, *chadoris* are also figures of fear: historically, as well as in the present, there is an anxiety about what the chador may hide or efface (we see this fear ironically turned on its head and reversed in Offside, when young women abandon the *chador* in favour of another kind of disguise). A symbol both of overt religiosity and oftentimes associated with poverty, since it is in poorer areas that women commonly wear *chadors* and not just a *manteau-rupush*, it is also a cloak that allows these convicted women to pass as normal members of the society and to hide the criminality with which society seeks to label them. Panahi suggests to us that their treatment as convicts is, in fact, reflective of the broader prison conditions in which women in the IRI live: unable to travel without a chaperone, and so on, women are forced by necessity to become outlaws.

In *Crimson Gold*, Hossein is hidden inside a lumbering, heavy body and bloated face. In this body of a *janbaz*, a war veteran, he has become unrecognizable even to those who knew him. His robbery of the jewellery store, which opens the film, is an attempt to become visible to society, but it kills him; or rather, forces him to kill himself.

Hossein dies in the first minutes of the film – before the viewer has a chance to know him or to sympathize with him as a character. We simply watch as he botches the robbery of a jewellery store, murders the store owner and commits suicide. After these horrifying six minutes, the film then undertakes the business of showing us how Hossein has arrived at this moment, cutting back in time to follow Hossein's journey to the climactic moment that ironically opens the film. As the camera follows Hossein through his errands as a pizza delivery man, the viewer learns through his contact with different customers that he is a disabled veteran of the Iran-Iraq War. He has become invisible even to those who once knew him: while making a delivery, he meets a former officer who doesn't recognize him and then guiltily observes that Hossein has changed a great deal. Hossein responds that the cortisone shots he requires to treat his injury have changed him; he hardly recognizes himself. The officer, clearly anxious to not engage further with Hossein, overpays him for the delivery and quickly shuts the door.

Hossein's friend, co-thief and brother-in-law to-be, Ali, does see him and tries to intercede with others on his behalf. He begs the manager of the pizza parlour where they both work not to fire Hossein, reminding him that Hossein is 'sensitive' because of his war trauma, but that he is a good man. The sensitivity that Hossein exhibits is visible to all and seems to inspire fear – not the fear of someone who is overtly dangerous or violent, but the fear inspired by guilt.

Hossein, biking sombrely through the city, seen often by the camera from the front, through the cloudy windshield of his bike, passes by the murals on the walls and billboards of Tehran that immortalize the war's martyrs. In spite of this overt tribute to those who sacrificed themselves in the conflict, Hossein, a living martyr, has no place or respect. He continues to be damaged by a society that cannot or will not find or see him. Ali tells him not to be offended by the patronizing and rude fashion in which the owner of the jewellery shop they will later rob treats him, but Hossein cannot be assuaged, and indeed the overt way in which the shop owner snubs them is echoed in the interactions he has with people as he delivers pizzas and travels through the upper parts of the city, Farmanieh and Za'feranieh. Instead of the sympathy that should be extended to him as a *mostazaf* and *janbaz*, Hossein is treated with contempt or apathy.

Even when people in the moneyed classes who comprise his customer base attempt to be kind, they reveal their indifference to him: their inability to recognize him. The young man in a luxury apartment building who invites him in 'to listen' and 'to share a meal' really does not want to know anything about Hossein. He does not ask him why there are dark shadows under Hossein's eyes, or why he delivers pizza for a living (though he remarks that 'it's midnight, everywhere is closed and no one works now'), or anything about his own life, although he proceeds to reveal to Hossein the details of his failed seduction effort with the young women Hossein sees leaving the building in a huff as he takes up the pizzas. Throughout, Hossein is unfailingly polite, even when mistreated, though as witnesses to the indignities he encounters, the viewer expects him to explode. Although he should be the recipient of mercy, he is more often the one to offer it. He also extends charity to those around him, even those who have wronged him: as he waits under orders of the military police who are arresting young people as they leave a party in a building to which Hossein was to make a delivery, he engages the young soldier standing with him in sympathetic conversation, and finally shares the pizza among the detainees and the police themselves at his own expense.

As the film progresses, it becomes possible to recognize in Hossein the figure of the *luti*, who is woven in and out of Iran's literary and cultural traditions: the man of the street who is strong and able to fight, but who fights not out of pleasure but to defend the weak and the poor. He is both the original revolutionary in his protection of the *mostazafan* and a *mostazaf* himself. However, Hossein is a *luti* deformed by his experience of a world shaped by the Islamic Republic: he can indeed look back to a time before the revolution when women 'wore miniskirts in the street', but there is no place for him in this world. The way in which Hossein's indefinitely postponed marriage to Ali's sister is alluded to – the wedding ring in the stolen bag, the white 'wedding purse' that Hossein buys for her but never delivers, in his desire to steal the jewellery he thinks she deserves for their wedding – only affirms the point that Hossein is damaged beyond repair: if he could marry, he might be recognizable to society as someone with rights as a husband, but without that marriage, he is doomed. He is the excess of which society must now dispose.[14]

Here, Panahi draws on this remembrance of the *luti* as the righter of wrongs, making him the figure sacrificed to maintain the status quo in the system. He is the person most wronged in the system he tries to make right. Hossein tries valiantly to uphold the code of chivalry and honour that is required of the *luti*, but in a system as corrupt of that of the IRI, in which the members of the society he encounters are either complicit with the regime as its direct beneficiaries or have the means to live outside of its strictures within the walls of their beautiful homes. Panahi makes it clear that the only rational choice for a man like Hossein is to kill himself and thus dispose of the excess he constitutes. As Georges Bataille would have it, Hossein is the portion beyond what is necessary for remembering the war: the murals on the walls and billboards of Tehran remember the veterans, and no living spectacle such as that constituted by Hossein is necessary or desirable.[15]

Is attending a soccer game a human right? In *Offside*, the story of the Iran-Bahrain football match and a group of girls who are prohibited from attending, we see the re-enactment of Afsaneh Najmabadi's (2005) reading of anxieties about gender practices and conformity in a modernizing Iran replayed on the contemporary stage. [16] Najmabadi argues that the *amrad*, the beardless youth who is the subject of adult male desire in pre- and early modern poetry and art, becomes the site of modern anxieties about homoeroticism and markers of backwardness. As such, they are transformed from figures of desire to figures of repulsion and perversity.

In *Offside*, the girls featured in the film have dressed up as boys to get into the football match, which they feel is their right to watch. Detected and detained in a pen outside of the stadium by the police, they are suspect not simply because they are breaking the law by dressing as males to enter a space that has been designated as exclusively male but because, in some cases, they seem to be doing at least as good a job at imitating the effect of masculinity as the 'real' male soccer fans and soldiers among whom they are attempting to blend in. The young woman who has donned the uniform of a soldier and managed to get into the official seats is particularly unsettling to the soldiers, who initially also believe she is one of them as she is led to them handcuffed to be penned in with the other girls. Another persuasive prisoner asks the soldier from Tabriz why it is so objectionable for women to attend soccer matches, especially when men and women are permitted to attend movies together. He responds that women are only allowed to go to the cinema in the company of their male family members, and she retorts, 'Okay, what if we came to the matches with our families?' As he tries to explain why that would not be okay, since your husband is not *mahram* to other woman, he stumbles over the word *husband* and asks, 'Hey, are you married?' It is clear that he is attracted to her, and she knows it: boy or girl, she is utterly convinced of her appeal.

Though some critics view this film exclusively as a critique of women's status in Iran, that reading eschews a more complex picture.[17] *Offside* invites us not only into the subject position of the imprisoned girls, straining to participate in the spectacle of the game, but also into the subject position of the soldiers, who are themselves imprisoned by their conscription, serving principles they have been taught are religiously 'correct' but which they cannot reasonably or logically defend. The confrontation between these soldiers, who are meant to be hyper-masculine – the vanguard and symbol of the regime's strength in the masses – and the boy-girls, whose ability to mimic such masculinity with better success, is unsettling for the soldiers. One responds by yelling his replies to the girls' incessant questions about why they are not permitted to enter; another is alternately contrite, agreeing to narrate the game for the girls from his vantage point by the door and later shouting at them that they do not understand the position the soldiers are in. These boy-soldiers, themselves clean-shaven and thin, actually look a great deal like their female detainees. Indeed, the difference between the smooth talker who says she has been to Tehran and the soldier she is flirting with is almost non-existent. They could both be *amrads*.

By invoking the counterfeit *amrad* – a symbol perverted and converted here to new use – as the agent of justice in this story, the film offers a complex reading of the injustices committed by the regime in Iran. Though seemingly trivial in aim – a football match – the girls' efforts to subvert the patriarchal order have deeper resonances. The film ends with the crowd, in its ecstasy over Iran's victory in the football match, inadvertently intervening as the girls are driven to jail to be booked. Paused in traffic, a reveller boards the bus to offer around sweets and then the crowd outside begins to shout for the soldiers to join the dancing and pulls them off the bus. The prisoners quickly decide to make their escape. As they make their way through the crowd, now no longer criminals but just members of this common entity, the young woman with whom the journey by bus to the stadium began holds eight sparklers to commemorate the Iranians killed in the Iran-Japan match above her head as the anthem '*Ey Irān*' plays on a loudspeaker. The camera follows behind her as she disappears, but for the sparklers, the sound of the anthem heightens the effect of this small gesture of defiance even as the crowd seems to reduce it to being meaningless.

Refusing the spectacle

Although this chapter has focused narrowly on three films from the height of the reform era of Khatami's presidency, looking back to Panahi's first feature film, the celebrated *The White Balloon*, one can already see evidence of his interest in visibility and invisibility. The action of the film is compressed to a few hours – in fact, the last hours of the old year on the day before Nowruz – in a neighbourhood in lower Tehran. Child protagonist Razieh certainly is treated differently because she is a girl, but the film refuses easy identification as a 'women's rights' film. We watch Razieh's face in close-ups as she experiences the indignities of being a child and a girl, but Panahi refuses to let the viewer see her simply as 'oppressed'. Using what tools are available to her (tears, persistence, a winning smile), she prevails on her mother to get her a 'big fat fish' for the Nowruz sofreh, instead of the 'skinny' ones her mother offers from the family's own courtyard pool. Except for the specificities of the holiday and the setting, this scene of negotiation for a desired object between mother and child could occur anywhere. Its universality *and* its particularity are what make the film so important and effective. In the very beginning of the film, we hear, in a strange collapse or questioning of diegetic and extradiegetic sound, the radio broadcasting the New Year's countdown and see Razieh in the streets near their home, holding the blue balloon her mother has purchased for her, perhaps as a reward for good behaviour (which we see is premature, given what follows) during a shopping trip. As Panahi has noted, 'I wanted people to wonder why the balloon we see is blue when the title is *The White Balloon*.'[18] In fact, the title is meant to draw our attention to the balloon seller, an Afghan refugee who, unlike all the other characters in the film, is utterly without refuge. At the end of the film, the soundtrack again collapses the distance of diegetic and extradiegetic sound with the fatuous, familiar voice of the radio broadcast, now counting down the final seconds of the old year as everyone runs home except the Afghan boy, who sits down with his lone balloon.

These films are not exclusively a critique of the IRI and its hypocritical stance with regard to the *mostazafan*; they are also critical of that very human rights discourse which ostensibly defends the rights of the dispossessed worldwide but may also, ironically, enable perpetuation of abuses of human rights and evasion of justice. Further, although Panahi's films depend fundamentally on the visual to incite viewers to sympathy, they do not traffic in the 'spectacular rhetoric' of conventional human rights activism, eschewing representations of outright violence against purported human rights victims. Instead, Panahi uses the opportunities, if they can be called that, afforded by both systems – what Slaughter calls 'Human Rights, Inc.' (the internationalist human rights movement) on the one hand, and on the other, the IRI's insistence on indigenous, Islamic human rights whose object of ministration is the *mostazafan* – to criticize the ideation of human rights both by the IRI and by the international human rights movement. Panahi is particular but not unique, part of a broader panoply of Iranian filmmakers who are engaging the hypocrisies of both systems. Through cinematic performance of injustices that cannot be remediated, Panahi's films put the lie not only to the "indigenous" human rights discourse asserted by the IRI but also to the hypocrisy of an international human rights movement that refuses to acknowledge its own paradoxes and hypocrisies.

9

PERSISTENCE AS PERFORMATIVE: A BRIEF HISTORY OF THE EVOLUTION OF TWO ROCK MUSIC SCENES IN IRAN

Siavash Rokni

Introduction

This chapter traces the rise of rock music as a scene in Iran from the early 1990s until the first decade of the twenty-first century. I look at two generations of rock musicians. The first consists of musicians that were active during the 1990s and early 2000s. This includes a look at the rise of music produced by those who saw the revolution in their childhood. The second period covers the timeline typical of most articles written about rock music in Iran. This is the period of the presidency of Mohammad Khatami (1997–2005) and the cultural thaw that followed it. Here, there will be a focus on two main rock music scenes that developed in this period of time, namely Tehran and Mashhad. I conclude by looking at how the bases laid by these two generations of musicians paved the way for the acceptance of rock as a permitted genre of music in Iran. Taking the argument of Laudan Nooshin on the subject of fetishization of resistance, I propose the term 'persistence' as a terminology that better suits the cultural and musical practices of Iranian rock musicians at the time.[1] I thus argue that Iranian rock musicians performed 'persistence', the practice of constantly persisting their presence as an inevitable reality while negotiating it with the Iranian authorities through different cultural practices. Persistence, in this context, is part of what Michel de Certeau calls 'tactics', a set of practices of finding different ways to adapting to an environment proposed by a given power. This is important because the notion frames a scene around ideas of negotiations and adaptations to different situations instead of framing it within a continuum of antagonism. The main reason why I am attracted to this subject in the first place is because I am a musician who has followed the developments in Iranian music since the late 1990s. As someone who learned music in Iran and grew up there till the late 1990s, I experienced the changes that took place in regard to the relaxation of music during this decade. As a small kid, I performed in places like Bahman Cultural Centre and I had the pleasure of experiencing my first live music show in Iran when I went to see the band Avizheh in Arasbaran cultural centre with my friend Kaveh. The constant in all of these experiences has been that I have followed the evolution of music genres in Iran even though I have not been there since 2003.

As a performer, my understanding of performance comes with a baggage of experiences that have framed performance as a rehearsed act that one merits to showcase by way of perfecting a craft through repetition and continuous learning. As an academic, I came to open my mind about performance when I was exposed to performance studies as a subject, whereby looking at performance goes beyond just looking at an artist performing an act. In *Performance Studies: An Introduction*, Richard Schechner[2] broadens the definition of performance from an artistic/aesthetic perspective and looks at how the ways of doing and being in everyday life can be treated as different forms of performances. Thus, performance is not simply limited to a practice that requires a stage or an audience whereby a performer performs an act and an audience observes the performance. Instead, one can broaden the idea of performance by looking at how different activities can be treated as performances. In this sense, different forms of practices can be treated as performances depending on how we observe the practices and the framework that we use to look at them. For the purpose of this chapter, I understand performative as the way one embodies certain behaviours and articulates them using different texts. I observe the way the musicians from two rock music scenes in Iran embodied persistence as performative and used it as a way to exist and negotiate their existence with a rigid power structure, the Ershad.

Before the revolution

One of the most prominent features of the Pahlavi dynasty (1925–79) was the decision of both monarchs, Reza Shah (1925–41) and his son Mohammad Reza Shah (1941–79), to drastically modernize the country not only in terms of infrastructure (building of roads, bridges, etc.) but also culturally (development of cinema, radio and later television). The cultural modernization revolved around the idea of Westernizing cultural products and practices introduced in the Iranian society. Music did not escape this process. By the mid- to late 1960s, Iranian popular music slowly formed its particular genre. This music was heavily promoted in the radio and television and supported by the state. The idea behind funding and promoting this music was in accordance with the cultural politics of the Pahlavi regime, which was looking at different ways of modernizing Iran. This promoted a peculiar ideology whereby modernization and Westernization became 'inextricably linked, creating a polarisation that can still be felt today'.[3] The 1960s and 1970s gave rise to a new kind of popular music where many pop musicians, such as Googoosh, Ebi and Hayedeh, became stars.[4]

While not as popular, the first signs of rock music in Iran began during the same period. For instance, the band Black Cats began covering Western music and performing it in different venues in Tehran. At the same time, garage bands began to pop up in urban centres and performed original music based on the Western garage rock riffs mixed with Persian 6/8 rhythms. Bands such as Littles, Owjubehā, Mohājemin, The Rebels and The Golden Rings are a few names that can be mentioned here. One of the most important rock musicians who reached stardom during this time was Kourosh Yaghmaie. Known as one of the founding fathers of rock music in Iran, Kourosh reached a level of popularity that other rock bands did not achieve with hit songs such as 'Gol-e Yakh' (Ice Flower) and 'Leila'. While the influence of Western rock and its techniques is clearly heard in Yaghmaie's music, it has very distinct characteristics that are Iranian, including the usage of Persian poetry as well as modal melodies. Other notable artists of the time are Fereydoon Forooghi and Farhad Mehrdad (who popularized the singer-songwriter genre) and Abbas Mehrpouya (who was one of the first fusion musicians of Iran).

After the revolution

The 1979 revolution gave rise to a new regime that saw Western culture as something toxic that was destroying and plaguing authentic Iranian culture.[5] The new regime began a project of societal disciplining in order to create an ideal society that is in line with the values of Shi'i Islam. Music, and specially Western-influenced music such as pop and rock, was heavily impacted after the revolution because it was associated with Westernization, imperialism and moral corruption.[6] Hence, the 'entire industry of popular culture went underground or into exile'.[7] Lost Angeles, having the biggest population of Iranians outside of the country, became the cultural centre of popular culture, including popular music.[8] Many pop stars, musicians, composers and producers from pre-revolution Iran moved there to continue producing music and keeping the music scene that was created during the Shah period alive by turning Los Angeles into the hub of Persian pop music from the 1980s onwards.[9] Interestingly, Iranian rock music did not continue its work in Los Angeles, and there was, to my knowledge, no Los Angeles Iranian rock music scene that developed in the 1980s. Indeed, there is no clear analysis of why such an event did not happen. One explanation may be that most rock musicians of the time did not leave the country and were silenced for at least the first decade and a half after the revolution.[10]

In Iran, almost all forms of music were banned. Any music 'that suggested dance movement or included solo female singing was prohibited'.[11] Western popular music in the broadest sense and Iranian pop were targeted and banned outright immediately after the revolution.[12] At the time, right after the revolution, we see the emergence of a new set of vocabulary whereby the influence of *farhang-e Biganengān*, or foreign culture, needed to be addressed through *nowsazi- ye farhangi*, or cultural reconstruction.[13] In 1979, addressing the state's radio employees, Ayatollah Khomeini compared music to opium and stated, 'If you want your country to be independent, from now on you must transform radio and television into educational instruments – eliminate music.'[14] Only certain music such as religious music or the military-style choir music, *Sorud*, was permitted to be performed and played publicly or on national television.[15] Meanwhile, many Iranians continued listening to non-official music in private since 'despite all measures designed to combat music, it could not be eliminated from Iranian culture'.[16]

The new proper and the Ershad

The post-revolution government in Iran created its own ways of instituting the normalization of cultural practices by establishing organizations that acted as what Michel de Certeau calls *Strategies*: 'the calculus of force-relationships which becomes possible when a subject of will and power, a proprietor, an enterprise, a city, a scientific institution, can be isolated from an environment'.[17] The regime that came into power after the 1979 revolution in Iran spent a great amount of energy and resources on controlling and managing culture and cultural practices of Iranians in every aspect of their lives. This began with the creation of the Cultural Revolution Committee.[18] During the first half of the 1980s, control over cultural production as well as cultural practices increased. By 1986, the Ministry of Culture and Islamic Guidance, known as Ershad, was created as the largest governmental body for the management of cultural practices.[19] Besides Ershad, two other governmental bodies are responsible for the evaluation and distribution of music: Seda va Simā (Iranian Radio and Television), and Howze-ye Honari (Arts Foundation).[20] What this did was to institutionalize censorship in the country by means of transferring the control of decision-making regarding music in the hands of these official organizations. Another impact of this was the confusion that it created in terms of the interpretation of what music can be allowed in the country. What I mean by this is that while one organization may reject an album, another may decide to accept and publish it. This was indeed the case of Mohsen Namjoo's album *Toranj*, whereby the album was rejected by the Ershad but was published by Howze-ye Honari.

As de Certeau states, 'strategy' is a 'calculus of force-relationships' that is 'isolated from an environment' and that it 'assumes a place' in the proper. From this, we can treat Ershad as a governmental body that functions as a strategy within the proper, the Islamic Republic system. What is important about Ershad as a 'strategy' is that it, first, exists as a physical entity that is representing the interests of the power in place; second, manages and controls any cultural practice by means of evaluating its accordance with Sharia law and approving it for public distribution; and third, functions as part of a larger power relationship that decides on the accordance of different cultural practices with Sharia law. As one of the three organizations that evaluate cultural products and practices and make a final decision on their publication and distribution publicly, Ershad has certain authoritative power when it comes to determining suitable cultural practices. However, it is part of a larger power relationship that rises from the interpretation of different religious leaders, organizations and authorities in the country in regard to the permissibility of different cultural practices. This is the difference between the second and the third point, because while Ershad has a certain authority that gives it power, such authority is not really fixed, and it is dependent on the power relationship that it functions within.

Towards a different direction

In 1989, Ayatollah Khomeini decided to 'go back on his absolute ban on music by issuing a *fatwa* (a religious decree establishing the licit or non-licit character of an act) authorizing the purchase and sale of instruments'.²¹ We see the instability of strategy in action here since what seemed to be completely forbidden at the beginning of the revolution became somewhat more legal by the end of the first decade following it. Interestingly, what became legal was the purchase and sale of instruments since the permissibility of music in Islam is an ambiguous topic. The main argument against music in Islam comes from the verses in Qur'an which advise Muslims to abstain from *lahw al-hadith* (idle talk), which 'conservative Islamic scholars have interpreted to mean music, espousing the view that music is "futile folly".'²² What seems to be at issue in the interpretation of the lawfulness of music is the content of the music, the lyrics. As Ayatollah Khamenei states, 'Profane singing (*ghana*) which is unlawful in the Islamic Shari'a, indeed refers to content not to form. Basically, when you are searching for instances of profane singing (*ghana*), you should study the song with regard to its content and not form, to ascertain whether it is lawful or unlawful.'²³ Another issue that normally comes up in the discussion on permissible music in Islam is that music should not provoke or promote activities that are un-Islamic or sinful. For example, Ayatollah Khomeini has stated that 'music that is *motreb* [causes *tarab*] is *haram* (not permissible), and voices that are *mashkuk* (doubtful, open to interpretation, questionable) are not prohibited'.²⁴ Such line of thinking exists among other religious leaders, such as Abdul-Karim Mousavi Ardebili and Yousef Saanei, who take cautious positions in regard to music by stating that music that causes unlawful activities or that has satanic or anti-religious nature is not permissible.²⁵ Added to all this is an agreement among Islamic scholars that the responsibility of determining the way music impacts one is on the individual who listens to it.

There are two issues at hand here. The first is that even though the responsibility of the judgement on the way music would influence an individual is on the individual, the Iranian government leaves that judgement to an institution. More importantly, this institution does not have clear guidelines as to what is or is not acceptable.²⁶ On one side, this has left musicians in a sort of bureaucratic limbo, whereby they would not know whether their music is accepted by the authorities. At the same time, this lack of clarity has left a space for negotiation for many genres of music, including rock. I look at the history of rock in Iran from two main perspectives. The first shows that rock in Iran has been evolving as a collection of multiple music scenes since the early 1990s. By giving attention to Tehran and Mashhad rock scenes, I show how they contribute to the development of the music genre in Iran in their own way. In this sense, they are as much separated as they are connected to one another in shaping the development of rock music in Iran.

Early 1990s

The earliest rock album that I was able to find in my research is called *Khodā* and was produced in 1991 by Arash Mitooie. A well-respected Iranian guitar player, Arash recorded the album on a two-track reel-to-reel tape and distributed it within a network of close friends.[27] The album was greatly influenced by the late 1970s and early 1980s rock as well as by blues. It was recorded in collaboration with another important Iranian musician, Babak Khiavchi, who later started the famous rock band Kiosk with Arash Sobhani. Mitooie released a second album, *Hafez*, in 1993 with Shahram Sharbaf, who later formed O-Hum. *Hafez* was probably one of the first attempts to mix the poetry of Hafez with rock music. The album was very important in inspiring many Iranian musicians to try to mix rock music with Persian poetry. In fact, the band O-Hum did exactly that in late 1990s. It is heavily influenced by 1970s rock music from bands such as Pink Floyd and Camel and musicians such as Eric Clapton and Mark Knofler. At the same time, the elements of Persian music are very evident in the music, especially in the rhythm section. For instance, while the song *Zahed* takes influence from Pink Floyd's music in its guitar solo, it is composed in 7/4 rhythm, a common meter in Persian traditional music. Also, the song *Ta ze meykhaneh* begins in the Persian style 6/8 rhythm and continuing with a guitar solo while it shifts to a 12 bar blues in 4/4 in the second half of the song.

The creation of Bam Studio, later Bamahang Productions, in 1996–7 was an important event that helped shape the post-revolution rock scene in Iran. The studio was created as a hobby project by a group of musicians and sound engineers in a bunker that was used during the Iran-Iraq War in Tehran.[28] It became the regular practice space for a band called Avizheh. The band was a *talfiqi* (fusion) music group that mixed Western instrumentation and musical style with Persian classical music and instrumentation. The term *talfiqi* was very important at the time since it implied that the seriousness of music is not being lost to the usage of Western instrumentation and musical styles. What I mean by this is that the association to Western instrumentation and musical genres as something that is negative was being negotiated through *talfiqi* as a discourse. *Talfiqi* was exploring the fusion of traditional Iranian music with genres such as jazz and rock while escaping the labelling game that would limit its activities publicly. The terminology also fitted the discourse of President Khatami at the time around the notion of the 'dialogue between civilizations'. Avizheh's music experimented greatly with timber and rhythm in order to fuse Persian classical music with jazz and rock. The song *Balooch*, from Avizheh's album by the same name, begins with a musical phrase played by the *santoor* (the Persian hammered dulcimer) that is accompanied by drums and bass. The phrase is then developed by the *kamancheh* (a Persian bowed string instrument) and is then followed with a question response between the two instruments. The song takes great influence from jazz music in its form in that it begins with a melody and is followed with improvisations by each instrument. What makes this music interesting is that it blurs the borders between traditional Iranian, rock and jazz music. Avizheh's music was the result of a need for creating transnational conversations in a very limited Iranian music scene due to governmental restrictions.

According to Reza Moghaddas, one of the founders of the studio, the space was largely used for recording and mixing music for film, while some days were set aside to invite local bands to practise their music and record them. Many of the first generations of Iranian rock bands came out of this studio because of two obvious reasons. First, the space was provided to them for a low price in order to help them do what they normally would not be able to do, which is playing music loudly. Hence, it provided many rock musicians with the space they needed for practising and recording their music. Second, it became a networking space for musicians to meet and exchange ideas with one another. This led Bam studio to become a hub for a variety of genres of music.

The development of Bam Studio and the rise of *talfiqi* music in the mid-1990s can be seen as tactics in relations to strategies developed since the 1980s. De Certeau provides certain characteristics for tactics. Tactics function within the proper and they are part of everyday life. However, they do not assume space within the proper in the same way that strategies do. Instead, they belong to 'the other' and they insinuate themselves 'into the other's place,fragmentarily, without taking it over its entirety, without being able to keep it at a distance'.[29] What de Certeau means by this is that tactics do not control space because the space is already dominated by strategies. Instead, they depend on time. As he states, 'a tactic depends on time- it is always on the watch for opportunities that must be seized 'on the wing'. Whatever it wins, it does not keep. It must constantly manipulate events in order to turn them into opportunities.[30] Therefore, tactics manoeuver around strategy by constantly proposing new ways of thinking and doing. They do so by using opportunities and opportune moments. In other words, tactics use what the Greeks call *Kairos*. *Kairos* is a concept used commonly in rhetoric as a technique of seizing the opportune moment. One can understand it by looking at it in relation to *chronos*, or chronological time. However, the two concepts are not oppositional but relational in the sense that they complement one another. Miller argues that 'Kairos refers not to the specific responsiveness of discourse to situation but to the dynamic relation between discourse and situation'.[31] De Certeau's idea about how tactics manipulate events in order to turn them into opportunities ties greatly with the notion of *kairos*. Tactics seek to constantly seize the moment, the opportunity, in order to use it to their advantage. According to Miller, *Kairos* 'tells us to look for the particular opportunity in a given moment, to find – or construct – an opening in the here and now, in order to achieve something, there and then'.[32] Hence, it is not just the moment but also the usage of the moment, and how it is used, that makes the moment precious.

The musicians who began Bam studio were using the opportune moment created by the changes in the attitude of the government in power towards music in order to develop a space for producing new genres of music. By using *talfiqi* as a discourse, they were able to introduce the jazz and rock sounds without calling the music by those names. Thus, they were able to negotiate sounds through the usage of an ambiguous discourse, *talfiqi* music. This was an effective way to negotiate without articulating. *Talfiqi* became an exploratory movement in creating a new Iranian sound that respected its past while adding elements from different music genres such as rock, which was at the time not officially sanctioned by the Ershad. What is very apparent in the development of *Bamahang* studio is the fact that those who created it were an interconnected group of musicians who were slowly developing a music scene.

The release of Nahal-e Heyrat

The election of President Khatami in 1997 saw many changes within the cultural politics of Iran. For music, the most important change was the reduction of government restrictions on cultural products.[33] In terms of communication infrastructure, an increase in access to the Internet and mobile phones had great social impact on the way people communicated with one another inside and outside of the country. In addition, the government's cultural thaw paved the way for the introduction of official pop music in the country. Musicians such as Shadmehr Aghili and bands such as Aria Band were given permission to produce and distribute their albums legally with music that resembled the more upbeat pop rhythms that would be found in *Los angelesi pop*.[34] Efforts such as dedicating a radio channel to music, an increase in the number of permissions for public concerts and a boost in the cassette and CD industry were implemented to create a local music industry. Rock music, however, stood in the periphery and was considered mostly illegal. In 1999, the bassist of Avizhe, Babak Riahipour, Shahram Sharbaf and Shahrokh Izadkhah formed a band called O-Hum, recorded the album *Nahal-e Heyrat* and went to Ershad for acquiring permission. Describing their music as 'western' and 'cheap', Ershad rejected the album by arguing that it is 'out of their music standards'. Seeing that they cannot get permission, the band launched their own website and released the album on the Persian new year for free as a new year's gift to Iranians around the world.[35] Indeed, the release of the album online was not as surprising considering the fact that the internet was being commonly used for other reasons, such as blogging, for several years. What was interesting was the usage of the opportune moment in order to gain visibility and show others the possibility of using the internet as a music distribution tool. This is indeed linked back to the idea of *kairos* and the usage of an opportune moment as a way to navigate a situation. Moreover, O-Hum's move was under the pretence that such an action is not illegal considering that no laws were written to ban musicians from using the internet as a channel of distribution. Lastly, we can look at the role of the affective relationship of musicians to their labour in music production as a motivation for releasing the album online. Producing a music album is an extremely time-consuming and labour-intensive process, and not being able to release an album after its production is extremely heart-breaking and frustrating for those who worked on it. Hence, the band took the opportunity of using the internet to at least release their album so that the labour used in its production was not completely wasted. In other words, the economy of music production and the affective relationship to the work put in producing music have as much of a role in Oh-Hum's album release as the politics of it. Thus, the release of the album was part of a process of finding new avenues to share and distribute music so that the labour of music production does not go to waste.

O-Hum did not profit from releasing their album online. However, they did open a Pandora's box by showing the possibility of the usage of the internet as a place to share music. One year after the release of *Nahal-e Heyrat*, Tehranavenue. com, an Iranian blog managed and ran from Tehran, launched Underground Music Competition (UMC) as an avenue for Iranian artists to submit their music for competition.[36] Its aim was to 'introduce new talents and non-official musical currents, the centralisation of scattered efforts to encourage synergy between various bands'.[37] Since most bands were recording their music in DIY studios, the recording quality of much of the music was not professional. However, the festival's 'reception among Iranian youth was nothing less than spectacular'[38] since the festival 'provided a venue through which underground artists obtain recognition and feedback from the audience'.[39] This showed many Iranian artists that they are not alone in producing homegrown music.

The emergence of rock music, and other genres such as rap, was a natural response to a vacuum of Iranian musical genres between the *los angelesi* music and official pop music industries. By the 1990s, these genres were no longer satisfactory for many Iranian youth who were listening to diverse genres of music from different parts of the world. These factors really fuelled a generation of musicians to seek different sounds. The Iranian post-revolution rock scene began as a grassroots movement of artists who made the best of what was available to them in order to negotiate with the *strategy* in a governmental system that seemed to be resistant to change. The development of Bam Studio began a core network of musicians who formed the first generation of rock bands in Iran. The early to mid-2000s came to represent a new generation of rock musicians in Iran. This is the time when an exponential growth in the rock music scene began to emerge in the country. In the next sections, I examine the Tehran and Mashhad Rock scene as examples of music scenes that evolved during this time.

Tehran's scene

Will Straw provides three main characteristics for determining a scene. First, they are cultural unities with an imprecise and ambiguous boundary.[40] Second, they are anti-essentializing in the sense that those who follow them need to 'observe a hazy coherence between sets of practices of affinities'.[41] The word 'anti-essentializing' is important here because it tries to escape from a pure and concrete definition of a scene. Instead, one feels that they belong to a scene on the basis of the practices and cultural affinities that they share with others in the same scene. Finally, scenes evoke a sense of community and cosmopolitan lifestyle. When looking at what was happening in Tehran since mid-1990s with Bam Studio, what we see is indeed the rise of a rock music scene in Tehran. With the release of *Nahal-e Heyrat* and the Tehran Avenue music competition, Tehran's music scene slowly expanded to include new bands that were not part of the core group from Bam Studio. Most of the academic and journalistic literature on the topic of rock music in Iran starts from this point forward.

Tehran's rock scene is the most studied music scene in Iran. For one, Tehran is the most populated and cosmopolitan city in Iran. Furthermore, many of the first bands that were able to share their music online came from Tehran. Another reason was the fact that being a rock musician is not cheap. Thus, those who were able to play rock music came from more affluent families since they were the ones with enough financial capacity to afford musical instruments and spaces needed for performing this type of music. As Robertson observes, 'the unofficial music scene constitutes a small minority of Tehran's vast population and its visibility within Iran is limited'.[42] Lastly, being in the largest city and the capital of the country has its advantages since there are more people and more venues to play music. Hence, musicians began to find different places to perform for a small public. Meanwhile, many rock musicians began releasing their live performances on YouTube and creating and sharing music videos online.

Tehran rock musicians at this stage were trying to challenge 'the aesthetic norms of mainstream pop' while offering 'a space for the expression of a growing youth consciousness'.[43] This began to create a discussion on what Iranian rock means and how one must approach it. Do Iranian rock musicians have to sing in Persian? What kind of sound is considered Iranian rock? How can the Iranian identity be seen in rock music? All these questions revolved around the themes of music and identity. Bronwen Robertson explores these questions in her book by speaking with several Tehrani rock musicians. Robertson observes how Tehran shaped the sound of the music that came out of the city. One of her research participants reiterated that '[Tehran] makes me, and therefore my music, a little angrier and more depressed. Although I must say there's no guarantee that if I was playing music in another country, I'd be any happier'.[44] Official Bands such as Meera and Barad kept on pushing the boundaries of *talfiqi* music by mixing rock with *sonnati* and folk music, respectively. Others, such as Mirza, took to the route of exploring blues music with Persian poetry. Some bands preferred imitating a genre of music. For example, Ballgard's music greatly resembled that of Red Hot Chilli Peppers.

In the quest for identity, 127 Band, and their album *Khal Punk*, was probably one the greatest examples of mixing the question of identity and music together. 127 was one of the bands that was able to have a long-term presence in Tehran's rock scene and extended this presence internationally while staying an unofficial band the whole time. The band's first two albums were in English, while they made a switch to Persian in their third and fourth album. 127 was successful in attracting international attention by producing original music that had 'an Iranian air'.[45] The music style was also unique. While the first two albums were more of a classic rock style that sounded like 'Odes to Bob Dylan',[46] their later music albums were more of a critique of *los angelesi* pop music and an ode to *motrebi* and *ruhowzi* music. In this sense, they not only had a critique of life as a young person in Iran but also satirically critiqued both LA and official popular music of the time.

What Tehran's rock scene did in the early 2000s was to create a musical identity that came out of a cosmopolitan city. Besides the cosmopolitan sound, this scene used the internet to their advantage for promoting themselves and sharing their music. Moreover, with the introduction of YouTube, many of these bands began to share their music videos and live sets online. Hence, the visual followed the sound as platforms such as YouTube made sharing of videos online easier. Lastly, Tehrani rock musicians used different avenues to make their music heard and available to the public. Besides using the internet, many bands tried performing at venues that didn't require government authorization, such as Farabi Hall in Tehran's Daneshgah-e Honar (Art University) or Honarestan-e Melli (Tehran Conservatory).[47] In this sense, these bands practised tactics by using multiple ways of doing what they could within the rigid structure of Iran in order to find ways to reach their audience and negotiate their legitimacy.

Mashhad's scene

Mashhad is a city in Iran in the northeastern province of Khorasan. It is a religiously important city because of the presence of the tomb of Imam Reza, the eighth Shi'i Imam. This means that the city homes a large religious community. Since the city is small, its rock scene consisted of a close network of musicians and music enthusiasts that began finding each other and collaborating with one another. As Abdi Behravanfar states in his interview with Manoto1 channel, 'Mashhad, in comparison to Tehran, is a smaller city and we know the musicians of the city [...] so we could attract an audience. Also, from experience, we saw that this music could be attractive to the public as well'.[48] This closeness produced a music scene that was different in sentiment from Tehran. On one side, many musicians in Mashhad were university students who were temporarily there for school. As Kaveh Afghan, one of the members of The Ways, recalls, 'some strange and fascinating people gathered together, each with their own thoughts and desires and as everyone knows about rock music one can act better in rock atmosphere for some idealisms so everybody was attracted to rock music [...] and we were not exception. It was actually an unintentional effect from the atmosphere'.[49]

Just like Tehran's music scene, which was supported by the core group that began Bam Studio in the mid-1990s, Mashhad had its own core group and the person who held this together was Abdi Behravanfar. Abdi, originally from Mashhad, began playing music in Tehran, where he was studying industrial engineering at Azad University. When he returned to Mashhad, to make a living, he began to sell copies of his CD collection to music enthusiasts. This allowed him to meet local musicians and collaborate with them on different musical projects. To put it in his own words, 'any of the musicians in Mashhad regarded my house as their hangout. There virtually wasn't a musician in Mashhad who didn't know that house'.[50] While he was constantly harassed by the police, he continued to use his house as a space for exploring and playing music. By the early 2000s, Abdi began forming a band that was later named MudBand. The band began performing in different venues around the city such as Golestan and Helal-Ahmar Hall in the early 2000s.[51] It is at this time that he began collaborating with Mohsen Namjoo and co-wrote many songs with him in the span of a few years. Sonically, MudBand was heavily influenced by blues, rock and folk music. Moreover, the music was also influenced by the folk music of Khorasan. The band was innovative in many ways in pushing the sonic boundaries of rock music in Iran by trying to find a unique sonic identity that was local and yet part of a larger movement. By 2003, MudBand was banned by the government. Although they never succeeded in releasing an official album, they continued to play and record music together and released two unofficial albums: *Shalamroud* and *Kokheo & Kalakhet,* in 2008 and 2009, respectively. The song *In!*, for instance, in the album *Kokheo & Kalakhet*, explores unique usage of timber by using a traditional instrument with modern Western instruments. It begins with a riff by guitar, bass and drums as accompaniments to a solo by Zorna (a Persian double reed instrument with a very high pitch sound). The usage of the Zorna solo in the music adds a flavour of regional Khorasani in the timber of the song. MudBand's only official recordings were made with Mohsen Namjoo when the band played on Namjoo's *Toranj* album.[52] Released in 2009, Toranj was probably the most popular and influential *Talfiqi Rock* (Fusion Rock) albums of the twenty-first century in Iran. By deconstructing Persian classical music and poetry and mixing it with rock and blues music, the album created controversies in the music scene in Iran.[53] While the album was rejected by Ershad, it was given permission for public release by *Hozeh Honari* in 2008 since the institution was working on a project called 'Three Mohsens'.[54]

Besides having an active role in motivating the rock scene in Mashhad, Abdi was one of the first musicians who took his music to the streets as a street musician. Abdi's act of performing with his guitar in the streets of Iran was something very new at the time. The act was very influential in demystifying music performance as a private experience by bringing it to the streets. This was indeed a very important contribution not only to Mashhad's rock scene but also to the Iranian music scene in general.

There were many similarities between what happened in Mashhad in comparison to Tehran. For one, the use of spaces that did not require permission by both scenes allowed musicians to perform live for an audience, albeit small. While both scenes saw multiple crackdowns of many of their shows, their persistence in continuing regardless of the consequences was key in normalizing the sound of rock in Iranian public space. While the process was slow and faced many struggles, its continuation was key in negotiating for the existence and legitimacy of rock in the public sphere. Mashhad played a key role in bringing folk and traditional Iranian music (*sonnati*) into Iranian rock music. MudBand's usage of Khorasani folk music and instrumentation as well as Mohsen Namjoo's experiments in mixing blues and *sonnati* played important roles in developing Iran's musical identity in profound ways. Also, its heavy emphasis on experimentation, especially with poetry and instrumentation, provided a great space for musicians such as Mohsen Namjoo to find their sound. Lastly, Mashhad scene, with Abdi's lead, was one of the first scenes that introduced the possibility of performing street music in the country. This was indeed an important step in demystifying rock, as the art form moved from a studio or live experience to a street experience. In the United States, we can think of Woody Guthrie and Bob Dylan as people who did similar work. In this sense, Mashhad was extremely influential in bringing music to the streets.

2010 Onwards

By 2010, rock music was more and more demystified in the eyes of Ershad. Many of the bands that were able to weather the storm in the first decade of the 2000s began gaining permissions to distribute their albums publicly. Many of the bands that were able to weather the storm in the first decade of the 2000s began gaining permissions to distribute their albums publicly while others were not able to survive. Some whose members began their careers in Iran, like Kiosk, started new careers abroad as independent artists. Others tried to recover the past by forming new bands abroad and singing the music that they made in Iran.[55] By the beginning of the first decade, we see the rise of a new wave of rock musicians reaching stardom, including Reza Yazdani and Kaveh Yaghmaie, the son of Kourosh Yaghmaie. Meanwhile, the styles of rock started to diversify as well to include genres such as heavy metal (Kahtmayan), progressive rock (Obour Band), hard rock (Nioosh) and *Talfighi* rock (Milad Derakhshani) to name a few. Rock also became a topic of discussion in music circles. For instance, the 160th edition of Honar-e-Musiqi was dedicated to the topic of rock music in Iran with articles discussing various issues that touch the music scene. As time passed, more record labels began supporting rock musicians and recording their albums. One of these labels, SiLahn-e Bārbad, concentrates solely on recording rock bands. Rock musicians also began tackling social issues. For example, the band Khorshid-e Siah, meaning The Black Sun, focuses their songs solely on environmentalism by concentrating their lyrics on the subject matter. With the advent of podcasts, several podcasts were created to address different issues surrounding rock in Iran. Among these, the podcast *rāk-va-risheh* (Rock and Roots) on Beeptunes.com has over twenty-four hours of extensive analysis as well as interviews with rock musicians.

While these changes are positive, rock musicians, and musicians in general, still face harassment and crackdowns by the government. For instance, in 2013, the Iranian police raided a concert by the band Down of Rage without any explanation 'despite organisers having received a permit from the Ministry of Culture and Islamic Guidance sanctioning the event'.[56] This is to say that while rock is now considered an official genre of music, rock musicians still face hardship in terms of the acceptance of their music. This is because one may never know when one's music is permitted and when one's career can end. With all this in mind, Iranian rock musicians continue to work and find ways to make their music heard.

Conclusion

What emerges from the close examination of Iranian rock music between the early 1990s and 2010s, the three decades in which the genre emerged and matured, are several key points. First, the significance of what was accomplished by the early rock musicians of the 1990s must not be understated. These musicians were able to lay the foundation for many other musicians who came in the early 2000s. Second, using Will Straw's notion of scenes allows us to blur the lines between official and unofficial and look at a genre of music and the activities of its participants within a context of an interconnected network that include musicians, fans, producers, distributors and others. However, the notion misses one important point. Scenes have leaders and they revolve around sources of inspiration. Hence, to think of scenes as an ambiguous coming together of different people is to forget the important effort put in organizing and inspiring those who contribute to a scene. Scenes are indeed cosmopolitan, and they have a certain coherence. However, what makes that coherence happen is contributed to the efforts of a core group that continues to make spaces for the scene. Third, I purposefully left out the internet in my chapter to focus on the importance of physical networks that contributed to the slow growth of the rock music scenes in Iran. Without spaces such as Bam Studio or Abdi's house, the rock scene of Tehran and Mashhad would not have been able to grow into something larger. The internet was important as a platform of sharing and a space of realizing the existence of others. However, what held the Tehran and Mashhad scene together was the physical presence of musicians and their networking capacities in those spaces. Finally, when thinking of rock history in Iran, we need to think of the notion of time as *kairos* and not *chronos*. The difference between these two terms is in the way we understand time and history. *Chronos* is the understanding of time chronologically. It is the way we look at time in everyday life. *Kairos* is to look at moments instead of just time. These moments are recognized, sought and used. The reason why I use this distinction is because cultural negotiation never happens at an exact day or time; it happens when opportune moments are seen, captured and used. It is for this reason that the notion of tactic by de Certeau is key in my analysis since tactics use opportune moments and function in *Kairos*. From early on, with the creation of Bam Studio, Iranian rock musicians have been using different opportune moments to gain grounds. In doing so, they have been persisting on the legitimacy of their music and the assumption that they never did anything wrong by playing music.

In his article on the subject of censorship in Iran, Babak Rahimi looks at how censorship in the country is not only reactive but also proactive.[57] What he means by this is that the government not only reacts to cultural products by stating whether they are legal or not but also generates an environment where censorship becomes an inherent part of the creative process of an artist. What I would like to add to this is that persistence, and tactics used in performing persistence, is located in the negotiations that happen within this model of censorship in Iran. Iranian musicians may self-censor when they create. However, they also negotiate their way with the system by trying to reconfigure the non-articulated parameters of censorship. In doing so, they continually negotiate the boundaries of what is or is not accepted. Persistence consists of a set of tactics that uses and mixes available materials (physical and discursive) in order to come up with new ways of doing culture. In doing so, they negotiate with power instead of resisting it. Moreover, persistence is a process of self-recognition, whereby those who are performing it are also learning about their own selves. This is why Iranian rock musicians were constantly trying to find their sound and their identities in this process of negotiation because they had to do so in order to articulate it better.

Finally, in her recent article, Laudan Nooshin argues how speaking about music in Iran from an occidental perspective has mainly been framed around the romanticized discourse of 'freedom' and 'resistance'.[58] This idea is largely stemmed in the politicization of the practice of music due to the heavy control of the Iranian regime over the production and distribution of music. The notion of resistance politicizes the activities of musicians in Iran, when, in fact, many of them articulate quite clearly that their activities are not in any shape or form political. Bronwen Robertson's book on the subject emphasizes this idea over and over again through interviews with many of the Iranian rock musicians in Tehran.[59] The question that remains is the following: if resistance does not do justice in framing the activities of Iranian musicians, how should we then look at this?

My answer to the question is to look at how Iranian musicians in the rock music scene embodied persistence, the act of firm continuation of a discourse in spite of difficulty in acceptance or opposition to that discourse, as performative. Persistence is a performance, a tactic, suited to manoeuver the strategy that occupies the proper in Iran at the moment. It is also a framework by which one can think about performance in Iran. In this framework, one is not thinking about performance as something that happens on the stage, but as an embodied experience that takes place off the stage in the minds and bodies of artists who continue to persist on the legitimacy of their craft. As a performative, persistence is a cultural practice that is the result of a thirty-odd years' relationship between Ershad and Iranian artists. In the song *Anthem*, Leonard Cohen famously utters the following words: 'there is a crack in everything, and that's how the light gets in.' If culture is the light, persistence is the force that locates the cracks in a rigid systemic structure. It does not resist the system; it finds new ways of getting through the system through different performative tactics.

Part III

RESTAGING IRAN IN DIASPORA SPACES

10

PROBING THE WOUNDS OF HISTORY: *444 DAYS*, A WORLD PREMIERE IN SAN FRANCISCO

Babak Rahimi and Torange Yeghiazarian

Diaspora is generally understood and analysed in terms of displacement and, by extension, the experience of trauma, nostalgia and longing for or a loss of an imagined homeland.[1] As a concept that seeks to capture the experience of displacement, diaspora is 'elusive by design', and this is so because defining diaspora would entail the imprecise enunciation of dispersion, travel and mobility of communities undergoing self-definition in shifting historical settings.[2] Such elusiveness equally underscores ambiguity in theorizing diaspora that reflects tenuous ways in which dispersed communities stage self and homeland in displaced contexts.

However, the experience of diaspora also opens up the possibility of self-affirmation and solidarity marked by a transformative force to rethink identity and home in expressive ways.[3] Such process of rethinking emphasizes the fluidity of diasporic identity, but more importantly, the performative ways in which identity, beyond the mere indication of heritage, can be reconfigured through art, literature and theatre. The appropriation of diaspora into expression of cultural practices, in particular, theatrical ones, could be understood to be a consequence of socio-political context in which a diasporic community is situated. But what remains integral to the diasporic experience is the intersection of multiple forms of performances that seek to reassemble boundaries that separate citizen from the alien, self from the other and ultimately strange from the familiar.

Since the conquest of Americas and colonization of Africa and Oceania in the early modern period, waves of migration, either forced or voluntarily, have seen the rise of diverse diasporic communities, displaced in varied geographies and with distinct performance traditions of subaltern orientation that range from ritual to dramatic staging of plays. From working-class Irish immigrant neighbourhoods in New England, America, to Turkish-German performances at Theater Ulüm in Ulm, Baden-Württemberg, Germany, from Black (African, African American and Caribbean) dramatic practices to 'Indic Theatre' in South Africa, theatre has served to communicate diasporic identity and its otherness in artistic, popular and commercial settings, often with the host country as the audience, and yet equally influenced by global theatrical trends and artistic production industries.

Yet the local has served an essential feature of diasporic theatre. In the American context, for example, since 1965 the Los Angeles-based East West Players, as the country's longest-running professional theatre founded by Asian American playwrights, has represented an alternative form of theatrical tradition that embraces questions of culture, identity and diversity. By staging performances of Asian-Pacific American artists, East West Players has also been celebrated for its community-based collaboration in a Southern Californian urban neighbourhood, where diasporic communities negotiate identity in a changing national cultural context. Theatre, as a collaborative art, is always tied to the local, whereby memory, kinship and solidarity are revived through performance in local terrains of belonging.

The following interview with Torange Yeghiazarian, the founding artistic director Golden Thread Productions in San Francisco, the first American theatre company devoted to plays from or about the Middle East, was conducted with the aim of including the voice of a playwright and theatre director in a volume that is meant to illustrate the transcultural life of theatre. Though theatrical production is, by and large, a response to the hegemony of national culture operating as the paradigm of belonging to a nation state, the interview reflects Yeghiazarian as a diasporic playwright of Middle Eastern heritage based in North America, whose distinct works emanate from a new staging and processes of diaspora theatre construed within a liminal space of performance. In a sense, the following conversation is informed by the diasporic condition that is located at the junction of mixtures, negotiations, revealing the dialogic nature of language through which diverse forms of expressions give rise to the transcultural awareness of connective lives, though situated in national and global sets of power relations.

For Yeghiazarian, theatrical performance marks a paradigm of diasporic anxiety in terms of 'otherness', caused by immigration and, moreover, the possibility in the dynamic of rethinking and rewriting to which the meaning of performance for a variety of audiences becomes a matter of recognition. With theatrical focus on the Middle East, Golden Thread Productions, as Yeghiazarian explains, is modelled after 'the legacy of Asian-American and Latino-American theatres', by which her theatre group has aimed to move 'towards building a Middle Eastern-American theatre'. The quest for such a unique form of American theatre has been a challenging one, but, as Yeghiazarian reminds us, it is with the very practice of theatre by which agency through the other can be affirmed. 'Theatre', she explains, 'provides an intimate space where we discover ourselves in someone else's story'.

In *444 Days*, a play about the 'reunion' twenty-five years later of a former hostage and a hostage-taker during the Iran Hostage Crisis, 1979–81, Yeghiazarian provides a unique perspective on the question of interrelatedness of identity through theatrical performance. *444 Days* invites us to a provocative theatre, opening up space to voices that are shut off in mainstream US theatrical culture. The play also opens to interconnective subjectivities that are inherently dispersed through despair, distance and flight of meaning. Home is the theatre of disjoint.

> **BR:** *Could you give an account of your artistic activities in the Bay Area? And how do you understand your diasporic identity, as an Armenian-*

Iranian-American, playing a role in your writings and theatrical productions?

TY: These days I mainly write, direct and produce at my company, Golden Thread Productions in San Francisco. Because my start in theatre was in acting, I carry that perspective in my writing – which is very character-driven – and in my directing, where I build on the actors' strengths. Much of my writing reflects my Armenian-Iranian-American triple identity and the experience of displacement. It is interesting to place myself within the larger context of diasporic writers. In a way, that experience actually began in Iran, where, as an Armenian, I lived in diaspora. I had to explain what it meant to be Armenian, to be Christian, to my non-Armenian, non-Christian friends. The experience of immigrating to the United States added a new layer of 'otherness' to my identity. I found myself constantly having to explain about Iran, its history and politics, women's lives, the lives of members of religious minority communities. I found it astonishing that in 1979, in the middle of the Hostage Crisis, many Americans did not know where Iran is, let alone have any knowledge about the lives of people there.

In my writing, I continue to examine the jarring effects of the 1979 revolution in Iran and its aftermath in the Iranian American community. My earliest produced play, *Waves*, tells the story of a friendship between two women political activists torn apart by the revolution. Both begin as leftist activists, but one gradually aligns herself with the Islamic factions and after the revolution finds herself in a position of leadership. While the other is arrested, tortured and ultimately exiled. The play takes place in the United States in the 1990s when both women have very different lives, but they still carry the wounds of the past. Feelings of suspicion and betrayal colour their reunion and leave the audience wondering if the love they once felt for each other would bring about any kind of salvation or understanding. *Dawn at Midnight* is the second in what I now understand is a trilogy about women and the revolution. It examines a turning point in the life of a successful Iranian television personality in Los Angeles who discovers she is HIV-positive. She has worked hard to hide the truth about her past as a refugee-turned-prostitute in Turkey. But it may no longer be possible to keep her secret, the revelation of which, she fears, will result in the loss of all that she has worked for: her film contract, her fiancé and, most importantly, the respect of her community. *444 Days* is the third and final play in the trilogy.

Thematically, a lot of my plays explore the intersection of sex and politics. I often use a personal relationship to reflect on broader social and political issues. Perhaps the fact that my parents' marriage was met with huge opposition has coloured my perspective. My father came from a prominent Armenian Christian family and my mother from an Iranian Muslim family. Both families were secular and progressive in their social values, but they were also very proud. They may have also worried about the clash of cultures in a mixed marriage: how would the children be raised? Not surprisingly, as a child growing up, I was always asked if I am Muslim or Christian, or which religion I prefer, which seemed like a ridiculous notion to me. There were so many perceived differences and incorrect assumptions. I grew up feeling frustrated by that and often felt the need to set the record straight. That urge has only increased living in the United States and having to deal with myriad misunderstandings about Iran and the Middle East, particularly when it comes to women.

Despite all claims to the contrary, I find the United States a surprisingly hostile environment for women. The #MeToo expose unveiled some of the more direct and illegal aspects of this. But on a very basic level, I see women in the United States being told we can have it all but the social structures have not been modified to support women in achieving their full potential. For example, women can have a job and a family – but without affordable childcare this opportunity is meaningless. Women who choose to stay home to raise their children continue to face judgement and are frequently rejected when they try to re-enter the workforce. Professionally, many previously closed doors have been forced open but glass ceilings and earning seventy cents on the dollar are facts. As is the fact that a man alleged to have assaulted and even raped multiple women has been elected as president. The election of many first-timer congresswomen in 2018 is promising. We will see if the trend continues and if these women leaders can actually be effective.

In theatre, there are significantly fewer opportunities for women than men. I began writing my own material early on because I was unhappy with the choices. Today, I strive to elevate the position of women in all areas of my theatre work: dramatically, artistically and financially. This is relatively easy because there are amazing women professionals out there but finding well-written parts for women continues to be a challenge. The near absence of Middle Eastern voices on the American stage and the lack of strong women narratives continue to fuel my work.

BR: *As the founding artistic director of a leading North American theatre company dedicated to exploring Middle East cultures and identities, can you elaborate on the history, objectives and activities of Golden Thread Production?*

TY: In 1996 when Golden Thread began its activities, the idea of an American company only producing plays from or about the Middle East seemed extremely limiting. In fact, my graduate advisor worried that it would 'box me in'. I think he was right. It did box me in, but that box was where I wanted to play. Our first two productions were plays by me staged with local artists. By 1999, we realized a season of two productions wasn't enough to convey the diversity that we knew was an important feature of the Middle East. That is when we launched an evening of short plays, which in the second year became the ReOrient Festival. This allowed us to include classics and contemporary works from the Middle East, translations, experimental work and new plays by Middle Eastern and Middle Eastern American playwrights. Because plays from or about various countries were being presented in one evening, ReOrient also became a community gathering and a frequent site of passionate debates particularly around Palestine-Israel.

It is worth noting that from the beginning, our vision was an inclusive one. Building on the legacy of Asian American and Latino-American theatres, we were moving towards building a Middle Eastern American theatre. We struggled with the best way to define our inclusive mission. The term 'Middle East' is loaded with political baggage, but other terms such as MENA (Middle East-North Africa) or SWANA (South West Asia-North Africa) seemed obscure; 'Near East' or 'The Levant' seemed inadequate. We chose to move ahead with 'Middle East' because at the time it was the most familiar and widely used term to refer to most of the countries we are dealing with. In 1999, we developed the following explanation to describe our approach: 'In our vast imagination, the Middle East is defined not by geographical boundaries and political separations, but as the shared experience of the people, who throughout history have been touched by its stories and culture.'

Golden Thread Productions celebrates its twenty-fifth anniversary in 2021. In our history, we have produced more than 100 new plays, hired more than 1,000 artists and reached over 50,000 audiences. Our programmes include the development and production of full-length plays, the ReOrient Festival of Short Plays, New Threads staged reading series, *What Do the Women Say?*, an annual curated evening featuring the work of women artists of Middle Eastern heritage in celebration of International Women's Day, and Golden Thread Fairytale Players, a Theatre for Young Audiences programme to create and tour original plays based on Middle Eastern fables.

> **BR:** *Could you explain the historical context of the play* 444 Days *and how it relates, or perhaps seeks to respond, to the 1979 Revolution? Also, what was your intention in writing and staging this play?*
>
> **TY:** I began working on *444 Days* soon after *Waves* and *Dawn in Midnight*. But I did not complete the play until my sabbatical in 2010, which I spent in Tehran with my family. In 2012, Golden Thread staged the world premiere of *444 Days*, directed by Bella Warda. The play title is a reference to the fifty-two Americans that were held hostage in Tehran for 444 days from November 1979 to January 1981. In my mind, the hostage taking of Americans at the US Embassy in Tehran is one of two critical moments in the history of US-Iran relations. The other is the 1953 coup that toppled the government of Mohammad Mosaddegh. Some argue that the 1979 incident was in retaliation to the 1953 coup: one slap in the face leading to another slap in the face. Nations, like humans, have personalities. They can hold a grudge. Iran held a grudge for twenty-six years then 'got even'. The United States is still holding a grudge, after more than forty years.

Set in an intensive care unit hospital room in an affluent suburban town in the United States in 2004, the play opens with Laleh sitting beside the bed of her daughter, Hadyeh, who is in a coma and in need of a bone marrow transplant. Harry walks in wearing sunglasses. The last time Harry and Laleh spoke to each other was in January 1981, when Harry along with fifty-one other hostages were being released. We learn that Harry heard about Laleh on the news which showed demonstrators outside the hospital chanting anti-Islamic Republic slogans. The news reported that the hospital administration had received criticism for aiding a known terrorist, meaning Laleh, and was being pressured to transfer the patient. This is an excerpt from the very beginning of the play:

LALEH: *You look good, Harry.*
HARRY: *You too.*
LALEH: *No need to lie. I know how I look.*
HARRY: *There are so many people outside.*
LALEH: *There are?*
HARRY: *Outside the building. Haven't you seen them?*
LALEH: *I haven't, no. What do they want?*
HARRY: *You don't know?*
LALEH: *Because of us? I guess it was wishful thinking to come and go unnoticed. Were you wearing sunglasses?*
HARRY: *I was afraid your bodyguards might recognize me.*
LALEH: *I'm no longer a government official.*
HARRY: *Isn't the new President an old friend?*
LALEH: *Harry…*
HARRY: *You're all over the news.*
LALEH: *Ah…*
HARRY: *You've been here over a month!*
LALEH: *Yes, I think so.*
HARRY: *You didn't contact me.*
LALEH: *No.*
HARRY: *No. No… why?*
LALEH: *Harry, my daughter is dying.*

The play is set up as a puzzle; I invite the audience to put the plot together one puzzle piece at a time. The dialogue is minimal and intentionally cryptic. The characters go only as far as they are prepared to go and not a step farther. Later in the same scene, Laleh confronts Harry about the past and criticizes his memoir.

LALEH: *We spent 444 days together, you and I.*
HARRY: *Extraordinary times…*
LALEH: *In all the interviews you gave, you never mentioned the positive things. Not even in your memoir.*
HARRY: *We were held against our will.*
LALEH: *You left so much unsaid.*
HARRY: *I was protecting you!*
LALEH: *You were protecting yourself.*
HARRY: *You would have preferred it if I shared all the details?*

As the play unravels, we are pulled deeper and deeper into Laleh and Harry's secret past; through flash backs, we meet their younger selves and experience their hopes and aspirations. Back in 1979, Laleh was an idealistic university student, an eighteen-year-old revolutionary who belonged to a group calling itself University Students Following the Line of the Imam [Khomeini]. They stormed the American Embassy in Tehran, which they called 'the den of spies'. They accused the Shah's government of behaving like a client state of the United States and believed they could find documents proving their case in the Embassy vaults. Harry was an attaché at the US Embassy in Tehran. He was young, charming and sympathetic to the young revolutionaries' aspirations. Harry was familiar with many aspects of the US activities in Iran and curiously, was quite willing to share his information – with Laleh. It did not take long for Laleh and Harry to find common ground, and eventually become intimate. This scene is a flashback:

LALEH: *Your help has been invaluable. Thank you, Harry.*
HARRY: *You know I would do anything for – I mean, I support the revolution – not this – not, you know – this! But yes, the Shah was getting out of hand, something had to be done. And we, I mean Americans are the first revolutionaries, right? So, I totally get the 'get rid of the king' thing. I just hope – I mean, it's good to see someone like you among them.*
LALEH: *And surprising to see someone like you among – them.*
HARRY: *We're not really enemies, you know.*
LALEH: *You're right. We would have to be equals to be enemies. No, Iran has been a slave to the US all these years. That will never happen again.*
HARRY: *America would welcome an equal partnership.*

By the time the hostages are released, Iran is at war with Iraq and the US policy towards Iran is murky at best. Harry's freedom is bittersweet, but he has every intention of returning. They make each other a promise of solidarity. They believe their love can survive the political rift between their countries. We witness for a brief moment many years ago, Laleh and Harry's love and trust for one another. But none of that is presently visible. Only bitterness and hurt remain where love once lived. In the present, Laleh and Harry seem entangled in national pride and self-righteousness, which leaves no room for reconciliation. When Harry shows up at the hospital room offering to help, Laleh rejects him outright.

LALEH: *Harry, Harry... always looking for solutions. For common ground. No, thank you. We don't need your help. Not then, not now, not ever. Do you understand? We have nothing in common. Betrayal, Harry, does that sound familiar to you? Hopes shattered, dreams thrown to the wind. An entire nation, betrayed! And now you stand here, a noble representative of your noble nation, extending a hand to us who are in dire need. Is this how you will describe it in your next book? I was there to help. I had a responsibility to do the right thing. Such simple words. Such generosity. So American!*

The hospital room is stark white, sterile. Its deafening silence is broken only with the faint beeping of the monitors: the only sign that Hadyeh is still alive. Olivia, the ICU nurse in charge of Hadyeh's care, performs her daily maintenance routine. Olivia is warm and caring but also has a no-nonsense attitude. In the play, she is a kind of 'everyman', the average American whose interest political leaders claim to represent. I always imagined Olivia being from the South, an example of Southern charm and hospitality, balancing Harry's East Coast formal sophistication. At one of the early workshops, we cast an African American actress as Olivia, and it made perfect sense. It opened up new possibilities; it endowed Olivia with the African American experience and personal narratives of social justice. In the following scene, Olivia confronts Laleh about being one of the hostage-takers.

OLIVIA: *You better calm down.*
LALEH: *I wish I could.*
OLIVIA: *I'll get you a couple of Valiums.*
LALEH: *That's right. Pop a pill, the American solution to everything. Maybe you should get your doctors to put me on Prozac. Then I'll be out of your hair for good.*
OLIVIA: *Now listen here you. You're a mother and you got the world weighing on your shoulders and I understand what that's like. But don't go around disrespecting my people who happen to be offering you shelter and care for your daughter even though you and your people put a gun to our head twenty-five years ago and still go around yelling Death to America!*
LALEH: *We had good reason for doing what we did twenty-five years ago.*
OLIVIA: *There is no reason in the world good enough-*
LALEH: *You hold a gun to our head every day! The whole world system is subjugated to America's imperatives, and we must bow to it or suffer the consequences. Your media and education system brainwash you to expect this delusion of superiority as the norm. You would never understand how oppressive American domination feels, how suffocating; so, don't sit there in judgment. I respect you as a person, Olivia but your country is a giant elephant that is so big, strong and remote that nothing can touch it. Like some island you float on your dream ocean gobbling up the world's resources and we pay for it with our lives. You ruin our future in the name of security and justice, then leave us with shattered pieces of a homeland and expect us to thank you!*
OLIVIA: *You've got some nerve lecturing me on Oppression!*
LALEH: *Please just leave me alone.*

It was important for Olivia to stand up both to Laleh's political sermons and to Harry's diatribes justifying his actions. She became the necessary third leg of the triangle that represented the shape of the play to me. I needed all three sides to be equally strong and opinionated. In this scene, Olivia confronts Harry about his real intentions:

OLIVIA: *Do I look stupid to you?*
HARRY: *No – what –*

OLIVIA: *I've been a registered nurse for twenty-five years. You think nurses are stupid? Just because hanging a drip looks easy or moving a patient so she doesn't get bed sores. Let me tell you something –*
HARRY: *I didn't mean to –*
OLIVIA: *Listen. I know why we're in Iraq and I don't like it. What's more, even though I hate the moron sitting in as president right now, if Canada one day invaded us to get rid of the stupid ass, I wouldn't be none too happy about Canadians telling me my own good.*
HARRY: *Hey, I'm with you.*
OLIVIA: *Are you? Because for a second there I saw the shadows of condescension in your eyes and I didn't like it.*

Olivia's focus is entirely on Hadyeh, who is at the centre of the dramatic triangle. Everyone claims to have Hadyeh's best interest in mind, but it quickly becomes clear that to Laleh and Harry, Hadyeh is the prize they are not willing to let the other win. The word *Hadyeh* means 'gift' in Persian. The choice, presumably made by Laleh, implies a sense of hope, perhaps of a new beginning. The battle over Hadyeh is centred on her need for a bone marrow transplant. Laleh is not a match. Unfortunately, Hadyeh does not have any siblings, or does she?

As the web of lies and deceit unravels, Olivia, and with her the audience, discovers that Harry's son is being evaluated as a potential donor. Harry claims this as a victory; it will prove his parental right. Laleh is not amenable to a public revelation of Hadyeh's true lineage. Laleh accuses Harry of bullying his way back into their life and blackmailing Laleh. Harry sees it differently. As far as he is concerned, he is doing Laleh a favour; he is saving Hadyeh's life. Laleh welcomes his help but would prefer the identity of the donor to remain anonymous. Laleh sees this as the best solution. It would keep Harry and Laleh's past private and allow both of them to continue their lives as they have. But that is not what Harry wants. He claims to be unhappy in his marriage; 'I never got over us', Harry confesses and asserts that Laleh too has been living a lie all these years.

But why is Harry so insistent on making a public display of his support, Laleh wonders. When he knows it will only bring shame to Laleh and her family. Could that actually be his intention? To shame Laleh and her husband, who happens to be a leading official in the Islamic Republic government? Is this Harry's way of getting even? Laleh is suspicious of Harry's motives; she is not one to be outplayed. She rejects Harry's pleas and reciprocates his threats of taking legal action. There is no shortage of damning evidence against both of them, and as it happens, Laleh and Harry are not shy about throwing past mistakes in each other's face. Like the jilted lovers that they are, Laleh and Harry go at each other in increasingly appalling fashion. Harry and Laleh are self-righteous and intransigent. They are unwilling to acknowledge their own mistakes or concede on any point.

This is not unlike the two nations Harry and Laleh represent. A number of US presidents have threatened Iran with military intervention and regime change. The 1979 hostage-taking is like a wound in the body of the United States: a wound that has festered for years and is now putrid. In the United States, Iran is represented in mainstream media and political debates as the United States' worst enemy. The Iranian nuclear programme, which was in fact built by the United States back in the 1970s, is paraded as the biggest threat to US security. There is no real national debate or meaningful analysis of the facts. During the George W. Bush years – and again today under the Trump administration – Iran's nuclear programme is used to justify harsh economic sanctions and military manoeuvring in the Persian Gulf. This makes for major schizophrenia for Iranian Americans. I may not be a fan of the Islamic Republic, but I certainly do not want Iran bombed back to the Stone Age, as some Generals are suggesting. But politicians seem to have failed where USA-Iran relations are concerned.

444 Days is an example of exploring a political conflict through a personal relationship. Behaving like jilted lovers, the United States and Iran accuse each other of lying and betrayal. Instead of writing a political essay or a play about politicians failing to negotiate, I wrote a play about secret lovers unable to face their political failures. Creating a personal story offers the opportunity to focus on the human cost of political decisions. In this case, Hadyeh's illness symbolizes the problem. In a fantastical moment, Hadyeh directly addresses the audience.

> HADYEH: *For the longest time they didn't even know what was wrong with me. We went to so many doctors but each one said something different. They said I wouldn't last very long, that my own cells would eventually destroy my body. Others said it's a kind of cancer and it will never leave my system. Finally, they figured out that it's something hereditary. It's been in both sides of my family for generations. It stopped being dormant when it got to me. Thanks a lot! I guess we can't always know what kind of poison we might release from one generation to the next.*

Hadyeh suffers from a genetic condition that she inherited from both parents. Left unaddressed, repressed political conflict can fester in the body of a nation and lead to terminal disease. I suppose I hold Iran and the United States equally responsible for the political mess we find ourselves in. For many Iranians, the 1979 revolution was a gift, a promise of better days to come. Unfortunately, that promise was broken by the leaders of the Islamic Republic. The country is suffering from political repression and corruption all the while its leadership maintains a stance of superior morality. Similarly, the United States continues to apply political and economic pressure on Iran, having effectively surrounded it with military forces in Afghanistan, Iraq and the Persian Gulf. Both sides have failed to take advantage of opportunities to negotiate and reconcile. Hadyeh also symbolizes the potential of USA-Iran reconciliation: the future generation that may overcome past mistakes and build a positive alliance.

> HADYEH: *[My mom] used to say, Hadyeh jān, you are God's gift to me. But then they found out I was sick, and she stopped saying that. I guess it's not the kind of gift you can return to the store.*

BR: *The play revolves around themes of suspicion, mistrust and perhaps longing for renewed intimacy as Harry and Laleh as key performers in reflecting this tension. 444 Days in a way seeks to uncover an unspoken pain that is now confronted by the key actors. What is the role of theatre in this complicated process? Is theatre cathartic by providing psychological relief through open expression of buried emotions? Or does this play specifically express a diasporic act of self-determination by bringing to light a lost history that needs to be confronted?*

TY: This is a very personal play. It's an internal dialogue between my American and my Iranian sides. As an immigrant, I'm broken-hearted by the animosity between the two countries I call home. Writing *444 Days* was a way for me to explore the roots of that animosity. I do see Iranians and Americans suffering from this long festering conflict and missing the opportunity for an amicable and mutually fruitful relationship.

Theatre provides an intimate space where we discover ourselves in someone else's story. Empathy is inherent to the theatrical experience, for the creative team as well as the audience. By watching Harry and Laleh tear each other down, we see our own families and examine personal issues. But because of its political context, *444 Days* also inhabits an additional geopolitical layer. Theatre enables us to experience complex global conflicts from a personal, more intimate lens. It highlights the human cost of global conflict, which so often is missing from news analyses and political debates. And because there are many characters in a play, the writer can give voice to conflicting narratives. Through this play, I am claiming my own narrative as an Iranian woman but also expressing my concerns as an American. It goes without saying, however, that this is one play and ultimately an expression of one mind. There are many different ways of telling this very same story. I have no claim to 'correctness' only to my personal truth. It either resonates with audiences or it doesn't. And that is the extent of its impact.

11

PERFORMING GLIMPSES OF THE PAST: THE POLITICAL IMPLICATIONS OF DANCE IN NOWRUZ PARADES

Rana Salimi

The rehearsal rooms at the Iranian School of San Diego (ISSD) are packed with dancers donning colourful outfits and sparkly scarves. The girls practise their routines one more time, checking out their bold make-up and perfect curls in the mirror. The backstage for another Nowruz production is full of vibrant-coloured fabrics, exotic fragrances, tantalizing fragments of rehearsals, a mixture of English and Persian, and excited parents with cameras in hand. The dancers are enthusiastic, as are their chaperones, who have performed on the same stage to the same routine over the years. Each year the repertoire includes folkloric *Gilaki*, *Āzari*, *Khoraasani*, *Kurdi*, *Bandari*, *Tehrani* and a couple of pop culture dances.[1] North American Programs that celebrate Nowruz, the Persian New Year, are filled with Persian dance, whether it involves hiring a professional dance troupe or involving amateur student dancers of all ages.[2]

As an Iranian American scholar of performance studies and a teacher at Iranian School of San Diego (ISSD), I have always been curious to know why dance has played such an integral part in the lives of second-generation Iranian Americans. At what point did dance come to dominate performance stages within the diasporic Iranian community and become a means of self-identification for that group? How does the community in exile reimagine itself through dance for the world at large? And to what extent is the public performance of bodies in rhythmic movement, especially female bodies, a political gesture? It is this political reimagining of a community and how the very precise and selective use of music, images, colours, costumes and movements define and redefine a new nation distanced purposely from its government back home that interest me the most.

Why dance?

As murals, paintings, texts, European travelogues and other historical evidence prove, dance has had a long tradition in Iranian culture. Even though at times this art form has been confined to the domains of harems or private spaces, including dance in happy occasions is an unbroken custom for Iranians to this day.³

Nowruz celebrations, some of the most joyous events for Iranians, are the ground for such festive ceremonies. Therefore, following this popular tradition, Nowruz in the United States is also filled with Iranian folklore and pop dance music. The absence of Persian⁴ classical music, *radif*, in Nowruz celebrations proves the favouritism of faster rhythms, upbeat tempos and less sombre lyrics. There are several possible explanations for the popularity of dance routines for the Iranian community in diaspora. First, pop music and improvisational solo or group dances are perhaps the most common features of any festive Iranian gathering. Pop singers gain swift popularity as the community listens to their songs at private parties and weddings, in Persian grocery stores and restaurants and even when riding in a friends' car. This wide exposure to pop music creates a sense of familiarity with the scores and encourages the members of the community to sing along or dance whenever the occasion arises. Involving the audience is one of the major goals of Nowruz organizers who use music and dance to engage their bystanders. A good example of an audience member's enthusiastic participation is seen in a short YouTube video of a Nowruz celebration in Ormond Beach, Florida. The video shows a group of professional female dancers in costume on an open stage. After dancing to two songs, the dancers pick partners from the audience and begin to dance with them. Interestingly, one woman who is close to the camera dances more passionately to Leila Forouhar's music than the professional dancer who follows her lead.⁵

Second, what is noticeable in Nowruz-related live performances is that young dancers imitate the professional movements while recognizing the type of dance they perform and the music they dance too. This is despite the fact that the cultural and historical context of such dances is unknown to the dancers. Not only do they not speak the vernacular of the region where the song is from, a large number of them cannot even speak Persian fluently. A large number of dance students at ISSD enrol in the dance classes with no intention to learn Persian. Ali Akbar Mahdi, whose sociological research focuses on second-generation Iranian Americans, states that 'given the low level of proficiency of these youths in this language [Persian], it is difficult to imagine how [they] can maintain the elements of a culture that they cannot fully understand'.⁶ Anthony Shay draws upon Mahdi's findings in his book, *Choreographing Identities*, and concludes that 'because of low linguistic skills in the Iranian community, many parents, seeing children of other ethnicities, have begun to look increasingly upon dance as a vehicle for cultural representation in school and civic folk dance festivals'.⁷ Dance can overcome such language barriers by not denying access to those who are not proficient in Persian. This is indeed a tremendous advantage in introducing the culture to the younger generations. Moreover, it has enabled Persian dance groups to form at colleges and universities throughout the country. Yet, one cannot overlook the fact that the lack of professional training and academic knowledge of Persian dance has resulted in low-quality performances in the majority of events.

Further, along with abiding with the customs, generations of bystanders have used dance as a bridge. Kambiz Mofrad, president of New York Persian Day Parade

(NYPP), agrees that there are three groups of spectators: the second and third generations of Iranians, their parents who are there to witness traditions being preserved and the rest of the world who are there to watch the parades.[8] The young and old generations of Iranian Americans see this as a chance to get together and revisit the traditions of their homeland, while the second- and third-generation Iranian Americans along with the American spectators enjoy the festivities and learn the customs of a faraway land. As a way of getting in touch with the younger members of the community, the event organizers ensure that Iranian pop music is played in every celebration. Professional DJs are hired to convey the message that they are well up-to-date in their musical taste. The use of familiar tunes creates fresh energy and attracts everyone. This helps the Iranian American organizations in realizing their plans of attracting future generations in order to continue the tradition. This also helps in building an affiliation with their culture. By using the more familiar tunes, the crowds of bystanders are reenergized. This corresponds with the mission of Iranian American organizations to attract younger generations and eventually have them run the events. As the familiar music to the stage derives young and old members of the community, they bond with one another and confirm their affiliations with their cultural heritage.

The fourth aspect is that the abstract world of dance and music welcomes various segments of the community to mingle with one another without risking ideological or political conflicts as parents are reassured that their children are not under any political influence. This is in accordance with the public belief that many, if not all, forms of arts are inspired by politics whether it be modern poetry, contemporary literature, Iranian cinema, theatre or photography. On the contrary, the Iranian community has usually treated dance as an apolitical entity, performed for entertainment only. This is reassuring for the second- or third-generation Iranian Americans, who may not have been exposed to Iran's history and politics and thus may have difficulty connecting with Iranian visual art forms, giving them a chance to represent their culture enjoyably without being categorized based on their language skills or their ideo-political views.

This chapter, however, challenges the notion of dance as an apolitical art form arguing that dance, when performed to showcase the Iranian national identity and culture, becomes an embodiment of political signs and signals. Dancers, as well as spectators, convey political messages, subconsciously or otherwise; their performance, thus, is a political statement. I argue that it is the intention of the organizers to create a new image and re-culturate a new nation through dance in Nowruz parades. However, this attempt, the re-culturation of the diasporic community, cannot be realized unless in its political implications.

The political implications of dance genres in Nowruz ceremonies

Emphasizing on dance in Nowruz ceremonies implies defiance of rules of law currently observed in Iran by Islamic Republic government. It also reimagines the exilic community against the international portrayal of Iran.

Different dance genres used in the ceremonies and parades make pronounced references to pre-revolution Iran. Pop music is to the young as classical Persian music is to the older generations; both genres nostalgic references to the pre-1978 Iran that celebrated its rapid modernization. Satisfying parents and grandparents is among the most important goals of Nowruz celebrations, which also happens to be a cultural Iranian value.[9] Persian classical dance is an enjoined style brought about by combining the Safavid- and Qajar-style court dances. These were modernized in the 1920s by Pahlavi regime and thus can be considered a direct reference to pre-revolution Iran. The dances are visually appealing as they are well-rehearsed, delicate and improvised solo or as group performances. The dancers, professional and amateur, are dressed in bright-coloured long silk dresses wearing bejewelled tiaras, long sparkly scarves and shiny braided hair that enhance their majestic looks and on-stage manoeuvres. Groups usually dress in identical or colour-coordinated costumes and are odd-numbered.

The Pahlavi era is also referred to in Nowruz performances through *raqs-e Jahel* (*Jaheli* dance), which showcases the *jahel* or *luti*, a street wanderer dressed in a black suit, a white dress shirt and a black hat. *Jahel* became a cinematic personality in the late 1960s and 1970s with stories of him and his lover, his large-heartedness, his readiness to sacrifice everything for friendship and love, his macho character and his willingness to fight for honour and dignity. Before the Islamic Revolution, the famous dancer Jamileh introduced the *Jahel* dance as an imitation of the character of the *jahel*. She performed the hypersexual *Jahel* dance while dressed in tight, shimmering black pants, a white dress shirt and high heels. Her femininity was admired by her male audience who were taken in by her open neckline, long blond hair that flowed beyond her fedora hat, full make-up and her broad smile.[10] This impersonation of the *Jahel* character has been repeated since then. Male and female dancers wear black suits and fedoras; while male dancers show *Jahel's* manliness, female performers emphasize feminine sexuality.

Regional folkloric dance, another popular genre, provides visual, pedagogical and communal values while challenging the laws imposed by the Iranian government. Examples can be seen in NYPP 2018 when men and women holding to one another dance a beautifully choreographed Kurdish variation. Another group of men and women as whirling Sufis take the stage shortly after and perform their traditional dance of *sama*. The Islamic law prohibits women from dancing in public. Even though men and women may dance together during festivities in provincial areas, such activities are forbidden by law and subject to severe punishment.

As explained by Kambiz Mofrad, the dance and the colourful outfits demonstrate the diversity of the Iranian culture and the community's appreciation of it. At least fifteen groups of dancers perform annually at NYPP, representing the multiple ethnicities living together in modern-day Iran. There are floats with signs and replicas of monuments and tourist attractions in every major city in Iran. The parade celebrates unity in spite of cultural differences, in addition to the religious and ideo-political challenges and struggles within the community. This is showcased by banners that carry the message 'We are one'. It seems that there is a possibility of achieving such harmony through dance and music. To quote Mofrad, 'the parade is a platform. We cannot see eye to eye, but we can walk side by side.'[11] The sight of Iranians of all social classes, political views, religious backgrounds and ethnic origins, marching together, holding flags and singing national anthems[12] unifies and re-culturates the community in exile. A strong nation is portrayed to the world and to younger generations, who learn the value of staying united and pay homage to the home country and its customs. And yet, portraying the image of Iran as one unified nation can be quite contradictory: both against the reality of all the existing turbulences among the various ethnicities in Iran and against the memories of the Islamic revolution, the hostage crisis, fundamentalist policies and human rights violations.

Many of the organizers, volunteers and audience members who participate in public events believe that cultural programmes such as Nowruz celebrations reframe the image of a tarnished Iran as a 'terrorist' or 'evil' nation and present a new version for the audience members who watch the parades. Amy Malek, who has done extensive research on the NYPP from 2004 to 2011, argues that Iranian Americans have 'adapted a popular American genre of public performance to interpret, represent and display selective understandings of Iranian culture'.[13] Malek is interested in the historical, cultural, socio-political and visual signs and symbols that are presented in parades. She concludes that NYPP organizers want to redefine the diasporic community through new images, educate second-generation Iranian Americans about their cultural heritage and ultimately send a message of unity to a community that has many ideological and political differences.[14] Analysing the ornaments used on the floats during the parades, Malek points to references to the Achaemenid Empire and ancient sources from other periods as 'a form of participatory didactic entertainment' for bystanders.[15] This paper, my research on the parades in New York, 2014–18, and Los Angeles, 2015 and 2016, confirms Malek's analysis. I also argue that Nowruz celebrations have taken a new route towards a more political stance. Subconsciously or not, these new developments are taking precedence in the community's attempts at self-identification.

Nowruz parades as political statements

Public celebrations, such as Nowruz parades, redefine the boundaries of the nation, a process that I refer to as re-culturation. Parades are political as they 'territorialise public space by establishing differential access to it'.[16] Nowruz public ceremonies in the form of parades, exhibitions and bazaars are practices of group identity and visibility to construct a sense of cultural and historical belonging that marks out terrains of commonality among Iranians living in diaspora. Thus, we can say that Nowruz ceremonies have always been political too. In *Sufis on Parade*, Zain Abdullah argues that 'parades allow immigrants to act out their presence and communicate their sensibilities to others'.[17] For the Iranian community living in diaspora, the public performance of identity in the form of cultural celebrations did not begin until March 2004, when a group of philanthropists in New York started the parade. This parade took place shortly after the war with Iraq had begun and preceded many anti-war and pro-war demonstrations that took place in New York and elsewhere throughout the country. The attempt to re-culturate Iran is a response to the view that took prominence after the Islamic revolution and especially after 9/11, which identified Iran as a 'terrorist country'. Even though the Iranian community living in diaspora has shown solidarity with the resistance against fundamentalism back in Iran, it has not been enough to alter Iran's image in the eyes of the international community. It is no surprise that the diasporic community of Iranians claims the public stage to present its national identity and pride in increasing numbers each year. In 2015, the NYPP drew more than 160,000 spectators of all ages and backgrounds to Manhattan.[18] These spectators watched the images of Iran's glorious past refurbished by the images of the new country: a united nation, practising its colourful traditions and inviting the world to take part in their jubilation. When Iranians paraded in Manhattan, they contested their marginal status as a minority group, but even more, they imagined their identity against the backdrop of a stigmatized Iran. The NYPP acted as a platform of a social movement that converted shame, loneliness and alienation into pride, solidarity, familiarity and an appreciation of diversity. It thus increased the emotional energy of the community, a resource it needed very much.

It is against this backdrop and through a semiological study of the parades that one may find answers to questions that inevitably arise. Are references to the great Achaemenid dynasty that highlight millenniums of civilization and emphasize an ancient declaration of human rights responses to the wartime characterization of Iran as the 'axis of evil'?[19] Are they attempts to segregate Iranian heritage and identity from Arab heritage and create distance between these cultures? What was the impetus for creating a parade that showcased the origins of a nation that stood for humanity, equality and peace when the world screamed violence, segregation and war?

We should first look at the performativity of Nowruz celebrations and the communication tools used at such events. The community re-culturates itself in two ways: by selecting moments of the past that it sees as worthy of commemoration and by encouraging the world to remember those segments of its history instead of the current connotations. The second and third generations of Iranians are constantly reminded of Iran's ancient past and its cultural, artistic, scientific and humanitarian history. Since access to linguistic knowledge limits the participation of second- and third-generation Iranian Americans, visual representations along with some abstract forms of communication have been used to acquaint the youth with their cultural heritage. For instance, the Zoroastrian ideals of 'good thoughts, good words and good deeds' have been recurrently displayed on banners as proof of the Iranian commitment to peace.

The emphasis on the Cyrus Cylinder in the 2015 parades in New York is a new addition that coheres with the goal of constructing an identity of peace for younger generations.[20] On the first float, young men and women surrounded a reproduction of tomb of Cyrus the Great at Pasargadae. A couple who represented Cyrus the Great and his wife, Cassandane, stood in the back dressed in royal blue and gold. The Pasargadae float was escorted by a group of women who were also dressed in royal blue and gold robes and rode white and brown horses. The float was also followed by a group of young men dressed as Achaemenid soldiers, also known as the *Jāvidān* guards, and armed with bow and arrows and shields. Next came the flag bearers and marchers carrying a sign that bore the *Faravahar* symbol. The next float was titled 'The Gate to the Nations', which carried a replica of the Cyrus Cylinder and a young couple who were also dressed as Cyrus the Great and his wife. On the side of the float was a sign that bore slogans such as 'The First Declaration of Human Rights, Abolish Slavery, Freedom of Worship, Choice of Homeland; Respect of Human Rights and Freedom of Speech'. Finally, two groups of marchers carried huge flags, one was the flag of Iran with the lion and sun emblem and the other was the *derafsh*, popularly ascribed to the Achaemenids.[21] Replicas of these flags were distributed among the spectators. Similar floats paraded Manhattan in April 2016 and 2018.[22] The friendship float which carried flags of many nations including Israel, Iran, the United States and Mexico was a new addition in 2018.

Another example with the same connotations occurred in 2015 at the first Nowruz Parade in Los Angeles. This parade was organized by Iranian actress Mary Apick, a group of Iranian artists, and various corporations. The parade began with the national anthem of the United States, followed by the Pahlavi national anthem both of which sung by a female performer. A group of marchers dressed in white carried wooden *Faravahars* and white flags that read 'good thoughts, good words, good deeds' as Zoroastrian priests followed them in their traditional garments. A replica of the Cyrus Cylinder was displayed on a float, along with a slate demonstrating Cyrus the Great's humanitarian laws while martial band and a group of drummers preceded the float. Finally, Parviz Sayad, the Iranian comedian, actor and director, appeared on top of a fire truck as his legendary TV character Samad Aqā. The presence of Samad on top of a fire truck beating his famous drum was received with much enthusiasm by the crowd.[23] Samad's films were comic criticisms of the social and economic conditions of life in pre-revolution Iran. Ironically, however, Samad's character has remained popular among audiences regardless of their political opinions of the Pahlavi regime.

Once again, references to the pre-revolution Iran portray a disconnect with the current regime of Iran. It is indeed a proclamation of a nation's desire to tie itself with humanity and civilization as far as the exilic community can remember. Also, a woman singing the national anthem nullifies the Islamic rule that women soloists must not perform in public for a mixed crowd.

Samad, the pre-revolution character, was enthusiastically welcomed in Nowruz parades. Yet, many of the popular characters of the Islamic Republic's television, whose programmes are voraciously watched by new and old immigrants daily, are not. Indeed, Samad and other Los Angeles-based stars and celebrities who attended the first Nowruz parade in Los Angeles in 2015 celebrated their cultural, ethical and visual differences with modern-day Iran.

NYPP parades include floats that carry representations of each major city in Iran. Amy Malek mentions the replica of the Azadi Tower, formerly known as

The Shahyad Tower, as one that the NYPP celebrates.[24] This building is indeed an architectural phenomenon, yet it is neither the newest nor the tallest building in the city.[25] In 2007, thirty-six years after the completion of Azadi Tower, they built the Milad Tower in Tehran. At 1,033 feet, it is the sixth tallest tower in the world, approximately 869 feet taller than Azadi. Both towers are architectural phenomena and house restaurants, coffee shops and gift shops. The Milad Tower has a revolving restaurant on the top floor and houses a convention centre and a five-star hotel as well. However, it has never appeared in any of the pictures or architectural representations that appear in Nowruz celebrations in the United States.

As Malek rightly observes, 'Islam remains awkwardly absent from this [the NYPP] parade.'[26] I would add that everything related to modern-day Iran is more or less absent from Nowruz parades and other Iranian American public ceremonies held in the United States. In the 2016 NYPP, the designers of the floats went as far as dedicating a float to the traditional Iranian sport, *varzesh-e bastani*, carrying the sign of Nowruz 2575 instead of 1395 (2016).[27] Dating the parade with a calendar that goes back to the Persian civilization in the ancient times, instead of the modern-day Iran's calendar that starts with Prophet Mohammad's migration from Mecca to Medina, once again tries to dismiss the nation's association with Islam. Is it possible to end the history of a nation at a certain time? Does negating the reality of modern-day Iran eradicate four decades of fundamentalist fascism? If not, then what purpose does this disconnection serve?

Dance and pop music are not the only sources of political statements during the Nowruz celebrations. The celebrations are organized by secular groups with no religious affiliation, even though the majority of the Iranian population is Muslim. For example, no woman marches in parades or stands behind a booth in a Nowruz market wearing hijab prior to 2019 when a single woman in hijab appears in NYPP. The only religious reference that has been represented during festivals is to Zoroastrianism. The Jewish Community of Iranian Americans, who was represented in 2016 NYPP for the first time, is an exception. By excluding more conservative or more stigmatized segments of the exilic community, the organizers draw an imaginary line between Oriental Iran as it is portrayed in the West (backward and fundamentalist) and an idealized Iran (Europeanized and modernized) as it was imagined by the Pahlavi kings of the twentieth century. This is obvious in many references to the twentieth century, even though that century should include Islamic Iran as well as the Pahlavi era.

The majority of popular hit songs that are commonly heard at Nowruz events do not have the musical or artistic sophistication necessary to categorize them as pedagogical tools. It is unfortunate that music is heard as a means of pleasure only and does not register as a way of communicating cultural messages to listeners. The same applies to performers who dance to the insistent and repetitive choreographies of folklore dances without learning the language, the stories and the cultural backgrounds of the dances. In addition, the absence of Iranian hip-hop and rock, which are underground art forms in Iran, and expressionist dance reveal a bitter truth about a diasporic culture that follows the institutions

11. Performing Glimpses of the Past 177

and traditions of the home country closely with little to no desire for novelty. The exclusion of Iranian hip-hop and rock singers may be due to the content of the lyrics of Soroush Lashkari (HichKas), Shahin Najafi, Yaser Bakhtiary (YAAS) and Mohsen Namjoo who are perhaps too political or simply too audacious to deal with during festive occasions. However, the expressionistic performance pieces these artists have created refer directly to social conditions in Iran of today and thus can have educational value for young Iranian Americans, who are always eager to know about the 'real' Iran.

A forbidden art for a forbidden body

In their mission statements, the Iranian cultural organizations emphasize on their non-political affiliations.[28] This emphasis intends as an encouragement for involving the wider range of participants and highlights the cultural, professional and artistic strength of the community. And yet, the event organizers' attempts to re-culturate the community make undeniable political statements by saturating Nowruz productions with music and dance. Celebrating a joyous event without music and dance is as unthinkable as distancing these art forms from the politics of the homeland. Music and dance, among some other art forms, have been subject to severe punitive measures since the Islamic Revolution of 1978–9. Khomeini prohibited rhythmic music as soon as he landed in Iran in February 1979, and dance was banned from public stages for many years. Even today, music that excites the listener is prohibited in Iran.[29] When dance was allowed a few years after the revolution, it was renamed *harekat-e mowzun*, meaning rhythmic movements. It can be performed by men and women on public stages as long as the performers abide by the Islamic rules concerning appropriate clothing, gender segregation and dance movements.

It should be noted that the so-called 'appropriate movements' is very open to the interpretation of censors whose responsibility is to issue permits for any live performance.

When young dancers, men and women, in colourful clothes and make-up sing happy tunes and make exotic movements in Nowruz celebrations in the United States, they defy the Islamic Republic's fundamentalist laws and portray a new image for the world to see. Professional dance groups and audience members who dance to the music, on the one hand, perform freedom to engage in a collective dance of celebration and, on the other, demonstrate rebellion against the Islamic Republic's law that prevents opposite sexes from dancing in ensembles. A cultural movement thus turns into a form of subconscious social activism. The same thing, however quite consciously, happens in the streets of Iran whenever a national sports team wins a game overseas. People pour into the streets and celebrate the victory by blocking the roads and dancing in the streets even though they risk arrest and imprisonment. This performs the people's unified victory not only in a sporting event but also over a fundamentalist government. Group dancing thus turns into a joyful social movement.

Public dance is a political performance for the diasporic community that offers an alternative view of the home country to the world by portraying it as docile, colourful, peaceful and approachable. An image that is galaxies away from the darkness of Islamic Republic's foreign policies, dogmatic worldviews and dehumanizing treatment of its citizens. It is certainly the goal of the organizers to welcome and involve non-Iranians to these events. Occasionally, one can recognize a non-Iranian face among the dancers and often among the audience members. On the surface, this is a mission accomplished, but knowing the disconnectedness of the dancers to the culture and the reality of modern-day Iran presents a few problems.

In US media, the ideal body is advertised as eternally young, healthy and perfectly fit. Nowruz dancers' picture-perfect presence on stage coheres with the ideal image of the immortal and unblemished young body. It is notable that the body of the dancers, specially the female dancers, at Nowruz celebrations is another demonstration of defiance of the rules of the Islamic Republic. The perfectly groomed young women in embroidered silk dresses, wearing meticulous makeup, always smiling, energetic and happy, mesmerize the crowd with the smooth movements of their hands and torsos. Their feminine presence stands against the desexualized, covered and militarized body of the 'ideal woman' who was imagined for the nation at the beginning of the Revolution.[30] The dancers in bright-coloured outfits who smile at American bystanders contrast sharply with military women in black hijabs armed with machine guns who shout 'death to America' slogans. Thus, the presence of female dancers on Nowruz stages is a political, anti-Islamic Republic statement and a demand for visibility of those who do not support the Islamic Republic. Simultaneously, the performativity in which the dancers are involved leans towards the self-orientalization of the female body that unintentionally deconstructs the discourses of feminism and postcolonialism. Is this part of the intended pedagogy of Nowruz for Iranian American youth to adhere to the binary gender norms of the previous century? How does the embellished female bodies allow for the individual dancers' recognition of their role in making a political statement? Is this an attempt to follow the Pahlavi's modernization plans for the country based on the Orientalist, Europhile and ignorant understanding of the cultures and traditions of Iran? Can we assume that imitating the rudimentary movements allow for a deeper connection with cultural roots of Iranians living in homeland? And if not, how the silent participation of the dancers not aligned with the Orientalist view of Middle Eastern women voiceless and in need of salvation?

Not only the dancers do not get a chance to create an art that is rooted in self-expression and creative emancipation of the mind, but also their participation in this craft is distanced from the reality of the cultures they try to represent. The young dancers who dance to the same tunes every year abide by the Orientalist view of Middle Eastern women as docile, available for the white culture's pleasure, and voiceless although visible. To summarize, we have our young generations practise a performance of public visibility and participate in a political statement without getting the chance to make real changes either among the diasporic community or in the world that watches them.

Dancers' costuming has the same effect. On the one hand it challenges the fundamentalist laws, while on the other, the choice of costuming in the parades falls into a self-orientalism that defies the purpose of visibility as power. Traditional Iranian costumes, which today are rarely seen in rural areas and tribes, are loose fitting, long and multi-layered. Although hijab rules are not imposed in rural areas as strictly as in metropolitan cities, women do cover their hair and bold make-up is not commonly seen. The costuming for dancers in the parades has been exoticized with shiny and see-though fabrics, high-heel shoes, bejewelled hairdos and make-up. Iranian American dancers barely cover their hair either. The vibrant colours and recreated costumes trespass the reality of what people in Iran wear daily and portray a picturesque image of the otherwise-dark imbued country. And yet, the choice of having young male and female dancers in gaudy and at times inauthentic costumes is in effect a theatricalized exhibition of an ancient culture that has been the victim of Orientalism for so long. The beginning of the twentieth century saw a shift in clothing when Iran moved rapidly towards modernism. Today, instead of traditional costumes, men and women wear outfits that can be seen anywhere in the world in private spaces. The image of the multi-coloured, domesticated, always dancing marchers while breaking through the stereotypes of dark, gloomy and aggressive media coverage of Iran does not do justice to the very real people who struggle every day for their fundamental rights.

Young women who appear on floats, march on the streets, tend the booths, perform dance onstage, host Nowruz programmes, organize events or sing the national anthem are all new but not necessarily real images of Middle Eastern women.[31] The groups of female dancers who display their bodies, delicate movements and uncovered hair and consciously choose to dance engage their viewers. Such extensive and active presence of women in Nowruz productions, against the patriarchal backdrop of its culture, presents a powerful image of women. The presence of Miss Universe 2009 in the New York 2015 Parade points to the same direction. The Islamists who advocate for hijab and women's modesty and virtue dismiss any possibility that Iranian women can participate in beauty pageants. As the ideas of beauty and the female body concerning male desire and feminine power were discussed in the context of Islamic doctrine and Islamic feminism, the Islamic Republic prohibited women from appearing in public without hijab. Consequently, displaying one's beautified appearance in public in Iran could have met with punitive results. In this context, when Miss International 2009 stood on a float, waving to the crowd, her presence was an act that constituted a challenge to the Islamic Republic. Miss International 2009 is another reference to the Pahlavi era when Iran would proudly host and participate in beauty pageants regularly. It is not hard to see that the young generations who participate in the routines of the Nowruz ceremonies each year are subconsciously part of a cultural identification that is based on nostalgia and idealization of the new self of older generations. The presence of Miss 2009 also presents the young members of the Iranian community with a commercialized version of beauty that is idealized on the floats. This particular depiction of Iranian cultural heritage in the form of vibrant colours, exotic dances and music is a form of self-objectification, regardless of the organizers' intention, that feeds into the orientalist image of the Middle East while creating a non-existent fantasy world – a new image that claims visibility while refraining from being entirely truthful about itself.

Conclusion: Where is the real Iran?

Performing national identity is a relatively new concept for Iranians living in diaspora. The exilic community has adhered to public performances such as parades, social gatherings, cultural events and artistic expressions to reclaim its national dignity and to re-culturate itself. Either a reflection on the age of communication or an attempt to survive the global stigmatization, the diasporic community has wisely recognized the power of performance for gaining visibility. And yet this visibility falls short of its time and the community's needs.

Perhaps it is time to think about the next step for the Iranian American community's cultural representations. Instead of creating an imaginary Iran that can only exist in the memory of the first-generation exilic community and thus present conflicts with the reality of the home country, we need to make bridges between contemporary Iran, its current population and the diasporic community: not necessarily as one unified nation but as multifaceted, dynamic and fluctuating members of the global community. It is not enough to educate our next generations about an ancient past that, although worthy of preservation, has ceased to exist. Neither does it prove productive to start from ancient Persia and end at an ambiguous moment in Iran's history year after year. Disregarding the most recent ground-breaking events that have transformed Iran forever has not offered a permanent solution for the ideological conflicts among the members of the community. How can we remain truthful in our very selective choice of pedagogy and remembrance? Also, more importantly, how can we, a minority group living in diaspora, unite with one another and transfer the message of unification and inclusiveness to the next generations when various segments of our society are deliberately being excluded?

12

NEW MEDIA PERFORMANCE AND (AR)TICULATIONS OF THE SELF: CONVERSATION WITH AMIR BARADARAN

Heather Rastovac-Akbarzadeh

Born in Iran and raised in Montreal, Amir Baradaran is a conceptual artist currently based in New York City. Baradaran draws upon a variety of artistic mediums, including performance and augmented reality (AR) technology, to invoke 'a provocation and a proposition' of an artistic movement he calls FutARism.[1] According to Baradaran, FutARism 'seeks to explore the experiential, conceptual and legal shifts suggested by the advent of AR within the modalities of contemporary art, its practice and reception'.[2] AR is a technology that has the ability, through the mediation of a Smartphone and other forms of display, to modify any given view of real-world environments by overlaying computer-generated input onto that view with video, sound and other graphics. Unlike virtual reality, which completely replaces the real world with a simulated one, AR remains in semantic context with physical environments in real-time, thereby enhancing one's perception of and interactive experience with their own physical world. For Baradaran, AR provides artists with the ability to use public spaces as 'white canvases' for artworks.[3] Through his critical art practice, Baradaran's commissioned and infiltratory AR performances such as *Frenchising Mona Lisa* (2011) and *Manam Na Manam: {AR}ticulations of the Self* (2015) offer spectator-participants speculative and performative experiences for critically engaging with the body, technology, curatorial authorship and the gendered racializations of (trans)national and diasporic identities.[4]

In *Digital Performance: A History of New Media in Theater, Dance, Performance Art, and Installation*, Steve Dixon broadly defines digital performance as 'all performance works where computer technologies play a *key* role rather than a subsidiary one in content, techniques, aesthetics, or delivery forms'.[5] While computer technologies are fundamental to the form, Dixon resists the fetishization of technology at the expense of artistic content.[6] Focusing instead on the dialogic relationship between form and content, he situates digital performance as an '*emergent* avant-garde' akin to the praxes of Dadaism, Futurism and other early avant-garde movements.[7] Indeed, digital performance praxis is nascent, and the form's greater social impact still remains to be seen.⁸ However, Baradaran's pioneering AR performances make valuable contributions towards the development of this emergent avant-garde, particularly for how his performances push the boundaries of both form and content, call conventional conceptions of performance into question and engage with pressing political and social concerns.

Cinema scholar Robert Stam refers to Baradaran's AR performances as a form of *détournement* (literally 'rerouting' or 'hijacking') for the ways in which they appropriate visual and digital content in aesthetically and politically innovative ways.⁹ While all of Baradaran's performance works 'reroute' an array of visual content and cultural repertoires in aesthetically and politically salient ways, *Frenchising Mona Lisa* is a particularly poignant illustration of Baradaran's formal and political interventions. First, I will briefly show how the content of *Frenchising Mona Lisa* provokes polemic debates on national identities, immigration politics and Islamophobia in France. Second, I will discuss how this AR performance revitalizes central questions in the field of performance studies through the ways in which it troubles conventional formulations of performance as it pertains to liveness, presence, legality and affect. Finally, the chapter concludes with a conversation with the artist himself.

Abigail Esman, contributor to *Forbes* magazine, begins her review of *Frenchising Mona Lisa* with a provocative question, 'Mona Lisa, a Muslim?' On 27 January 2011, Baradaran infiltrated the Louvre Museum in Paris to permanently install a fifty-two-second augmented reality performance streaming live over Leonardo da Vinci's *Mona Lisa*.¹⁰ In Esman's review, titled 'The rape of the Mona Lisa', she elaborates:

> This Thursday, before your very eyes, the beloved La Jaconde will replace her exquisite gossamer veil for an Islamic headscarf, or hijab. Simply [...] train your Junaio-loaded Smartphone camera at any image of the painting [...] and watch as Leonardo's lovely sitter places a scarf made from a French flag around her head.¹¹

By means of AR technology and the mediation of a Smartphone or tablet, the viewer witnesses, in real-time, Mona Lisa's transformation into a 'Muslim woman', which is enabled through the digital splicing of Baradaran's animate performing body and the inanimate representation of hers.¹² Abigail Esman disapprovingly continues:

> Poor bella Gioconda, it would seem she has been hijacked [...] Baradaran aims to see the hijab become as much a symbol of La France as is the Mona Lisa [...] he wants a France defined as much by Islam as by *pain chocolat* [...] the true implications of his art seem clear enough: a call for the Islamization of the West – of its nations and the magnificent achievements of Western culture.

For Esman, Baradaran's AR performance is nothing less than a 'rape of the Mona Lisa', as the title of her review proclaims. The review's inflammatory title together with Esman's opening question – 'Mona Lisa, a Muslim?' – lay bare the operating framework through which Esman perceives Baradaran's work, one that conflates Muslim masculinity with violent and perverse sexual tendencies. In this case, the rape of Mona Lisa by a Muslim man (Baradaran, more specifically) does not merely violate any Western woman but violates the woman who has come to represent France itself, thereby becoming an assault on the nation and its 'magnificent achievements'.

While digital media forms are often believed to be post-racial or colour-blind, digital media theorist Lisa Nakamura argues that digital media, particularly the internet, are, in fact, sites of what she calls 'digital racial formation'.[13] Building on Michael Omi and Howard Winant's formulation of racial formation, Nakamura's theorization parses 'the ways that digital modes of cultural production and reception are complicit with this ongoing process [of racial formation]'.[14] While Baradaran's AR enactment of Mona Lisa actively veiling draws critical attention to the racialized constructions of Muslim and immigrant subjects in France, Esman's reception of *Frenchising Mona Lisa* exemplifies the very racialized discourses that Baradaran's performance attempts to question: those that place Muslim subjects within an Enlightenment frame as temporally and geographically distant, unchanging, unassimilable and a threat to the fabric of Western civilization.

As a performance experience that is contingent upon video documentation and mobile mediation, *Frenchising Mona Lisa* and its use of AR trouble conventional and influential definitions of performance that have been predicated upon a particular ontology of bodily liveness and presence. Within this established paradigm of performance, forms of reproduction such as video recording and other modes of archiving 'betray' and 'lessen' the ontological promise of performance.[15] According to Peggy Phelan's earlier theorizations of performance, once performance participates in the economy of repetition and the circulation of representations, 'it becomes something *other* than performance'.[16] Philip Auslander, on the other hand, argues 'against ontology' and instead insists on the 'mutual dependence of the live and mediatized'.[17] Auslander further suggests:

> It may be that we are at a point at which liveness can no longer be defined in terms of either the presence of living beings before each other in physical or temporal relationships. The emerging definition of liveness may be built primarily around the audience's *affective* experience.[18]

Auslander's framework theorizes live performance not as inevitably or ontologically contingent upon bodily co-presence in time and space, but rather as defined by its affective impact and its reception as liveness. *Frenchising Mona Lisa* contributes to this debate in two particularly interesting ways, especially with regard to (1) what I suggest would be the affective failure of its original 'live' performance and (2) the performance's legal implications as a performance that could not legally materialize in the institutional space of the Louvre if it were not for the AR technology and the 2D video archiving that constructs it.

First, I argue that what would conventionally be considered *Frenchising Mona Lisa*'s original performance – Baradaran's 'live' body enacting a standard drag rendition of Mona Lisa actively veiling – would fail in its affective and performative impact. In other words, while Baradaran's drag performance would impart a particular political statement about the politics of the hijab in the secularized public sphere in France, it would likely fail to garner the same affective response as the AR performance. Instead of the perception that it is 'really' Mona Lisa actively veiling in one's spatial and temporal midst, the audience would more likely affectively perceive the performance as Baradaran himself actively veiling in drag as Mona Lisa. I further suggest that this 'live' performance would then also lack the performative quality of Mona Lisa *becoming* a Muslim woman and would instead remain at the level of representation.

Frenchising Mona Lisa also complicates Phelan's claim that performance's ontological character is contingent upon disappearance, which, as Auslander describes, would therefore make performance 'exempt from control by the forces that govern […] [a cultural] economy, including the law'.[19] With regard to legal ownership of space, however, AR as a performance art medium currently provides the means to perform in spaces otherwise inaccessible to the practitioner. Referring to *Frenchising Mona Lisa* as a form of graffiti, Baradaran explains that AR as art installation 'confounds current definitions of physical property ownership, rupturing the relationship between the ownership of a space and the agency of its alteration'.[20] Along similar lines, Baradaran refers to graffiti artist Banksy, who is known for placing subverted artworks in institutional spaces such as museums, which were predictably quickly removed.[21] In *Frenchising Mona Lisa*, it is precisely the performance's lack of material and bodily presence that enables the performance to infiltrate the institutional space of the Louvre, circumvent removal from that space and to sustain itself as a performance (therefore establishing it as part of the museum's 'permanent collection', as Baradaran describes in his conversation with me).

It is questionable whether or not Baradaran would have been able to successfully infiltrate the Louvre museum with his 'live' drag performance as Mona Lisa engaged in the act of veiling. Yet, if one is to consider the choreography of space that museum institutions such as the Louvre typically sanction, it is perhaps safe to assume that the museum's security would have prevented or quickly halted Baradaran's live performance. While it may be argued that this hypothetical 'live' performance between Baradaran and the security guards could have had a particular affective impact on the viewers that AR could not – conjuring, perhaps, a spectacle of injustice or even simply an annoying spectacle that disrupts visitors' experiences at the Louvre – this is not the performance that Baradaran intended. Rather, the performance that Baradaran wished to enact – Mona Lisa actively veiling herself in the institutional and national space of the Louvre – could only be actualized (affectively, performatively and legally) through the use of AR and its concomitant video archiving.[22]

The following conversation between Baradaran and me took place in November 2015. As an artist and performer working at the intersection of technology and identity formations, Baradaran is a theorist in his own right. This is evident not only in his artworks but also in his astute conversations about art and technology and the everyday worlds and markets within which they exist.

HR: *How do you define your performance works or yourself as an artist?*
AB: I consider myself a conceptual artist since I don't limit myself to one specific artistic medium. I choose a concept that leads my path and then, based on that, I choose a medium that best helps me articulate those set of thoughts, ideas or concepts. I do performances where my body is the primary medium. Sometimes I use painting, sometimes silkscreen and sometimes video or other spatial installations. I've concentrated a lot of my focus towards the new augmented reality (AR) technology as an artistic medium, which often helps me bring together a variety of concepts and the diverse range of mediums I play with.

HR: *Across most, if not all, of your work, you engage with performance, liveness, mediation, bodies and spectatorship in very interesting ways. Do you have any comments on what it means to bring together 'performance' with the title 'conceptual artist'? Would you also call yourself a performance artist?*
AB: There's a power that comes with the label of being called a performance artist. It opens up a whole set of privileges and allows for me and the performativity of my presence to be framed as a work of art. Also, it frames that which is being displayed as art. I want to turn that question on its head and ask: what is performance art anyway? What is art anyway? Does it need a signature at the bottom of the piece that has been created? Is it whatever I produce at the moment I call myself an artist? Is it a title that allows me to enter the art market or enter a specific social scene? I think it's interesting to see how we arrive at these titles and how these titles inform the theoretical framework through which the works of art are created. I have the tendency of breaking away from these frameworks of 'what is performance art'. Let me give you an example. In *Man Na Manam: The {AR}ticulations of the Self*, the participant and I are supposed to stand on opposite sides from each other, divided by two digital screens. If I feel that the participant may need some extra love, I would go stand beside them, leaving my screen empty. In some types of performance art, breaking the sanctity of the artist/audience dichotomy is not encouraged. Some may allow for an open encounter between the artist and the audience, but it is usually framed in a manner that is oriented towards limited aspects of the experience, thus creating a very sterile engagement. It is often a very scientific-like environment where you may talk to the artist, but you cannot touch them. Or you may exchange energy but cannot verbalize your thoughts as you do so. I've come to feel more comfortable breaking away from the sanctity of these prescribed roles. I don't oppose the possibility of a participant who would want to come and give me a hug. I grew up in a large family where serious conversations about politics could be held concurrent with kids playing and screaming. It's real. It's always changing. I like the idea of embracing

the unpredictability and moving away from the stoic and scientific performance laboratories that many like to create.

I do have a tenuous relationship with these titles, but at the same time, I'm cognisant of the fact that these very titles provide social mobility and allow me to get funding, to be given the spaces to share my ideas and thoughts and to lend legitimacy to my praxis as a conceptual artist, a performance artist, an augmented reality artist.

HR: *You have said that you see performance and performance art as a contract between the artist and the spectator or participant. More specifically, you have called it a contract of marriage, a temporary marriage. Can you speak to the source from which you draw? What is the cultural reference to temporary marriage?*

AB: Often performance art is discussed in secular terms within 'Western' narratives of performance. Temporary marriage provides the space to address the changing nature of desire and bodily, emotional and spiritual engagement.

I've always been fascinated by temporary marriage (*sigheh* or *mut'a*), which is mainly a Shi'i tradition in Islam. It is the legal means within a religious framework that allows for two bodies and minds to come together and negotiate a specific reason (sexual and beyond), a specific, renewable period of time and a specific exchange of money. For me, it addresses the political economy of the institution of marriage or the transactionality of the contract that it represents.

In this Shi'i view, it is important to note that sexuality is not only for the sake of procreation. Temporary marriage is one way to mediate the different ways in which two bodies could temporarily live an experience together.

For me, it's interesting to think about performance in relation to temporary marriage. It allows us to think about the temporality and the contractual nature of that interaction. We usually don't talk about the contract, but there's an unspoken contract between the artist, the space and the audience in performance. For example, [when] you go to a theatre you are taught to behave in a certain way, which may be different from the way you would behave if you go to the cinema.

The contractual aspect of temporary marriage provides a way to shed light on the very transactional nature of performance. Temporary marriage becomes this generative conceptual platform for me to talk about participatory desires and about bodies coming together to co-create a live sculpture. Drawing from a Muslim theoretical paradigm about body, time and desirability also help me to interject religiosity into and thus unsettle the secular or at times spiritual lexicon of performance art.

HR: *What is augmented reality (AR)?*

AB: By looking through the camera of your smartphone, imagine if you could see a butterfly materializing itself from thin air on the palm of my hand.

AR is the technology that allows us to insert virtual, computer-generated content like text, photo, video or 3D animation onto the space in real-time. To make this happen, you usually need a computer, a screen, a camera and sometimes internet, all of which are now available in a smartphone. There are two ways of doing augmentations. The first way is to augment an object, which, at the advent of AR, meant photos (2-dimensional objects) serving as 'markers'. Now we can recognize three-dimensional objects and even faces and body parts. Once the camera recognizes the object or the body, it can overlay on top of it or fully replace it with specific computer-generated content.

The second way of augmenting the world is to do so in a specific point in space. Of course, every point in space has three coordinates: X, Y, Z. The computer now has the capability to recognize its positionality in relation to the space and recognize the coordinate of every possible point in space around it. So, you could possibly place an elephant in a specific point inside of a room, which could then be viewable through your phone, glasses or eventually contact lenses.

> **HR:** *You've done quite a few AR performances since 2011 but I am particularly interested in knowing about two of your AR projects,* Frenchising Mona Lisa *(2011) and* Man Na Manam: The {AR}ticulations of the Self *(2015). What inspired these projects? What were their contexts and the pleasures and challenges in creating and performing them?*
> **AB:** I like the fact that you have chosen these two projects because, firstly, they chronologically represent my earliest and most recent {AR}t works. But also, these two installations sit diametrically opposed from one another in terms of the ways I used the technology which, in turn, reflects the progress of the AR technology throughout the last few years.

Frenchising Mona Lisa is personally one of my favourite projects because it allowed me to think about space, performance and installation art in different terms. I was excited by the possibilities of AR because of the way in which any space could be used as a white canvas for artists to place their art works, thus breaking through the legal and curatorial challenges of art institutions.

AR technology allowed me to place an artwork in the Louvre museum without their permission as a way to instigate questions about the role of AR in our choreography of the social and to shed light on paradigms shifts happening regarding the legal utilization of augmentable spaces. I have claimed that until the Louvre finds the legal means of kicking me out, I'm part of the permanent collection of the museum.

Infiltration art has existed for as long as institutions have. Up to now, trespassing has meant that the very body of the artist had to be present or the artwork had to be physically placed inside the space. For example, when Banksy inserted his work inside the Tate and the British Museum, authorities removed it upon recognizing that the work was not part of the curated collection. It is in this context that AR technology became exciting for me as it allowed me to infiltrate iconic institutions and literally unsettle their existing curatorial authorship. AR provides a paradigm shift here as it complicates the modes of display, authorship and ownership over institutional art spaces. However, it is only a matter of time before the market puts its grip on the augmentable volume and creates the necessary laws that will control where and how this technology can be used. These laws will soon regulate stakeholders and their agency over alteration of spaces. It won't be free for all. In other words, the existence of the world as an augmented white canvas for everyone to play with has an inevitable expiration date.

Frenchising Mona Lisa was a very interesting project for me also because of the way that I interjected my queer Muslim immigrant subjectivity into the performance. At the time, questions dominated the news about hijab in France and Sarkozy's banning of the burqa in public areas. Speculations abounded about the French secular identity and its relationship to its evolving immigrant demographics. So, I wanted to think about the ever-changing object history of the veil and its role as a sartorial signifier of woman's piety, class and religiosity. If you look carefully at Davinci's painting, you see that she was painted with a thin veil over her hair. It was common practice to represent Catholic women of a certain class through the veil. So, I pondered: here is Mona Lisa, an immigrant woman, originally Italian, painted by an Italian artist and she is wearing a 'hijab', right? So, I asked: 'What is Sarkozy going to do?' Mona Lisa is literally a veiled immigrant woman in a public space. Will Sarkozy kick her out of the Louvre?

Man Na Manam, on the other hand, utilizes and plays with the latest available developments of AR. The data sculpture is made of two digital mirrors that are standing back to back at the eye level. Both are fully equipped with microphones, cameras, depth sensors, colour sensors and computers with customized AR algorithm that has the capacity of recognizing seventy points on your face. The AR sculpture, the machine, is thus empowered to perform facial detection and to understand and react to participants' facial expressions. It can understand if you're smiling, if you're sticking your tongue out, if you're kissing or if you're frowning. In other words, through artificial intelligence, the camera not only sees but it understands what it sees by analysing the input and computing its meaning.

Frenchising Mona Lisa sits within a genre of {AR}t works that I have called BYOD – requiring the audience members to bring their own device. These bodies of my works include *FutARism Manifesto*, *mARkers*, *Takeoff* and *Little Buzzz*. I have moved away from that genre and have been working on pieces that are fully equipped with all that's needed to experience the {AR}twork. *Man Na Manam* is the latest iteration of my praxis. For one, it makes the work more accessible, and more importantly, when people bring their own devices, they are relying on the capability of a small processor that's in the smartphone, which has very limited capacity for rendering and executing binaries. Whereas when I do installations for what I call data sculptures, then it includes devices of which I am fully in control. I can use heavy-duty computers and processing systems that allow me to do all kinds of acrobatics with algorithms and processing data that would never be feasible on smartphones. With growing technological advancement in AR, I can now better flex the muscles of AR to create much more complex experiences.

HR: *For* Man Na Manam, *you use a few lines of poetry from the thirteenth-century Persian poet Jalaleddin Rumi. Why did you choose this particular poem? Does it speak to a particular experience enabled through AR performance? Is there any relationship between the poem and AR?*

AB: I'm not an expert on Rumi and I certainly don't claim to have the capacity of fully grasping the layers of meaning in his writing. Despite the fact that his work has been appropriated by the new age genre of spirituality, somewhat turning the poem into a commodity, I think Rumi's work is very radical and has many more layers than what one may usually grasp. I particularly love this poem because it formulates the notion of self in relation to the other in a very moving and complex way. The refrain I chose could be translated as 'I am not I, neither am I, I'. The poem goes on to say, 'and you are not you, neither are you, you'. It essentially shatters the identity of both the poet and the reader and then brings them together only to shatter them again. Even though Rumi wrote this eight centuries ago, it feels poignantly relevant with regard to politics of identity and identity formation.

I'm particularly interested in the poem for it enables a fresh way of thinking about the notion of self versus the other, which I refer to interchangeably as both the participant and the machine. This allows me to engage with the concept of AR within a larger narrative and phenomenon of artificial intelligence (AI) as a way of understanding our relationality to one another and to the machine. In the piece, I simply see myself in my own mirror before my face gets merged with that of the participant. There is a representation of myself that's being produced through the machine. It really makes me think about 'I' in relation to the machine and to the algorithm that's written for the machine.

If you look at programming language, you see that there is a resemblance between codes and modern poetry in the way they both use letters, words, phrases, digits and symbols alongside the negative space. Every element of the syntax has a particular spatial configuration that is communicated as much through its textual formation and meaning as its visual representation. For me, writing in binary codes is a lyrical way of communicating through the language of AI. It is modern poetry. It is poAItry. I work with technologists and programmers who write for me and I call them my poAIts. In *Man Na Manam*, my aim was to juxtapose a classical genre of Persian poetry with the writing of contemporary poAIts.

It's also interesting to note that, like any textual creation, poAItry is framed by and represents the moral value systems of those who are producing it as much as it also acts as a new site through which cultural paradigms are mobilized and articulated.

HR: *You mentioned the term 'data sculpture'. Can you tell me more about that?*

AB: Yes, it really speaks to the joys and pains of using a medium that has yet to be framed theoretically. There really is no vocabulary for using AR in art. We have to come up with ways of talking about it, practising it, showing it, exhibiting it, conceptualizing it, materializing it and visually executing it. Everyone is very familiar with a painter's tools – a brush, paint and canvas. We have gained familiarity with that artistic medium, its techniques and different ways of displaying it because people have been using it for centuries. But when it comes to using AR as an artistic medium, how do I refer to my 'finished' pieces? Are they sculptures? I like the idea of using the word 'sculpture' because it denotes a certain realness and object-driven physicality, which is a stretch from the way we usually think of AR.

So, when I talk about {AR}t as data sculpture or installation, it is a tongue-in-cheek commentary on the corporeality of the AR experience as opposed to its virtual contents. I like to think about sculpture and AR in the same phrase because I believe that it pushes us to think of the space in which the {AR}t is installed, displayed and/or experienced.

> **HR:** *Can you talk a little more about the role of the materiality of your own body or that of other bodies, even if the 'live body' is perhaps questionable in your works?*
>
> **AB:** Some of my performance pieces don't incorporate my corporeal presence or even its representation. But some of them still do require a bodily presence, even if it's not my own. For me, performance art is more about choreographing the way bodies come together in space, in relation to one another and in relation to an object or multiple objects in a particular space. My *SamovAR* installation piece is one example. Basically, the piece consists of this antique Russian royal samovar that I acquired through eBay and that I placed on the wall inside of a Plexiglas box. At the foot of the samovar, there was an inclined digital mirror equipped with a camera, computer and custom algorithms. Audience members were given a saucer with the painting of a marker in the middle of it that was recognizable and augmentable by the camera.

As the participant put the saucer beneath the samovar, they would experience an AR drop of tea dripping onto their saucer. Although my own body is not present in that space, I'm choreographing the way in which the participant's body should perform specific corporeal tasks – such as standing, holding, looking and interacting – for the participant to experience the {AR}t.

In that sense, because I'm curating or choreographing audience's bodily participation, I consider this a performance, even though in this case my own body is absent. I tend to explore the overlaps between interactive art and performance. I'm interested in the way these mediums may brush against, and in turn inform, one another. For me, {AR}t installations provide the site to curate a spatial choreography that forces the body of the audience into particular contortions and ultimately into an AR experience. So, in a way, I am always using the concept of performance as I encourage a specific choreography for bodies to react to and interact with other bodies, objects and (intelligent) machines surrounding them.

Usually it's the body of the performance artist that's fully in action or in motion. This is not the case in *SamovAR* or other BYODs ('bring your own device') installations, such as the *Frenchising Mona Lisa*. The participant must operate the phone and hold it in a particular way and at a specific height, distance and angle, thus allowing for the machine to affect the reality and to unsettle the body/object and real/virtual dichotomies. For me, these bodies of work propose a shift away from performances where the audience may not be given a lot of space to interact other than being present or gazing at the performance artist. I like to conceptually explore the space where experiencing the piece predicates forcing a specific choreography of the space through, and by, the body of the participant.

> **HR:** *You have mentioned to me in a previous conversation how the failures of technology are nonetheless generative. Can you elaborate?*
>
> **AB:** I love thinking about the promise of technology as much as its failures. In fact, for me, talking about the promise already insinuates a certain room for improvement, which is often linked to its experiential or conceptual failures. I'm not technologically deterministic. I do not believe in a particular salvation through technology. At the same time, I'm not dystopian. I prefer to create within a heterotopian framework where I engage with both ends of that spectrum to create a contemplative and generative space. I enjoy playing with the technology itself while momentarily thinking about that very process of engagement. It helps me create knowledge that positions itself within the larger metanarrative of technology.

I'm particularly interested in what I call the 'adjacent potentiality of technology', a generative space right at that juncture of where any idea initially blossoms and/or fails, a space from where many other possibilities can emanate. It is the space that juxtaposes rise and failure. It's the procreative space where thought formation happens, where we extrapolate from that very technology or innovative idea to build upon and/or move away from what is initially created. It's seeing the potential in that adjacent space in which the limitations of the created things or the produced knowledge push us to tangentially conceive new sets of thoughts and paradigms.

> **HR:** *Can you describe the intersections between form, in this case AR technology, and the content? How do they enable each other?*
>
> **AB:** What I realized about the few artists working with AR is that a lot of them come from very technical backgrounds. They get very excited about the novelty effect of AR, so their interaction and engagement with the medium can be limited.

Knowing that the art world has always had an aversive reaction towards new forms of technologies, I was excited about creating a platform where I could challenge the art world to understand the merits of AR technology as a new medium for artistic creation. My interest has been in finding ways of marrying the form with the artistic content. Explorations of the form are certainly very important as we need to pave the way and come up with creative uses of the medium: how to display it, how to engage with it, how to create an experience through it. So when creating {AR}t works, there's a necessity for engaging with the form for form's sake. There's a need for the type of art making that solely evolves around form. Such works help us extend our knowledge and experimentation with the medium itself.

But that is not enough. For AR to be truly considered as a new medium for {AR}tistic creation, we also need to push for finding ways of creating powerful content that is unique to the form while transcending it at the same time. That is something that I have tried to pursue as a goal. For me, there are important questions: Can we use this technology to think about technology? How does the medium affect our bodies or our sense of self/otherness? How does AR affect other forms of art making? What about performance art and the role of our body inside AR experiences? How will it affect theatre, installation art and sculpture? How will it affect photo, video and animation? What's the difference between experiencing a video that lives through augmented reality and seeing it through traditional screens? How does this medium change the reception of the content but also the very making of it as it does so?

> **HR:** *What is most interesting about your work for me is how it so intelligently uses and pushes technology while also speaking to political concerns and/ or drawing upon a wide range of cultural references. Do you consciously consider the political implications of your very specific body in the making of your work?*
>
> **AB:** Absolutely. Even if I didn't want to consider it, the consideration would be imposed upon me. The question of identity is less about how you position yourself and more about how others position you in relation to them. Twenty-first-century representations and treatment of Muslim bodies, and those who pass for Muslim, have been more unified and exacerbated in their characterization. Let us be reminded that if you choose to frequent a mosque or participate in any religious practices in New York City, chances are that you will be placed under a not-so-secret governmental surveillance programme. My position as a Muslim person is affected by all of that. My body is continuously subjected to these power dynamics. I'm very conscious of that and I take great joy in utilizing references to Muslim religious and cultural practices. I do so as a way of confronting that positionality with an emphasis on the very assemblages that construct my sense of self.

When I did *The Other Artist Is Present*, which was an infiltration into Marina Abramović's 2010 MOMA performance *The Artist Is Present*, I played a lot with my position as Iranian and as Muslim. One act of my performance was called *The Other Trance*, which aimed to trouble the pseudo-secular sanctity of a museum experiences. In Marina's performance, her trance involved silence based on her long engagement with Buddhist traditions of meditation. But that's not the only way of achieving a transformative metaphysical experience. My way, the way I grew up, the way I learned about spirituality was precisely the opposite of that. It was never that sterile. It's messy and not at all stoic. It involves singing, dancing and eventually sweating or bleeding. So, whether it's the whirling of Sufi dervishes or the flagellations in Shi'i processions, it's all about corporeal movements and the tensions between the space and sound through vocal and participatory experiences. In *The Other Trance*, I chant across from her by positioning my body as the other artist, the queer Muslim immigrant of colour. The chanting I do also references one of Marina's earlier works where she combs her hair while uttering, 'Art is beautiful, and artists must be beautiful'. The repetitive act is powerful as far as it critiques standards of beauty in the (art) world. As a reference to that work, I used a Sufi saying that I learned from my grandfather: 'God is beautiful and loves beauty.' It comes from a story that describes how an elderly Sufi master kneels down in front of a beautiful adolescent boy to show his love of God by praising the beauty of the young boy.

> **HR:** *Can you tell me more about the relationships between your various self-identifications and your performance work?*
> **AB:** It's a very tenuous relationship particularly because of how the art world functions. Class, gender, race, nationality and cultural affinities affect the way one navigates through the webs of power inside the art world and its market. Questions of centre versus periphery are essential to the ways artists are produced, appreciated and marketed. The binary paradigm mimics that of the larger world order, which, in turn, affects the way in which art markets respond to, commodify, appraise, circulate and exchange those bodies of work and ultimately the bodies of the artists that produce those works.

I was born in Iran, a place that, despite and maybe because of its cultural and geopolitical significance, is considered as part of the periphery, not the centre. Although I was transplanted as an adolescent to Canada and have been living in in New York for almost a decade, I will always be seen and framed as the other. Because of that, I constantly have to renegotiate my positionality in relation to the centre. It is in this context that, playfully and purposefully, I bring in glimpses of 'peripheral' religious traditions into my performances, as 'dated' as they may seem, in order to disrupt the West-centric and often pseudo-secular lexicon of the art world. There's this constant struggle, constant tension, constant negotiation that takes place every time I start a project because of the intersection of the spaces I inhabit.

It is a very contentious space to inhabit that I share with many other artists of colour in the West. It is one that concurrently positions us as part of the centre and outside of it. It is a peculiar space as it directly affects the way in which one experiences access as privilege.

Who has access to institutions that define art? What does it mean to be a part of the dialogue that happens within the mainstream art world? Does the scene still belong, and cater, to specific social and economic demographics? With that power comes a sense of cultural superiority through which the value systems within the art world get to be evaluated and defined. Access to it determines agency over its representation. If members of communities of colour are not allowed to be actively a part of those scenes, then somebody else is likely speaking for those communities. Somebody else is creating the visual vocabulary to represent those communities. So, then the question is: how much agency do communities of colour have over their own representation? Through perpetual Orientalist discourses, the media's recurring image of a Muslim man remains equated with violence, lack of rationality and often over-sexualization. The question is, who writes and produces those stories? Who funds them and ultimately for whose consumptions are they made? Taking ownership over one's representation is required in much more systematic ways than the few token spaces that are sporadically made available to them.

I'm also excited to carve out my own way of addressing these challenges and to contribute to dialogues within the art scene. Particularly, I am cognisant of the fact that as an Iranian immigrant Muslim queer body of colour, I happen to be one of the few artists in the world who are thinking and talking about technology, artificial intelligence and how AR will affect our understanding of our bodies, objects around us and our body-machine interactivity. This is a very privileged space that I have come to colonize. Although I have been privileged enough to gain some kind of a position of authority within this field, I remain conscious of the way in which I have forced myself into that space. I'm taking this conscious road of forcing myself into that narrative, into that space, and making myself relevant by literally infiltrating the mainstream discourses around art and technology. Otherwise, the usual platforms given to Middle Eastern artists basically expect that we regurgitate a certain set of existing Orientalist and Islamophobic tropes about our identities. For instance, as a queer Iranian Muslim, I'm often expected to orient my work around articulations of sexual freedom that position Canada or the United States as the 'land of liberty' where I'm allegedly able to freely express my sexuality (narrowly framed as gay). I stay away from these types of narratives in my work, even though I would definitely be much more successful in the art market if I did express these themes. Instead of that, however, I tap into spaces, conceptually and otherwise, in which I'm not supposed to be. It's a conscious and constant struggle of infiltration.

Aside from the challenges of my specific positionality in relation to the art market, another important thing to consider is that the art world has historically had difficulties accepting new forms of technologies. The market's strong grip over the art world particularly manifests itself through its concerns over archivability and collectability of art. The notion of archive has been a long-time challenge for performance artists and especially for those who work with any form of new media. The question comes down to 'What is it that we are collecting?' The market needs to hold it in its hands, quantify it and then put a value it. At this point, data sculptures and {AR}t installations particularly disrupt these models. What is it that can be owned and sold? Is it the augmentable point in space that you are selling? Is it the content? Or the experience as a whole? What's the final product that has been created? And can we quantify it? Make it into limited editions? Can we put a name on it, touch it, hold it, collect it and ultimately sell it? Those are also the big questions.

Conclusion

As this chapter has illustrated, Baradaran's AR performances complicate conventional ontologies within theatre and performance studies that perceive performance to require embodied liveness. Moreover, his performances critically engage the impossibility of his queer, Iranian Muslim body within social, geopolitical and market spheres. While Euro-American geopolitics construct the Muslim male as homophobic, perverse and a threat to women's and gay rights,[23] 'the repeated and socially sanctioned modes of behaviour'[24] within dominant diasporic Iranian social repertoires also marginalize 'presentations of self'[25] that deviate from norms of heterosexuality and 'non-Islamiosity'.[26] Baradaran's interventions into these dominant scripts are mobilized through astute form, content and corporeality that coalesce into critical {AR}ticulations of the self: augmented reality technology, 'undesirable' Islamic practices, Iranian cultural archives and Baradaran's queer, Muslim immigrant body. In *Frenchising Mona Lisa*, for instance, Baradaran creates AR-enabled performance assemblages through which his body becomes the *Mona Lisa* as a Muslim woman veiling herself with the French flag in the institutional space of the Louvre Museum. At once, Baradaran mobilizes his veiling body to interrogate the xenophobic political landscape of contemporary France and to create emergent relationalities between his racialized body and the bodies of the performance participants, a process Baradaran refers to as 'choreographing the social'. Baradaran's other performances reconfigure dominant national iconography of Iranianness, such as utilizing Rumi's poetry in juxtaposition with the programming language for artificial intelligence, or what Baradaran refers to as poAItry. In *Manam Na Manam: {AR}ticulations of the Self*, Baradaran uses Rumi's stanza *man na manam na man manam* ('I am not I, neither am I, I') as a point of departure for exploring contemporary identity politics more broadly, and the relation between self, other and technology more specifically. Across all of his performances, Baradaran brings together the repertoires of (dominant and marginal) Iranianness with emergent AR technologies to construct queer diasporic Iranian archives and to generate new forms of belonging.[27]

NOTES

Introduction

1. As part of a former garden, which also included a zoo, and originally located outside of the city walls, Lalehzar was built in the process of urban expansion under the reign of Nasser al-Din Shah (1831–96). For an oral account of Lalehzar under Naser al-Din Shah, see Hossein Shahidi Mazandarani, *Sargozasht-e Tehran* (Tehran: Entesharat-e Mana: 2004), pp. 63–4.
2. It is likely that Abbas Rasam Arjangi (1892–1975), known for fusing European and Iranian themes in his artistic works, was the architect of the bass-relief statue. I am grateful to Behnam Aboutorabia for his suggestion about Arjangi as a possible architect.
3. The theatre space originally grew into existence from one of the entrances of the Grand Hotel of Tehran, which was established in 1916, one of the most luxurious buildings in the capital. Golbarg Rekabtalaei, *Iranian Cosmopolitanism: A Cinematic History* (Cambridge: Cambridge University Press, 2019), p. 54. Also, Theatre Tehran was burnt down in 1962, the same year when Nasr passed away.
4. Established in 1940 as 'Theatre Tehran', though after damage caused by fire in 1962 was renamed after Nasr, the Nasr Theatre served as the only permanent theatre space under Reza Shah's reign. Saeed Talajooy, 'The Impact of Soviet Contact on Iranian Theatre', in *Iranian-Russian Encounters: Empires and Revolutions since 1800*, Stephanie Cronin ed. (London; New York: Routledge, 2013), p. 340. For an audio documentary on the theatre in Persian, see http://radionist.com/. Last accessed 15 October 2020. I am grateful to Ida Meftahi for informing me of the informative audio documentary.
5. Tehran municipality briefly opened the theatre for public view in mid-April 2019. As of 2020, there are plans to turn the theatre into a museum. See https://www.tehrantimes.com/photo/434755/Historic-Tehran-Nasr-Theater-to-undergo-renovation (last accessed 25 September 2020).
6. Eric J. Hobsbawm, *The Age of Extremes: A History of the World, 1914–1991* (New York: Vintage Books, 1996).
7. Written by Hasan Moqaddam (1897–1925), the play is a critique of the Iranian failure to appropriate modernity in its intellectual core rather than mere superficial display. For a historical account of the play, see Maryam Shariati, 'Jaʿfar Ḵān az Farang Āmada', January 2000. http://www.iranicaonline.org/articles/ja-far-khan-az-farang.
8. Talajooy, 'The Impact of Soviet Contact', p. 340.
9. Ibid., pp. 342; 353–4.
10. The political satirical play about the conflict between two families, members of rival political groups though later reconcile in alliance against economic repression, ended with the call for workers' solidarity. The production was an adaptation with the title *The Workers Alternative*. The play was twice performed at the theatre, packed with mixed audiences of students, intellectuals and regular Lalehzar spectators. According to Nasser Rahmaninejad, the anniversary of the revolution was celebrated by an

'anti-imperialist theatre festival'. Interview with Nasser Rahmaninejad, 20 September 2020. See also Nasser Rahmaninejad, A *Man of the Theatre: Survival as an Artist in Iran* (New York: New Village Press, 2020), pp. 224–5 and Nasser Rahmaninejad, 'Yadat mandegar aghaye vahdat', *Asr-e, No. 7*, October 2020 http://asre-nou.net/php/view.php?objnr=50531 last accessed 16 October 2020.

11 For a comprehensive list of theatres, festivals, educational venues and libraries related to the study of theatre in contemporary Iran, see Mashhood Mohsenian ed., *Ketab-e Avval Te'atr-e Iran* (Tehran: Entesharat-e Namayesh, 2016).

12 Alain Badiou has underscored the theatre's value, unique among the arts, as a site of immanence and transcendence, by which depicted ideas transcend our reality and yet are of our most immediate reality, an 'art of possibilities' as its highest expression. Alain Badiou, *In Praise of Theatre* (Cambridge, UK; Malden MA: Polity Press, 2015), p. 2.

13 Theatre, Samuel Weber has argued, is a unique medium, an interval in that ambivalences about space and subjectivity emerge. Samuel Weber, *Theatricality as Medium* (New York: Fordham University Press, 2004).

14 For a study of theatre, spectrality and modernity, see Marvin Carlson, *The Haunted Stage: The Theatre as Memory Machine* (Ann Arbor: The University of Michigan Press, 2003) and Mary Luckhurst and Emilie Morin, eds., *Theatre and Ghosts: Materiality, Performance and Modernity* (Houndmills, Basingstoke, Hampshire [England]; New York: Palgrave Macmillan, 2014).

15 Note that 'modernity' should be understood as a concept formation tied to disciplinary institutional transformations that gave rise to its first written articulation in France in the middle of the nineteenth century. See Matei Calinescu, *Five Faces of Modernity: Modernism Avant-Garde, Decadence, Kitsch, Postmodernism* (Durham: Duke University Press, 1987), pp. 42–3.

16 Augusto Boal, *Theatre of the Oppressed*, trans. by Charles A and Maria-Odilia Leal Mcbride (New York: Theatre Communication Group, 1985), p. IX.

17 See Emmet Kennedy, *A Cultural History of the French Revolution* (New Haven, Conn: Yale University Press, 1989).

18 See Mohammad Tavakoli-Targhi, *Refashioning Iran: Orientalism, Occidentalism and Historiography* (Houndmills, Basingstoke, Hampshire; New York: St. Antony series, Palgrave, 2001), pp. 113–34.

19 Quoted in Saeed Talajooy, 'A History of Iranian Drama (1850–1941)', in *Literature of the Early Twentieth Century: From the Constitutional Period to Reza Shah: A History of Persian Literature*, Ali-Asghar Seyed Gohrab, ed. (London; New York: I.B. Tauris, 2015), pp. 373–4.

20 Ibid., 374. For the statement in the original Persian, see Jamshid Malekpoor, *Adabiyat-e Namayeshi Dar Iran: Dowran-e Enqelab-e Mashruteh*, Vol. 1 (Tehran: Tus Publication, 2006), p. 1.

21 *Etela'at*, No. 3771, 18 Esfandmah, 1317 (8 March 1939).

22 The notion of 'performing Iran' is an attempt to go beyond the limits of society-state binaries and a conception of culture, perceived as implicitly distinct from national identity, that negotiates civic space with territorial state power. A mere focus on 'national identity' in textuality of stories or narrative as repertoires of social action that content, negotiate or at times appropriate state territoriality is itself a discursive performance; its social imaginary sustains the prominence of the 'state', sovereign in territorial definition, though in its revolutionary context perpetually under the threat of collective action. For an example of a nation-state paradigm approach, see Farideh

Farhi, 'Crafting a National Identity Amidst Contentious Politics in Contemporary Iran', in *Iran in the 21st Century: Politics, Economics and Conflict*, Homa Katouzian and Hossein Shahidi eds. (London; New York: Routlege, 2008), pp. 13–27.

23 For a classic study of cinema as commodity, see Jean-Luc Comolli and Paul Narboni, 'Cinema/Ideology/Criticism', *Screen*, Vol. 2, No. 1, Spring 1971, pp. 27–38.

24 Not all chapters in this book adopt this conception of culture. See for example, Chapter 5, by Mahmood Karimi Hakak. Also for an example on the study of culture as resistance, by and large, in post-revolutionary Iran, see Annabelle Sreberny and Massoumeh Torfeh, eds. *Cultural Revolution in Iran: Contemporary Popular Culture in the Islamic Republic* (London; New York: I.B. Tauris, 2013).

25 For a recent example in the study of culture, or rather 'popular culture' in post-revolutionary Iran, see Sreberny and Torfeh, eds. *Cultural Revolution in Iran*.

26 Williams rejects the notion of 'culture' in exclusive terms of activities such as art, music, literature or theatre, known as 'high culture', and interprets the concept through inclusive terms of everyday practices based in the systems of production. For Williams's two conceptions of culture, see Raymond Williams, 'Culture Is Ordinary', in *Resources of Hope: Culture, Democracy, and Socialism* (London: Verso, 1989), pp. 3–8.

27 Here by 'Iranian theatre' I refer to a European-inspired theatre that attained a distinct Iranian socio-cultural character in its various formations from the late nineteenth century.

28 Mohammad Ali Pirzadeh Na'ini, *Safarnameh Haji Pirzadeh*. edited by hafez-e Farmaniyan (Tehran: Moasseseh-ye Entesharat-e va chap-e daneshgah-e Tehran, 1963), p. 227.

29 For literary reference to theatre's popularity, see the short story, *Mademoiselle Pearl*. Guy de Maupassant, *Mademoiselle Pearl* (Read Books Ltd, 2012).

30 For nineteenth-century Iranian accounts of theatre in Europe, see Tavakoli-Targhi, *Refashioning Iran*, pp. 59–61; and Nile Green, *The Love of Strangers: What Six Muslim Students Learned in Jane Austin's London* (Princeton; Oxford: Princeton University Press, 2016), pp. 37–8.

31 The Opera House was built at the behest of Napoleon III from 1861 to 1875.

32 For a study on the relationship between city space and theatre, see Marvin Carlson, *Places of Performance: The Semiotics of Theatre Architecture* (Ithaca and London: Cornell University Press, 1989), pp. 14–36.

33 Pannill Camp, 'Theatre Optics: Enlightenment Theatre Architecture in France and the Architectonics of Husserl's Phenomenology', *Theatre Journal*, Vol. 59, No. 4 (December 2007), pp. 615–33.

34 Richard Preiss, 'Interiority', in *Early Modern Theatricality*, Henry S. Turner ed. (Oxford: Oxford University Press, 2013), p. 51.

35 For a historical account of gaslight technology in pre-Edisonian theatre, See Gundula Kreuzer, *Curtain, Gong, Steam: Wagnerian Technologies of Nineteenth-Century Opera*, (Oxford: Oxford University Press, 2018).

36 Glynn Wickham, *A History of the Theatre* (Cambridge; New York; Port Chester; Melbourne; Sydney: Cambridge University Press, [1985]1992), p. 182.

37 Henry James, 'The Parisian Stage, Letter from Henry James, Jr', in *Parisian Sketches: Letters to the New York Tribune*, 1875–1876, Leon Edel and Ilse Dusoir Lind eds. (New York: New York University Press, 1957), p. 44.

38 See Fredrick Brown, *Theatre and Revolution: The Culture of the French Stage* (New York: The Viking Press, 1980), pp. 5–8.

39 The sociological category 'middle-class', and its associated cultural practices, should be understood in limitation to regional and historical settings, and therefore not be

universalized based on a European model of social structure-if such imagined model even has coherency. In its late Qajar context, I primarily refer to 'middle-class' in segmentations, from propertied classes, such as merchants, shopkeepers, craftsmen, to some local notables, small landowners and even waged artisans. The added complexity of Qajar 'class system' lies in the status of the clerical establishment and tribal linkages, with the former cross-cutting into commercial class segments through familial ties. See Ann K.S. Lambton, *Qājār Persia: Eleven Studies* (Austin: University of Texas Press), pp. 194–222. Ervand Abrahamian, *Iran: Between Two Revolutions* (Princeton, New Jersey: Princeton University Press, 1982), pp. 33–6; Ahmad Ashraf and Ali Banuazizi, 'Class System v. Classes in the Qajar Period', *Encyclopaedia Iranica* https://iranicaonline.org/articles/class-system-v.

40 See 'Emile Durkheim's Remarks on Late Nineteenth-Century Rural-Urban Transformation', in *The Division of Labour in Society* (1898), Emile Durkheim, trans. G. Simpson (New York: Free Press, 1933), p. 172.
41 On the concept of theatrical environment in the context of nineteenth-century England, see Raymond Williams, *Culture and Materialism: Selected Essays* (London; New York: Verso, 2005), pp. 125–47.
42 For a study of Tehran's population and districts, see Nabuaki Kondo, *Islamic Law and Society in Iran: A Social History of Qajar Tehran* (London; New York: Routledge, 2017), pp. 14–15.
43 Similar to Hamid Amjad, I make a distinction between *namayesh*, though not an ideal equivalent but translated here as 'ritual spectacle', and 'theatre', for the interchangeability of audience and spectator as a cultural institution. Note that the Greco-Roman notion of 'theatre' (*theatron* [Greek] and *theatrum* [Latin]), in its purpose-built staging location form, meant a 'space of viewing', and hence in terms of denotation shared a similar meaning with *namayesh*. See also Chapter 3 in this volume for a discussion on the distinction between 'ritual' and 'theatre'. Moreover, see Hamid Amjad, *Te'atr-e Qarn-e Sizdahom* (Tehran: Nila Publications, 2002), p. 13. Among numerous urban performances ranging from animal games to athletic competitions, one could also mention *Sho'badeh-bazi* (magic show), which most likely saw its growth in popularity during the Safavid period. For a historical account, see Yagoob Azhand, *Namayesh dar dor-ye Safavi* (Theatre and Popular Entertainment in the Safavid Period]) (Tehran: Moasseseh Ta'lif, 2009), pp. 113–20.
44 Farokh Gaffary, 'baqqal-bazi', *Encylopaedia Iranica* 1988 http://www.iranicaonline.org/articles/baqqal-bazi-lit (last accessed, April 30). For a short account of *pahlavan kachal* performances, see Talajooy, 'A History of Iranian Drama', pp. 358–9; see also Willem Floor, *The History of Theater in Iran* (Washington, DC: Mage, 2005), pp. 305–10.
45 See Anthony Shay, 'Bazi-ha-ye Nameyeshi: Iranian Women's Theatrical Plays', *Dance Research Journal*, Vol. 27, No. 2, 2014, pp. 16–24.
46 Talajooy, 'A History of Iranian Drama', p. 357.
47 For a general study of Iranian performance traditions, see William O. Beeman, 'A Full Arena: The Development and Meaning of Popular Performance Traditions in Iran', in *Modern Iran: The Dialectics of Continuity and Change*, Michael Bonine and Nikki Keddie eds. (Albany: State University of New York Press, 1981), pp. 361–82 and William O. Beeman, *Iranian Performance Traditions* (Costa Mesa, Calif: Mazda Publishers Inc, 2011). For a comparative study of blackface minstrel traditions with reference to its Iranian practice, see Angelita D. Reyes, 'Performativity and Representation in Transnational Blackface: Mammy (USA), Zwarte Piet

(Netherlands), and Haji Firuz (Iran)', *Atlantic Studies*, Vol. 16, No. 4, 2019, pp. 521–50.
48 Mahroo Rashidirostami, 'Performance Traditions of Kurdistan: Towards a More Comprehensive Theatre History', *Iranian Studies*, Vol. 51, No. 2, 2018, pp. 269–87.
49 Vanessa Martin, *The Qajar Pact: Bargaining, Protest and the State in Nineteenth-Century Persia* (London; New York: I.B. Tauris, 2005), p. 150.
50 See Philippe Rochard and Denis Jallat, 'Zurkhaneh, Sufism, Fotovvat/Javanmardi and Modernity: Considerations about Historical Interpretations of a Traditional Athletic Institution', in *Javanmardi: The Ethics and Practice of Persianate Perfection*, Llyod Ridgeon ed. (London: Gingko Library, 2018), pp. 232–62.
51 There were two forms of Takkiyeh Dowlat prior to the construction of the larger Naseri version, commissioned in 1868. See Floor, *The History of Theater*, pp. 140–5. Babak Rahimi, 'Takkiyeh Dowlat: The Qajar Theater State', in *Performing the Iranian State: Visual Culture and Representations of Iranian Identity*, Staci Gem Scheiwiller ed. (London; New York; Delhi: Anthem Press, 2013), pp. 55–71.
52 For a discussion on why the Parisian Opera House was a possible site of inspiration instead of the Royal Albert Hall in London, see Rahimi, 'Takkiyeh Dowlat', p. 63; 70 ft. 33. See also Abbas Amanat, *Pivot of the Universe: Nasir al-Din Shah and the Iranian Monarchy* (London; New York: I.B. Tauris 2008), p. 435.
53 Vahid Vahdat, 'Spatial Discrimination in Tehran's Modern Urban Planning 1906–1907', *Journal of Planning History*, Vol. 12, No. 1, 2013, pp. 49–62.
54 For a history of Dar al-Fonun, see Maryam Ekhtiar, 'Nasir al-Din Shah and the Dar al-Funun: The Evolution of an Institution', *Iranian Studies*, Vol. 34, No. 1/4, 2001, pp. 153–63.
55 Floor, *The History of Theater*, p. 213.
56 Hasan Shirvani, *Honar-e Namayesh* (Tehran: Vezarat-e Farhang va Honar, 1976), pp. 21–7.
57 Ibid., p. 215.
58 Ibid., pp. 214–15.
59 Talajooy, 'A History of Iranian Drama', pp. 372–3.
60 Rekabtalaei, *Iranian Cosmopolitanism*.
61 For an account of Akhondzadeh's plays, see Talajooy, 'A History of Iranian Drama', pp. 360–3; Floor, *The History of Theater*, pp. 219–21. For Akhondzadeh's critique of gender and marriage in its Qajar context, see Afsaneh Najmabadi, *Women with Mustaches and Men without Beards* (Berkeley, Los Angeles, London: University of California, 2005), p. 156, and for a more in-depth study, Sahar Allamezade, *Men Writing Women: 'The Woman Question' and Male Discourse of Iranian Modernity* (Dissertation: University of Maryland, 2016), pp. 34–68.
62 Mohammad. R. Ghanoonparvar and John Green, compiled and eds., *Iranian Drama: An Anthology* (Costa Mesa: Calif. Mazda, 1989), pp. xi–xii.
63 A similar trend can also be identified with the tradition of naturalism, in particular Anton Chekhov's plays, which continues to enjoy popularity in contemporary Iran.
64 See Malekpoor, *Adabiyat-e Namayeshi*, pp. 194–210. Also, see Hasan Javadi and Farrokh Gaffary, Āqā Tabrīzī, *Encyclopaedia Iranica*, 1986, accessed 20 June 2020. http://www.iranicaonline.org/articles/aqa-tabrizi-mirza.
65 See Talajooy, 'A History of Iranian Drama', p. 365.
66 Farrokh Gaffary, 'Evolution of Rituals and Theatre in Iran', *Iranian Studies*, Vol. XVII, No. 4, Autumn 1984, p. 375.
67 Malekpoor, *Adabiyat-e Namayeshi*, pp. 249–52.

68 Other venues were the hall in Mas'udiyyeh Park, the hall of the Armenian school in Hasanabad and the hall of the Grand Hotel in Lalehzar Street. Floor, *The History of Theater*, p. 257.
69 Llyod Ridgeon, 'Revolution and a High-ranking Sufi: Zahir al-Dowleh's Contribution to the Constitutional Movement', in *Iran's Constitutional Revolution: Popular Politics, Cultural Transformations and Transnational Connections*, H.E. Chehabi and Vanessa Martin, eds. (London; New York: I.B. Tauris, 2010), pp. 156–8.
70 *Lal-bazi* shared a family resemblance with *ruhowzi* genre. See Gaffary, 'Evolution of Rituals', p. 373.
71 Karman Sepehran, *Te'atr-krasi dar asr-e mashruteh: 1285–1304* (Tehran: Golshan, 1387[2008]), p. 61. For a historical account of print culture in Tehran, see Afshin Marashi, 'Print Culture and Its Publics: A Social History of Bookstores in Tehran, 1900–1950', *International Journal of Middle East Studies*, Vol, 47, No. 1, 2015, pp. 89–108.
72 Talajooy, 'A History of Iranian Drama', p. 374.
73 Hamid Naficy, *A Social History of Iranian Cinema: The Artisanal Era, 1897–1941*, Vol. 1 (Durham; London: Duke University Press, 2011), p. 323. Also see Malekpoor, *Adabiyat-e Namayeshi*, pp. 251–2.
74 Sepehran, *Te'atr-karasi*, p. 59. See also Yahya Aryanpour, *Az Saba ta Nima: tarikhe-e 150 sal-e adab-i Farsi* Vol. I (Tehran: Kitabha-ye Jibi, 1350 [1971]), p. 291.
75 Edward G. Browne, *A Literary History of Persia: Modern Times*, Vol. IV (Cambridge: Cambridge University Press, 1969), p. 464. It is likely that Brown formed his general opinion on Iranian cinema based on an Orientalist bias in favour of European dramaturgy, echoed best by Johann Wolfgang von Goethe's observation about the absence of drama in Persian literature with the following remarks: 'Had a dramatic poet made his appearance, the whole literature would have assumed a different appearance.' Quoted in Peter Chelkowski, 'Popular Entertainment, Media and Social Change in Twentieth-Century Iran', in *The Cambridge History of Iran: From Nader Shah to the Islamic Republic*, Vol. 7, Peter Avery, Gavin Hambly, and Charles Melville, eds. (Cambridge: Cambridge University Press, 1991), p. 782.
76 For a study of the early Pahlavi theatre, see Nasser Aghai, *The Development of Western Theatre in Iran*, (Saarbrüken, Germany: LAP Lambert Academic Publisher, 2012), pp. 66–88.
77 Zeinab Stellar, 'From "Evil-Inciting" Dance to Chaste "Rhythmic Movements": A Genealogy of Modern Islamic Dance-Theatre in Iran', in *Muslim Rap, Hala Soaps, and Revolutionary Theatre: Artistic Developments in the Muslim World*, Karin van Nieuwkerk ed. (Austin: University of Texas Press, 2011), p. 239.
78 For a study of post-Constitutional operettas, especially in relation with the rise of 'national dance' and the hetero-normalization of the theatre stage, see Ida Meftahi, 'Dancing Angels and Princesses: The Invention of an Ideal Female National Dancer in Twentieth-Century Iran', *The Oxford Handbook of Dance and Ethnicity*, Anthony Shay and Barbara Seller-Young, eds. July 2016. https://www.oxfordhandbooks.com/view/10.1093/oxfordhb/9780199754281.001.0001/oxfordhb-9780199754281-e-002. Last accessed 12 October 2020.
79 See Tavakoli-Targhi, *Refashioning Iran,* pp. 122–34. See also Talajooy, 'A History of Iranian Drama', p. 397. Naficy, *A Social History of Iranian Cinema*.
80 Talajooy, 'A History of Iranian Drama', pp. 367–8.
81 Browne, *A Literary History of Persia*, pp. 459–62.

82 This is best evident in changes made to the Persian translation of William Shakespeare's *Hamlet* where Hamlet, the King and the Queen are all poisoned in the final act.
83 Farzin Vejdani, *Making History in Iran: Educational, Nationalism, and Print Culture* (Stanford: Stanford University Press, 2015), p. 28. For a history of print during the Iranian Constitutional period, see Ali Gheissari, 'Despots of the World Unite! Satire in the Iranian Constitutional Press: The Majalleh-ye Estebdad, 1907–1908', *Comparative Studies of South Asia, Africa, and the Middle East*, Vol. 25, No. 2, 2005, pp. 360–76.
84 Here we can acknowledge the photographic depiction as a performance act. Interperformativity of expressive genres becomes best visible with the development of graphic art in advertisements of cinema and theatre later in 1950s.
85 See https://shahrefarang.com/en/the-merchant-of-venice-in-tehran-1928/. Last accessed 15 October 2020.
86 See Talinn Grigor, *Building Iran: Modernism, Architecture, and National Heritage under the Pahlavi Monarchs* (New York: Periscope Publishing, 2009) and Pamela Karimi, *Domesticity and Consumer Culture in Iran: Interior Revolutions of the Modern Era* (London; New York: Routledge, 2013), especially pp. 51–83.
87 Ida Meftahi, 'Sacred or Dissident: Islam, Embodiment, and Subjectivity on Post-Revolutionary Iranian Theatrical Stage', in *Islam and Popular Culture*, Karin Van Nieuwkerk, Mark Levine, and Martin Stokes, eds. (Austin: University of Texas Press, 2016), p. 258.
88 The nineteen-year-old Qamar al-Moluk Vaziri would sing 'Ode to the Morning Bird', a poem by the Constitutionalist Mohammad-Taqi Bahar (1886–1951). See Hossein Kamaly, *God and Man in Tehran: Contending Visions of the Divine from the Qajars to the Islamic Republic* (New York: Columbia University Press, 2018), pp. 1–2.
89 Malekpoor, *Adabiyat-e Namayeshi*, p. 37.
90 Ida Meftahi, *Gender and Dance in Modern Iran* (London; New York: Routledge, 2016), p. 36.
91 For a study of *motrebi* musical culture, its close association with *ruhowzi* and Lalehzar Street, see GJ Breyley and Sasan Fatemi, *Iranian Music and Popular Entertainment: From Motrebi to Losanjelesi* (London: New York: Routledge, 2016).
92 See Meftahi, *Gender and Dance*.
93 I borrow the term 'Sovietisation' from Jamil Hasanli's study of the South Caucasus, in particular Azerbaijan, where the Bolshevik Revolution first pushed a twofold policy of accessing the oil-rich fields on the Caspian Sea and also spreading Marxist-Leninist revolutionary ideology into the southern coast of the Caspian Sea with the establishment of the Gilan Province in 1920–21. Jamil Hasanli, *The Sovietization of Azerbaijan: The South Caucasus in the Triangle of Russia, Turkey, and Iran, 1920–1922* (Salt Lake City: University of Utah Press, 2018).
94 For a detailed study of Nooshin, see Talajooy, 'The Impact of Soviet Contact'.
95 Ibid., pp. 347–9.
96 Talajooy, 'The Impact of Soviet Contact', p. 349.
97 Note that Stanislavki's system was known to Nooshin and Shahin Sargsyan. However, it was Oskyoos who first trained actors according to the system. Mahin Oskyooi's contribution to the introduction of Stanislavki's system in Iran has been overlooked, opening up space for further research on her theatrical activities in this period. See, for example, Floor, *The History of Theatre in Iran*, p. 286.
98 The nation-building process tied to cultural memory formation through urban space is not unique to post-1953 Iran. Consider urban history of numerous state operas and

theatres across the globe, from Prague Opera House to Théâtre municipal de Tunis, most of which built in the nineteenth to early twentieth centuries.

99 For an in-depth analysis of the Celebrations, see Robert Steele, *The Shah's Imperial Celebrations of 1971: Nationalism, Culture and Politics in Late Pahlavi Iran* (London; New York; Oxford; New Delhi; Sydney: I.B. Tauris, 2021).

100 The inauguration of the festivals on September 11 1967 at Shiraz-Persepolis followed the establishment of the National Iranian Radio and Television (NIRT) in 1966, led by Reza Ghotbi (1940–), who was project manager of the festivals, appointed by Farah Pahlavi. Gaffary, 'Evolution of Rituals', p. 38.

101 Consider the proliferation of radio and television theatre between 1950s and 1970s. For a sample of radio theatre, see Khosrow Hakimrabet, *Namayeshye Radioyi* (Tehran: Rozbahan, 1395 [2016]) and for a study of television theatre, see Gholamhossein Lotfi, *Te'atre Televisioni dar Iran* (Tehran: Soroush, 1387 [2008]).

102 Here we can also speak of the theatrization of Iranian cinema, best exemplified by Asghar Farhadi's 2016 *The Salesman*.

103 Mofid's tale shares resemblance with George Orwell's 1945 *Animal Farm* and yet there are echoes of ancient allegorical fable in which animals serve as satirical characters that address political and existential problems in life.

104 Saeed Talajooy, 'Indigenous Performing Traditions in Post-Revolutionary Iranian Theater', *Iranian Studies*, Vol. 44, No. 4, 2011, pp. 497–519 and Amin Sharifi Isaloo, *Power, Legitimacy and the Public Sphere: The Iranian Ta'ziyeh Theatre Ritual* (London; New York: Routledge, 2017), pp. 78–82. It is important to note that Javanmard also directed the country's first teleplay of Armand Salacrou's 1941 play *La Marguerite*.

105 Chelkowski, 'Popular Entertainment', p. 788. Don Rubin, ed., *The World Encyclopedia of Contemporary Theatre: Asia/Pacific*, Vol. 5 (London; New York: Routledge, 1998), p. 261.

106 For an account of Tudeh's critique of post-1953 theatre, see Ida Meftahi, 'The Sounds and Moves of *ibtizāl* in 20th-Century Iran', *International Journal of Middle East Studies*, Vol. 48, 2015, pp. 153–4.

107 For a study of Chekhov's influence on Radi, see Maryam Heydari Fard, 'A Study of Chekhovian Elements in Radi's Drama', *International Letters of Social and Humanities Sciences*, Vol. 42, pp. 88–97. For a study of Ibsen's influence on Iranian theatre, see Farindndokht Zahedi, *Henri Ibsen and Iranian Modern Drama: Reception and Influence* (Oslo: Fagbokforlaget, 2006).

108 For an introduction to Beyzaie's theatre, see Saeed Talajooy, 'Beyzaie's Formation, Forms and Themes', *Iranian Studies*, Vol. 46, No. 5, 2013, pp. 689–93.

109 For a study of Sa'edi's 1960s plays, see Eden Naby, *Gowhar-e Murad: A Persian Playwright* (M.A. thesis: Columbia University Press, 1971).

110 Chelkowski, 'Popular Entertainment', p. 787.

111 Talajooy, 'Indigenous Performing Traditions', p. 499.

112 For a study of Abbas Nalbandian's works, see Atefeh Pakbaznia and Javad Atefeh, *Digaran-e Abbas Nalbandian* (London: H&S Media, 2013).

113 Parviz Tanavoli is best known for his *Heech* (Nothing) bronze sculpture. See Shiva Balaghi, 'Iranian Visual Arts in "The Century of Machinery, Speed, and the Atom": Rethinking Modernity', in *Picturing Iran: Art, Society and Revolution*, Shiva Balaghi and Lynn Gumpert eds. (London; New York: I.B. Tauris, 2002), pp. 25–8. For a general account of the 1960s artistic movement known as '*Saqqakhana*', which Tanavoli also belonged, and artistic exhibit during the period, see Maryam Ekhtiar, 'Artists of the *Saqqakhana* Movement', https://www.metmuseum.org/toah/hd/saqq/

hd_saqq.htm. Last accessed 28 October 2020. Also note that intellectual currents also interacted with theatre, in particular absurdist drama. Jalal Al-e Ahmad's translation of one-act play, *The Wedding Party on the Eiffel Tower* by Jean Cocteau (1921) is a case in point.

114 Pakbaznia and Atefeh, *Digaran-e Abbas Nalbandian*, pp. 6–10.
115 *Arus* (The Bride), a one-act play, is about a barren woman caught in a marriage where the husband seeks another, young wife. See Chelkowski, 'Popular Entertainment, Media, and Social Change in Twentieth-Century Iran', p. 791.
116 See Babak Rahimi, 'Introduction', in *Theater in the Middle East: Between Performance and Politics*, Babak Rahimi ed. (London; New York: Anthem Press, 2020), pp. 1–3.
117 For a study of late Pahlavi modernization and the changing cultural status of Iranian women, see Liora Hendelman-Baavur, *Creating the Modern Iranian Woman: Popular Culture Between Two Revolutions* (Cambridge: Cambridge University Press, 2019).
118 See Ghanoonparvar and Green, *Iranian Drama*, pp. 1–61.
119 Nasser Rahmaninejad, *A Man of the Theater: Survival as an Artist in Iran* (New York: New Village Press, 2020), pp. 106–8; 191.
120 Ibid., p. 101.
121 Shahla Talebi, *Ghosts of Revolution: Rekindled Memories of Imprisonment in Iran* (Stanford: Stanford University Press, 2011), p. 202.
122 Interview with Shahla Talebi, via email, 20 November 2020.
123 For an account of revolutionary demonstrations at the cemetery, see Sa'edi's 1983 account. Gilles Peress, *Telex Iran: In the Name of Revolution* (Millerton, N.Y: Aperture, 1983), p. 101.
124 For one of the best studies on the centrality of visual culture in the 1979 revolution, see Peter Chelkowski and Hamid Dabashi, *Staging a Revolution: The Art of Persuasion in the Islamic Republic of Iran* (New York: New York University Press, 1999).
125 See Annabelle Sreberny-Mohammadi and Ali Mohammadi, *Small Media, Big Revolution: Communication, Culture, and the Iranian Revolution* (Minneapolis: University of Minnesota Press, 1994), especially pp. 139–62 and also Mehdi Mohsenian Rad, 'Diwar neveshtehay-e dowran enghelab khiyabanha-ye Tehran', in *Dar Hasrat-e fahm-e dorost [Longing for the True Understanding]* Mehdi Mohsenian Rad ed. (Tehran: Entesharat-e Simay-e Shargh va Nashr-e Sani, 2015), pp. 90–146.
126 Rahmaninejad, *A Man of the Theater*, pp. 204.
127 On the street staging of *Days of the Commune* and the epic parable play, *Round Heads and Pointed Head*, see Rahmaninejad, *A Man of the Theater*, pp. 203–6.
128 Seyed Habiballah Lazgee, *Post-revolutionary Iranian Theatre: Three Representative Plays in Translation with Critical Commentary* (University of Leeds: Dissertation, 1994), p. 18.
129 See Mohsen Azimi's interview with playwright, Nasser Hosseini Mehrm, on theatre in the early revolutionary years. https://www.chistart.com/theater/t_interview/%D9%86%D8%A7%D8%B5%D8%B1-%D8%AD%D8%B3%DB%8C%D9%86%DB%8C-%D9%85%D9%87%D8%B1-%D8%B3%D9%86%D8%AF%DB%8C%DA%A9%D8%A7%DB%8C-%D8%AA%D8%A6%D8%A7%D8%AA%D8%B1/, last accessed, 16 October 2020.
130 Meftahi, 'Sacred or Dissident', pp. 269–73.
131 Hashimi-Rafsanjani, quoted in Meftahi, 'Sacred or Dissident', p. 260. It is important to note that following the formation of the Islamic Republic theatre did not become, as argued by Willem Floor, 'socially, religiously and, above all, politically suspect'.

Floor, *The History of Theatre in Iran*, p. 297. The shared cultural policy among elites in the regime was rather a revolutionary kind, which ultimately saw theatre not merely as a propaganda device but a radical aesthetic means for changing Iranian society.
132 Lazgee, *Post-revolutionary Iranian Theatre*, pp. 15.
133 For a study of Arzeshi genre, see Marjan Moosavi, 'Desacralizing Whispers: Counter-Conduct in the Iranian War Theatre', *New Theatre Quarterly*, Vol. 34, No. 3, 2018, pp. 235–48.
134 Amin Sharifi Isaloo, *Power, Legitimacy and the Public Sphere*, pp. 96–115 and Meftahi, 'Sacred or Dissident', p. 263; pp. 265–9. For a study of Sacred Defence cinematic culture and its performance implications, see Pedram Khosronejad (ed.) *Iranian Sacred Defence Cinema: Religion, Martyrdom and National Identity* (Canyon Pyon, UK: Sean Kingston Pub, 2012).
135 Liliane Anjo, 'Contemporary Iranian Theatre: The Emergence of an Autonomous Space', in *Cultural Revolution in Iran: Contemporary Popular Culture in the Islamic Republic*, Annabelle Sreberny and Massoumeh Torfeh eds. (London; New York: I.B. Tauris, 2013), p. 86.
136 In 1982 festival, eleven plays were staged for forty-seven times, all written and performed by Iranians. The number of audiences: 8279. By 1989, despite relatively low number of performances (39 plays), the festivals saw a sharp increase in audiences: p. 72, p. 170. Lazgee, *Post-revolutionary Iranian Theatre*, p. 21.
137 Here we can make an analytical distinction between monumental and ceremonial performances, with the latter an ephemeral practice on an annual basis, although still involved in the staging of state power.
138 Marjan Moosavi, 'Performing and Conforming: Iran's Fadjr International Theatre Festival', *TDR: The Drama Review*, Vol. 60, No. 1, Spring 2016 (T299), p. 81. One can add that internationalization of the festivals also served as a way to legitimize a regime of cultural officialdom that integrated Iranian theatre within the broader globalizing processes.
139 The original name of the institution was the Ministry of Guidance, changed to the Ministry of Culture and Islamic Guidance in 1986.
140 Censorship continues to be a negotiated practice between theatre practitioners and the ministry, even protests and boycotts as evident in the 2020 festivals. See 'Iran Film, Theatre, Music Artists, Broadcasters Boycott State TV, Festivals', *Radio Farda*, 13 January 2020. https://en.radiofarda.com/a/iran-film-theater-music-artists-broadcasters-boycott-state-tv-festivals/30375019.html. Last accessed 28 October 2020. For a study on post-revolutionary censorship regimes, see Babak Rahimi, 'Censorship and the Islamic Republic: Two Modes of Regulatory Measures for Media in Iran', *Middle East Journal*, Vol. 69, No. 3, Summer 2015, pp. 358–78.
141 Hamid Keshmirshekan, 'Reclaiming Cultural Space: The Artist's Performativity versus the State's Expectations in Contemporary Iran', in *Performing the Iranian State: Visual Culture and Representations of Iranian Identity*, Staci Gem Scheiwiller ed. (London; New York; Delhi: Anthem Press, 2013), p. 147.
142 Floor, *The History of Theatre in Iran*, p. 298.
143 Nahid Siamdoust, *Sound Track of the Revolution* (Stanford, California: Stanford University Press, 2017), pp. 263–81. *Bidad* could also mean 'fabulous', 'frenzy' and also 'ecstasy'. I'm grateful to Ali Gheissari for his help with the translation.
144 For a detailed history of Rafsanjani-era economic and social changes, see Ali Gheissari and Vali Nasr, *Democracy in Iran: History and the Quest for Liberty* (Oxford: Oxford University Press, 2006), pp. 105–26.

145 I am grateful to Marjan Moosavi for pointing out the political importance of shortage in theatre venues.
146 See 'Yek vaghiyat-e degargoon konand-eh ya nesbathay-e dorost ba jang', 30 September 2018. https://theater.ir/fa/111765. Last accessed 28 October 2020. As Marjan Moosavi has argued, the tension over Alireza Nader's play was reflective of a major change that took place in mid-1990s in the narrative of war. The shift from a realist, best represented by the play, *Kanal-e Komeil* (*Komeil Canal*), to an abstract or universal aesthetics identified a 'desacralized' process that challenged the official narrative of the war. See Moosavi, 'Desacralizing Whispers'. For a more in-depth study of this shift, also see Marjan Moosavi, 'B for Badan, Blessed, and (B)othered: the Counter-Sacred in the Iranian Theatre of War', *Ecumenica*, Vol. 11, No. 2, Fall 2018, pp. 28–45.
147 Mohsen Namjoo, 'The Revolution and Music: A Personal Odyssey', in *Politics and Culture in Contemporary Iran: Challenging the Status Quo*, Abbas Milani and Larry Diamond eds. (Boulder; London: Lynne Rienner Publishers, 2015), p. 193. For an account on Namjoo's musical career, see Siamdoust, *Sound Track of the Revolution*, pp. 160–5. Between 1990s and 2000s, Iran would also see rise of a new rock musical culture, some of which became active underground in urban centres. As Bronwen Robertson has shown in her ethnographic study, the middle-class and youth-driven rock music became a disruptive expression of new, transgressive Iranian identities. See Bronwen Robertson, *Reverberations of Dissent: Identity and Expression in Iran's Illegal Music Scene* (New York: Continuum, 2012).
148 See Eskandar Sadeqhi-Boroujerdi, *Revolution and Its Discontents: Political Thought and Reform in Iran* (Cambridge: Cambridge University Press, 2019).
149 Siamdoust, *Sound Track of the Revolution*, p. 167.
150 See Laudan Nooshin, '"Our Angel of Salvation" Toward an Understanding of Iranian Cyberspace as an Alternative Sphere of Musical Sociability', *Ethnomusicology*, Vol. 62, No. 3 (Fall) 2018, pp. 341–74.
151 Floor, *The History of Theatre in Iran*, p. 299.
152 Javad Arabi, 'Hasht Sal Te'atr-e Iran ba Mohammad-eKhatami', BBC, August 3, 2005. https://www.bbc.com/persian/arts/story/2005/08/050803_pm-ja-theatre-khatami. Last accessed 29 October 2020.
153 See Ramin Farhadi, 'Adapting Shakespeare's Richard III: A political reading of hamid-Reza Naeemi's Richard,' *Cogent Arts and Humanities*, Vol. 7, No. 1, 2020. https://www.tandfonline.com/doi/full/10.1080/23311983.2020.1823599.
154 Moosavi, 'Performing and Conforming, pp. 79–80.
155 Jacques Derrida, *Monoligualism of the Other or the Prosthesis of Origin*, trans. Patrick Mensah (Standford: Standford University Press, 1996), p. 63.
156 For a study of early translation of Shakespeare into Persian, see Abbas Hori, *Influence of Translation on Shakepeare's Reception in Iran: Three Farsi and Suggestions for a Fourth*, (Ph.D Dissertation, Middlesex University, 2003), especially pp. 88–91.
157 Chrisoph Werner, 'Drama and Operetta at the Red Lion and Sun: Theatre in Tabriz 1927–41,' in *Culture and Cultural Politics under Reza Shah: The Pahlavi State, New Boureoisie and the Creation of a Modern Society in Iran*, Bianca Devos and Christoph Werner eds. (London; New York: Routledge), pp. 208–10.
158 See in particular the study of post-Reformist theatre, many in translation, by Torange Yeghiazarian, also a contributor to this volume. Torange Yeghiazarian, 'Dramatic Defiance in Tehran: Reflections on a Society of Contradictions', *TDR: The*

Drama Review, Vol. 56, No. 1, Spring 2012 (T213), pp. 77–92. See also Anjo, 'Contemporary Iranian Theatre', pp. 81–94.

159 See also Mahmood Karimi Hakak, 'Exiled to Freedom: A Memoir of Censorship in Iran', *Theatre Drama Review*, 47, No. 4, 2003, especially pages 31–3. For an interview, see https://www.emptymirrorbooks.com/literature/interview-mahmood-karimi-hakak-bill-wolak. Last accessed 28 November 2020.

160 See Ali-Reza Mirsajadi, 'Reading Hamlet in Tehran: Neoliberalism and the Politics of Politicizing', *Theatre Journal*, Vol. 72, No. 1, March 2020, pp. 39–60. For another study on restaging Shakespeare in post-revolutionary context, see Amin Azimi and Marjan Moosavi, 'Mystic Lear and Playful Hamlet: The Critical Cultural Dramatugy in the Iranian Appropriations of Shakespearean Tragedies', *Asian Theatre Journal*, Vol. 36, No. 1, 2019, pp. 144–64.

161 See Mirsajadi, 'Reading Hamlet in Tehran', p. 48.

162 See Marjan Moosavi, ' "Unpermitted Whispers": Reflections on the Originality of "Hopscotch" Performance', *Theatre Times*, 19 January 2018. https://thetheatretimes.com/unpermitted-whispers-reflections-originality-hopscotch-performance/. Last accessed, 15 January 2021.

163 See Anoushiravan Ehteshami and Mahjoob Zweiri, *Iran and the Rise of Its Neoconservatives: The Politics of Tehran's Silent Revolution* (London; New York: I.B. Tauris, 2009).

164 In the post-Reform period, changes in theatre production were partly due to limitations in state financial support, especially in the second phase of the Ahmadinejad government as government funds shifted towards religious centres and events. See Reihaneh Mazaheri, 'Ahmadinejad's Cultural Priorities', *Tehran Bureau*, https://www.pbs.org/wgbh/pages/frontline/tehranbureau/2010/04/ahmadinejads-cultural-priorities.html. Last accessed 29 October 2020.

165 Founded by Kaveh Mahdavi (1978–), *Goruh-e Te'atr-e Lahzeh* represents a post-Reformist theatre troupe that engaged with key dramatic texts in alternative translations. Mahdavi's reappropriation of *Waiting for Godot* was the street theatre production of *Dar-e Bedun-e Charchub* (*A Frameless door*), a play with two male characters who, against a neutral background and next to a frameless door, engage in absurd conversation while waiting for someone to enter through the door.

166 The September 2013 version went onto stage with the title *Dar Entezar-e Guni* (*Waiting for Guni* [meaning a 'sack']). The play also features a female actor who also performs in the genre of *ruhowzi*. For another study of *ruhowzi* in post-2009 period, see Erum Naqvim, 'Reinventing Ruhowzi: Experiments in Contemporary Iranian Musical Theater', *Middle East Journal of Culture and Communication*, Vol. 13 2020, pp. 28–48.

167 Interview with Kaveh Mahdavi, Tehran, 24 September 2013.

168 For a 2014 account of the plays at the City Theatre, see Rana Salimi, 'Waiting for Godot in Tehran', *Theatre Forum,* No. 24, July 2014. For a post-Ahmadinejad report on the play in relation with economic and political conditions, see Deborah Amos, '"Waiting for Godot" Strikes a Chord in Tehran', 14 March 2014. https://www.npr.org/sections/parallels/2014/03/14/289831124/waiting-for-godot-strikes-a-chord-in-tehran. Last accessed 29 October 2020.

169 For variation of songs during the 2009 uprisings, see Siamdoust, *Sound Track of the Revolution*, pp. 263–81. For the visual culture of protests with relation to memory, see Aleida Assmann and Corinna Assmann, 'Neda-the Career of a Global Icon', in *Memory in a Global Age: Discourses, Practices and Trajectories*, Aleida Assmann

and Sebastian Conrad, eds. (New York: St Martin's Press, 2010), pp. 225–42. For the complex relationship between age and class in the Green Movement, see Kevan Harris, *A Social Revolution: Politics and Welfare State in Iran* (Oakland, California: University of California Press, 2017), pp. 196–211.

170 For an account on the self-critical features of post-revolutionary Iranian diaspora theatre, see Hamid Dabashi, 'Introduction: Parviz Sayyad and His Theater for the Diaspora', in *Theater of Diaspora: Two Plays: The Ass and the Rex Cinema Trial*, Parviz Sayyad ed. (Costa Mesa, Calif: Mazda Publishers, 1992), pp. xi–xxiv.

171 'Interview: Whose Theatre?' *Index on Censorship*, Vol. 14, No. 4, 1985, pp. 16–20.

172 See Hamid Dabashi (ed.), *Parviz Sayyad's Theatre of Diaspora: Two Plays, the Ass and the Rex Cinema Trial* (Costa Mesa: Mazda Publishers, 1992).

173 The original play, based on *kheimeh-shab-bazi* performance, is an allegorical story about four characters dressed in different colours, each representing clergy, intellectuals, worker and merchants, who create a scarecrow to protect themselves against an external enemy. The scarecrow, after coming alive, becomes an authoritarian monster and puts the characters into four boxes. The US version, performed in Santa Monica, California, 1987, has the boxes as coffins and has the black character include a gun into one of the coffins so as to provide a weapon for a future fight against the monster, representing the Islamic Republic. Interview with Nasser Rahmaninejad, 20 September 2020. For a brief account of the play, see M.R. Ghanoonparvar, 'Persian Plays and the Iranian Theatre', in *Colors of Enchantment: Theatre, Dance, Music, and the Visual Arts of the Middle East*, Sherifa Zuhur, ed. (Cairo; New York: The American University of Cairo Press, 2001), p. 97.

174 Interview with Mahmood Karimi Hakak, 12 December 2020. For an interview with Mahmood Karimi Hakak, see https://www.emptymirrorbooks.com/literature/interview-mahmood-karimi-hakak-bill-wolak and also www.mahmoodkarimihakak.org. Last accessed 28 November 2020.

175 See Ursula Lindqvist, 'Staging Migration and Post-national Identities: Swedish-Iranian Feminist Playwright and Director Farnaz Arbabi visits UCLA', https://escholarship.org/content/qt7d17f6rv/qt7d17f6rv.pdf. Last accessed 28 November 2020.

176 Majran Moosavi, 'Moments of Encounter: Iranian-Canadian Immigrant Theatre with Art Babayants', in *Performing Canadian Frontiers: Theatre and (Im)Migration*, Yana Meerzon ed. (Toronto: Playwright Canada Press, 2019).

177 Note that post-2009 censorship was selective to certain plays that the ministry had deemed problematic. However, theatrical works still grew, as evident with the inauguration of new theatre space such as Tamashakaneh-ye Iranshahr in Tehran in the immediate aftermath of the election crackdowns. See Anjo, 'Contemporary Iranian Theatre', pp. 91–2.

178 For example in a range of pelatoos, see https://pelatoo.com/centers. Last accessed 25 November 2020.

179 For a fictional-ethnographic study of underground theatre, see Roxanne Varzi, *Last Scene Underground: An Ethnographic Novel of Iran* (Stanford, CA: Stanford University Press, 2015).

180 The term 'non-governmental' specifically underlines the absence of government financial support, which became apparent in the second term of Ahmadinejad's administration. Interview with Mostafa Koushki, Tehran, 24 September 2020. For a critical analysis on 'independent theatre' as 'private', see Marjan Moosavi, 'Defunded and Defiant, Iranian Theatre's Path to Become Independent and/or Private', *The*

Theatre Times, 8 June 2017. https://thetheatretimes.com/defunded-defiant-iranian-theatres-path-become-independent-andor-private/. Last accessed 18 October 2020.

181 Prior to its closure during the 2020 pandemic, the theatre, located in centre of the capital city and in proximity to the University of Tehran, staged a single play for fifty nights. One exception was Shakespeare's *A Midsummer Night's Dream*, which was staged 260 times in 2016, also restaged in 2019. Interview with Mostafa Koushki, Tehran, 24 September 2020. See also https://www.tehrantimes.com/news/438028/Shakespeare-Midsummer-Night-s-Dream-Coriolanus-coming-to. Last accessed, 20 November 2020.

182 'Avalin pelatooy-e tea῾atr-e dar Ilam eftetah shod', *Iranian Student's News Agency*, 30 September 2019. https://www.isna.ir/news/98070805621/%D8%A7%D9%88%D9%84%DB%8C%D9%86-%D9%BE%D9%84%D8%A7%D8%AA%D9%88%DB%8C-%D8%AA%D8%A6%D8%A7%D8%AA%D8%B1-%D8%AF%D8%B1-%D8%A7%DB%8C%D9%84%D8%A7%D9%85-%D8%A7%D9%81%D8%AA%D8%AA%D8%A7%D8%AD-%D8%B4%D8%AF. Last accessed 25 November 2020. For Bushehr, see The Ministry of Culture & Islamic Guidance's report on Farhang.gov.ir. 'Naghshe-he pelatoo jadid majmoe-ye tea῾atr-e shahr mojtama-e farhangi honari bushehr amadeh shod', 22 March 2020. https://www.farhang.gov.ir/fa/news/517969/%D9%86%D9%82%D8%B4%D9%87-%D9%BE%D9%84%D8%A7%D8%AA%D9%88-%D8%AC%D8%AF%DB%8C%D8%AF-%D9%85%D8%AC%D9%85%D9%88%D8%B9%D9%87-%D8%AA%D8%A6%D8%A7%D8%AA%D8%B1-%D8%B4%D9%87%D8%B1-%D9%85%D8%AC%D8%AA%D9%85%D8%B9-%D9%81%D8%B1%D9%87%D9%86%DA%AF%DB%8C-%D9%87%D9%86%D8%B1%DB%8C-%D8%A8%D9%88%D8%B4%D9%87%D8%B1-%D8%A2%D9%85%D8%A7%D8%AF%D9%87-%D8%B4%D8%AF.

183 Such development was less evident beyond Tehran, especially in smaller towns where local state involvement operates on a weaker extend in cultural productions such as theatre.

184 https://www.tehrantimes.com/news/417327/Iranian-director-to-stage-Oliver-Twist-musical-in-Tehran. For an online photo gallery from the performance, see https://en.mehrnews.com/photo/130084/Oliver-Twist-musical-on-stage-in-Tehran. Last accessed 10 October 2020.

185 Interview with Mostafa Koushki, Tehran, 24 September 2020.

186 David Harvey, *Paris, Capital of Modernity* (New York and London: Routledge, 2003), p. 113.

187 Kaveh Bassiri, 'Privatization and the Changing Landscape of Iranian Theatre', *International Journal of Middle East Studies*, vol. 52, 2020, pp. 52, 363.

188 See John Thornton Caldwell, *Production Culture: Industrial Reflexivity and Critical Practice in Film and Television* (Durham; London: Duke University Press, 2008).

189 See Reza Abedini and Hans Wolbers, *New Visual Culture of Modern Iran* (West New York, NJ: Mark Batty, 2006).

190 The poster was distributed in Tehran and also exhibited in Japan. Interview with Faranak Irani, via email, 18 November 2020.

191 Reza Kouchek Zadeh, ed. *Te῾atr va Jame-eh* (Tehran: Farhang-e Nashr-e No, 1398 [2019]).

192 See John B. Thompson, *Merchants of Culture: The Publishing Business in the Twenty-First Century*, second edition (Cambridge: Polity Press, 2012), pp. 326–39.

193 Marjan Moosavi, 'Bird's-eye View on Iranian Theatre in 2016', *The Theatre Times*, 25 January 2017. https://thetheatretimes.com/birds-eye-view-iranian-theatre-2016/. Last accessed, 18 October 2020.
194 Ibid.
195 For the theoretically informed study on the relationship between theatre and performance studies, see Marvin Carlson, *Performance: A Critical Introduction*, Third edition (London; New York: Routledge, 2018).

Chapter 1

1 http://www.goodreads.com/quotes/525822-stories-live-in-your-blood-and-bones-follow-the-seasons.
2 Hezar Afsan is a non-extant collection of tales believed to have been popular in ancient Iran. The oldest reference to this collection is made by Mas'udi. See, Charles Pellat, 'Alf Layla Wa Layla', in Encyclopædia Iranica, I/8, Ehsan Yarshater ed., accessed 10 July 2005, http://www.iranicaonline.org/articles/alf-layla-wa-layla.
3 While Shahrzad is a fictitious character, her role as a female acquainted with epic and heroic tales of her people is an enduring example of the existence of such women in ancient Iran. There is no evidence of any restrictions placed on women acting as storytellers or musicians in this period. Moreover, Tabari writes that Khosro II had numerous maids and female servants who were individually responsible for singing and playing musical instruments. Mohammad b. Jarir Tabari, History of al-Tabari: The Sasanids, the Byzantines, the Lakhmids, and Yemen, vol. 5, trans. and annotated by C.E. Bosworth (Albany, NY: SUNY Press, 1999), pp. 376–7. In addition, archaeological findings portray females engaged in what could be categorized as minstrelsy. For example, The Louvre Museum holds a figurine of a female harpist, found at Susa and believed to belong to the Seleucid or Parthian period. See, http://cartelen.louvre.fr/cartelen/visite?srv=car_not_frame&idNotice=13924. Also, a mosaic panel, from the third century CE, discovered at Bishāpur, depicts a female harpist. See, http://www.louvre.fr/en/oeuvre-notices/mosaic-woman-playing-harp.
4 Richard F. Burton, The Book of the Thousand Nights and a Night: A Plain and Literal Translation of the Arabian Nights Entertainments (London: Burton Club, 1925), pp. 14–15.
5 The first chapter of Hezar Afsan takes us to the turbulent bedchambers of a mad king, whose mental and emotional insanity had driven him to spill the blood of many of his female companions. Shahrzad, the young daughter of the Vizier, implores her father, to task her with the mission of curing the king's madness. See, Ibid.
6 Xenophon, Cyropaedia, volume I, books 1–4, Trans. Walter Miller, Loeb Classical Library 51 (Cambridge: Harvard University Press, 1914), p. 11. Rawlinson also adds: 'Persian authors to whom he [Herodotus] refers in several places as authorities on the subject of their early national history were poets, the composers of those national songs of which Xenophon, Strabo and other writers speak, wherein were celebrated the deeds of the ancient kings and heroes, and particularly those of the hero-founder of the empire, Cyrus.' See, George Rawlinson, History of Herodotus, vol. 1–4 (London: John Murray, 1862), p. 42.
7 See, Mary Boyce, 'The Parthian Gōsān and Iranian Minstrel Tradition', Journal of the Royal Asiatic Society, Vol. 89, 1957, pp. 10–45. For the term used in the Romance

of *Vis and Ramin*, see Fakhraddin Gorgani, *Vis and Ramin*, trans. Dick Davis (New York: Penguin Classics, 2008), p. 265. Regarding the etymology of the term *gosān*, W. Floor makes mention of Georg Goyan's argument that the Armenian theatre evolved out of funeral rites dedicated to the divinity Anahita-Gisane – *Gisane* meaning the long-haired one. Floor further argues that these *gosān* transformed into bards and minstrels, as they would sing the heroic deeds of the deceased as singing mourners and wailers. Moreover, their singing role later took on a more dramatic effect rendering them as actors. Willem M. Floor, *The History of Theater in Iran* (Odenton, MD: Mage Pub, 2005), p. 16. While we cannot say for sure that the *gosān* of the Parthian and later Sasanian era developed out of the same Anāhitic cult, but the linguistic similarity is fascinating, what we can be relatively sure of is that Armenians, Parthians, and Georgians referred to gosān as magusāni. The Middle Persian term *khunyāgar is* translated by medieval authors as musician or minstrel. A question-and-answer episode between the Sasanian king Khosro II and a young progeny (*redag*) reveals the Sasanians' mindset regarding the term *khunyāgar*, its scope of meaning and its significance. Khosro asks the progeny about whom he believes to be the best and the most desirable of the *khunyāgar*. The youth responds by saying that '*huniyāgar hamāg xwaš <ud> nēk*', meaning that *khunyāgars* are all delightful and pleasant. He then goes on to list all of those skilled at playing a musical instrument and those skills at certain arts that we would categorize as 'circus performances'. While here we see the term encompassing a broad range of performers and artists in the late Sasanian period, we see that by the medieval era, authors are translating *khunyāgar* as singer, poet, minstrel. It is not clear why by the ninth-century term had shrunk in its scope of meaning, becoming limited to minstrels. For the Pahlavi text, see *Corpus of Pahlavi Texts*, ed. Jamaspi Dastur M. Jamasp-Asana (Bombay 1913), p. 32. For the transliteration of the text, see http://titus.uni-frankfurt.de/texte/etcs/iran/miran/mpers/jamasp/jamast.htm.

8   In this specific instance, the term 'Persian' is used, and not Iranian, as Xenophon's experience took place amongst the Achaemenid royal family who claimed to be of the Pārsa- clan, referred to the Greeks as the Persians. They were inhabitants of the plains of Pasargadae, located in the modern-day province of Fars.

9   See, 'Alī Āl-e Dawūd, 'Coffeehouse', in Encyclopaedia Iranica, vol. 6, fasc. 1, ed. Ehsan Yarshater, 1992, accessed online 5 July 2015, http://www.iranicaonline.org/articles/coffeehouse-qahva-kana. Coffee Houses in the early modern period became a fascinating social space that brought together the elite and the non-elite members of the Safavid society. Mirza Mohammad Taher Nasrabadi (1618–78 CE) mentions a coffeehouse in Isfahan by the name of Qahve-khāneh Arab-e Qahve-chi, where Shah Abbas I is known to have frequented. Mirza Mohammad Taher Nasrabadi, Tazkareh Nasrabadi (Tazkerat al-Sho'arā), Vahid Dastgerdi ed. (Tehran: Armaghan Publishers, 1938), p. 255. *Naqqali*, meaning to recount, is the term used to refer to the dramatic reading or recitation of tales. Hannaway defines the difference between the storyteller and the *naqqal* by arguing that while storytellers mainly performed and narrated folkloric tales, naqqals were skilled at performing stories popular romances and epic collections of poetry such as the Shahnameh, the Abumoslemnāmeh and more. See, William Hannaway, 'Dārāb-nāma', in Encyloapedia Iranica, vol. 7, fasc.1, 1994, accessed 5 July 2015, http://www.iranicaonline.org/articles/darab-nama. An essential element of *naqqali* that needs to be pointed out here is its performative and dramatic nature. *Naqqali* and *Shahname-khwani* are also differentiated in the sense that on the one hand the latter is believed to 'be an exact recitation or reading of the *Shahnameh*',

and on the other hand, the former retells the account heroic tales in poetry or prose, while having the liberty to diverge from written story and its plot. See, Sajjad Aydenlou, *Tumar-e naqqali-e Shahnameh* (Tehran: Behnegar Publishers, 2012), p. 23. Omidsalar is of another opinion; he argues, 'Professional storytellers do not deviate from the Shahnameh narrative in significant details. However, they freely elaborate and reorganise.' Omidsalar looks at the different version of *tumār* and states that the order of Rostam's trials has been altered, an alteration which has a 'literary logic of its own'. Mahmoud Omidsalar, 'Rostam's Seven Trials and the Logic of Epic Narrative in the Shāhnāma', *Asian Folklore Studies,* Vol. 60, No. 2, 2001, pp. 259–93; (275).

10 Boyce argues that storytellers and minstrels of ancient Persia served as preservers and transmitters of mythology and history, thus playing an important role in the construction of the Iranian identity and 'preserving the Iranian national tradition'. See, Boyce, 'The Parthian Gōsān', p. 12. Omidsalar, on the other hand, believes that Boyce's argument regarding the role of Parthian minstrels or *gosan* in transmitting the Iranian tradition has been 'taken to fanciful extremes by contemporary scholarship'. He strongly disagrees with the *gosan* being the main transmitters of the traditions. He also does not believe that the epics were originally in the form of poetry and were sung. Omidsalar states that 'such an argument would be similar to proposing that because there is some professional race car driver in the united states, all of the driving in that country is of necessity accomplished by Mario Andretti's colleagues'. Mahmoud Omidsalar and Teresa Omidsalar, 'Narrating Epics in Iran', in *Traditional Storytelling Today: An International Sourcebook*, Margaret R. Macdonald ed. (Chicago: Fitzroy Dearborn Publishers, 1999), pp. 326–40; (327).

11 Ibid.

12 Strabo, *Geography*, vol. 1, books 1–2, trans. Horace Leonard Jones, Loeb Classical library 49 (Cambridge: Harvard University Press, 1917), p. 179.

13 Later literature such as *Qābusnāmeh* and *Tāj*, which fit into the mirror for princes genre, give us examples of the types of chivalric and honourable behaviour that would have been preached during the pre-Islamic period. We also see traces of such codes of ethics in the concept of *javanmardi* or *fotowwa*, specifically in the Sufi tradition. Scholars believe that the origins of this code of ethics can be found in the pre-Islamic period, specifically the Sasanian era. See L. Ridgeon, *Morals and Mysticism in Persian Sufism: A History of Sufi-Futuwwat in Iran* (Abingdon: Routledge, 2010). For an overall study of *javānmardi*, see, Mohsen Zakeri, 'Javānmardi', in *Encyclopaedia Iranica*, vol. 14, fasc. 6, Ehsan Yarshater ed. 2008. Accessed 5 July 2015, http://www.iranicaonline.org/articles/javanmardi.

14 Hannaway, 'Dārāb-nāma', 1994.

15 From an Iranian point of view, the best performances are those that prove to be 'useful'. This outlook might have its roots in the fact that the earliest performed acts were ritualistic, aiming to appease the gods and, in return, receive their blessings or divert their wrath. The happiness of the gods (audiences) would result in something and thus prove the performance to be 'useful': in the form of receiving a blessing such as victory and rain or eliminating something evil, such as sickness and war.

16 '[S]trewn here and there and shining like stars on that background, so that the clever and the great read it and learn from it many conceits, while men of low and middle state swallow it for the sake of the story'. Vladimir Minorsky, 'Vīs u Rāmīn, a Parthian Romance', *Bulletin of the School of Oriental and African Studies, University of London*, Vol. 11, No. 4, 1946, pp. 741–63 (743), accessed 6 July 2015, http://www.jstor.org/stable/608589.

Notes 213

17 For the use of the term 'safety valve' in modern politics, see https://www.mtsu.edu/first-amendment/article/1014/safety-valve-theory.
18 For example, the Parthian Minstrels or *gosan* 'was a person of considerable social standing, on a level with a district judge'. Boyce, 'The Parthian Gōsān', p. 12. Also, Sasanian *khunyāgar* and *rāmeshgar* (singers) constituted one of the officially recognized social classes. Jahez, *Tāj (Ketāb Al-Tāj)* (Arabic to Persian) trans. Mohammad Ali Khalili (Tehran: Ibn Sina Publications, 1964), pp. 66–7. The Sasanian king Bahram V is famed also for holding court entertainers and minstrels at a very high position Ibid., p. 70.
19 Athenaeus, *The Learned Banqueters*, vol. VII, books 13–14, ed. and trans. S. Douglas Olson, Loeb Classical Library 345 (Cambridge, MA: Harvard University Press, 2011), p. 205. Athenaeus is quoting a passage from Homer's *Odyssey* which reads, 'Then, as the tears filled her (Penelope) eyes, she spoke to the divine minstrel: "Phemius, many other things you know to charm mortals, deeds of men and gods which minstrels make famous. Sing them one of these, as you sit here, and let them drink their wine in silence."' Homer, *Odyssey*, volume I: books 1–12, trans. A. T. Murray, rev. George E. Dimock, Loeb Classical Library 104 (Cambridge: Harvard University Press, 1919), p. 37.
20 This is most especially studied in the context of *naqqali*. The extensive interaction between storyteller and *naqqal* in Iran gives the audience a sort of ecstatic power over destiny, if not their own but that of the protagonist. For example, there are accounts of how the audience would meddle and ask the *naqqāl* to change the plot of the story, sparing their favourite character from death. A similar interaction happens when important news is received through the channel of minstrelsy – music and storytelling. The receiver and the messenger both become agents involved in the news, rather than one being a passive reviver and the other the active party. See, Aydenlou, *Tumār-e naqqali*, 2012. Jahez emphasizes the importance of being patient with kings when they show signs of boredom or are in a bad mood. He believes that entertainers, buffoons and humourists are as essential to the well-being of the king as are brave warriors and men of wisdom. He provides an example of how Khosro's clown, Māziār, responded in a unique way to an instance of the king's bad mood: 'he [Maziār] got himself close to the King's chamber and hid. He then started barking like a dog [...] and howling like a wolf [...] until everyone gathered around him and pulled him out of his hiding place and told the king that it is Māziār the clown and the king laughed so hard that his mood became joyous.' Jahez, *Tāj*, p. 185.
21 Athenaeus, *The Learned Banqueters*, p. 205.
22 For a translation of the passage, see Gorgāni *Vis and Ramin*, pp. 265–7.
23 Regarding the skill and specialization of Bārbad, it is said that 'he is represented as a minstrel rather than a poet; he is not a mere musician like his comrade Nakisā, but essentially a singer, an improvisator, who, in the form of ballads, brings to the king's notice what it is desired that he should know'. Edward G. Browne, 'The Sources of Dawlatshāh, p. 61; With Some Remarks on the Materials Available for a Literary History of Persia, and an Excursus on Bārbad and Rūdagī', *Journal of the Royal Asiatic Society of Great Britain and Ireland (JRAS)*, 1899, pp. 37–69, accessed 9 July 2015, http://www.jstor.org/stable/25208066.The influential role of the minstrel at court is also stressed when Brown compares the character of Barabad to that of the Samanian poet Rudaki, who is the only person at court who is able to persuade the Samanian prince Nasr ibn Ahmad to return to Bukhara (Ibid., pp. 61–2).

24 Abumansur Tha'ālebi, *Shahnameh Tha'alebi*, trans. (from Arabic to Persian) Mahmood Hedayat (Tehran: Asatir publications, 2005), p. 339.
25 For example, Mas'udi, when speaking of performers and entertainers, expresses outward distaste towards them and says that he shows his disappointment in people who gather to watch and enjoy such performances by saying, 'One of the traits you find a lot among the masses is that they choose unworthy men as their leaders, and… can not distinguish right from wrong… and are either only interested in following bear whisperers, *daf* players, and monkey tamers or are busy being entertained by the lying and deceiving illusionist and magicians and those lie-weaving storytellers'. Ali b. Hussain Mas'udi, *Moruj al-Dhahab*, 2 vols (Arabic to Persian) trans. Abolghasem Payandeh (Tehran: Elmi va Farhangi Publications, 2003), p. 38. Mas'udi's distaste in entertainers is not that different from Mandakuni's opinion on them. While the two men lived almost four centuries apart, the mentality they held regarding performers was similar. Mas'udi brands performers and their followers as 'ignoble and vile' (*forumayegan*) and adds several hadith from the Prophet Mohammed to religiously back and legitimize his criticism (Ibid., p. 39). Mas'udi is not the only voice in the medieval world of Islam who displays a sour attitude towards performers. Ghazali (eleventh century), the great jurist, philosopher and theologian, advises against any humour jesting or singing (unless it is mystical *samā'*), categorizing such acts as the plague of humanity, and supporting his argument with words and advice from the prophet. He holds a very puritan stance on the subject of entertainment that leads to laughter and proclaims anything beyond a smile as evil, stating that '*mezāh* (humour) has been strictly prohibited by the prophet, however, a small bit of it is okay… under the condition that it does not turn into a habit… as excessive humour ruins one's life and causes undue laughter, which darkens the heart and results in the loss of prestige and esteem.' Abu Hamed Ghazali, *Kimiya-ye Sa'adat*, 2 vols, Hossein Khadiv-Jam ed. (Tehran: Elmi va Farhangi Publishers, 2001), p. 75. He then adds several hadith from the Prophet Mohammad in this respect. For example, 'those who say things to make people laugh will fall from esteem and lose their respect… moreover, anything that causes laughter is vile, and laughter should not exceed a light smile.' Ibid. Ghazvini-Razi (twelfth century), a theologian, from Ray, writing almost a century later, tries to illustrate non-religious storytelling as evil, by politicizing it. He states that 'after the murder of Hossein, the bigoted men of the house of Umayyad and the house of Marvan, could not stand the praise and honour that was placed upon the family of Ali, thus they gathered… a group of infidels to weave false tales and groundless stories about Rostam, Sorkhab, Esfandiyar, Kavoos, Zal, and others of this crowd. They then sent out singers, storytellers, and minstrels to the four corners of this land… and this heretical innovation is still alive and practiced'. Abdoljalil Ghazvini-Razi, *Naghz*, Mir-Jalaleddin Ormavi Mohaddes ed. (Tehran: Anjoman Asar-e Melli Publishers, 1980), p. 67.
26 Anthony Shay, *The Dangerous Lives of Public Performers: Dancing, Sex, and Entertainment in the Islamic World* (Palgrave Macmillan, 2014), p. 95.
27 This daunting view is found mainly among men of books and monotheistic theologians. For example, the Babylonian Talmud (approximately sixth-century Sasanian Iran) states that 'the ear which listens to song should be torn off… when there is song in a house there is destruction on its threshold; as it is stated: their voice shall sing in the windows, desolation shall be in the thresholds… when men sing, and women join in it is licentiousness; when women sing and men join in it is like fire in tow' (Babylonian Talmud, Sotah 48. Retrieved at: http://www.come-and-hear.

com/sotah/sotah_48.html). While the rabbis of Babylon are warning against music, its broad scope encompasses musicians, minstrels, storytellers and all gatherings that involve any performance along with music. A similar antagonist view is expressed by Catholicos Yovhannes Mandakuni, the fifth-century Catholicos of Armenia, hoping to lead his audience to the 'right path' and open their eyes to what he calls 'the lawless theaters of the demonic'. James R. Russell, 'On an Armenian Word List from the Cairo Geniza', *Iran and the Caucasus,* Vol. 17, No. 2, 2013, pp. 189–214 (202), accessed 10 July 2015, http://nrs.harvard.edu/urn-3:HUL.InstRepos:10880590. While doing so, he provides us with information on Armenian *gosan* of his time. Mandakuni's description illustrates a scene that involves drama, minstrelsy, storytelling and stunt performances, all working together to create a night of entertainment and pleasure, which, put in the context of *Khosro ud Rēdag,* could all be called *khuniyagars.* Mandakuni then warns his audience against minstrelsy and dramatic performances and says that 'where jesters and minstrels and lewd play and satire be; there the demons, too, join in the dance… the custom itself is evil and so are those who encourage it: wine, the minstrel (*gosan*), and Satan' (Ibid). He then adds more detail to what such gatherings entailed: 'women are cast into the role of prostitutes; and men, as rutting stallions mounting mares' (Ibid, pp. 202–3). He continues to paint the performances of his time with a bolder brush of evil saying that 'the theaters of the play are the encampments of the demons, as are all the immoral, minstrel-mad wine-imbiber, too… they pour more into the mouths of the lewd minstrels – many clownish jests and moronic speeches' (Ibid, p. 203). The Christian Armenian dislike of such performances goes beyond the *gosan* and their wining, dining, singing, and dancing festivities and even blacklists simple storytelling performances. Moses Khorenatsi (fifth century), writing at almost the same time as Mandakuni, reproaches his audience and asks, 'what then is your delight in the obscene and ridiculous fables […] and why do you trouble us for those absurd and incoherent Persian stories, notorious for their imbecility? […] But you ask us to explain the reason for their irrationality and to embellish what is unadorned.' Revise to Khorenatsi, History *of the Armenians*, trans. and commentary by Robert W. Thomson (Cambridge: Harvard University Press, 1978), pp. 126–7. Even earlier sources are not any more sympathetic or kind to performers. A Manichean Parthian text (fourth-fifth century) states that 'a Gosan, who proclaims the worthiness of kings and heroes of old, and himself achieves nothing at all'. Boyce, 'The Parthian Gōsān', p. 11. Here, although not seen as demonic, evil and promiscuous, minstrels and *gosāns* are viewed as not quite as worthy as other classes, such as the military and the royalty.

28 Ibrahim Moseli is believed to have originally been from Kufa and was only referred to as Moseli after a trip to Mosel, Iraq. He is reported to have passed away in 828 CE. Mohammad Hasan Khan Etemad-o Saltaneh, *Tarikh-e Montazem-e Naseri,* vol. 2, Mohammad Esmail Rezvani ed. (Tehran: Donya-ye Ketab, 1988), p. 182. An interesting incident that took place at the Abbasid court can further depict what is meant by the 'high status' of minstrels. The incident is narrated by Eshaq ibn Ebrahim Moseli, a Persian musician of the Abbasid era. Eshaq states that he had been deeply shocked and disrespected when an Arab courtier called him over and asked him 'in a drunkard fashion' to sing and play a piece of music. He then adds that he is a courtier and a servant of the caliph, and a noble and wise man should not dare speak to him in such a manner. See, Sadegh Sajjadi, *Tarikh e Barmakian* (Tehran: Bonyad Mowqufat Dr Mahmoud Afshar, 2006), p. 237. Minstrelsy and musical performance, like many other jobs of the time, was usually a hereditary job, as the case of Ibrahim

and his son Eshaq. However, there were also others who would be educated in the art of performance. For example, we know of Danānir, one of Yahya Barmaki's maids and a highly skilled *khunyāgar*, who had been trained by Eshaq and his father, Ebrahim. Ibid. p. 456. There were also instances of strong bonds and loyalty between performer and patron. For example, after the death of Yahya Barmaki the grand vizier of the Abbasid court, Danānir, his minstrel, rejected Harun's request to play at his court and 'spent the rest of her life singing elegies and dirges' for the house of the Barmakis. Ibid.

Chapter 2

1. 'The Scarlet Stone' is a literal English translation of the Persian words '*Mohreye Sorkh*'. However, as the stage production uses both segments from *Shahnameh* (by Ferdowsi), and only parts of *Mohreye Sorkh* (by Kasrai), for clarity in this article we refer to the poem as *Mohreye Sorkh*, and to the production as *The Scarlet Stone*.
2. Ahmad Karimi-Hakkak, *An Anthology of Modern Persian Poetry* (Boulder, Colorado: Westview Press, 1978), p. xiii.
3. Ahmad Karimi-Hakkak, *Recasting Persian Poetry: Scenarios of Poetic Modernity in Iran* (Salt Lake City: University of Utah Press, 1995), p. 247.
4. Charles Kurzman, *The Unthinkable Revolution in Iran* (Cambridge, Massachusetts: Harvard University Press, 2005), p. 122.
5. Michael Axworthy, *Revolutionary Iran: A History of the Islamic Republic* (New York: Oxford University Press, 2013), p. 235.
6. Abolqasem Ferdowsi, Shahnameh: the Persian book of kings / by Abolqasem Ferdowsi; translated by Dick Davis; with a foreword by Azar Nafisi (New York: Viking, 2006), p. 190.
7. The long-poem form in the Persian literature refers not only to the length of the poem but also to the depth of its literally and philosophical investigations.
8. Siavash Kasrai, *Mohreye Sorkh* (Vienna, Austria: Kara Publications, 1995), p. 34.
9. Kasrai, *Mohreye Sorkh*, p. 42, 43. All translation of excerpts of *Mohreye Sorkh* are by Sia Nemat-Nasser.
10. Kasrai, *Mohreye Sorkh*, p. 48.
11. Ibid., p. 51.
12. Ibid., pp. 56–7.
13. Ibid., p. 62.
14. Ibid., p. 7.
15. Beeman, *Iranian Performance Traditions*, p. 30.
16. Mark Coniglio, *Isadora's User's Manual* (Portland, OR: Troika Ranch, 2002–2013).
17. According to the only recording of the poem recited by Siavash Kasrai, http://kasrai.com.
18. *The Scarlet Stone* had two sets of performances in 2011 and 2015 in San Diego (Mandel Weiss Forum), Los Angeles (UCLA, Freud Playhouse and Royce Hall) and Toronto (Harbourfront Fleck Dance Theatre). The project was conceived by the author, who adapted, directed and composed the piece, and Shahrokh Moshkin-Ghalam, who choreographed the dances, designed the costumes and performed as the protagonist Sohrab. The *Shahnameh* sections were adapted in collaboration with Gordāfarid, who performed the role of the *naqqal* and that of Ferdowsi. Other

performers were Afshin Mofid as Rostam, Ida Saki as Gordāfarid and Miriam Perez as Tahmineh. Ian Wallace designed the set and interactive projections and Omar Ramos, Kristin Hayes and Wen-Ling Liao designed the lights. English renditions of all text were by Sia Nemat-Nasser. *The Scarlet Stone* has been in production since 2009 and has been generously funded by grants such as the MAP Fund, a programme of Creative Capital supported by the Doris Duke Charitable Foundation, the University of California Research in the Arts Institute Production Grant, UCSD Arts and Humanities Innovation Fund, and a grant from Chehre-Azad Endowment Funds at UC San Diego.

Chapter 3

1. Abbas Kiarostami, *Bad va barg*, trans. Fatemeh Esmaeili (Tehran: Chap va Nashr-e Nazar, 2010), p. 272.
2. For a study of diverse dramatic traditions in Islamdom, see Marvin Carlson, *Theatre & Islam* (London: Macmillan Education: Red Globe Press, 2019).
3. The question of 'theatre' goes beyond the present study. But the wide-ranging features that characterize theatre distinct from ritual, as Richard Schechner notes, are not clear-cut. To classify a performance as 'theatre' one needs to study its specific context and circumstances where it is staged. There are aspects of theatre production, for example, that go beyond 'entertainment' and acquire the efficacy of ritual practice, such as the socio-economic structure of theatre procedures. See Richard Schechner, *Performance Theory* (London; New York: Routledge, 2003), pp. 130–1. What I would like to underline, though, is the historicity of the theatre formation as a distinct cultural and urban industry that emerged in early modern Europe, although with ancient roots across Eurasia. For a study on the intricate relationship between ritual and theatre, which is not 'neither necessarily opposed normutually exclusive', see Eli Rozik, *Rethinking Ritual and Other Theories of Origin* (Iowa City: University of Iowa Press, 2002).
4. For an ethnographic and theoretical study of the relationship between Moharram rituals and space, see Reza Masoudi, *The Rite of Urban Passage: The Spatial Ritualisation of Iranian Urban Transformation* (New York; Oxford: Berghahn, 2018).
5. The proposed definition is similar to Catherine Bell's ritual theory. However, the theoretical idea that informs my understanding of ritual also emphasizes the notion of play as misrule and transgression based on disjointedness of the subjunctive 'as if', as described by Henri Lefebvre. See Catherin Bell, *Ritual Perspectives and Dimensions* (New York; Oxford: Oxford University Press, 1997).
6. Here a distinction should be made between ritual performers and theatre audiences. Both forms of dramatic performances can have their distinct communities. As for theatre, Jacque Rancière's notion 'being apart together' identifies the collective experience of audiences in range of audio-visual performances that may include being silent together. The audience as an ensemble of observers can become a community of present bodies in proximity of a shared experience of an event. See Jacque Rancière, *The Emancipated Spectator*, trans. by Gregory Elliott (London; New York: Verso, 2009), p. 59.
7. Shiʿi Twelver (Imami) Islam is the largest Shiʿi branch and with the most adherence in Iran. Also, *taʿzieh* performances are wide, and they can be staged for other male and female descendants of the Prophet throughout the year, especially the month of Safar.

8   For a history of Karbala and its importance to Shiʻi history, see Andrew J. Newman, *Twelver Shiism: Unity and Diversity in the Life of Islam, 632–1722* (Edinburgh: Edinburgh University Press, 2013), pp. 19–25.
9   Here I diverge from a historical-nationalist view that understands the roots of *taʻzieh* in pre-Islamic Iran. It should be made clear that there is no single evidence that suggests it is an extension of ancient Iranian ritual traditions, as though ritual narratives with an imagined primordial national character can reincarnate in historical temporality. Though there are certainly symbolic and thematic resemblances, including universal myths of martyrdom and in particular the legend of Siyavush/Siavash, *taʻzieh* is a (late) Safavid formation that reflects the distinct socio-religious realities of a society under construction of a Perso-Shiʻi Imami identity. For a critical study of Moharram studies, see Babak Rahimi, *Theater State and the Formation of Early Modern Public Sphere in Iran: Studies on Safavid Muharram Rituals, 1590–1641 CE* (Leiden; Boston: Brill, 2012), pp. 31–62.
10 See Rahimi, *Theater State and the Formation of Early Modern Public Sphere in Iran*, pp. 199–234.
11 Peter J. Chelkowski, 'Taʻziyeh: Indigenous Avant-Garde Theatre of Iran', *Performing Arts Journal*, Vol. 2, No. 1 (Spring) 1977, p. 33 and Rahimi, *Theater State*, pp. 215; 307–20.
12 Bahram Beyzaie views the birth of *taʻzieh* in the late seventeenth-century Safavid era. However, the Safavid versions of the dramatic rituals were primarily processional and dependent on the Moharram repertoire performed in urban spaces. See Bahram Beyzaie, *Namayesh dar Iran* [Theatre in Iran] (Tehran: Entesharat-e roshangaran va motaleat-e zanan, 1965), pp. 111–17.
13 Peter J. Chelkowski, 'Time Out of Memory: Taʻziyeh the Total Drama', *Drama Review*, Vol. 49, No. 4 (Winter), 2005, p. 16 and Sadeq Humayuni, *taʻzieh va taʻzieh-Khwani* (Shiraz: Navid, 1991), p. 19; Farrokh Ghaffary, *Theatre Irani* [Iranian theatre] (Tehran: Shiraz Arts Festivals, 1971); and Bahram Beyzaie, *Namayesh dar Iran* [Drama in Iran] (1965–66; repr. Tehran: Entesharat-e Roshangharan va Motaliat-e Zanan, 2001), p. 122.
14 There is also the mid-eighteenth-century depiction of the German explorer, Carsten Niebuhr, who depicts a mock battle between Yazid and Imam Hossein's armies on Khark Island in the Persian Gulf. See Carsten Niebuhr, *Reisebeschreibung nach Arabien und andern umliegende Ländern* (Zurich: Manesse Verlag, 1992), pp. 575–8.
15 A collection of handwritten *taʻzieh* manuscripts from the Zand period suggests that the ceremonies had been widely practiced in Iran by the mid-eighteenth century. See Beeman, *Iranian Performance Traditions*, p. 122, n10.
16 Matthew Arnold, 'A Persian Passion Play', *Cornhill Magazine* (December), 1871, p. 676.
17 Rahimi, 'Takkiyeh Dowlat', pp. 55–71.
18 See Iraq Anvar, 'Peripheral Taʻziyeh: The Transformation of Taʻziyeh from Moharram Mourning Ritual to Secular and Comical Theatre', *Theatre Drama Review (TDR)*, Vol. 49, No. 4 (Winter), 2005, pp. 61–7. https://www.jstor.org/stable/4488681?seq=1#metadata_info_tab_contents and also Talajooy on the incorporation of *taqlid* play in *taʻzieh*, Talajooy, 'Indigenous Performing Traditions in post-Revolutionary Iranian Theater', pp. 497–519.
19 See Pahlavi prohibition of *taʻzieh*, see Floor, *The History of Theater in Iran*, pp. 196–9.
20 For a thorough study of *taʻzieh*'s impact on post-revolutionary Iranian theatre, see Talajooy, 'Indigenous Performing Traditions in post-Revolutionary Iranian Theater',

pp. 497–519. In the post-war period, a similar trend can be also identified in Arab theatre in case of Tayeb Saddiki (Morocco) and Sa'dallah Wannous (Syria), who employed *al-halaqa*, which heavily rely on audience participation with the spectators circling around the actors.
21 Peter J. Chelkowski, 'From Karbala to New York City: Taziyeh on the Move', *The Drama Review*, Vol. 49, No. 4, 2005, pp. 12–14. *ta'zieh* influence is also evident in the work of Claude Confortès, *Le Marathon* (1972). Gaffary, 'Evolution of Rituals and Theatre in Iran', p. 371. For the Shiraz-Persepolis Festivals of Art and performance of *ta'zieh Horr* in 1967, see Mahasti Afshar, "Festival of Arts, Shiraz-Persepolis, 1967–1977," Iran Namag 4, no. 2 (2019): pp. 4–64.
22 See Sharifi Isaloo, *Power, Legitimacy and the Public Sphere*, pp. 71–150.
23 See Abbas Amanat, *Iran: A Modern History* (New Haven: Yale University Press, 2017), p. 290 and Rahimi, 'Takkiyeh Dowlat', p. 63.
24 For a detailed study of *ta'zieh* narrative structures, in particular an account of prologue, episode, sub-episode and comic episodes, see Jamshid Malekpour, *The Islamic Drama* (London: Frank Cass, 2004).
25 See J. L. Austin, *How to Do Things with Words* (Cambridge, Massachusetts: Harvard University Press, 1975).
26 See Schechner, *Performance Theory*, pp. 126–9.
27 'Sug-e Azadegi, Elham Gerefte az Sakhte-ye "Taziyeh" Kiarostami', *Mehr News*, 10 October 2019 (last accessed 30 April 2020): https://www.mehrnews.com/news/4742886/%D8%B3%D9%88%DA%AF-%D8%A2%D8%B2%D8%A7%D8%AF%DA%AF%DB%8C-%D8%A7%D9%84%D9%87%D8%A7%D9%85-%DA%AF%D8%B1%D9%81%D8%AA%D9%87-%D8%A7%D8%B2-%D8%B3%D8%A7%D8%AE%D8%AA%D9%87-%D8%AA%D8%B9%D8%B2%DB%8C%D9%87-%DA%A9%DB%8C%D8%A7%D8%B1%D8%B3%D8%AA%D9%85%DB%8C).
28 Diana Taylor, *The Archive and the Repertoire: Cultural Memory and Performance in the Americas* (Durham; London: Duke University Press, 2003), p. 20; 37.
29 Erving Goffman, *Interaction Ritual: Essays on Face-to-Face Behavior* (New York: Pantheon Books, 1967), pp. 5–45.
30 One must bear in mind that the element of 'stage' entered *ta'zieh* most likely in the late Naseri period (1848–96) with the construction of Takkiyeh dowlat, partly modelled after European theatre architecture. In its Qajar development, the circular stage is a distinct architectural platform feature from central Iran, especially Kashan and Tehran. The incorporation of *ta'zieh* stage in cinematic works of Bayza'i, as innovatively described by Negar Mottahedeh, is reflection of a development that took place in late Qajar and Pahlavi periods, in particular during the Shiraz Arts Festival (1967–1977). See Negar Mottahedeh, *Displaced Allegories: Post-Revolutionary Iranian Cinema* (Durham; London: Duke University Press, 2008), pp. 18–19.
31 Peter Brook, *The Empty Space* (New York: Touchstone, 1968), p. 9.
32 Hamid Dabashi, *Shi'ism: A Religion of Protest* (Cambridge, Massachusetts; London; England: The Belknap Press of Harvard University Press, 2011), p. 220.
33 Lee Marshall, 'People Watching', *The Guardian*, July 14, 2003. Last accessed, 30 April 2020: https://www.theguardian.com/film/2003/jul/14/theatre.artsfeatures.
34 Reza Ale-Mohammad, 'An Iranian Passion Play: "Taziyeh" in History and Performance', *New Theatre Quarterly*, Vol. 17, No. 1, February 2001, p. 58.
35 Peter J. Chelkowski, 'Ta'ziyeh: Indigenous Avant-Garde Theatre of Iran', *Performing Arts Journal*, Vol. 2, No. 1, 1977, p. 37.

36 Here I diverge from a symbolist approach on Shi'i rituals advanced by William Beeman in that the 'system of symbols' define the ritual culture under study. William O. Beeman, 'Cultural Dimensions of Performance Conventions in Iranian Ta'ziyeh', in *Ta'ziyeh: Ritual and Drama in Iran*, Peter J. Chelkowski ed. (New York: New York University Press, 1979), pp. 24–31.

37 Sadegh Homayouni, 'A View from the Inside: The Anatomy of the Persian Ta'ziyeh Plays', in *Eternal Performance: Ta'ziyeh and other Shiite Rituals*, trans. by Iraq Anvar, Peter J. Chelkowski ed. (Calcutta; London; New York: Seagull Books, 2010), p. 124. The post-revolutionary *ta'zieh* has undergone a change in the minimalist character of the plays with the introduction of theatrical decors and props on a stage setting.

38 Naficy, *A Social History of Iranian Cinema*, p. 189.

39 Talajooy, 'Indigenous Performing Traditions in Post-Revolutionary Iranian Theatre', p. 510, f.20.

40 For an account of Kiarostami's notion of 'disappearance of direction', or in what can be called as anti-film filmmaking, see Alberto Elena, *The Cinema of Abbas Kiarostami*, trans. by Belinda Coombes (London: Saqi in association with Iran Heritage Foundation, 2005), pp. 174–9.

41 Paul Cronin, *Lessons with Kiarostami* (New York: Sticking Place Books, 2015), p. 159.

42 Kiarostami would describe *Shirin* as his most 'artificial film' but also 'the most honest and truthful'. See Cronin, *Lessons with Kiarostami*, p. 160.

43 Ibid., p. 159.

44 Hamideh Razavi, *Taste of Shirin* (2008). https://vimeo.com/322922297.

45 Here I agree with Abbott Matthew, who regarding facial performances in *Shirin* argues, 'For it isn't quite that the women are "acting," in the usual sense of performing a role. Perhaps what we see is the condition of acting, that which renders possible the act of performing.' Matthew Abbot, *Abbas Kiarostami and Film-Philosophy* (Edinburgh: Edinburgh University Press, 2017), p. 101.

46 John Berger, *Ways of Seeing* (London: British Broadcasting Corp.; London; New York, N.Y. Penguin Books, 1977), p. 61.

47 When *Shirin* was screened in 2008 Venice Film Festival, audiences were uncertain if the women were watching a play or a film, making room for audience interpretation of negative spaces in the film. Henry K. Miller, 'Shirin', *Sight and Sound*, July 2009.

48 Cronin, *Lessons with Kiarostami*, p. 160.

49 Michael Price, 'Imagining Life: The Ending of *Taste Cherry*', 17, November 2001. (Last accessed 30 April 2020: http://sensesofcinema.com/2001/abbas-kiarostami-17/cherry/).

50 'Kiarostami Photos Displayed in Louvre in Tehran', *Islamic Republic News Agency*, 26 February 2018. Last accessed 29 September 2020: https://en.irna.ir/news/82844722/Kiarostami-photos-displayed-in-Louvre-in-Tehran.

51 For an account of the 2003 performance, see Anna Vanzan, 'Ta'ziyeh in Parma', *Eternal Performance: Ta'ziyeh and Other Shiite Rituals*, Peter J. Chelkowski ed. (Calcutta; London; New York: Seagull Books, 2010), pp. 280–3. According to Mohamamd Ghaffari, the 2003 *ta'zieh* performers were mostly comprised by performers in 2002 production, directed by Ghaffari, in the New York's Lincoln Center Festival. Interview, Mohamamd Ghaffari, 21 Februrary 2021.

52 Nacim Pak-Shiraz, *Shi'i Islam in Iranian Cinema: Religion and Spirituality in Film* (London; New York: I.B. Tauris, 2011), p. 162.

53 The film version includes three screens, with the two large screens depicting the spectators watching the performances.

54 Pak-Shiraz, *Shi'i Islam in Iranian Cinema*, p. 161.
55 Ibid.
56 Ibid.
57 Lee Marshall, 'People Watching', *The Guardian*, July 14, 2003 (last accessed, 30 April 2020: https://www.theguardian.com/film/2003/jul/14/theatre.artsfeatures).
58 Rahimi, *Theater State*, pp. 273–320.
59 I have discerned similar personal motivational features in other ethnographic studies on Moharram in Iran.
60 Erving Goffman, *The Presentation of Self in Everyday Life* (Garden City, N.Y: Doubleday, 1959), pp. 208–37.
61 Kiarostami sums up the element of agency with the following account: 'I never told any of them to be sad or gloomy and certainly didn't ask them to cry, though the agreement was that everyone would finish on a sad note. I filmed each woman for five minutes, so ended up with several hundred minutes of footage. Two minutes later it was over. There were several instances when the women had stood up and removed themselves from the camera lens, yet were still deeply involved. The five-minute shoot had ended but the tears hadn't. I found it extraordinary how the vivid imaginations of these women had created and summoned to consciousness such powerful and consequential imagery.' Cronin, *Lessons with Kiarostami*, p. 159.
62 Lee Marshall, 'People Watching', *The Guardian*, 14 July 2003 (Last accessed 30 April 2020: https://www.theguardian.com/film/2003/jul/14/theatre.artsfeatures).
63 As Dabashi has correctly argued, there is an ethical dimension to the second audience. He writes, 'Making a European seasonal spectacle out of the ritual piety of the Shi'i spectators, who are participating in the sacrosanct moment of their collective faith, is all the more troubling when Iranian peasants caught in a moment of their sacramental rites are offered up for the passing entertainment of bored urban Europeans, who might attend a Russian circus next week and a film or theater festival the week after.' He adds, 'Along the same lines, marking the dangerously slippery slope down which aesthetic formalism may slide, there is also an aggressive (violent even) anthropologization of rural areas for the benefit of urban spectators (whether in Tehran or Paris, it makes no difference).' Dabashi, *Shi'ism*, p. 221. The purported voyeuristic tendency in Kiarostami's *ta'zieh* is critique that overlooks the element of empathy in cosmopolitan attempt to bridge cultural distance through human emotions, which can underline not an anthropologization but a transculturalization of the performances.
64 According to an account, some of the Italian audiences who attended the *ta'zieh* in Rome wore veils and even cried during the performances. 'Vaghti Kiarostami Ta'ziyeh ra dar Italia Ejra Kard' (When Kiarostami staged *ta'zieh* in Italy), *Asr-e Iran*, 9 July 2016, last accessed 6 May 2020: https://www.asriran.com/fa/news/478852/%D9%88%D9%82%D8%AA%DB%8C-%DA%A9%DB%8C%D8%A7%D8%B1%D8%B3%D8%AA%D9%85%DB%8C-%D8%AA%D8%B9%D8%B2%DB%8C%D9%87-%D8%B1%D8%A7-%D8%AF%D8%B1-%D8%A7%DB%8C%D8%AA%D8%A7%D9%84%DB%8C%D8%A7-%D8%A7%D8%AC%D8%B1%D8%A7-%DA%A9%D8%B1%D8%AF).
65 A similar inter-perspectivist strategy can also be detected in Kiarostami's photographic works.
66 For a study of the relationship between the Brechtian theatre and *ta'zieh*, see Parviz Mamnoun, 'Ta'ziyeh from the Viewpoint of the Western Theatre', in *Ta'ziyeh: Ritual and Drama in Iran*, Peter J. Chelkowski ed. (New York: New York University Press and Soroush Press, 1979), pp. 154–66. For a more detailed study of Brecht's

distancing effect (*Verfremdungseffekt*) in comparison with *ta'zieh*, see Mohd Sasir Hashim and Farideh Alizadeh, 'A Comparative Study: The Principles of the Distancing Effect in Bretchtian Theatre and Ta'ziyeh', *Cogent Arts & Humanities*, 7, No. 1, 2020.

67 Majid Fallahzadeh, *Tarikh-e Ejtemayi-Siasi-ye Te'atr-e Iran: ta'zieh* (The Social-Political History of Theatre in Iran) (Tehran: Nashr-e Pezhvak, 2014), p. 192. See John Willett, ed. and trans. *Brecht on Theatre: The Development of an Aesthetic* (New York: Hill and Wang, 1964).

68 Consider again Kiarostami's photographic selections, *Look at Me*, in which the photos of Louvre Museum visitors overlap with the displayed paintings, breaking the boundary between viewership subjects and the viewed objects (last accessed 5 May 2020: https://www.tehrantimes.com/news/421618/National-Museum-of-Iran-to-showcase-Louvre-visitors-in-Kiarostami-s).

69 Nassia Hamid, 'Near and Far', *Sight and Sound*, Vol. 7, No. 2 (February) 1997, p. 24.

70 Rancière, *The Emancipated Spectator*, p. 13.

71 Zsolt Gyenge, 'Subjects and Objects of the Embodied Gaze: Abbas Kiarostami and the Read of the Individual Perspective', *Acta Univ. Sapientiae, Film and Media Studies*, Vol. 13, 2016, pp. 127–41.

72 For an account of 'averted gaze', understood in the limits of strategic practice of subverting external limitations for 'visual modesty', see Mottahedeh, *Displaced Allegories*, pp. 121–6.

73 For the concept of 'scopic regimes', a term originally borrowed from film theorist Christian Metz, see Martin Jay, '*Force Fields: Between Intellectual History and Cultural Critique* (New York: Routledge, 1992), pp. 114–33.

74 Ibid., p. 134.

75 Kenta McGrath, 'Unseen Voices in Abbas Kiarostami's *The Wind Will Carry Us*', *Mise-en-scène: The Journal of Film & Visual Narration*, vol. 1, No. 1, winter 2016. Last accessed 23 November 2020. https://journals.sfu.ca/msq/index.php/msq/article/view/19/pdf.

76 Commenting on omission as a narrative technique, Hemingway would explain his theory as 'that you could omit anything if you knew that you omitted and the omitted part would strengthen the story and make people feel something more than they understood'. Ernest Hemingway, *A Moveable Feast* (New York; London; Toronto; Sydney: Scribner, [1964] 2009) p. 71.

77 See Jean-Luc Nancy, 'On Evidence: Life and Nothing More, by Abbas Kiarostami', *Discourse*, Vol. 21, No. 1, 1999, pp. 85–6.

Chapter 4

1 Farah Pahlavi, *An Enduring Love: My Life with the Shah* (New York: Miramax Books, 1987), pp. 151–8.

2 National Iranian Television (NITV) became National Iranian Radio and Television (NIRT) in 1971.

3 Farah Pahlavi, *An Enduring Love: My Life with the Shah*, p. 227.

4 Gholam Reza Afkhami, *The Life and Times of the Shah* (Berkeley: University of California Press, 2009), p. 248.

5 Farah Pahlavi, '"Lecture," Asia Society Shiraz Arts Festival Symposium', *New York*, 5 October 2013.

6 Ibid.
7 Mahasti Afshar, 'Festival of Arts Shiraz-Persepolis: Or You Better Believe in as Many as Six Impossible Things before Breakfast', Paper presented at the *Asia Society Shiraz Arts Festival Symposium* (New York, 5 October 2013), pp. 4–5.
8 Farah Pahlavi, *An Enduring Love*, pp. 228–9.
9 Ibid.
10 In Michael Axworthy's *Revolutionary Iran*, he refers to the 1970s as a period when the country was on a 'slide to revolution'. See, Michael Axworthy, *Revolutionary Iran: A History of the Islamic Republic* (London: Allen Lane, 2013).
11 Hamid Dabashi, 'Ta'ziyeh as Theatre of Protest', *TDR*, Vol. 49, No. 4, 2005, pp. 91–9.
12 Robert Gluck, 'The Shiraz Arts Festival: Western Avant-Garde Arts in 1970s Iran', *Leonardo*, Vol. 40, No. 1, 2007, pp. 20–47 (25).
13 Iannis Xenakis and Sharon Kanach, *Music and Architecture: Architectural Projects, Texts, and Realizations* (Hillsdale, New York: Pendragon Press, 2008), p. 219.
14 Ibid.
15 Maryam Kharazmi, 'World Premiere of "Persepolis" by Xenakis', *Kayhan International* (17 August 1971), p. 6.
16 Iannis Xenakis and Sharon Kanach, *Music and Architecture*, p. 221.
17 Ibid., p. 223.
18 Afkhami, *The Life and Times of the Shah*, p. 420.
19 Parisa Parsi, 'Xenakis Attempts to Burn Persepolis', *Kayhan International* (28 August 1971), p. 6.
20 Ibid.
21 Parisa Parsi, '"Persepolis" Controversy a Greek Fury', *Kayhan International* (August 30, 1971), p. 6.
22 Ibid.
23 Ibid.
24 Amir Taheri, 'Empress Defends Celebration as National Target', *Kayhan International* (August 29, 1971), p. 4.
25 Sven Sterken, 'Towards a Space-Time Art: Iannis Xenakis's Polytopes', *Perspectives of New Music*, Vol. 39, No. 2, 2001, pp. 262–73 (269).
26 Amir Taheri, 'Empress Defends Celebration as National Target', p.1.
27 Ibid.
28 Michael Axworthy, *Revolutionary Iran*, p. 77.
29 William O. Beeman, *Culture, Performance and Communication in Iran* (Tokyo: Institute for the Study of Languages and Cultures of Asia and Africa, 1982), p. 189.
30 Afshin Molavi, *The Soul of Iran: A Nation's Journey to Freedom* (New York: W.W. Norton & Company, 2002), p. 14. Also see Sadegh Khalkhali's, *Kourosh-e Doroughin va Jenayatkar* (Besat, 1981).
31 Elaine Sciolino, *Persian Mirrors: The Elusive Face of Iran* (New York: The Free Press, 2000), p. 168.
32 Iannis Xenakis, Sharon Kanach, *Music and Architecture*, p. 223.
33 Robert Gluck, 'The Shiraz Arts Festival', p. 26.
34 Ervand Abrahamian, *Iran between Two Revolutions* (Princeton: Princeton University Press, 1982), pp. 480–1.
35 Beeman, 'Cultural Dimensions of Performance Conventions in Iranian Ta'ziyeh', pp. 185–6, 189.
36 Ervand Abrahamian, *Iran between Two Revolutions*, p. 443.

37   Victor S. Navasky, 'The Moral Question Boycott', *New York Times* (15 August 1976), p. 169.
38   Gholam Reza Afkhami, *The Life and Times of the Shah*, p. 457.
39   Peter J. Chelkowski, 'Ta'ziyeh: Indigenous Avant-Garde Theater of Iran', in *Ta'ziyeh: Ritual and Drama in Iran*, Peter J. Chelkowski ed. (New York: New York University Press, 1979), pp. 1–11 (2).
40   Maryam Kharazmi, 'Scholars Discuss Art of Tazieh', *Kayhan International* (18 August 1976), p. 3.
41   Peter J. Chelkowski, 'Ta'ziyeh: Indigenous Avant-Garde Theater of Iran', pp. 3–4.
42   Dabashi, 'Ta'ziyeh as Theatre of Protest', p. 98.
43   Peter J. Chelkowski and Mohammad Ghaffari, 'Mohammad B. Ghaffari: Ta'ziyeh Director', *TDR*, Vol. 49, No. 4, 2005, pp. 113–29 (114).
44   Mahasti Afshar, 'Festival of Arts Shiraz-Persepolis', p. 21.
45   Mahraz Khavari, 'Theatrical Feasts at Shiraz Festival', *Kayhan International* (19 August 1971), p. 6.
46   Peter J. Chelkowski and Mohammad Ghaffari, 'Mohammad B. Ghaffari: Ta'ziyeh Director', p. 113.
47   Ibid.
48   Ibid., p. 115.
49   Ibid., p. 116.
50   Andrzej Wirth, 'Semiological Aspects of the Ta'ziyeh', in *Ta'ziyeh: Ritual and Drama in Iran*, Peter J. Chelkowski ed. (New York: New York University Press, 1979), pp. 32–9 (38).
51   Ibid., p. 37.
52   William O. Beeman, Mohammad Ghaffari, 'Acting Styles and Actor Training in Ta'ziyeh', *TDR*, Vol. 49, No. 4, 2005, pp. 48–60 (49).
53   Afkhami, *The Life and Times of the Shah*, p. 417.
54   Sharmeen Battat, 'Empress Launches 10th Shiraz Festival', *Kayhan International* (21 August 1976), p. 1.
55   Sharmeen Battat, 'ta'zieh – A Distinct Theatrical Tradition', *Kayhan International* (28 August 1976), p. 3.
56   Michael Kirby, 'An Editorial: The Shiraz Festival: Politics and Theater', *The Drama Review: TDR*, Vol. 20, No. 4, 1976, pp. 2–5 (5).
57   Peter J. Chelkowski, Mohammad Ghaffari, 'Mohammad B. Ghaffari: Ta'ziyeh Director', p. 117.
58   Ervand Abrahamian, *Iran between Two Revolutions*, p. 425.
59   Dabashi, 'Ta'ziyeh as Theatre of Protest', pp. 95–6, 99.
60   Afkhami, *The Life and Times of the Shah*, p. 422.
61   Robert Gluck, 'A New East-West Synthesis: Conversations with Iranian Composer Alireza Mashayekhi', *eContact*, Vol. 14, No. 4, 2013. http://econtact.ca/14_4/gluck_mashayekhi.html.

Chapter 5

1   ABC News Nightline, Iran Crisis: America Held Hostage, Day 26.
2   *Bombing the Cradle* was a one-person theatre production written by David Willinger and Mahmood Karimi Hakak, produced at Theatre for the New City, 1992.

3   During the 1980s Iran's authorities demanded bullet money from relatives of executed political prisoners before they released the whereabouts of their unmarked graves.
4   In July 1988 accepting the cease-fire demanded by the UN, Khomeini said, 'Taking this decision was more deadly than taking poison. I submitted myself to God's will and drank this drink for his satisfaction.'
5   Jerzy Grotowski (11 August 1933–14 January 1999), Polish theatre director and theorist whose innovative theatrical approach, Poor Theatre, has significantly influenced today's theatre practices.
6   A reference to 'Earthly Verses', a poem by Forugh Farrokhzad.
7   Gordāfarid is one of the heroines of the Ferdowsi's Shahnameh. She confronted the unparalleled hero, Sohrab, thus delaying the enemies march on Iran. *Another Birth* by Forugh Farrokhzad.
8   Molla-Sadra (1571–1640), Islamic theologian and philosopher of the Islamic Golden Age who is credited for the transition from essentialism to existentialism.
9   *Qameh-zani* is a religious practice where one lightly stabs himself/herself on the forehead using a dagger, *qameh*.
10 *'ashura* is the tenth day of the month of Moharram. On this day Hussein, the grandson of the Prophet Mohammad was martyred in 680 CE.
11 *Amr-e be ma'ruf va nahy az monkar*, promotion of virtue and prevention of vice. It is one of the ten secondary principles of Islamic doctrines according to Shi'i.
12 *Sineh-zani* is a form of self-flagellation, where men hit themselves on their bare chests while chanting verses in support of Hossein's cause. *Zanjir-zani* is a form of self-flagellation, where men use metal chains to hit themselves on their shoulder, reminding them of the suffering of Hossein on the day of *'ashura*.
13 *Shabih-khwani* is a reenactment of the treatment Hossein and his family after their defeat, where their tents were burnt, women and children beaten, and young men killed, their bodies dragged through the streets. Chador is a long black cape covering from head to foot, and the Islamic outdoor clothing of females.
14 'Jesus on his way, Moses on his way. Each on his own belief'.
15 Mao Tse-tung.
16 Darakeh is a short hill in northern Tehran. It is a popular hiking place, especially on Fridays and at nights when there is a full moon.
17 Previously known as Rudaky Hall.
18 *The Epic of Gilgamesh* is a long poem about Creation discovered in Mesopotamia. It is regarded as the first great work of literature. Mahmood Karimi Hakak co-authored and directed a stage adaptation of this epic, entitled *Gilgamesh Con/Quest* at Towson University in 1990.
19 The story of this production, dubbed as 'Midwinter Nightmare', is told in the article 'Exiled to Freedom', published in Winter 2003 issue of *The Drama Review* (TDR-180).
20 Ministry of Culture and Islamic Guidance (Ministry of Culture and Art).
21 Dizi is a traditionally working-class stew.
22 English translation for '*barkhiz ke vaqt-e ettehād ast!*'
23 English translation for '*hezb faqat hezb-e rahbar faqat Khāmenei*'.
24 English translation for '*bizāram az din-e shomā, nefrin be āyin-e shomā, az pine-ye pishāni o del-hā-ye sangin-e shomā*'.
25 One of the two young men who knocked at my mother's apartment two decades ago and also served as the assistant director for our production of *A Midsummer Night's Dream*.
26 Pueriarchy: a social system in which children dominate.
27 In Ferdowsi's Shahnameh, Rostam kills his son Sohrab in a battle.

Chapter 6

1. The Iran-Iraq War (1980–9) began when Saddam Hussein attacked Iran, thinking it would be easy to take Iran while it was just recovering from the aftermath of the Revolution. On the contrary, the war consolidated the power of the new state.
2. Khatami was three years into his presidency. He was forward-thinking and interested in opening relations with the West. He re-opened the theatres, allowed music concerts, gave visas to American students, allowed non-governmental newspapers to flourish – to print colour photos and reviews of cultural events, but he was not able to stand up to the central government which shut down many of his reforms which led to protests.
3. Taheri never uses a dramaturge. He has a very personal relationship with the texts: Grotowski, the Bible, The Torah, Simone Weil, T. S. Eliot, Dostoevsky, Walter Benjamin and Hanna Arendt. He is like Benjamin who uses quotations to build a new text – like an archivist, an archaeologist of language from which he builds a new space, a new understanding of the world.
4. Jean Genet, *The Blacks, A Clown Show* (New York: Grove Press, 1960).
5. A play must be approved before the government grants permission to begin rehearsals, and then, often the rehearsals will also be screened by the censors. Film directors in the past have tricked the government censors by giving them a script to get a permit and then go on to shoot an entirely different film. At the end the film is sometimes exported: if it gains attention, the director pays the price in jail time or a ban on their films and filmmaking. In theatre there is no material product to export, only bodies, which means this loophole doesn't work for the theatre.
6. See Roxanne Varzi, *Warring Souls: Youth, Media, and Martyrdom in Post Revolution Iran* (Durham: Duke University Press, 2006). Revolutionary cultural policy in every sector of the Islamic Republic (visual and print media, Islamic rules for behaviour and the education of youth) was aimed solely at creating and projecting an Islamic identity on and to the public. Producing an Islamic identity is inextricably tied to the project of creating an Islamic social space; in a revolutionary state, space is as much a part of ideology formation as ideology is a part of spatial formation. The Iranian government has created a visual state that promotes an Islamic ideology. Back then the ultimate foundation of social space was prohibition. This was especially true of Tehran, where restrictions and bans defined a bound public space.
7. See Ibid.
8. Jerzy Grotowski, *Towards a Poor Theatre* (New York: Simon and Schuster, 1968), p. 211.
9. Interview with author, July 2005.
10. Jerzy Grotowski, *Towards a Poor Theatre*, p. 218.
11. See Roxanne Varzi, 'Pulling Focus on Kiarostami's Iran', *Eastern Art Report*, Vol. 5, No. 2, 2005, pp. 19–24.
12. See Varzi, *Warring Souls*, 2006.
13. See Ibid.
14. See Ibid.
15. Jerzy Grotowski, *Towards a Poor Theatre*, p. 21.
16. See Varzi, *Warring Souls*, 2006.
17. Jerzy Grotowski, *Towards a Poor Theatre*, pp. 211–18.
18. Ibid., p. 21.
19. Ibid., p. 22.

Chapter 7

1. My sincerest gratitude goes to my treasured colleagues for all their assistance (listed in Latin alphabetical order): Bavand Behpoor, Siamak Delzendeh, Barbad Golshiri, Andrea D. Fitzpatrick, Sohrab Kashani, Nazila Noebashari, Neda Razavipour, Hamid Severi, Donna Stein and Farhad Tamadon. I am also appreciative of Babak Rahimi's enduring support, friendship and mentorship. Thank you.
2. Ali Ettehad, 'Therapeutic Effect and Experimental Interaction: Neda Razavipour', *Honar-e Farda* [*Art Tomorrow*], Vol. 2, 2010, p. 75.
3. RoseLee Goldberg, *Performance Art: From Futurism to the Present*, third edition (repr. 2011; London: Thames & Hudson, 1979), p. 8.
4. See Frazer Ward, *No Innocent Bystanders: Performance Art and Audience* (Hanover, MD: Dartmouth College Press, 2012), pp. 4, 9–10, 17.
5. Thomas J. Berghuis, *Performance Art in China* (Hong Kong: Timezone 8, 2006), p. 8; Francesca Dal Lago et al., 'Space and Public: Site Specificity in Beijing', *Art Journal*, Vol. 59, No. 1 (Spring), 2000, pp. 74–87.
6. Nermin Saybasili, 'Gesturing No(w)here', in *Globalization and Contemporary Art*, Jonathan Harris ed. (Chichester: Wiley-Blackwell, 2011), pp. 418–19.
7. See Goldberg, *Performance Art*, chapter 8, which approaches performance art in several countries in a similar manner to that of Europe and North America.
8. See Michel Foucault, *The History of Sexuality: An Introduction*, trans. Robert Hurley (repr. 1990; New York: Pantheon, 1978), pp. 92–3.
9. Berghuis, *Performance Art in China*, pp. 2, 17–18.
10. Bavand Behpoor, 'Tajrobeh-yeh avvalin dadgah-e ejra [The experience of the first court of performance]', 8 Khordad 1391 SH/28 May 2012, http://fa.behpoor.com/?p=1117 (accessed 4 September 2015).
11. Barbad Golshiri, 'About your work' (17 February 2014), email.
12. See Mohammad Baqer Rezai, 'Moruri tarikhi bar performance az aghaz ta avvalin qarn-e bist o yekom [A historical review of performance from the beginning to the early twenty-first century]', *Honar o resaneh* [Art and media], 2–3, (1392 SH/2013), pp. 6–7.
13. See Amitis Motevalli, 'Artist statement', http://amitismotevalli.com/statement/(accessed 4 September 2015).
14. Amir Esfandiari, 'Kutah darbaryeh Festival-e "Si performance, si honarmand, si ruz" [A little about the "30 performances, 30 artists, 30 days" Festival]', *Honar o resaneh* [Art and media], 5, (Ordibehest 1394 SH/April 2015), p. 54. Video art as a genre is also translated directly as 'video art'. There is no Persian equivalent for its purpose and context. See also Mohammad Baqer Rezai with Mohammad Parvizi and Amir Rad, 'Performance, honar-e tajasomi ya teater [Performance, visual art or theatre]?' *Honar o resaneh* [Art and media], 2–3, (1392 SH/2013), p. 44. For those using the term *honar-e ejrā* as performance art, see Bavand Behpoor, 'Honar-e ejrā', http://fa.behpoor.com/?cat=12 (accessed 1 September 2020).
15. Ali Madanipour, *Tehran: The Making of a Metropolis* (Chichester: Wiley, 1998), pp. 94–6.
16. Varzi, *Warring Souls*, pp. 146–7.
17. Diba's interest in the Neo-Dadaists was also noted by Karim Emami. See Houra Yavari, ed., *Karim Emami on Modern Iranian Culture, Literature, and Art* (New York: Persian Heritage Foundation, 2014), p. 211.

18 Hannah Crawforth, 'About Kamran Diba', in *Kamran Diba: Good News, Bad News, No News*, Negar Diba ed. (Dubai: Gallery Etemad, 2012), pp. 8–11; Kamran Diba with Janet Rady, 'Janet Rady in Conversation with Kamran Diba', *Contemporary Practices: Visual Arts from the Middle East*, v, (January 2009), p. 192.
19 Kirby, 'An Editorial', p. 5.
20 Susan Habib and Helia Darabi, 'Video Art as a Rising Medium in Iranian Contemporary Art' (paper presented at the seventeenth meeting of the International Association of Aesthetics, Ankara, Turkey, 9–13 July 2007).
21 Ali Ettehad and Joobin Bekhrad, 'Street Fighting Man', *Reorient Magazine*, 2 June 2015, http://www.reorientmag.com/2015/06/performance-art-iran/(accessed 4 September 2015).
22 Helia Darabi and Elahe Helbig, foreword to *Unanonymously Condemned: Video Art and Performance Documentary from Iran* (Bonn: Bonner Kunstverein, 2012), p. 3.
23 Ettehad and Bekhrad, 'Street Fighting Man'.
24 Ibid.
25 Ibid.
26 Ibid.
27 Bavand Behpoor, 'Question' (18 February 2014), email.
28 Behpoor, 'Tajrobeh-yeh avvalin dadgah-e ejra'.
29 Behpoor, 'Question'.
30 See Mohammad Hosseini, 'The Lady in Red', Aaran Gallery, *Limited Access Festival*, January 2013, https://vimeo.com/76218718 (accessed 29 December 2015).
31 Tara Fatehi Irani and Mariam M., 'The Women behind Tehran's Mysterious "Ladies in Red"', *France 24 International News*, 21 October 2011, http://observers.france24.com/content/20111021-iran-women-behind-tehran-mysterious-lady-in-red-performance-art-yaqut-ruby-legend-ladies (accessed 4 September 2015).
32 Siamak Delzendeh, 'Taksir-e kitsch, Tekrar-e hich [Reproducing kitsch, repeating Heech]', *Herfeh honarmand* [Professional artist], 40, (1390/2012): p. 128.
33 Ibid.
34 Ibid.
35 Fatehi Irani and Mariam N., 'The Women behind Tehran's Mysterious "Ladies in Red."'
36 Anonymous, conversation with the author, 5 June 2015.
37 Sohrab Kashani, conversation with the author, 3 June 2014.
38 Nazila Noebashari, conversation with the author, 3 June 2014.
39 John Seed, 'A report from the Assar Gallery: Contemporary art in Iran', *The Huffington Post Arts & Culture*, 19 February 2013, http://www.huffingtonpost.com/john-seed/a-report-from-the-assar-gallery-iran-contemporary-art_b_2702578.html (accessed 4 September.2015).
40 Pantea Karimi, artist talk, California State University, Stanislaus, 19 March 2014.
41 Esfandiari, 'Kutah darbaryeh-yeh Festival-e "Si performance, si honarmand, si ruz,"' 54–5; Ettehad and Bekhrad, 'Street fighting man'.
42 East Art Gallery, 'Performance art, Euphoria, Alireza Amirhajebi' (2013), https://www.youtube.com/watch?v=h0OqV8WNF4U (accessed 4 September 2015).
43 Relational aesthetics relate to performances or happenings, in which the gallery space becomes the last bastion of contact between human beings in a world that has become mechanized and dominated by capitalist relations. The gallery then becomes a place to critique those social 'relations'. See Nicolas Bourriaud, *Relational Aesthetics*, trans. Simon Pleasance and Fronza Woods (Dijon: Les Presses du réel, 2002), pp. 8–9.

44 Ettehad, 'Therapeutic Effect and Experimental Interaction', p. 76.
45 Andrea D. Fitzpatrick, 'Female Trouble: Melancholia and Allegory in Contemporary Iranian Art', in *Performing the Iranian State: Visual Culture and Representations of Iranian Identity*, Staci Gem Scheiwiller ed. (London: Anthem Press, 2013), pp. 163–5.
46 Ettehad, 'Therapeutic Effect and Experimental Interaction', p. 76.
47 Fitzpatrick, 'Female Trouble', p. 164.
48 Amitis Motevalli, conversation with the author, 17 February 2014.
49 Saeed Kamali Dehghan, 'Iran's artists warn US and European sanctions are affecting their work: Tehran-based artist Sohrab Kashani could not visit US due to visa "complications" – and he's not the only one', *The Guardian*, 31 October 2013, http://www.theguardian.com/world/2013/oct/31/iran-artists-sanctions-affecting-work (accessed 4 September 2015).
50 Golshiri, 'About Your Work'; Aaran Gallery, 'Barbad Golshiri Presents Cura; The Rise and Fall of Aplasticism this Friday 16 December for 4 Days', 16 December 2011, http://www.aarangallery.com/news/barbad-golshiri-presents-cura-the-rise-and-fall-of-aplasticism-this-friday-16-december-for-4-days/ (accessed 4 September 2015).
51 Barbad Golshiri, 'کورا/Cura*; The Rise and Fall of Aplasticism' (2011), http://www.barbadgolshiri.com/Cura/Cura;-The-Rise-and-Fall-of-Aplasticism.htm (accessed 4 September 2015).
52 Abbas Daneshvari, 'Seismic Shifts across Political Zones in Contemporary Iranian Art: The Poetics of Knowledge, Knowing and Identity', in *Performing the Iranian State: Visual Culture and Representations of Iranian Identity*, Staci Gem Scheiwiller ed. (London: Anthem Press, 2013), p. 111.
53 Hamid Keshmirshekan, 'Reproducing Modernity: Post-Revolutionary Art in Iran since the Late 1990s', in *Amidst Shadow and Light: Contemporary Iranian Art and Artists*, Hamid Keshmirshekan ed. (Hong Kong: Liaoning Creative Press, 2011), p. 61.

Chapter 8

1 P. 7, Shiva Rahbaran, 'An Interview with Jafar Panahi', *Wasafiri*, Vol. 27, No. 3, 2012, pp. 5–11.
2 Wendy Hesford, *Spectacular Rhetorics: Human Rights Visions, Recognitions, Feminisms* (Durham, London: Duke University Press, 2012).
3 Internationalist discourse is animated, in the view of its critics, by US and Western humanism, while the IRI's human rights discourse is based on a rejection of the internationalist discourse and an insistence on an indigenous, Muslim rights.
4 See Reza Afshari's, *Human Rights in Iran: The Abuse of Cultural Relativism* (Philadelphia: University of Pennsylvania Press, 2011) for a more extensive discussion of the IRI's human rights discourse.
5 For a fuller discussion of this process, see Naficy, *A Social History of Iranian Cinema*, esp. pp. 116–22.
6 Among these may be mentioned several films by Majid Majidi, who has remained loyal to the regime and recently directed a major regime pet project in a wildly expensive biographical film about the Prophet Mohammad, as well as Abbas Kiarostami.
7 Abbas Kiarostami, *Khaneh-ye dust kojast*? (*Where Is the Friend's House*), Tehran, Fadjr, 1987; Jafar Panahi, *Badkonak-e sefid* (*The White Balloon*), Tehran, October Films, 1996; Majid Majidi, *Bacheh-ha-ye aseman* (*Children of Heaven*), Tehran, The Institute

for the Intellectual Development of Children and Young Adults, 1997; *Rang-e khoda* (*The Color of Paradise*), Varahonar, 1999.
8   For example, while the Family Protection Law was initially struck down, parts of that law have been reinstated.
9   See Arzoo Osanloo, *Forgiveness Work: Mercy, Law, and Victims' Rights in Iran* (Princeton, New Jersey: Princeton University Press, 2020). Chapter 2 is particularly useful for understanding this principle in Islamic law and its interpretation in contemporary Iran.
10 Exploring mercy as a foundation of the IRI's response to pressures to conform to international standards concerning human rights, Arzoo Osanloo discusses the case of Morteza Amini Moqaddam, who had been sentenced to execution for killing Hadi Mohebbi, a *Basiji* who had reprimanded Moqaddam for smoking in public during the month of Rameżān in 1999. Swiftly sentenced to public execution, Moqaddam was pardoned at the last moment by Mohebbi's father. Osanloo sees this case as a performance of the IRI's defensive policies on human rights, which are, at once, a reply to international pressure to conform to international standards and an insistence on 'local' or 'indigenous' forms of human rights – namely, mercy. Tracing the practice or invocation of mercy both in the contemporary IRI and in other cultures, Osanloo points out that one problem with construing mercy as a foundation for human rights is that it is both conditional and connected to religious discourses. As such, mercy contravenes the possibility of consistent results and undermines the universality that international human rights proponents emphasize. Drawing on the arguments of Giorgio Agamben in *Homo Sacer* (1998) to demonstrate that it is the exceptions invoked by the sovereign (state) that establish the inexorability of sovereign power, Osanloo asserts that the 'mercy' performed through the pardoning of Moqaddam is not to exclusively demonstrate the IRI's commitment to 'human rights'. Arzoo Osanloo, 'The Measure of Mercy: Islamic Justice, Sovereign Power, and Human Rights in Iran', *Cultural Anthropology*, Vol. 21, No. 4, 2006, pp. 570–602.
11 *The White Balloon* (Tehran: October Films, 1995); *The Circle* (Tehran: Jafar Panahi Film Productions, 2000); *Offside* (Tehran: Sony, 2006).
12 *This Is Not a Film* (Paris: Kanibal Films, 2011).
13 In an interview, Panahi disclosed that Solmaz has, in fact, escaped from prison: by bookending the film with her name (in the hospital, in the prison), he intends for her to be the 'one who screams, who is never destroyed' (91). 'Jafar Panahi', *Cinemas of the Other: A Personal Journey with Film-Makers from the Middle East & Central Asia* (Bristol; Chicago, IL: Intellect, 2012), pp. 90–6.
14 Hamid Dabashi suggests that Hossein's suicide is the symbolic death of the revolution, as well as the murder of the revolution's father; because the son cannot kill the father, he kills himself:

> So, the bullet that Hossein puts into his head is also the bullet that lolls the charismatic memory of Khomeini. In a classic case of masochistic violence, the son replaces his own body for the body of the father and by inflicting (the ultimate) pain on himself revenges himself against the father. See, Hamid Dabashi, *Masters and Masterpieces of Iranian Cinema* (Washington, DC: Mage Publishers, 2007), p. 395.

15 Bataille Georges, *The Accursed Share* (New York: Zone Books, 1988). Bataille's ideas of exchange and excess are further explored in productive ways by Baudrillard in *Symbolic Exchange and Death* (London: Sage Books, 1993).

16 Najmabadi Afsaneh, *Women with Mustaches and Men without Beards: Gender and Sexual Anxieties of Iranian Modernity* (Berkeley, CA: University of California Press, 2005).
17 See, for example, Boris Trbic, 'Stranded Offside: The Compulsive and Compassionate Discourse of Jafar Panahi', *Metro*, Vol. 2006, No. 150, pp. 96–100.
18 *Cinemas of the Other*, pp. 94–5.

Chapter 9

1 Laudan Nooshin, 'Whose Liberation? Iranian Popular Music and the Fetishization of Resistance', *Popular Communication*, Vol. 15, No. 3, (July 3, 2017), pp. 163–91, https://doi.org/10.1080/15405702.2017.1328601.
2 Schechner Richard, *Performance Studies: An Introduction*. Second edition (New York: Routledge, 2006).
3 Laudan Nooshin, 'Subversion and Countersubversion: Power, Control and Meaning in the New Iranian Pop Music', in *Music, Power, and Politics*, Annie Janeiro Randall ed. (New York: Routledge, 2005), p. 233.
4 Nooshin, *Subversion and Countersubversion*.
5 Jalal Al-e-ahmad, *Occidentosis: A Plague from the West*, ed. Hamid Algar, trans. R. Campbell, Contemporary Islamic Thought (Berkeley: Mizan Press, 1983).
6 Shahram Khosravi, *Young and Defiant in Tehran* (Philadelphia: University of Pennsylvania Press); 2009, p. 19, http://www.aspresolver.com/aspresolver.asp?ANTH;1759351.
7 Ibid.
8 Sanam Zahir, *The Music of the Children of Revolution: The State of Music and Emergence of the Underground Music in the Islamic Republic of Iran with an Analysis of Its Lyrical Content* (ProQuest, 2008) http://hdl.handle.net/10150/193427.
9 Farzaneh Hemasi, 'Iranian Popular Music in Los Angeles: A Transnational Public beyond the Islamic State', in *Muslim Rap, Halal Soaps, and Revolutionary Theater: Artistic Developments in the Muslim World*, Karin van Nieuwkerk ed. (Austin: University of Texas Press, 2011), pp. 85–107.
10 Both Kourosh Yaghmaie and Farhad Mehrdad were artists who stayed in Iran. While they did try to perform after the revolution, they were not successful in receiving permissions until after the presidency of Mohammad Khatami.
11 Hemasi, *Iranian Popular Music in Los Angeles*, p. 89.
12 Nooshin, *Subversion and Countersubversion*.
13 Ameneh Youssefzadeh, 'The Situation of Music in Iran since the Revolution: The Role of Official Organizations', *British Journal of Ethnomusicology*, Vol. 9, No. 2, (January 2000), pp. 35–61, https://doi.org/10.1080/09681220008567300.
14 Nahid Siamdoust, *Soundtrack of the Revolution: The Politics of Music in Iran*, Stanford Studies in Middle Eastern and Islamic Societies and Cultures (California: Stanford University Press, 2017).
15 Namjoo, 'The Revolution and Music: A Personal Odyssey', pp. 179–216.
16 Youssefzadeh, *The Situation of Music in Iran since the Revolution*.
17 Michel De Certeau, *The Practice of Everyday Life*, trans. Steven Rendall (Berkeley: Univ. of California Press, 1984), p. xix.
18 This was a council that was responsible for closing down all higher education institutions and reforming the curriculum so that it was in accordance with the Sharia law.

19. Refer to the Ministry of Culture and Islamic Guidance website at https://www.farhang.gov.ir/fa/intro/history.
20. Heather Rastovac, 'Contending with Censorship: The Underground Music Scene in Urban Iran', *The McNair Scholars Journal*, 2009, p. 273.
21. Youssefzadeh, *The Situation of Music in Iran since the Revolution*, p. 39.
22. Siamdoust, *Soundtrack of the Revolution*, p. 7.
23. Ali Khamenei, *The Cultural Viewpoints of the Leader of the Islamic Revolution of Iran Ayatollah Seyed Ali Khamenei* (Tehran: Center for Cultural and International Studies, Islamic Culture and Relations Organization, 2000).
24. Siamdoust, *Soundtrack of the Revolution*, p. 19.
25. Robertson, *Reverberations of Dissent*.
26. Siamdoust, *Soundtrack of the Revolution*.
27. See Arash Mitooie's official Bandcamp account, https://soundcloud.com/arash-mytouei.
28. For Interview with Reza Moghaddas see, https://www.youtube.com/watch?v=Vfx0dpYheL0.
29. de Certeau, *The Practice of Everyday Life*, p. xix.
30. Ibid.
31. Carolyn R. Miller, 'Opportunity, Opportunism, and Progress: Kairos in the Rhetoric of Technology', *Argumentation*, Vol. 8, No. 1, 1994, p. 84.
32. Miller, *Opportunity, Opportunism, and Progress*, p. 83.
33. Nooshin, *Subversion and Countersubversion*.
34. Ibid.
35. See O-Hum's biography for more information, http://www.playityet.com/artists/o-hum/about.
36. Tehran Avenue was a small online magazine that began in 2001. The website began a series of online music competitions that exposed the diversity of unofficial music in the country beginning in 2003. The website was later shut down by the government of Iran.
37. Zahir, *The Music of the Children of Revolution*, p. 14.
38. Morad Mansouri, 'The Underground Rises', *Payam Ashena*, 2011, accessed 2016-05-27 http://www.ashena.com/english/culture-art-history/2540-the-underground-rises.html.
39. Zahir, *The Music of the Children of Revolution*, p. 14.
40. Will Straw, 'Scenes and Sensibilities', *Public*, No. 22–23, 2001, p. 248 http://public.journals.yorku.ca/index.php/public/article/viewFile/30335/27864.
41. Ibid., p. 248.
42. Robertson, *Reverberations of Dissent*, p. 134.
43. Laudan Nooshin, 'Underground, Overground: Rock Music and Youth Discourses in Iran', *Iranian Studies*, Vol. 38, No. 3, (September) 2005, p. 11, https://doi.org/10.1080/00210860500300820.
44. Browen Robertson, 'I Am an Original Iranian Man: Identity and Expression in Tehran's Unofficial Rock Music', in *Cultural Revolution in Iran: Contemporary Popular Culture in the Islamic Republic*, Annabelle Sreberny and Massoumeh Torfeh, ed. International Library of Iranian Studies 41 (New York: I.B. Tauris), p. 140.
45. Laudan Nooshin, 'The Language of Rock: Iranian Youth, Popular Music, and National Identity', in *Media, Culture and Society in Iran: Living with Globalization and the Islamic State*, Mehdi Semati, ed. Iranian Studies (New York: Routledge, 2008), pp. 1–30.

46 Robertson, I Am an Original Iranian Man, p. 144.
47 Nooshin, The Language of Rock.
48 Please consult Abdi Behravanfar's in interview with Manoto1 channel, https://www.youtube.com/watch?v=2xXOr589X_g.
49 For a detailed interview with Kaveh Afghan, see https://www.youtube.com/watch?v=r2FBcsGtRLs.
50 F. Shams and E. Sadeghi-Boroujerdi, 'Q&A | Head to Head with Abdi Behravanfar, Khorasan Blues Pioneer', *Tehran Bureau | Frontline | PBS*, 12, https://www.pbs.org/wgbh/pages/frontline/tehranbureau/2012/01/qa-head-to-head-with-abdi-behravanfar-pioneer-of-the-khorasan-blues.html.
51 Ibid.
52 MudBand is credited on the back of the album of Toranj that was released by *Hozeh Honari*.
53 Siamdoust, *Soundtrack of the Revolution*, p. 192.
54 For a detailed interview with Reza Mahdavi, the then general director of *Hozeh Honari*, please visit https://www.khabaronline.ir/news/697940/%D8%AA%D8%A8%D8%B9%D8%A7%D8%AA-%D8%A7%D9%86%D8%AA%D8%B4%D8%A7%D8%B1-%D8%AA%D8%B1%D9%86%D8%AC-%D9%86%D8%A7%D9%85%D8%AC%D9%88-%D9%85-9%86%D8%AA%D9%81%DB%8C-%D8%B4%D8%AF%D9%86-%D8%A7%D9%86%D8%AA%D8%B4%D8%A7%D8%B1-%DB%B1%DB%B3-%DA%86%D8%A7%D9%88%D9%88%D8%B4%DB%8C-%D9%88-%D9%86%D8%B1%D8%B3%DB%8C%D8%AF%D9%86.
55 The singer of the band Gachpaj, Hooman Hamedian, performed his music with a new band outside of Iran called 'also Gachpaj'. The videos of their performance are now available on YouTube: https://www.youtube.com/watch?v=_Rw3OW2pLlk&list=PLjYqNf9XLeGl878EX7D6PuaKbqx-Lkm6_.
56 Freemuse, 'Iran: Over 200 Rock Fans Arrested at Concert', *Freemuse* (blog), 2013, accessed 2019-06-25, https://freemuse.org/news/iran-over-200-rock-fans-arrested-at-concert/.
57 Babak Rahimi, 'Censorship and the Islamic Republic: Two Modes of Regulatory Measures for Media in Iran', *The Middle East Journal*, Vol. 69, No. 3 (July 15), 2015, pp. 358–78, https://doi.org/10.3751/69.3.12.
58 Nooshin, *Whose Liberation?*
59 Robertson, *Reverberations of Dissent*.

Chapter 10

1 Brian Keith Axel, 'The Diasporic Imaginary', *Public Culture*, Vol. 14, No. 2, 2002, pp. 411–28; William Safran, 'Diasporas in Modern Societies: Myths of Homeland and Return', *Diaspora*, Vol. 1, No. 1, 1991, pp. 83–100.
2 Alpha Abebe, 'Performing Diaspora', in *Routledge Handbook of Diaspora Studies*, Robin Cohen and Carolin Fischer eds. (London; New York: Routledge, 2019), p. 55.
3 See Celeste Fraser Delgado and José Esteban Muñoz, eds., *Everynight Life: Culture and Dance in Latin/o America* (Durham: Duke University Press, 1997);Anaya Jahanara Kabir, 'Music, Dance and Diaspora', in *Routledge Handbook of Diaspora Studies*, Robin Cohen and Carolin Fischer eds. (London; New York: Routledge, 2019), pp. 71–8.

Chapter 11

1. *Gilaki* dance is a type of dance from the northern region of Iran, close to the Caspian Sea; *Azari* refers to the dances of the north-western part of Iran; *Khorasani* dance is from the north eastern region; *Kurdi* is from the mountainous west region; and *bandari* is a dance from the coastal areas in the south.
2. A few examples of these dance groups are: *Aftab* dancers who performed Persian Day Parade in New York (NYPP); *Silk Road Dance Company* at Nowruz celebrations at the White House; children at ISSD, Northeastern University students and the audience in Ormond Beach, Florida, who were engaged in the dance. See videos below: Aftab Dance Group at the NY Persian Parade (2015). YouTube video, accessed 21 August 2015, https://www.youtube.com/watch?v=GfdJ6q1cFsw.

    Aftab Dance Group (Norouz 2015), NorthEastern University, YouTube video, accessed 21 August 2015, https://www.youtube.com/watch?v=TlBvQnKeiX4. Documentary video about Iranian New Year Festival in Reston, Virginia (2014). YouTube video accessed 17 August 2015https://www.youtube.com/watch?v=duQ9H L1NFZo. First Lady Michele Obama Celebrates Nowruz at White House, YouTube video, accessed 21 August 2015, https://www.youtube.com/watch?v=m2IIrwjmxUU. 4th Chicago Nowruz Parade 2013. YouTube video, accessed 19 August 2015, https://www.youtube.com/watch?v=dwtq_SxEegE.

    Persian Parade Los Angeles, YouTube video, accessed 26 September 2016, https://www.youtube.com/watch?v=xkBNB9AZVD0. New York Persian Parade, YouTube video, accessed 15 February 2019, https://www.youtube.com/watch?v=ycGabZ4U1iw. Nowruz Celebrations—Iranian School of San Diego—15 March 2015, YouTube video, accessed 17 August 2015, https://www.youtube.com/watch?v=2fXVEs23ht4.
3. In *Choreophobia: Solo Improvised Dance in the Iranian World*, Anthony Shay notes the historical evidence of dance in the Achaemenid Empire (559–330 BC), pointing out that 'when Parmenio, the Greek general, took Damascus, he captured several hundreds of [dancers and singers] from the court of Darius III'. See, Anthony Shay, *Choreophobia: Solo Improvised Dance in the Arab World* (Costa Mesa: Mazda Publishers, 1999), p. 71.
4. Persian classical music is a vast domain that includes traditional music from Iran, Tajikestan, Afghanistan, Kurdistan and other countries in Persian world.
5. Nowruz Festival 2015 in Ormond Beach, FL, Iranian American Society of Daytona Beach, YouTube video, accessed 17 August 2015, https://www.youtube.com/watch?v=udJ5T4OGc1A.
6. Shay Anthony, *Choreographing Identities: Folk Dance, Ethnicity and Festival in The United States and Canada* (Jefferson, N.C: McFarland Publishing, 2006).
7. Ibid., 147.
8. Kambiz Mofrad, telephone interview, 29 May 2015.
9. Ibid.
10. Jamileh, Jaheli dance. YouTube video, accessed 26 September 2016, https://www.youtube.com/watch?v=gSE7oJth06E.
11. Kambiz Mofrad, telephone interview, 29 May 2015.
12. Iranian community in exile, nationalists and opposition groups as well as other members of the exilic community, sing the pre-revolution national anthem even though the Islamic Republic has changed it after 1978.
13. See, Amy Malek, 'Public Performances of Identity Negotiation in the Iranian Diaspora: The New York Persian Day Parade', *Comparative Studies of South Asia, Africa and the Middle East*, Vol. 31, No. 2, 2011, pp. 388–410.

14 Ibid., pp. 390–401.
15 Ibid., 393.
16 Zain Abdullah, 'Sufis on Parade: The performance of Black, African, and Muslim Identities', *Journal of the American Academy of Religion*, Vol. 77, No. 2, 2009, pp. 199–237 (215).
17 Ibid.
18 Mofrad, Telephone interview, 2015.
19 The term 'axis of evil' was used by American president George W. Bush in his State of the Union Address on 29 January 2002, and often repeated it throughout his presidency, to describe governments that he accused of helping terrorism and seeking weapons of mass destruction.
20 In 2013, the authentic Cylinder toured five major cities in the United States in a period of nine months and was on displayed in Washington, Houston, New York, San Francisco, and Los Angeles.
21 New York's 12th Annual Persian Day Parade 2015, YouTube video, accessed 8 August 2015, https://www.youtube.com/watch?v=QjVYAr25ikI.
22 New York Persian Day Parade, YouTube video, accessed 26 September 2016, https://www.youtube.com/watch?v=GjyJcwv1mUs. Also see, https://www.youtube.com/watch?v=ycGabZ4U1iw, accessed 15 February 2019.
23 Parviz Sayyad appeared as Samad Aqa for the first time in an Iranian TV show in 1971. His character, a rural, funny simpleton, became so popular that even though Sayyad has performed many difficult roles and has created more sophisticated characters in various plays he has written and directed, Samad has remained his main cinematic persona for his entire career.Iranians parade in Los Angeles, YouTube video, accessed 8 August 2015, https://www.youtube.com/watch?v=pvRQYe34HL0.
24 An architectural monument associated with Tehran.
25 Shahyad tower was commissioned by Mohamad Reza Pahlavi as part of a much bigger project to celebrate Iran's move towards modernization. The task was given to the Iranian architect Hossein Amanat, who had won first prize in a contest to design a building that would be 'a gateway to a great civilization'. The Pahlavi regime was celebrating 2,500 years of Persian history in an extravagant series of spectacular ceremonies in Persepolis which reminded the nation and the world of Iran's historical heritage. The international dignitaries who were invited to these ceremonies would be able to view the tower on their way to or from Mehrabad airport. The Tower was renamed right after the Revolution as *Borj-e Azadi* or the Tower of Freedom.
26 Malek, 'Public performances of identity', p. 399.
27 See Part 4 of New York Persian Day Parade, YouTube video, accessed 26 September 2016, https://www.youtube.com/watch?v=MIYPODxHELA.
28 Persian Cultural Center (PCC) is a non-profit, non-religious and non-political 501(c)(3) national organization, established in 1989 in San Diego, California. https://pccsd.org AIAP (Association of Iranian-American professionals) is non-political. Yet, it strives to protect our professional interests, image and reputation. https://aiap.org The Iranian American Foundation (IAF) is a non-political and non-religious organization based in Florida. https://iafflorida.org.
29 Islamic republic banned variety of music genres as means of seduction and corruption. However, those genres of music with mythological or religious connotations were sanctioned.
30 Iranian Military Women Carrying AK4, YouTube video, accessed 21 August 2015, http://iranian.com/PhotoDay/1999/September/parade.html.
31 Iranians Parade in Los Angeles, author's translation.

Chapter 12

1. http://amirbaradaran.com/ab_futarism.php (accessed 25 February 2016).
2. Ibid.
3. Interview with author, conducted 23 November 2015.
4. Baradaran's other AR performances include *Takeoff* (2010), *Simple as Drinking Water* (2011), *Growing Panes* (2012) and *Facing the Cloud* (2017).
5. Steve Dixon with Barry Smith, *Digital Performance: A History of New Media in Theater, Dance, Performance Art, and Installation* (Cambridge and London: MIT Press, 2007), p. 3. Emphasis in the original.
6. Ibid., p. 5.
7. Baradaran cites the work of Dadaism and Futurism as inspirations for his own work with AR. Interview with author, conducted 23 November 2015.
8. Dixon, *Digital Performance*, p. 8. Emphasis in the original.
9. Robert Stam with Richard Porton and Leo Goldsmith, *Keywords in Subversive Film/Media Aesthetics* (Malden and Oxford: John Wiley & Sons, Inc, 2015), p. 282.
10. In Baradaran's artist statements and the personal interview included in this chapter, Baradaran refers to *Frenchising Mona Lisa* as part of the permanent collection at the Louvre. Although it is partially a playful statement, it also speaks to the fact that there is currently no legal way of removing Baradaran's AR performance artwork from the Louvre. It is expected that, at some point in the near future, lawmakers will convene to legally define this new technology, what it can do and how one can use it to alter a space. Interview with author, conducted 23 November 2015. Also see: http://amirbaradaran.com/ab_futarism_monalisa.php. For research on AR and the law, see, Brian D. Wassam, *Augmented Reality: Law, Privacy, and Ethics* (Waltham, MA: Syngress, 2015).
11. Abigail R. Esman, 'The rape of the Mona Lisa', *Forbes*, 24 January 2011, http://www.forbes.com/sites/abigailesman/2011/01/24/the-rape-of-the-mona-lisa/(accessed 1 September 2020).
12. I don't mean to suggest that Mona Lisa becomes a Muslim woman merely through the act of wearing a headscarf, nor do I believe this to be Baradaran's assumption or intent. To suggest this would further replicate a problematic discourse within which the veil stands in as a metonym for Muslim woman. Instead, I use scare quotes to highlight the discursive construction enacted in Esman's opening question 'Mona Lisa, a Muslim?'
13. Lisa Nakamura, *Digitizing Race: Visual Cultures of the Internet* (Minneapolis, MN: University of Minneapolis Press, 2008).
14. Nakamura, *Digitizing Race*, p. 14. Also see, Michael Omi and Howard Winant, *Racial Formations in the United States: From the 1960s to the 1990s* (London and New York: Routledge, 1994).
15. Peggy Phelan, *Unmarked: The Politics of Performance* (London and New York: Routledge, 1993), p. 146.
16. Ibid. My emphasis added.
17. Philip Auslander, *Liveness: Performance in a Mediatized Culture* (London and New York: Routledge, 2008), p. 11.
18. Ibid., p. 62. My emphasis added.
19. Ibid., p.128.
20. www.amirbaradaran.com/ab_monalisa.php (accessed 25 February 2016).

21 Interview with author, conducted 23 November 2015.
22 My argument about the legal implications of this AR performance can only be applied in the case of the original representation of *Mona Lisa* in the Louvre museum and doesn't quite hold true for other renditions of the painting (even though the performance can be enacted with any suitable replication). This thread of argument here speaks specifically to the ways in which AR complicates Phelan's claim that performance depends on disappearance and that, subsequently, performance necessarily circumvents legal parameters. Instead, here I argue that the lack of the 'live' performance as conventionally defined is actually what is needed to circumvent the legal parameters of the institutional space such as the Louvre.
23 Jasbir K. Puar and Amit S. Rai, 'Monster, Terrorist, Fag: The War on Terrorism and the Production of Docile Patriots', *Social Text*, 72, No. 3, (Fall) 2002, pp. 117–48.
24 Marvin Carlson, *Performance: A Critical Introduction*, Third edition (London: Routledge, 2018), p. 15.
25 Goffman, *The Presentation of Self in Everyday Life*.
26 Reza Gholami, *Secularism and Identity: Non-Islamiosity in the Iranian Diaspora* (Burlington, VT: Ashgate Publishing, 2015).
27 I borrow from J. Halberstam and Gayatri Gopinath conceptions of 'queer' in my reference to the queer diasporic Iranian archives that I contend Baradaran constructs through his performances. Halberstam refers to the notion of queer as 'nonnormative logics and organizations of community, sexual identity, embodiment, and activity in space and time'. J. Halberstam, *In a Queer Time and Place: Transgender Bodies, Subcultural Lives* (New York: New York University Press, 2005), p. 6. Gopinath explains that she uses '"queer" to refer to a range of dissident and non-heteronormative practices and desires that may very well be incommensurate with the identity categories of "gay" and "lesbian."' Gayatri Gopinath, *Impossible Desires: Queer Diasporas and South Asian Public Cultures* (Durham and London: Duke University Press, 2005), p. 11.

BIBLIOGRAPHY

Michael Axworthy, *Revolutionary Iran: A History of the Islamic Republic* (London: Allen Lane, 2013).
Edward G. Browne, *A Literary History of Persia: Modern Times*, Vol. IV (Cambridge: Cambridge University Press, 1969).
Richard F. Burton, *The Book of the Thousand Nights and a Night: A Plain and Literal Translation of the Arabian Nights Entertainments* (London: Burton Club, 1925).
Peter J. Chelkowski, 'Ta'ziyeh: Indigenous Avant-Garde Theatre of Iran', *Performing Arts Journal*, Vol. 2, No. 1 (1977), pp. 31–40.
Peter J. Chelkowski (ed.), *Ritual and Drama in Iran* (New York: New York University Press, 1979).
Peter Chelkowski and Hamid Dabashi, *Staging a Revolution: The Art of Persuasion in the Islamic Republic of Iran* (New York: New York University Press, 1999).
Paul Cronin, *Lessons with Kiarostami* (New York: Sticking Place Books, 2015).
Hamid Dabashi (ed.), *Parviz Sayyad's Theatre of Diaspora: Two Plays, the Ass and the Rex Cinema Trial* (Costa Mesa, CA: Mazda Publishers, 1992).
Steve Dixon with Barry Smith, *Digital Performance: A History of New Media in Theater, Dance, Performance Art, and Installation* (Cambridge and London: MIT Press, 2007).
Sasan Fatemi, *Iranian Music and Popular Entertainment: From Motrebi to Losanjelesi* (London: New York: Routledge, 2016).
Abolqasem Ferdowsi, *Shahnameh: The Persian Book of Kings*, trans. Dick Davis (New York: Viking Adult, 2006).
Willem Floor, *The History of Theater in Iran* (Washington, DC: Mage Publishers, 2005).
Robert Gluck, 'The Shiraz Arts Festival: Western Avant-Garde Arts in 1970s Iran', *Leonardo*, Vol. 40, No. 1 (2007), pp. 20–47.
Ahmad Karimi-Hakkak, *Recasting Persian Poetry: Scenarios of Poetic Modernity in Iran* (Salt Lake City, UT: University of Utah Press, 1995).
Siavash Kasrai, *Mohreye Sorkh* (Vienna, Austria: Kara Publications, 1995).
Hamid Keshmirshekan (ed.), *Amidst Shadow and Light: Contemporary Iranian Art and Artists* (Hong Kong: Liaoning Creative Press, 2011).
Shahram Khosravi, *Young and Defiant in Tehran* (Philadelphia, PA: University of Pennsylvania Press, 2008).
Charles Kurzman, *The Unthinkable Revolution in Iran* (Cambridge, MA: Harvard University Press, 2005).
Reza Masoudi, *The Rite of Urban Passage: The Spatial Ritualisation of Iranian Urban Transformation* (New York; Oxford: Berghahn, 2018).
Ida Meftahi (2016a), 'Sacred or Dissident: Islam, Embodiment, and Subjectivity on Post-Revolutionary Iranian Theatrical Stage', in *Islam and Popular Culture*, ed. Karin Van Nieuwkerk, Mark Levine and Martin Stokes (Austin, TX: University of Texas Press), pp. 259–77.
Ida Meftahi (2016b), *Gender and Dance in Modern Iran* (London; New York: Routledge).

Marjan Moosavi, 'Performing and Conforming: Iran's Fadjr International Theatre Festival', *TDR: The Drama Review*, Vol. 60, No. 1, Spring 2016 (T299), pp. 79–92.

Marjan Moosavi (2018a), 'Desacralizing Whispers: Counter-Conduct in the Iranian War Theatre,' *New Theatre Quarterly*, Vol. 34, No. 3, 2018, pp. 235–48.

Marjan Moosavi (2018b), 'B for Badan, Blessed, and (B)othered: the Counter-Sacred in the Iranian Theatre of War', *Ecumenica*, Vol. 11, No. 2, Fall 2018, pp. 28–45.

Laudan Nooshin, 'Whose Liberation? Iranian Popular Music and the Fetishization of Resistance', *Popular Communication*, Vol. 15, No. 3 (3 July 2017), pp. 163–91.

Arzoo Osanloo, *Forgiveness Work: Mercy, Law, and Victims' Rights in Iran* (Princeton, NJ: Princeton University Press, 2020).

Babak Rahimi, *Theater State and the Formation of Early Modern Public Sphere in Iran: Studies on Safavid Muharram Rituals, 1590–1641 CE* (Leiden; Boston: Brill, 2012).

Babak Rahimi, 'Takkiyeh Dowlat: The Qajar Theater State', in *Performing the Iranian State: Visual Culture and Representations of Iranian Identity*, ed. Staci Gem Scheiwiller (London; New York; Delhi: Anthem Press, 2013), pp. 55–71.

Babak Rahimi, 'Censorship and the Islamic Republic: Two Modes of Regulatory Measures for Media in Iran', *The Middle East Journal*, Vol. 69, No. 3 (15 July 2015), pp. 358–78.

Nasser Rahmaninejad, *A Man of the Theater: Survival as an Artist in Iran* (New York: New Village Press, 2020).

Staci Gem Scheiwiller, *Performing the Iranian State: Visual Culture and Representations of Iranian Identity* (London; New York; Delhi: Anthem Press, 2013).

Amin Sharifi Isaloo, *Power, Legitimacy and the Public Sphere: The Iranian Ta'ziyeh Theatre Ritual* (London; New York: Routledge, 2017).

Anthony Shay (2014a), *The Dangerous Lives of Public Performers: Dancing, Sex, and Entertainment in the Islamic World* (New York, NY: Palgrave Macmillan).

Anthony Shay (2014b), 'Bazi-ha-ye Nameyeshi: Iranian Women's Theatrical Plays', *Dance Research Journal*, Vol. 27, No. 2, 2014, pp. 16–24.

Nahid Siamdoust, *Soundtrack of the Revolution: The Politics of Music in Iran* (Stanford, CA: Stanford University Press, 2017).

Annabelle Sreberny and Massoumeh Torfeh (eds.), *Cultural Revolution in Iran: Contemporary Popular Culture in the Islamic Republic* (London; New York: I.B. Tauris, 2013).

Saeed Talajooy, 'A History of Iranian Drama (1850–1941)', in *Literature of the Early Twentieth Century: From the Constitutional Period to Reza Shah: A History of Persian Literature*, ed. Ali-Ashgar Seyed Gohrab (London; New York: I.B. Tauris, 2015), pp. 354–410.

Mohammad Tavakoli-Targhi, *Refashioning Iran: Orientalism, Occidentalism and Historiography* (Houndmills, Basingstoke, Hampshire; New York: St. Antony series, Palgrave, 2001).

Farzin Vejdani, *Making History in Iran: Educational, Nationalism, and Print Culture* (Stanford, CA: Stanford University Press, 2015).

Roxanne Varzi, *Last Scene Underground: An Ethnographic Novel of Iran* (Stanford, CA: Stanford University Press, 2015).

Sanam Zahir, *The Music of the Children of Revolution: The State of Music and Emergence of the Underground Music in the Islamic Republic of Iran with an Analysis of Its Lyrical Content*, Vol. 47, No. 2 (ProQuest: ProQuest Dissertations Publishing, 2008).

INDEX

Page numbers in *italics* indicate illustrations.

Aali, Ahmad 117
Abbasid dynasty 42, 215n28
Abdullah, Zain 173
Abramović, Marina 192–3
Abstract Expressionism 113, 116
Abumoslemnameh (epic poem) 211n9
Achaemenid dynasty 81, 173–5, 211n8, 234n3
Afghan 137
Afghanistan 166, 234n4
Agamben, Giorgio 230n10
Aghili, Shadmehr 146
Ahmadinejad, Mahood 25, 28
Akhondzadeh, Mirza Fath-Ali 11
Alexander the Great 80, 81
al-Halaqa 57, 219n20
Amirhajebi, Alireza 116, 122
Amjad, Hamid 199n43
amrad 135–6
amr-e beh ma'ruf 95
Anahita-Gisane 211n7
Anjoman-e Okhovvat 12
anthropolisation 221n63
'anti-essentializing' 147
Antigone 106, 124
Anvar, Iraj 18
Apick, Mary 175
Arab 42, 45, 49, 174, 215n28
Arbabi, Farnaz 27
Ardebili, 13, Abdul-Karim Mousavi 143
Aristotle 4
Arjangi, Abbas Rasam 196n2
Armenians 10, 17, 158–9, 211n7, 215n27
Arnold, Matthew 59
art galleries 114, 117, 118, 121–4, *123*, *124*
artificial intelligence (AI) 189
Arusi-ye Hossein Aqa 14
Ascetic Theatre 92, 100
Ashraf Khan 11
'*ashura* commemorations 95, 96, 225n10

Association of Iranian-American Professionals (AIAP) 235n28
Association of Theatre Lovers 10
Athenaeus 41, 213n19
augmented reality (AR) 35, 181–2, 185–92, 195
Auslander, Philip 183–4
Azad Gallery 122, 124
Azad University 149
Azadi Tower 175, 176
Azar, Alireza Sami 118
Azari 11
Azerbaijan 10, 202n93
Azimi, Hasan 20

Badiou, Alain 3–4
Bakhtiary, Yaser 177
Bam Studio 144–9
Banisadr, Abolhassan 91
Banksy (graffiti artist) 184
baqqal-bazi 9, 21
Baradaran, Amir 35, 181–95; *(AR)ticulations of the Self* 35, 181, 185, 187–9, 195; *Frenchising Mona Lisa* 181–4, 187, 191, 195; *FutARism* 35, 181, 188; *Little Buzzz* 188; *Manifesto* 188; *mARkers* 188; *The Other Artist Is Present* 192–3; *SamovAR* 190–1; *Takeoff* 188
Baraheni, Reza 83
Basij militia 22, 91, 95–6, 100, 121
Bataille, Georges 135
Baudrillard, Jean 230n15
Beckett, Samuel 18, 25–6, 116
Behpoor, Bavand 116–20, *119*, *120*
Behravanfar, Abdi 149–50
Bell, Catherine 217n5
Benjamin, Walter 226n3
Bentley, Eric 83
Berger, John 64

Berghuis, Thomas 115–16
Beyzaie, Bahram 17, 27, 59, 218n12
blackface 9, 25, 26, 199n47
Boal, Augusto 4, 69
The Bolshevik Revolution 202n93
Boyce, Mary 212n10
Brecht, Bertolt 19, 69, 70, 221n66, 222n67
Brechtian 69, 221n66
Brook, Peter 18, 59, 61, 84
Browne, Edward G. 12, 13, 201n75
Bush, George W. 166, 235n19
Butoh Theatre 108

Cage, John 116, 117
Caldwell, John T. 29
calendar, Zoroastrian 81, 169, 176. *See also* Nowruz parades
Camus, Albert 25
Carter, Jimmy 90
Caspian Sea 82, 202n93, 234n1
censorship: approval process of 97–8, 226n5. *See also* Ershad; Karimi Hakak on 93–4, 97–101; Motlagh on 130–1; of music 141; Rahimi on 152
Charmshir, Mohammad 23, 24
Charney, Joshua 33, 77–86
Chekhov, Anton 17
Chelkowski, Peter J. 58
Clapton, Eric 144
Coelho, Paulo 105
coffee houses 9, 40, 99, 211n9
Cohen, Leonard 153
Constitutional Revolution (1905–11) 4; theatre of 9, 11–12
counterculture 94–5, 105
Cunningham, Merce 83, 117
Cyrus the Great 81, 174–5

Dabashi, Hamid 61, 221n63; on 'theatre of protest' 78, 85–6
Dadaism 34, 113, 116–20, *119*, *120*, 126–7, 181, 236n7
Dal Lago, Francesca 115–16
Daneshvari, Abbas 126
Dante Alighieri 109
Dar al-Fonun school 10, 13
Darabi, Helia 118
'data sculpture' 189–90
Davis, Patti 39

de Certeau, Michel 139, 142, 145
Deihim, Mahin 15
Derrida, Jacques 23
diaspora 66, 103; Baradaran on 181, 237n27; Rahimi on 10–11, 26–7, 34–5, 157–9, 167; Salimi and 169, 173–4, 176–80
Diba, Kamran 117
Dickens, Charles 28
Dixon, Steve 181
Dylan, Bob 148, 151

East West Players (Los Angeles) 158
Ehteshmi, Anoushiravan 25
Eisenstein, Sergey 88
Entezami, Ezzatollah 17
epic poetry 211n9, 225n18
Ershad (Ministry of Islamic Culture and Guidance) 131. *See also* censorship; Karimi Hakak 99, 101; Rokni on 140, 142–3, 146, 150–3
Eshqi, Mirzadah 13
Esman, Abigail 182–3
Ettehad, Ali 118

Fadjr International Theatre Festival 20–1, 23
Fallah-Zadeh, Majid 69
Farabi Cinema Foundation 131
Farah Pahlavi 33, 77–8, 80, 81, 203n100
Farahani, Gholshifteh 111
Faravahar symbol 175
Farjam, Farideh 18
Farrokhzad, Forugh 92, 93, 225nn6–7
Ferdowsi, Abolqasem 32, 45–55, 225n7, 225n27
Ferdowsi Theatre 3
Fitzpatrick, Andrea 123, 124
Fleuret, Maurice 79–80
Floor, Willem M. 205n131, 211n7
Fo, Dario 3
Forooghi, Fereydoon 141
Forouhar, Leila 170
Forsi, Bahman 18
Francklin, William 59
fusion music 141, 144–6, 148, 150
FutARism 35, 181, 188
Futurism 116, 181, 236n7

Ganjavi, Nezami 63, 64
García Lorca, Federico 20

Garnier, Charles 7
Genet, Jean 98, 106, 110–11
Ghaffari, Farrokh 78
Ghaffari, Mohammad 78–9, 84–6, 220n51
Ghanizadeh, Homayoon 26
Ghotbi, Reza 78
Gilan 10, 202n93
Gilgamesh, Epic of 99, 225n18
Goethe, Johann Wolfgang von 201n75
Goffman, Erving 60, 68
Gogol, Nikolai 11
Goldberg, RoseLee 114–15
Golden Thread Productions 34, 158–61
Golshiri, Barbad 116, 125–6, *127*
Gooran, Reza 24
Gopinath, Gayatri 237n27
Gorgani, Fakhraddin 41, 211n7
gosan. *See* minstrels
Great Depression (1930s) 15
Green Movement (2009) 26, 27, 94, 102
Grigorian, Marco 117
Grotowski, Jerzy 18, 33, 59; acting method of 107–11; Karimi Hakak and 92, 225n5; Taheri and 106–11
Gyenge, Zsolt 71, 72

Hada, Reza 28
Hafez, Mohammad Shams al-Din 87, 144
Hakopian, Zaven 78
Halberstam, J. 237n27
Hamedian, Hooman 233n55
HamletIRAN 27
Hannaway, William 41, 211n9
Harvey, David 29
Hasanli, Jamil 202n93
Haussmann, Georges-Eugène 7
Hedayat, Sadeq 13
Helbig, Elahe 118
Hemingway, Ernest 72, 222n76
Herodotus 210n6
Hesford, Wendy 129–30, 132
Hezar Afsan 39, 210n2
HIV/AIDS 105, 159
Hobsbawm, Eric 1
Holocaust Memorial Museum (Washington, DC) 89–90
homeless children 99

Homer 213n19
homosexuality 35, 105, 135, 194–5, 237n27
Hossein ibn Ali (626–680) 10, 58
Hosseini, Mohammad 119–20
Howze-ye Honari Arts Foundation 142
human rights 131, 230n10; Hesford on 129–30, 132; Panahi on 132, 137
Human Rights Watch Film Festival 102

Ibsen, Henrik 17
Imam Khomeini Relief Foundation 20
'Indic Theatre' 157
infiltration art 181, 184, 187–8, 192, 194
interactive art 35, 52, 68, 181, 190–1, 217 n18
International Women's Day 161
invented traditions 7–12
Ionesco, Eugène 18
Iran Hostage Crisis (1979–81) 158–67
Irani, Faranak 29–31, *30*
Iranian American Foundation (IAF) 235n28
Iranian Comedy Company 14–15
Iranian nuclear program 166
Iranian Revolution (1979): human rights abuses of 89–91; Karimi Hakak on 87–94; Kurzman on 46; as reaction to Westernization 78; as street theatre 4, 19; theatre culture during 5, 16, 20–2
Iranian School of San Diego (ISSD) 169–70
Iranian Theatre Society (Paris) 26
Iran-Iraq War (1980–8) 3, 6, 226n1; films about 108–9; Karimi Hakak on 90, 91; Khomeini on 225n4; Naderi's play about 22; Sacred Defence theatre about 20
Isfahan 9, 10, 58, 211n9
Izadkhah, Shahrokh 146

Jalali, Alirez Koushk 27
Jallat, Denis 9–10
James, Henry 8
Javanmard, Abbas 16–17, 59
javanmardi 9–10
Javidan guards 175
jazz music 16, 144
Jewish Community of Iranian Americans 176
Jones, Allen 117

Kabir, Amir (1807–52) 13
kachalak-bazi 9
kairos 145, 152
Kamal, Reza "Shahrzad" 13
Kantor, Tadeusz 18
Kaprow, Allan 116
Karamustafa, Gülsün 115–16
Karbala, Battle of (680 CE) 10, 58
Kargah-e Namayesh Theatre Workshop 17–18
Karimi Hakak, Mahmood 24, *25*, 27, 33, 87–103; *Bombing the Cradle* 90, 224n2; *Common Plight* 99; *Gilgamesh ConQuest* 99, 225n18; *Seven Stages* 92
Karimi Hakkak, Ahmad 46
Kashan 219n30
Kashani, Sohrab *125*, *126*
Kasrai, Siavash 47; *The Scarlet Stone* 32, 45–55, *52–4*
Kermanshah 9
Kesey, Ken 91
Keshmirshekan, Hamid 125
Khalaj, Ismael 18
Khalkhali, Sadegh 81
Khatami, Mohammad 3, 118, 129–30; cultural policies of 21, 22, 99, 105, 139; election of 100
kheimeh-shab-bazi 9, 57, 208n173
Khiavchi, Babak 144
Khomeini, Ayatollah 85–6; Karimi Hakak on 88–91, 102; on music 141, 143, 177
Kiarostami, Abbas 57–73, 108, 220n40, 229n6; *ABC Africa* 63; *Close-Up* 62–3; *Look at Me* 65, 222n68; *A Look to ta'zieh* 33, 57–73, 221n61, 221n63; *Original Copy* 63; *Shirin* 63–5, 68, 220 n42, 220n47; *Taste of Cherry* 62; *Through the Olive Trees* 63, 71; *Where Is the Friend's House* 63, 71, 131, 229n7
Kiya, Khojasteh 18
Knofler, Mark 144
Koohestani, Amir Reza 22–3
Koushki, Mostafa 28
Kurdish culture 9, 52, 172, 234n4
Kurdistan 234n4
Kurzman, Charles 46

Lalehzar Street (Tehran) 1–3, 13–15, 20
Lashkari, Soroush 177
Lefebvre, Henri 217n5
LGBTQ community 35, 105, 135, 194–5, 237n27

Madanipour, Ali 117
Magritte, René 131
Mahdavi, Kaveh 207n165
Mahdi, Ali Akbar 170
Majidi, Majid 229n6
Makhmalbaf, Mohsen 20
Malek, Amy 173, 175–6
Malekzadeh, Soodabeh 32, 39–43
Malevich, Kazimir 126
Mamet, David 29–31, *30*
Mandakuni, Yovhannes 215n27
Manicheanism 79, 215n27
ma'rekeh-giri 9, 17
Marx, Karl 94
Mashayekhi, Alireza 86
Mashhad 91, 139, 147, 149, 150
Matthew, Abbott 220n45
McGrath, Kenta 72
Meftahi, Ida 14
Mehr Theatre Group 22–3
Mehrdad, Farhad 141, 231n10
Mehrpouya, Abbas 141
Mehrzad, Turan 15
#MeToo Movement 160
Middle East, terms for 161
Miller, Carolyn R. 145
minstrels 39–43, 215n27; Abbasid 42, 215n28; Parthian 211n7, 212n10, 213n18; women 210n3
Mirsajadi, Ali-Reza 24
Mitooie, Arash 144
Moberg, Vilhelm 27
Mofid, Bijan 16
Mofrad, Kambiz 170–3
Mohamedi, Manijeh 18
Mohammad Reza Shah Pahlavi 46; coronation of 77; exile of 86; on freedom of expression 83; human rights violations of 82–3, 90; modernization programme of 15–18, 77, 140, 235n25; *ta'zieh* under 59; White Revolution of 15–16, 77, 82

Molière 10, 13, 20
Molla-Sadra 94, 225n8
Momayez, Morteza 29
Monk, Meredith 106
Moosavi, Marjan 20–1, 23, 206n146
Morad, Gowhar (Gholam-Hossein Sa'edi) 17, 18
Mosaddegh, Mohammad 15, 161
Moseli, Ibrahim 215n28
Moshkin-Ghalam, Shahrokh 32, 50, 216n18
mostazafan 129, 130, 134, 137
Motevalli, Amitis 116–17, 125
Mother Homeland 13
Motlagh, Amy 34, 129–37
Mottahedeh, Negar 219n30
music, Islamic proscription of 141, 143, 177

Nader, Alireza 206n146
Nader Shah 59
Naderi, Alireza 22
Naeemi, Hamid Reza 24
Naficy, Hamid 62
Naficy, Nooshin 122, *123*
Nahavand, Battle of (642 CE) 42
Nai'ni, Mirza Reza Khan 4–5
Najafi, Ayat 102
Najafi, Shahin 177
Najmabadi, Afsaneh 135
Nakamura, Lisa 183
Nalbandian, Abbas 18
namayesh (popular entertainment) 9, 31, 199n43
Namjoo, Mohsen 142, 150, 177, 206n147
naqqali 9, 16, 32, 211n9, 213n20; in coffee houses 40; *Scarlet Stone* and 45, 50
Naser al-Din Shah 10, 59, 219n30
Nasirian, Ali 17
Nasr, Seyyed Ali 1, 14–15
Nasr Theatre 1, *2*, 20, 196n4
National Art Group (Goruh-e Honar-e Melli) 16–17
National Iranian Television (NITV) 77
National Performance and Conference Company 12
neorealism 108–9
New Media Art 119

New York Persian Day Parade (NYPP) 170–6
Niebuhr, Carsten 218n14
Nima Yushij 46
9/11 attacks 174
Nooshin, Abdolhossein 3, 15
Nooshin, Laudan 139, 153
Nowruz parades 34–5, 169–80

Oedipus myth 102, 230n14
Omi, Michael 183
Omidsalar, Mahmoud 212nn9–10
One Flew over the Cuckoo's Nest 91
One Thousand and One Nights 39–40
Ono, Yoko 115–16
Osanloo, Arzoo 230n10
Oskooi, Mahin 15
Oskooi, Mostafa 15
Ostrovsky, Alexander 10, 13
Ovanessian, Arby 16, 18

Pagnol, Marcel 15
pahlavan kachal 9
Pahlavi dynasty 82, 140; dance forms and 172; legitimation of 77, 81, 82; performance art during 117; theatre during 5, 12–18
Pak-Shiraz, Nacim 66
Panahi, Hossein 111
Panahi, Jafar 34, 108, 129–37; *The Circle* 131–3, 230n13; *Crimson Gold* 133–5, 230; *Offside* 131, 135–6; *This Is Not a Film* 131–2; *The White Balloon* 131, 136–7
pantomime 12
pardeh-khani (screen-reading) 50
pardeh-khwani (storytelling) 9
Paris 7–8, 12
patriarchy (*pedar-salari*) 102, 136
peacebuilding through art 97
pelatoo 28, 208n178
performance art 5–6, 113–27, 140; Auslander on 183; Baradaran on 185, 190; characteristics of 115–16; Persian name for 117, 227n14; theatre versus 114–15, 127
performance studies 140
Persepolis (multimedia spectacle) 78–82, 86

Persian Cultural Center (San Diego) 235n28
Persian New Year. *See* Nowruz parades
Pesyani, Atila 23
Phelan, Peggy 183–4, 237n22
Pink Floyd 144
Pirzadeh Nai'ni, Hajji Mohammad Ali 7–8, 12
Plato 123, 124
'poAItry' 189
Preiss, Richard 8
prison theatre 19
private spaces 95–6, 113, 120–1, 170
'private theatre' 28–9
prostitution 105
public sphere 105, 117–20, 226n6
puppet shows 9, 57, 208n173

Qajar dynasty 6–11, 23, 172, 199n39; *ta'zieh* of 59, 219n30
qameh-zaniz ceremony 95, 225n9
Qarachehdaghi, Mirza Jafar 11
quotidian logic 130

Rad, Amir 122
Radi, Akbar 17
radif 170
Rafsanjani, Akbar Hashemi 21, 22, 27
Rahimi, Babak 152
Rahimi, Mostafa 24
Rahmaninejad, Nasser 3, 19, 26
rap music 147
Rashidi, Davood 23–4
Rasht 3, 10, 18, 30
Rastovac-Akbarzadeh, Heather 181–95
Rawlinson, George 210n6
Razavipour, Neda: *Dream Sets* 113, *114*, 124; *Self-Service* 122–5, *124*
Reformist Period (1997–2002) 21, 22
Rekabtalaei, Golbarg 11
ReOrient Festival 160, 161
Reza Shah Pahlavi 161; modernization programme of 12, 140; *ta'zieh* banned under 59, 83, 84
Reza, Yasmina Evelyne Agnes 27
Rezai, Mohammad Baqer 116
Rezvani, Serge 81
Riahipour, Babak 146

Richard, Jules 59
Robertson, Bronwen 148, 153, 206n147
Rochard, Philippe 9–10
rock music 34, 139–53, 176, 206n147
Rokni, Siavash 34, 139–53
Rosenberg, Harold 116
Rostam and Sohrab myth 102
Rouhani, Hassan 27
rowzeh-khani 58
Royaee, Yadollah 110
ruhowzi shows 9, 21
Rumi, Jalaleddin 92, 94, 189, 195

Saanei, Youse 143
Sabzian, Hossein 62
Sacred Defence theatre 20
Saddiki, Tayeb 219n20
Sa'edi, Gholam-Hossein (Gowhar Morad) 17, 18, 26
Safavid dynasty 58, 67
Salimi, Rana 26, 34–5, 169–80
Samandarian, Hamid 17
Sarkissian, Shahin 17
Sasanian dynasty 212n13, 214n27
Sayyad, Parviz 26, 84, 175, 235n23
Schechner, Richard 140, 217n3
Scheiwiller, Staci Gem 33–4, 113–27
Sedaeva Sima (Iranian Radio and Television) 142
Sepehran, Kamran 12
shabih-khwani 58, 96, 225n12
Shahnameh 32, 45–55, 211n9, 225n7, 225n27
Shahnameh-khwani 32, 40, 212n9
Shahrestani, Mikail 24
Shahrzad 39–40, 210n3
Shajarian, Mohammad-Reza 21
Shakespeare, William 23–5; *Hamlet* 24–5, 27, 202n82; *Macbeth* 23, 24; *The Merchant of Venice* 13, *14*; *A Midsummer Night's Dream* 24, *25*, 99, 101, 102, 209n181; *Richard III* 23–4; *The Taming of the Shrew* 23
Shamlou, Ahmad 107
Sharbaf, Shahram 144, 146
Shay, Anthony 42, 170, 234n3
Shiraz Arts Festival 16, 18, 33, 59; boycott of 83; Charney on 77–86; creation of

77–8; Karimi Hakak on 97; Khomeini on 86; performance art at 117; Xenakis on 82
siah-bazi comedy 20, 21. *See also* blackface
sineh-zani 96, 225n12
slapstick comedy 9
Sobhani, Arash 144
socio-theatre 87–103
Soltanpour, Saeed 19
Sophocles 106, 124
Soroush, Abdol Karim 21
'Sovietisation' 202n93
Stam, Robert 182
Stanislavski's method acting 15, 202n97
Strabo 40–1, 210n6
Straw, Will 147
Sufism 92, 97; *sama* dance of 172, 212n13
Surrealism 116

Tabriz 3, 9, 10, 11, 23, 135
Tabrizi, Mirza Aqa 11
Taher Nasrabadi, Mirza Mohammad 211n9
Taheri, Hamed 33, 105–11
Tajikestan 234n4
Takkiyeh Dowlat theatre 10, 59, 219n30
Talebi, Shahla 19
talfiqi music 141, 144–6, 148, 150
Talmud 214n27
Tanavoli, Parviz 18, 117, 203n113
taqiya 88
Taste of Cherry (1997 film) 62
Tavakoli-Targhi, Mohammad 13
Taylor, Diana 60
ta'zieh 10, 16, 21, 117–18, 218n12; ban of 59, 83–4; Brook on 84; Dabashi on 61; Ghaffari's staging of 78–9, 84–6, 220n51; Kiarostami on 221n61, 221n63; music of 84–5; as passion play 83; post-revolutionary changes to 219n20, 220n37; in pre-Islamic Iran 218n9; during Qajar period 59, 219n30; Rahimi on 33, 57–73; Sayyad's staging of 84; as 'theatre of protest' 78–9, 85–6
te'atr-e arzeshi (value-laden theatre) 20
te'atr-e gheyre dolati (non-government theatre) 28, 208n180
Teatro Olympico (Vicenza) 7

Tehran viii, ix, x, 1–3, 5, 9, 12–15, 18, 20, 22, 25, 28, 33–4, 63, 65–6, 77, 88, 90–2, 95–7, 105, 107, 110–11, 113–27, 132, 134–136, 139, 140, 144, 147, 148–50, 152, 153, 163, 169, 176, 199n42, 201n71, 207n167, 207n168, 208n177, 209n180, 209n183, 209n191, 219n30, 221n63
Tehran Acting School 2–3, 5
Tehran City Theatre 107, 111
Tehran Museum of Contemporary Art 118
Tehran University 105, 209n181
Terian, Varto 2
Theatre Forum (Khaneh Te'atre) 22
Theatre Mon 28
'theatre of protest' 78–9, 85–6
30 Performances, 30 Artists, 30 Days Festival 122
Thompson, John B. 31
Tiwall app 29
Tudeh Party 15, 17, 46–7
Turkey 12, 83, 90, 101, 159

Underground Music Competition 147
underground theatre 105–11
United States 16, 22, 83, 85, 89, 90, 91, 99, 129, 150, 159, 160, 161, 163, 165, 166, 170, 175, 176, 177, 194, 235n20

Vahdat Theatre 98
Vahdat, Vahid 10
Varzi, Roxanne 33, 105–11, 117
Vaziri, Qamar al-Moluk 14, 202n88
Vejdani, Farzin 13
Vienna actionists 108
virtual reality 181. *See also* augmented reality
Vis o Ramin 41–2, 211n7

Wannous, Sa'dallah 219n20
Warda, Bella 161
Wedding of Mr. Hossein, The 14
Werner, Christoph 23
'Westoxication' (*gharbzadegi*) 78
What Do the Women Say? (festival) 161
'White Revolution' 15–16, 77, 82
William, Raymond 6, 8–9, 198n26
Wilson, Robert 117

Winant, Howard 183
women actors 15, 18
women minstrels 210n3
women's rights 12, 172, 177–9

Xenakis, Iannis 78–82, 86
Xenophon 40, 211n8

Yadegari, Shahrokh 32–3, 45–55
Yaghmaie, Kourosh 141, 231n10
Yahmaie, Kaveh 151
Yaqut ('lady in red') 120

Yarshater, Ehsan 46
Yazdani, Reza 151
Yeghiazarian, Torange 34, 157–67; *Dawn at Midnight* 159, 161; *444 Days* 158, 161–7; *Waves* 159, 161

Zadeh, Reza Kouchek 31
Zahir al-Dowleh 12
Zoroastrian Club (Tehran) 13, *14*
Zoroastrianism 79, 80, 174–6; calendar of 81, 169, 176
Zweiri, Mahjoob 25

www.ingramcontent.com/pod-product-compliance
Lightning Source LLC
Chambersburg PA
CBHW062131300426
44115CB00012BA/1881